MEDIATED SOCIETY

In Memoriam
Elva duFresne-Jackson
1930–2010

MEDIATED SOCIETY

A CRITICAL SOCIOLOGY OF MEDIA

JOHN D. JACKSON
GREG M. NIELSEN
YON HSU

OXFORD
UNIVERSITY PRESS

OXFORD
UNIVERSITY PRESS

8 Sampson Mews, Suite 204, Don Mills, Ontario M3C 0H5
www.oupcanada.com

Oxford University Press is a department of the University of Oxford.
It furthers the University's objective of excellence in research, scholarship,
and education by publishing worldwide in

Oxford New York
Auckland Cape Town Dar es Salaam Hong Kong Karachi
Kuala Lumpur Madrid Melbourne Mexico City Nairobi
New Delhi Shanghai Taipei Toronto

With offices in
Argentina Austria Brazil Chile Czech Republic France Greece
Guatemala Hungary Italy Japan Poland Portugal Singapore
South Korea Switzerland Thailand Turkey Ukraine Vietnam

Oxford is a trade mark of Oxford University Press
in the UK and in certain other countries

Published in Canada
by Oxford University Press

First Published 2011

Library and Archives Canada Cataloguing in Publication

Jackson, John D.
Mediated society : a critical sociology of media / John D. Jackson,
Greg M. Nielsen, and Yon Hsu.

(Themes in Canadian sociology)
Includes bibliographical references and index.
ISBN 978-0-19-543140-7

1. Mass media--Social aspects. 2. Mass media--Social aspects--Canada. I. Nielsen, Greg M.
II. Hsu, Yon, 1972- III. Title. IV. Series: Themes in Canadian sociology

HM1206.J33 2011 302.230971 C2010-907705-9

Printed in Canada

Oxford University Press is committed to our environment. This book is printed on
Forest Stewardship Council certified paper, harvested from a responsibly managed forest.

1 2 3 4 – 14 13 12 11

Sources mixtes
Groupe de produits issus de forêts bien
gérées et d'autres sources contrôlées
www.fsc.org Cert no. SW-COC-000952
© 1996 Forest Stewardship Council

Contents

Preface

On any given day problems with media regulatory systems, media content, democracy and citizenship issues, and free speech are brought to our attention. We are cajoled by the media, surrounded by the media, dominated by the media, and freed by the media. A constellation of media images not only forms and amplifies our imaginations but also mediates and constrains it precisely through the spread and use of media in everyday life. Indeed the media appears to generate its own sociological imagination insofar as it builds and organizes the terrain of social practices and processes through which negotiation between agency (the power of self-determination) and structure (relations that regulate social actors) takes place. In the twenty-first century the means of communication envelop us; it has become a powerful institution and a major resource used to make sense of everyday experiences.

Our objective in *Mediated Society: A Critical Sociology of Media* is to address the media and means of mass communications as fundamentally a social issue. We locate issues and questions concerning mass media and communications within a sociological framework and with a sensitivity to questions of democracy and citizenship, class, gender, and cultural diversity. To accomplish this we elaborate on the idea of a mediated society; i.e., society as representation experienced through exposure to media in all its forms and expressions. The expression 'mediated society' places an emphasis on the social, the political, and the societal as representations received through reading, listening, watching, and interacting with others. Our environments are mediated for us through various avenues of communication that tell us how to belong, feel, think, and act. We are not saying, of course, that we are mere putty in the hands of mass media institutions; we, too, identify, feel, think, and act in creative ways as we take from, give to, and alter received meanings. In other words, we construct images of the social and the political from materials gleaned from everyday life experiences—including those that emerge from mass media. It is the active construction and, thus, the critically real presence of society that distinguishes what can be male, female, human, non-human, or post-human. Identities, norms, and values—indeed, our very sense of humanity or inhumanity—are thoroughly mediated by images of interaction between citizens, non-citizens, and other actants, both human and non-human, and by the tensions between social order and disorder and between received meanings and creative acts, deeds, and events. These ideas are both traditional and still very current subjects of sociology but they are also subjects that have entered the study of mass media and the emerging field of citizenship studies.

The first section of *Mediated Society* illuminates issues of communication and citizenship and, as will become apparent to the reader, assumes an approach frequently referred to as critical sociology. The first chapter defines a variety of sources for a *critical sociology* that combine interactionist and structuralist sociology and communications literature with more recent interdisciplinary dialogical, deconstructive, and postructural theories. This stance enabled us to begin to pinpoint dialogic relations between the real and implied audiences that media address while also revealing both the most visible norms they generate and the often invisible ties between social, political, and economic institutions imbedded in the organization and output of media corporations. Although each type of media has a real audience, media content is influenced not only by the story genre but also by who the media producers, writers, directors, and creative formations *think their audiences are*, what kinds of publics they belong to, or, in other words, an *implied audience* which may or may not overlap with the real audience. In Part 1, we critically examine citizenship, audiences, advertising, and Web 2.0 technologies. Part 2 explores media events at the global, national, and urban levels—happenings that tend to interrupt our everyday routines and intensively capture the attention of thousands, perhaps millions, of people within a specific period of time and forge an historical sense of significance through participating and witnessing the unfolding of live, staged, mediated events. Part 3 tackles the issue of social problems as defined and presented by media by first presenting a discussion of social problems and then critically examining a series of issues as mediated events. Further examination will take the reader to Montreal and New York City, where journalistic norms of reporting on poverty and immigration as social problems are deconstructed and critically considered.

Communications and journalism are disciplines in and of themselves. This book is first and foremost a critical sociology of mass media in which the media, communications, and journalism are the objects of study. Paraphrasing a note in C. Wright Mills' classic *The Sociological Imagination*, we recognize that the individual can understand his or her own experience only by becoming aware of the institutional setting and its contractions in which they are located. We have tried to provide a framework for such critical thought on the organization of media in all its forms.

Finally we would like to note that all translations from French to English were done by the authors unless otherwise noted in the references section.

Acknowledgements

This was a team project; each author would like to thank the other two for their cooperation, willingness to compromise, and hard work. Our thanks go to Lorne Tepperman and Susan Daniels for the invitation to contribute to the Oxford University Press (OUP) Sociology Series. In addition we are very appreciative of the assistance provided by Nancy Reilly, the OUP Acquisitions Editor who was of considerable help during the proposal stage. We thank Jennifer Mueller, the first editor assigned to our project, Jessie Coffey, our copy editor, and, most especially, Allison McDonald, who was later assigned to our project and who devoted a considerable amount of time and energy shepherding our work through the system. We are truly indebted to Allison. Thanks as well to the Concordia University Centre for Broadcasting Studies for space and the means of production, and most especially thanks to the Centre Administrator, Mircea Mandache, for his help with the mechanics of pulling the manuscript together.

Finally, we must acknowledge several articles based on research funded by the Social Science and Research Council of Canada and published in various journals and books by the authors. Parts of these works appear in Chapters 2, 3, 8, 10, and 11. Reference to the publishers on Nielsen (2007, 2008, and 2009), Jackson and Rosenberg (2004), Saxton et al. (2004), Jackson (2002), and Fink and Jackson (1987) may be found in the bibliography.

Chapter-opening photo credits: page 3: Imagestate Media Partners Limited – Impact Photos/Alamy; page 30: ZITS © 2005 ZITS PARTNERSHIP, KING FEATURES SYNDICATE; page 55: Danita Delimont / Alamy; page 78: Bill Brooks / Alamy/GetStock; page 100: Art Kowalsky / Alamy/GetStock; page 123: David Crausby / Alamy/GetStock; page 145: Shaun Cunningham / Alamy/GetStock; page 165: Matt Harris Digital Photography / Alamy; page 194: AP Photo/Vincent Yu; page 215: John Kenney, The Gazette (Montreal); page 235: Peter Casolino / Alamy / GetStock.

Part 1

Sociology, Media, and Citizenship

In the twenty-first century media has become one of the world's most powerful institutions. Media influences corporate and government agendas, as can be seen in how it impacts official responses to epidemics, social policies, and boom-and-bust economic cycles. Media is capable of defining large sectors of the **public sphere**, thereby helping shape the meaning of identities that cut across race, gender, class, sexual orientation, and citizenship. Media is engaged in the production of commodities and services through the endless variety of advertising narratives it provides. Media itself is a major economic force that helps drive the invention of a steady stream of new technologies of communication. These same technologies appear to alter our most basic forms of association both from one generation to the next and, increasingly, among the same generation. This raises the question of whether 'the new' has ever been that 'new'.

When media technologies of production and distribution are mainly owned or controlled by companies in one powerful state and when programs are produced by that culture and then consumed by many different cultures around the world, as has been the case of US cultural products for many years now, then we have to begin to wonder if the deep traditions of various world cultures are being excluded from mediated society. This suggests that we need to be very careful about how we talk about any single mediated society.

We argue that there is no one global mediated society, although there might be a global culture in which some members of many societies commonly consume American cultural products. When we talk about mediated society we are talking rather about a form of society that has a specific regime of communication that expresses a certain regional or local angle on culture, that has a particular effect on the type of citizenship that is practised, and that has a specific **normalizing** impact on subjects that have been created by—and who also create—its institutions.

We begin with a chapter exploring the sources behind our critical sociology of media. We first refer to 'Media Centred Approaches'; media centred in that they treat mass media technologies either as the most important negative causes of domination in society or as the main centring force in the evolution of human culture and civilization. We then refer to 'Media Decentred Approaches'; decentred in that they tend to situate mass media in broader critical or deconstructive terms, also folded into affirmative and negative orientations. In the next chapter we continue the main theme of mediated citizenship through an exploration of media-constructed public spaces and the tensions arising as citizen, state, and corporate worlds collide over issues of content, control, and participation in the media. Chapter 2 takes gender into account as a highly contested space in the public sphere and entertainment programming. The citizen/state/corporate world tension is again introduced in Chapter 3, where we will discuss audiences and citizenship, and in Chapter 4 advertising is more fully considered in light of the **commodification** of women through advertising. The advertising or 'persuasion' theme is then continued in Chapter 5 as we consider what is really 'new' about new communications technologies.

We recognize that almost everyone born today will experience mass communications as an ongoing language of gestures or **discourse**. We also acknowledge that this is a phenomenon that has come to peoples around the world at different times over the last 60 years or so and through different technologies. Our aim is not to map what some call the global mediascape but to demonstrate how critical sociology puts into question the relationship between media and society and, in the process, how the critique reveals new ways to increase the diversity and **dialogic** qualities of communications and the quality of address to audiences that have been historically excluded. While this is an enormous task we believe the creation of a better world is not only possible by making communications media more inclusive but will also be necessary if we are to build more answerable democracies in the future.

Today's mediated societies have announced an unprecedented convergence of technologies of communications. Currently, in studies of mediated society this convergence implies ever more powerful instruments that carry and frame interpretation and representation. Representations saturate our way of thinking about others and ourselves. In and through these institutions, socio-political relations, and society itself, are constructed, imagined, and mediated into ways of thinking about others, our everyday social discourse, our sense of belonging, and our world views. Thus the institutionalized media of communication become objects for sociological study.

1 Sources for a Critical Sociology of Mediated Society

Learning Objectives

- To understand the meaning of mediated society and critical sociology
- To consider the gap between real and imaginary audiences
- To define instituted and instituting media programs
- To review classical sociological theories of society and culture, alienation, and the culture of domination
- To consider centred and decentred approaches to the study of media
- To think about the undoing of gender norms
- To think about society as communication, communicative action, deconstruction, genealogy, and performance

Introduction

This first chapter of *Mediated Society* outlines the sources for a critical sociology used to demonstrate how the institution of mass media evolved into both a dominating and a creative societal force. We will begin by examining a number of key questions. What is critical sociology? What is the advantage of its approach to the study of mediated society? What is an **institution**? Is the institution of mass media what centres a society or is it what allows society to decentre? How does classical sociology define the concept of society? How has this tradition transformed itself across the twentieth century and into the twenty-first century?

We then sketch the origins and development of two overlapping contemporary sources for a critical sociology of mediated society. We call the first set of sources 'Media Centred Approaches' because they treat mass media technologies either as the most important negative causes of domination in society or as the main centring force in the evolution of human culture and civilization. We call the second set of approaches 'Media Decentred Approaches' because they tend to situate mass media in broader critical or deconstructive terms, which are also divided into affirmative and negative perspectives.

Critical Sociology: Exposing the Gap Between Real and Imaginary Audiences

> When I say media I mean media: the mass, the globalized, the regional, the national, the local, the personal media; the broadcast and interactive media; the audio and visual and the printed media; the electronic and the mechanical, the digital and the analogue media; the big screen and the small screen media; the dominant and alternative media; the fixed and the mobile, the convergent and the stand alone media. (Silverstone, 2007: 5)

It seems obvious that almost everything that exists in society can be found represented in some kind of communications media. And yet, most of us think that our own voices, private thoughts, and emotions remain separate from media. This is one of the most striking paradoxes of mediated society that critical sociology examines. Critical sociology is interested not only in how events and private experiences become what Gilles Deleuze and Felix Guatarri (1987) call '**deterritorialized**' but also in how the institution of media 're-**territorializes**' **norms** and **values** in social life, democracy, and citizenship. As we will see in this and in following chapters, **critical sociology** contrasts real audiences and the audiences implied or imagined by media in order to expose the gap between communities and the imaginary, but not always fictional, representation of their stories transmitted in multiple contexts—global, national, and urban. In doing so, critical sociology also pinpoints how media practices carry norms and values that are performed and received, and how they can be deconstructed or uncovered, questioned, and upset. Finally, critical sociology contrasts tensions between already tried or instituted media technologies and creative or instituting media practices along with the anticipation of responses from their varied publics.

Norms and values remind us of how we should act toward each other and of what and how we should feel. These guidelines for conduct and emotional orientations toward the 'normal' or 'natural' way of acting are the basic elements of socialization. In mediated societies, the anticipation by media of our response to norms and values is an added defining feature of our subjection toward 'normalization' on a variety of levels. Consider the following example. Mainstream contemporary mass media see themselves as addressing an audience that is measured by ratings and then bought and sold for advertising revenues in the marketplace. Alternative media, new media, and most forms of public broadcasting address audiences that while often popular can also be marginal to the mainstream because they are not defined exclusively by a commercial imperative. Although each type of media has a real audience that can overlap, each media addresses an ideal or **implied audience** that doesn't always overlap. Media content is influenced not only by the story genre but also by who the media producers, writers, directors, and creative formations think their audiences are, what kinds of publics they belong to, and how they might be affected as consumers or citizens. In other words, your own private stories and emotions are already implicated in the media's anticipation of your response to their products. In mediated society we are socialized not only at a face-to-face first level of observation, but also at a more abstract or second level of mediated observation (Luhmann, 2000). To paraphrase an infamous media critic, 'You are not (only) watching media, it is watching you' (Baudrillard, 1983).

Thus the expression '**mediated society**' places emphasis on understanding 'society' as an intervening force in our lives and as being constructed from complex interests that extend far beyond our immediate experience. We receive images of ourselves and others through listening to and watching older media as well as by responding to and interacting with each other across always emerging newer media. *Mediate* means to represent, to come between, and to 'cover'. Similar to clothing, our choice of media can transmit a very personal sense of who we are or who we would like to be (Silverstone, 2007: 5). But the irony is that the more exquisite our choice in fashion, the more we are likely to exclude others from participating in the same pleasure.

Critical sociology looks for ways to expand communication toward the possibilities of addressing more receivers, not fewer. Reducing the gap between real and imaginary or implied audiences and between primary and secondary levels of observation is not about an expansion of the quantity of communication in society. It is about bringing others into what Russian cultural theorist Mikhail Bakhtin (1895–1975) called the **dialogic** quality of communication. By this we mean we need to expand the address media makes toward audiences who have been historically excluded from dialogue in their societies. The first step in this direction requires a critical evaluation of institutions that introduce new technologies, representations, divisions of labour, and complex forms of regulation that govern or dominate a citizenry. Reducing the gap between populations who are defined as social problems in media and the audience to which the media addresses itself is the second step that critical sociology proposes toward understanding the 'answerability' of media and prompting it toward a democracy that is yet to be achieved. While the former step is covered in the first and second sections of this book, the latter step is considered in the third section. Thus the critical sociology of mediated society does more than simply identify the dominating systems of media. It also does more than deconstruct or upset the claims of truth held in the exchange of norms and values carried by media practices. The promise of critical sociology for those who follow its path is that exercising both these steps will allow unique insights into the possibilities of a better world.

Instituted and Instituting Media

The alternative media activist and practitioner Amy Goodman—co-host of *Democracy Now*, a one-hour daily alternative radio news program from independent Radio Pacific's WBAI, produced in New York City—sets a crucial tone for the critical sociology of mediated society when she asks whether or not contemporary media can stand up to power and make it tell the truth so we can be better informed and so our democracy can be more just. Does it go where silences are? Does it make static 'criticism, opposition, or unwanted interference' (Goodman and Goodman, 2006)? Or, conversely, does it trade truth for access to power? Her answer is that while the institution of mass media has become the most powerful institution on the planet it almost never does these things.

For Goodman the power of the mainstream, or what she and others call '**corporate media**', is especially evident when it doesn't live up to the role it's supposed to play in a democratic society. Goodman maintains, for example, that mainstream journalists are increasingly trading access to government officials and politicians for interviews and quotes in exchange for not telling the whole truth about their policies. The most spectacular example of how journalists, as a group, traded access to information in exchange for not pursuing facts about the truth was seen in the lead-up to the American invasion of Iraq in 2001. At the time, journalists desperately sought access in order to report the breaking news. Officials from the White House regularly fed journalists information about weapons of mass destruction in Iraq. In other words, journalists accepted the politicians' claims that there were weapons and yet, because of security reasons, no independent verification could be offered. Only after the United States invaded Iraq did journalists begin to question the claim and, much later, force the White House officials to admit there had never been weapons of mass destruction in Iraq.

If you think this is restricted to or typical of American media, think again. Why don't we see images of mangled bodies of dead Afghans or Canadian soldiers on the CBC or SRC news? Who can recall a single emotionally or politically upsetting debate in English or French from the main Canadian public networks about the war? And yet we have more information programs and journalists working on stories than at any other time in our history. Two all-news channels—CBC News Network and RDI—begin programming at 5:00 AM and conclude late in the evening, seven days a week. Programs focus on smart star presenters who most often conduct interviews with personalities of the week or former politicians who come to present their 'points of view', provide 'special analyses', or give their 'take' on current events. Given that networks have to fill the airwaves all day, every day, seven days a week, can any of these programs afford to ask really hard questions? After all, if each interview were done in the tradition of hard-hitting journalism, with edge and research rather than style and finesse, who would come to talk?

It is important, though, when speaking about media and power to remember the sociological distinction between telling stories about the experience of individuals, groups, and communities within a given society and telling the events or acts as they emerge. In telling us what is true or what is normal, mediated society 'normalizes' events and creates an ideal sense of who we are or have been in relation to others within the same events or within other events yet to come. Media events do not normalize us by making us into robots nor do they convince us by bombarding us with a constant barrage of propaganda, as some critics of mediated society suggest. Media normalize us by reproducing attitudes across networks of power that often work only to the advantage of those who have power. Mediated society normalizes us by playing with our already 'instituted' sense of lifestyle, of what is taken for granted as acceptable and what is not, of what is fashionable and what is not, of what is male and what is female and what is not, of who is attractive and who is not, of who belongs and who doesn't, and of who is a citizen and who is an outcast. The institution of media endlessly transmits all these things 24 hours a day—things we think we need to know so we can be together, or at least so that we can be the best we can under the circumstances of our own time.

An institution in sociological terms is both a set of rules that normalizes and a creative site that helps shape events in which we act and from which subjects emerge. Schools teach us about the rules of how to lineup in an orderly fashion, how to read, how to be creative, and how to become citizens. Religion teaches us rules about the big questions we need to know and, eventually, about how to belong in a community. Families teach us about being loved and how to love. But what about those who don't get 'normalized' at school, by religion, or by the family?

There is little debate over the fact that the institution of mass media teaches us about citizenship, community, and love, but there is little agreement as to just how much it causes us to act or determines what we might hope for or what we might fail at. The late critical sociologist Cornelius Castoriadis makes a key theoretical distinction that helps get at this discrepancy between the instituted and instituting meanings of how society is imagined. To be instituting, he argues, means to invent or create something not previously imagined. To be instituted suggests a repetition of already regulated ways of doing things (Castoriadis, 1978). The institution of media is created between these two contradictory forces.

For example, a contemporary AMC television series like *Mad Men*, about advertising executives on Madison Avenue in Manhattan, gives us an instituted representation of what work and family life was like in 1961. The paradox of *Mad Men* is that anyone outside that normal sense of family life is feared or rejected; however, be it secretly or openly, almost all the characters are shown to act outside its norms. At the same time that it looks to conserve family values the series provokes an instituting response by showing us what we no longer imagine to be normal. We see scenes of male executives in their offices smoking and drinking alcohol during their meetings. Female secretaries are there to assist them as typists, telephone operators, or organizers but never as colleagues with equal status. Husbands cheat on their wives and the single women dream of getting married. A rigid colour line separates races and cultures. Homosexuality is deeply feared. The character of Betty, the wife of advertising executive Don Draper, is presented as the caregiver for their children as well as a partner. As the first season of the series progresses, we learn that Don believes she is in need of psychoanalysis for the treatment of hysteria—given the overwhelming force of a suburban lifestyle. Don is a 30-something post–Second World War husband who works, drinks, and drives; has affairs; dominates his other male colleagues; and is a candidate for a heart attack. In short, the show portrays an instituted set of rigid gender relations with a division of labour in which we can recognize the recent past.

Television programs have been presenting family life since their beginning in the 1940s in the US and the 1950s in Canada. The way we are normalized by media is easily seen when we study the themes from early American TV situation comedies that emphasize the importance of keeping the nuclear family together, like *I Love Lucy* and *The Dick Van Dyke Show* from the 1960s and the more conservative programs like *Father Knows Best*, *Leave It to Beaver*, and *My Three Sons*. In the 1970s *The Mary Tyler Moore Show* introduced an acceptable, single, white, adult working woman and her single, Jewish, female neighbour as normal lifestyles for the first time in mass media history.

*M*A*S*H**, *All in the Family*, and *Maude* broke cultural ground and put a new kind of politics into play that questioned American race relations, foreign policy, the nuclear family, and traditional gender roles. This laid the groundwork for the next decade of situation comedies that would push the norm of 'what is possible' to represent as normal even further. *The Jeffersons*, *The Cosby Show*, *Sanford and Son*, and other programs brought African American and Hispanic faces and political issues to the world's attention. A decade later shows like *Ellen* and *Will and Grace* set the stage for exposing a new culture of laughter that had not yet been instituted. The crop of programming that includes *The L Word* and *Queer as Folk* breaks through some of the last taboos on public drama related to homosexuality and transgendered subjects while series like *Sex and the City*, *Rescue Me*, *30 Rock*, *The Office*, and *Weeds* all play with a seemingly endless mixture of masculine and feminine norms and interchangeable sexual orientations. HBO dramas like *Big Love*, *Deadwood*, and *True Blood* introduce other kinship relationships and language use previously forbidden from being viewed or heard publicly.

Mediated references to work and family are presented as already instituted ways of doing things from the past. In doing this, television intervenes directly into the way we feel about both work and family. At the same time, the program can institute an effect that has not been previously experienced. Presenting graphic transmissions of what we were like not so long ago can have the simultaneous effect of getting us to imagine what it should be like in the future. In this way TV sends both an instituted and an instituting message that is about not just what we should feel but also how we should feel about work and the family life that is yet to come.

Critical sociology takes gaps between the real and imaginary audience, **first and second levels of observation**, and the instituted norms and the instituting creative forces of media as its objects of study. We know that the instituted representation of family life in 1961 is similar to today but also that it is very different. The instituting dimension of the media is located in this difference. What regulates this difference is the instituted. How we feel about what the family should be like has to do with our instituting values and norms with television and not only passively receiving its message. For example, our sense of the 'normal' family today doesn't have the same gender, racial, or sexual rules of orientation and division of labour—or at least we think it should not have the same divisions and fears. Instituting contemporary values favours mixed families, possibly a more diverse set of sexual orientations, organic foods, non-smoking environments, multiculturalism, moderate use of stimulants, and a post-racial Barack Obama world—or we think they should. Does mediated society centre these values and eventually help force all of us to respect corresponding norms so as to avoid disorder? Or does mediated society decentre norms and values to allow a variety of **lifeworlds** to create order out of disorder?

What Is a Society? Classical Sociology as a Dialogue on Media Culture

Although there is much disagreement among sociologists over exactly what a society is, whether or not it actually exists, and if it exists then how it should be studied, most would agree that a society is both a system of institutions created by people to solve various problems and a force in peoples' lives. Sociologists most often focus on a society defined at the level of nation-states like Canada or the United States. But there is almost no limit to the kind of society sociologists can study. The local student's society, European society, or global society—all are examples of just how specific and just how general a society can be. Societies are made up of institutions that are themselves expressions of everyday events.

Max Weber (1864–1920), Émile Durkheim (1858–1917), Georg Simmel (1858–1919), and Karl Marx (1818–1883) are among the most recognized early sociologists to have defined society as a centre for political contradiction and civic order. However, each of the classical sociologists has a different way of studying the question. When sociologists debate questions about 'how' to study an object like the media, they are talking about method. When they debate questions about 'what' the object of study is, they are talking about theory. For example, we might ask how we should study media products or programs, audiences or readers, technologies or various mediums of transmission and distribution. For each of these objects we need specific methods and theories that can help reveal both creative and organizing patterns. Once we have demonstrated the patterns we need to ask what they mean and how can we explain them.

Max Weber looked to understand and explain different patterns or types of meaning that emerged from the seemingly unrelated media of religion, culture, law, and economy. His sociology is focused on the historical relations between values and actions in each of these spheres. Émile Durkheim was the first to understand society as a collective consciousness that forced actors to conform to general norms so that society could reproduce itself. For Durkheim, sociology is the study of collective representations as social facts. Social facts 'are ways of acting and thinking external to the individual, and endowed with a power of reason that can control him or her' (Durkheim, 1966).

Simmel and Bakhtin: Media Culture as Dialogue

It was Georg Simmel, more than Weber or Durkheim, who developed the most helpful approach for our critical sociology of the institution of mass media. We refer here to Simmel's definition of objective and subjective culture. He saw objective culture as the representation of culture as a 'thing' and subjective culture as its 'unique experience'. Objective culture is everything that we create. Subjective culture is everything we feel. This is an important distinction that helps explain a key element of media as a contemporary institution whose representations are separate from our real life experiences and yet also intervene directly in them. Simmel (1998) calls this the 'tragedy of culture' which is about the loss of real subjective culture to the objective culture of representations created by all kinds of (media) industry.

On the other hand, if there is no finite number of experiences for the products of media, we might ask Simmel, how then can the complex of unique experiences of them be understood? Inspired and influenced in part by Simmel, Mikhail Bakhtin developed the concept of dialogue in his studies of the novel as a means to get at the subjective exchange that occurs in objective culture itself (1981, 1984). Participation in dialogue means that words and phrases anticipate rejoinders from an animated other and that the words themselves are, in a sense, 'half someone else's'. A dialogic form of communication (objective culture) has the capacity to be answered. Although many traditional print and electronic media appear to be non-participatory in the sense that most of their actual audiences are not involved in any direct question-and-answer exchange (other than a financial one in terms of buying access, or through letters or e-mails to the editor), the fact that even traditional media like newspapers anticipate rejoinders means they also imply what an audience 'ought to feel' (subjective culture) through the emotional and moral tones of address.

Answerability in communication suggests a two-sided process in which media themselves can be thought of as anticipating a general (objective) response to an event as well as a unique (subjective) rejoinder from the implied audience. A dialogic approach to a news article, as will be discussed in Chapters 10 and 11, locates the journalist's position in the tonality of the utterance. As Bakhtin notes, 'emotional–volitional tone . . . is a certain ought-to-be attitude, an attitude that is morally valid and answerably active' right there in what Simmel calls objective culture (1993: 36). In other words, treating media as dialogical, rather than as the transmission of information toward a passive receiver, means that media can be treated as participatory in orientation.

Marx: Alienation and the Culture of Domination

Critical sociologists understand societies, like institutions, as both a form of dialogue between objective and subjective cultures and as an evolving political and economic ordering force. Karl Marx, the first and most important critical sociologist, used the metaphor that society's general culture or superstructure is built on an economic base. He argued that all societies contain within them the seeds of their own destruction and rebirth (Marx, 1978). The internal contradiction that defines society for Marx is between the small number of wealthy people in a class that owns the means of production and most of the wealth versus the vast majority of people from classes that work for them or the even larger mass of people on the planet who have no work and are the least well off. For Marx, the bourgeois class has the greatest wealth; these are society's 'haves', while the middle and working classes, as well as the mass of the world's poor, are the 'have-nots'.

Society's main contradiction is created in the economic base and in the need for continual expansion and a non-ending search to earn more profits on investments. The search for profits leads capitalist societies to create a large class of workers that Marx thought would eventually rise up against the much smaller capitalist class of owners and establish a new society. Hence, we can say society intervenes in people's lives through all kinds of mediums while at the same time has within it creative forces that institute change.

Marx's labour theory of value argues that value is artificially ascribed to commodities. **Commodity fetishism** means that consumers project a value onto the commodity as if it were inherent to the object itself, whereas the real value of the commodity is in the labour that produces it. Workers are exploited by capitalists who always make more money for their product in the marketplace than it costs them to pay labourers. In this process workers are alienated on three levels. Firstly, as natural or artificially manufactured resources are appropriated and transformed into a commodity, workers become separate from that resource. Secondly, as specialization is required to reduce costs of production the work is more and more separated from the final product of the labour. In more holistic-type technologies, such as nursing or childcare, this level of alienation is reduced. Marx, however, predicted a massive increase in more specialized industrial technologies. Thirdly, specialization separates workers from other workers and ultimately turns workers into commodities or 'things'; Marx argues this final act of alienation separates humanity from its own 'species'.

As we will see in Chapter 4, the institution of mass media in capitalist societies gradually evolved with technologies of communication that divide specializations into increasingly minute tasks, similar to the production process described in Marx's theory of alienation and the labour theory of value. Technological shifts from the telegraph to the radio to television and to the computer, and to today's hand-held communications devices, play a central role in the accumulation of profits and concentration of wealth that now takes place on an ever more global scale. In many cases, parts of a transmission device might be made in one country because that is where labour is cheapest, assembled in another country, and sold in yet another where the prices are highest; the remainders are dumped back into cheaper markets at lower prices. As the division of labour increases in each of these media the labour becomes more specialized, older skills become worthless, and entire communities and ways of telling stories about them begin to disappear.

Critical sociology looks to analyze symptoms of alienation as a gap between imaginary and real audiences but it also looks to engage the creative instituting forces in dialogical forms of mediated society. Even when social actors in mediated society contradict each other in their adversarial struggles to be heard, they can't help but take on aspects of each other's voices, intonations, emotional–volitional attitudes, and orientations—whether they agree or disagree, are in solidarity or resentment, domination or subordination, good taste or bad. If we trace the foundations of these contradictions we begin to hear mediated society as an infinite number of embodied voices, each 'shot through' with (or in anticipation of) other voices, and each struggling to be heard over all others (Evans, 2008). Social actors or agents living in mediated societies have the capacity to organize and stand up against instituted ways of doing things.

Media Centred Approaches

Media centred approaches see contemporary societies as being driven by institutions of communications. These approaches can be divided between the poles of 'media negation' and 'media affirmation'. Extreme media negation sees mass media as a form of total domination or ideological mystification without any inherent creative potential to emancipate groups or change society. Marx, for example, understood mass-produced cultural creations as part of a dominant ideological, legal, and moral superstructure that supported the contradiction in the economic base of society described above. For Marx, social change comes from below and not from institutions of media and culture, which tend to support the dominant class. In contrast, affirmation of mass media attributes positive and creative functions to media and sees them as a central organizing force in human culture and society. Émile Durkheim, for example, saw communications media as key to society's deep structure. This meant that the management of the volume, density, and distribution of populations in complex modern societies could only be organized and achieved through various channels of communication.

Here we examine examples of a negative media centred approach that extends Marx's critical insights into the twentieth century across the work of Walter Benjamin, Theodore Adorno, and Max Horkheimer, all of whom were original members or associates of the Frankfurt Tradition. We also introduce the work of postmodern thinker Jean Baudrillard as an extension of both the negative approach to media and the more affirmative media centred approaches of celebrated Canadian communication scholars Harold Innis

> In contemporary societies, the myth of the centre is inseparable from the myth of the mediated centre: the myth that media institutions are our privileged, or central, access point to the social centre . . . yes media comprise one of the crucial centralizations of resources in society but that does not mean media are a centre of social value or coherence. (Couldry, 2006: 17)

and Marshall McLuhan, who can be seen to have extended Durkheim's basic idea.

Negations: Walter Benjamin and the Culture of Storytelling

The first lesson in the critical sociology of the institution of media is that although our reception of images of family or work seems direct, the organization of the media comes between us and the images in a variety of ways. Not only the representation but also the transmission technologies intervene into our emotions and effect how we think about things. Some of the twentieth century's most experimental intellectual projects that challenge a variety of disciplines—including sociology and media studies—are to be found in the Frankfurt Institute of Social Research, established in 1923. The original project, led by Max Horkheimer (1895–1973) and Theodore Adorno (1903–1969) and others, was conceived as a research centre for the social sciences and humanities that would be autonomous from private and public financing, although it would be affiliated with the newly formed University of Frankfurt.

Walter Benjamin (1892–1940) was an early analyst of mediated society and an associate of the Frankfurt School. His work remains one of the most important sources for developing a contemporary critical sociology of mediated society. For Benjamin, it is important to consider how technologies of transmission are handed down from one generation to another. For example, when contemporary music connoisseurs say they prefer the sound of long-playing (LP) vinyl albums to the tape or digital medium, they are saying that a sense of the authentic sound, an 'aura', is lost in the new technology. It is not important for the moment that the LP and the digital technologies are two different types of recording mediation that distort sound. Benjamin's point is that emergent technologies generate new 'auras' from sounds or images formed from the clash that occurs in the memory of what the original sound or image was like.

Knowing the way technologies come between our lives and the representations of how our lives should be lived is key to understanding how society itself intervenes into our acts and ways of thinking. Technologies of communication are mediated by the organizing and creative practices that have come before them. The organizing practices of communication technologies are composed of an historical and actual division of labour; a way of creating things; a particular administrative logic; and systems of ownership, distribution, production, and reception. Each of these processes is defined through the limits set by the transmission technologies available in the given time period.

Benjamin uses the example of the artisanal 'story teller' to illustrate the points about the processes involved in media production. He sees storytelling as allegorical in the sense that the characters and narratives in stories are a symbolic surface of some deeper social signification. The demise of oral storytelling means the loss of an 'aura' or beauty to newer technologies of mechanical or electronic media production and distribution that replaces the older technology. Storytelling continues in the new media but oral storytelling is no longer a dominant technology. It belongs to traditional cultures that are increasingly marginal to Western versions of mass mediated society.

Storytelling has always had both instituting and instituted effects. Telling stories is an art that is thousands of years old. Speaking of the ancient art of fairy tales, Jack Zipes says that 'from the very beginning tales were told to create communal bounds in the face of inexplicable forces of nature and to provide hope in a world seemingly on the brink of catastrophe' (Zipes, 1999: 1). Think of children's stories like 'Little Red Riding Hood'. It can easily be read as an allegorical form; that is to say that the story is the surface cover for some deeper meaning. It takes the form of remembrance of the past and how to understand relations with nature and gender. The story is there to correct the conduct of community members should they deviate from its norm. The point though is that storytelling is a mediating force in society that can also be an instituting force of culture promoting solidarity and cooperation.

The shift from oral storytelling to the novel is a key step in the history of mass media production. The rise of the printing press and the novel came about in the fifteenth century. The novel is a technology and a cultural form that borrows its storytelling structures from ancient tragedy and epics, the long tradition of folk tales, and the transposition of more than a thousand years of peasant cultural festivals and carnivals into a mediated literary form that could easily travel (Bakhtin, 1984). The Hungarian cultural and political activist Georg Lukacs (1885–1971) was the first sociologist and literary critic to explain this tradition (Lukacs, 1971). Lukacs observed that the hero of the epic was never problematic. Even though we know Odysseus from *The Iliad* and *The Odyssey* will be away at sea for more than 20 years and will encounter fantastic obstacles, we also know from the onset that he will eventually find his way back to his beloved Penelope. In the modern novel, though, the hero becomes deeply problematic. Joseph K in Franz Kafka's *The Trial* is a good example of a self-reflective hero who is an individual on a quest for authenticity in a corrupt and inauthentic world.

The theme of the problematic hero has not been the dominant cultural genre across contemporary media as it was in the modern novel but it has been present in contemporary media. Before discussing this further we need to first explain how the multiple transitions in the modes of media production and effects on the aura of cultural creations are organized in systematic ways across the twentieth century. This explanation will allow us to better grasp the state of new media in our own time.

The Culture Industry

Max Horkheimer and Theodore Adorno were among the first and best examples of the negative media centred approach. On the one hand, they deepened

Benjamin's critique of the loss of knowledge that comes with new technologies. On the other hand, they rejected the argument that new 'auras' would come along as new technologies were introduced. They were critical of Benjamin's conviction that mass media could take on a positive political identification. They also argued that great works of art retained the formal capacity to overcome the new domination brought on by mass media.

Unlike Benjamin, who took his own life rather than risk arrest by the Gestapo, Adorno and Horkheimer escaped into exile in Southern California, where they witnessed first-hand the phenomenon of American popular culture and its mass media. They recognized the United States as a fully mediated society driven by a culture industry based on the buying and selling of audiences in exchange for media content. Like Marx, they argued that the culture industry not only transforms every aspect of culture into a commodity but also creates 'mass mystification'. They argued that the modern media of the day—especially radio, television, and film—had already submitted its content to models that required standardization of technique and a repetition of forms and contents, just like in a factory. Here, the problematic hero on a quest for authenticity in an inauthentic world disappears into the Hollywood formula and the 'happy ending'. Whether it is a news announcer, a soap opera star, or a popular song, each element of the cultural product is carefully scripted using techniques of mass production and distribution. They conclude that, given the imperative of a uniformity of signs and images, the culture industry leaves nothing to creative chance. As they put it, the 'culture industry' creates a constant conformity that even regulates relations with the past.

Negative media centred approaches demonstrate that our environments are thoroughly mediated for us through various technologies of mass communication, which tell us how to belong, feel, think, and act. Although the approach gives us insight into just how deeply mediated society affects us, it tends to leave us with the impression that media consumers are mere putty in the hands of the culture industry. Positive media centred approaches move to an opposite extreme where technologies of mass communication can be seen in an almost euphoric light of endless possibility and innovation.

Affirmations: Harold Innis and Marshall McLhuhan

In sharp contrast to the Frankfurt School, two Canadians from the University of Toronto—Harold Innis (1894–1952) and his student Marshall McLuhan (1911–1980)—were among the first to view the significance of the affirmative relation between media technologies of communication and power in society. Innis is most famous for his argument that all media of communication carry a bias that actively organizes society toward more centralized or decentralized forms of power distribution and empire. Heavier durable technologies that go into architecture or sculpture, like in Ancient Egypt, are said to emphasize a time bias; lighter forms of communication, like writing or computers, press the advantage of a space bias. Mediated societies that have a strong time bias tend to operate through decentralized but hierarchical forms of communication. Mediated societies that favour a spatial bias lean toward more centralized but less hierarchical forms of communication (Innis, 1972).

A simple example of how media technology creates a space bias can be seen by looking at former President George W. Bush when he first came to office in 2000. One of the first things his administration did was to replace the land-based telephones used by White House staff with cell phones in order to have a more centralized and complete record of all incoming and outgoing calls. This meant any calls to the media could be traced to individual users. This was part of the administration's plan to control access to information. While the lighter technology allowed greater mobility, it also permitted greater centralized control.

Marshall McLuhan shifted from defining the political and economic bias in media to looking at its effect on culture and civilization as a whole. For McLuhan, the media of communication are either hot or cool. Hot media, such as radio or cinema, require less participation from the audience, have a higher definition of a single sense, and unlock a greater capacity for us to receive their messages. On the other hand, hot media allow less participation than cool media. The lecture you will attend in class this week requires less participation than a seminar. Similarly, reading a chapter from your book will require less participation than your MSN instant messaging. Cool media, like the cell phone, require higher degrees of audience participation. This is because the audience has to respond to the speaker. We see from these examples that McLuhan had an affirmative view of mediated society and the new patterns of human behaviour it was introducing. He believed the 'media is the message' and not the content, per se. The new phenomena of media were creating a world he called the global village: 'We now live in a global village. . . a simultaneous happening. We are back in acoustic space. We have begun again to structure the primordial feeling, the tribal emotion from which a few centuries of literacy divorced us . . .' (McLuhan, 1967: 14).

Fatally Media Centred: Jean Baudrillard

Jean Baudrillard (1929–2007), a French postmodernist and iconoclastic sociologist, was among the first thinkers to absorb both negative and affirmative media centred positions. He was an early admirer of McLuhan, whom he referred to as 'the Canadian Texan'—perhaps because of his 'shoot from the hip' style of writing. Baudrillard argued in favour of McLuhan's idea that 'the medium is the message' but added that the basic structure of emerging society is one of consumption and not production as Marx had predicted. 'The medium is the message' means that 'the real message that radio and television deliver, the one that is unconsciously and deeply decoded by audiences, is not the content that is apparent in the images and sounds. It is rather the technology itself. The message of the television is not in the images that it transmits but rather the new mode of perception that it imposes on traditional group and family structure' (Baudrillard, 1970: 187).

Baudrillard argued beyond McLuhan that the most important thing to understand about modern mass media is that they are not just about a spectacle or about a global village. They are about the virtual possibility of consuming and assimilating all possible spectacles that could be imagined. He reverses McLuhan's affirmative position and concludes that mass media are 'an all powerful ideological vehicle . . . and that is the totalitarian "message" of a society of consumption' (1970: 189). Baudrillard posits the negative media centred thesis of complete control with images of concentration camps instead of McLuhan's global village built out of an ethics of responsibility and care.

Baudrillard nonetheless draws both affirmative and negative positions together across his numerous commentaries on contemporary communications technologies and resulting forms of mass consumption. Combining sociology, communications studies, and semiotics (the study of signs), he develops what he calls fatal strategies, rather than a theory of media as a way to keep pace with the ever-changing technologies themselves. He arrives at this position by situating the modern history of media, spanning from the renaissance to the industrial revolution and to the present postmodern phase. What he calls the procession of the simulacrum spans across four periods: (1) the age of the Symbolic and the Counterfeit; (2) the age of the Sign and Production; (3) the age of Simulation; and (4) the age of Hyperreality (Baudrillard, 1983).

Baudrillard argues that the hierarchical structure of communication in feudal society meant 'there was no such thing as fashion' among the masses. Every media of communication was so fixed into a specific symbolic status that only counterfeit copies of dress or manners from the aristocracy could create fashion. According to Baudrillard, a symbol has a more fixed meaning than a sign. The symbol refers to something real, but this is not necessarily the case for the sign. For example, a wedding ring is a symbol that represents a person's real relation to another in the context of a real community; an ordinary ring has no such symbolic use value although it does have a monetary value. The shift from the practical use value of the symbol to the exchange value of the sign is most pronounced in an industrial society built on mass production.

Following the democratic and industrial revolutions the sign replaced the symbol as the dominant mode of communication. As technologies of communication, like photocopy machines and faxes, advanced and this process became more sophisticated, Baudrillard described a shift from sign-based culture to a culture of simulation. **Simulation** would be the twentieth-century form of communication based on copies of copies, literally without originals. Note that this is very close to Adorno and Horkheimer's earlier critique of the culture industry as an apparatus that requires all culture conform to standardized production techniques. But Baudrillard takes their negation of media as a totalizing force in society much further.

The rise of mass media shifts mediated society away from the problem of mass production and toward increased fragmentation of family and community life into a period of serialization and sign-based culture, only to shift again into more advanced problems of mass consumption and distribution. Along with the change in the economic base of society and in group and family life, there is a shift away from heavier symbolic forms of communication to lighter sign-based forms.

As technologies of simulation advance beyond the former sign-based culture it becomes increasingly difficult to distinguish between the original copy of a cultural product and its copies. The **hyperreal** is what Baudrillard calls the ultimate effect of simulation. Hyperreality is images that appear more real than the real. Think of how a great goal in a hockey game was experienced in 1946 and then compare that to how it was experienced in last year's Stanley Cup game. In 1946, still in the era of the sign, there was no instant replay. Instead there was only a description by the radio announcer. Now we wait to see the play again on a screen and then review it over and over. Even the fans at the arena want to see the simulated replay. When the simulation seems more real than the real, we are in hyperreality.

Each of the above negative approaches reducees the role of mass media to either a process that leads to the loss of cultural knowledge, a form of standardization that leads to mass mystification, or a dynamic that transforms social reality into the fatal strategies of the hyperreal. In contrast, affirmative approaches see not only that empires depend on technologies of communication to maintain power and influence but also that the new medium of communication is able to create a global culture virtually on its own. Critical sociology carries forward the insights from each of these approaches but makes them more flexible by decentring the approach to mass media and society while adding other everyday forms of communication in order to concentrate analysis.

Decentred Approaches

Affirmative decentred approaches limit the scope of media influence to its role as an intermediary institution that provides connections between individuals and groups across society's main institutions. Although they represent two generations of sociology, George Herbert Mead (1863–1931) and Jürgen Habermas (1929–) developed what is called a normative definition of communication. A normative definition states what a thing should be like under ideal conditions and not what it actually is. In the first section below we preview their theories and propose an extension of those theories toward a

> A decentered media approach—which openly considers the varying importance that media, among the whole range of causal factors, may have in society—reduces the risk of our assuming that the sites where most of our symbolic resources are concentrated are both value-centered and the starting point of social explanation. It should make us more skeptical also about whether a social center in this sense exists at all. (Couldry, 2006: 19)

discussion of the role media play in creating mediated society without focusing on technologies of communication as the primary force of intervention.

Norms also discipline and coerce agents to conform, which raises the crucial question of how to account for change and ruptures from norms. To get at this question we introduce the decentred negative approach of **deconstruction** developed by the French philosopher Jacques Derrida (1930–2004), the genealogical approach to power and discourse in the work of Michel Foucault (1926–1984), and a combination of both approaches applied to the area of gender studies by the contemporary scholar Judith Butler (1956–).

Affirmations: George Herbert Mead and Jürgen Habermas

Mead was a philosopher and sociologist at the University of Chicago and the first to define society as a regime of communication. This is different from the previous approaches, which perceived the technologies of media as supporting the dominant power structure of society. Society as a regime of communication comes about through the many everyday, practical ways in which actors communicate in what Mead calls a language of gestures. The 'generalized other' is the term Mead uses to describe the communication storehouse of the language of gestures built by communities that begins normalizing agents in early childhood. The generalized other informs an agent's social conscience in such a way that the agent is aware of the attitudes we can expect from a given community, an awareness that enters the conduct of a person throughout their life cycle as language is learned and as various roles are played out as a member of society.

Mead defines the person as a self made up of a creative 'I', a more receptive 'me', and a 'generalized other'. Recall that an institution in sociological terms is both a creative site and a set of rules that help shape the way we act. Whenever people communicate and share understandings together they are expressing an institution that is part of society. Mead argues that there are two stages in the socialization of the self within institutions. In the first stage, for example, a child learns through play and, eventually, through games to understand attitudes of others that are addressed toward her and through the response given to other individuals she participates with across various acts. In the second phase a fuller development of the self occurs when the attitudes of the generalized other or larger group to which she belongs are absorbed and responded to.

The 'I' is that deeper part of the self that acts or reacts to others and so is difficult to represent. Think of how you feel about yourself when you look in a mirror. You see an image of yourself that others see. We get a similar sense when we see a movie that is filmed in our hometown or in a place with which we are familiar. Yet you never quite see the 'I' in a mirror or in a locally produced film. Whereas the 'I' is the part of the self that is difficult to represent, the 'me' is my awareness of how others see my appearance or how I would like them to see my appearance. A person with a strong 'me' is keenly aware of others and often draws others toward himself, whereas a person with a strong 'I' is only partially aware of others, and may push others away. The 'I' is the part of yourself that gives you a unique agency or power to create, resist, or act on alternatives. The 'me' is that part of you that responds more cooperatively to the attitudes of others. When we assume an attitudinal stance in front of the mirror we imagine how we would like others to see us. Sometimes when we listen to our favourite music we imagine how others might see us in a similar way. This is the 'me' that anticipates the normalization of fashion or that absorbs the attitudes of many more people that make up a given group or complex of communities that Mead calls 'the generalized other'.

For Mead identity is formed in the search by the self to achieve understanding from the process of interpersonal communication. A person knows herself as a subject from the memory she has of herself and from what she sees in the gaze of others. In remembering the 'I' we are no longer in the experience of the 'I' but of the 'me'. 'The me is the organized set of attitudes of others which one assumes. This theoretical me represents a definite organization of the community there in our own attitudes, and calling for a response, but the response that takes place is something that just happens' (Mead, 1934: 175).

Mead was the first sociologist to explain how a mediated society is in fact possible. Though radio, for example, came to North America as a means to sell products through mass advertising, its basic assumption about socialization was very sociological. This assumption continues all the way through to today and the new media. Both sociologists and media producers continue to assume that whenever someone speaks with someone else, whether in virtual or real time and space, the speaker calls out an image in the mind of the person that is assumed to be the same image the speaker has in mind. For Mead, communication starts in the thinking process as a kind of interior dialogue. Thinking in the language of gestures leads to acts in the language of gestures. For communication to be possible, however, the symbols of communication have to be universal. For Mead, this minimum process of understanding through communication with others is not at the centre of human society and culture—*it is society*—which is itself an endlessly decentred regime of communication.

Communicative Action and the Public Sphere

Although Habermas has never directly treated the question of the status of mass media in a separate work, his commentary on the work of the earlier members of the Frankfurt School and his concepts of the public sphere and of communicative action provide an affirmative decentred approach to mediated society. Habermas connects the seemingly opposite conceptual strategies of a society composed of a system of institutions with a lifeworld, or the individual and community worlds of lived experiences. He connects these two dimensions by introducing the concept of the public sphere and of communicative action.

Communicative actions are defined as rationally motivated attempts to move toward shared agreements between people concerning norms that can be agreed on within limited lifeworlds or cultural contexts. 'In communicative action one actor seeks rationally to motivate another by relying on the illocutionary binding effect of the offer contained in his speech act' (Habermas, 1990: 58). In communicative action, the addressee accepts truth claims not only because of the logic of an argument but also because the speaker has invested a personal sincerity and guarantee of its validity. The guarantee enters into the coordination of the relation between the speaker and the addressee. The binding effect of communicative actions is not achieved through political or economic force but rather through the creation of unconstrained, unforced, mutual understandings.

The **public sphere**, discussed in more detail in Chapter 2, is, in a way, the collective result of communicative actions. Generated in large part by the institution of media, it is understood to be positioned between the multiple lifeworlds or everyday cultural contexts in a given society and institutions of power and money, such as the government and the economy. The public sphere is defined as working toward an ideal speech community wherein each potential speaker might have equal opportunity to be heard. Habermas traces the important role of mass media and public opinion to its genesis in the emergence of newspapers and coffee houses in the eighteenth century. Since then journalists have been reporting daily on the state of the economy.

The influence of media on the economy is most easily seen in the role advertising has played since the beginning of mass media in North America. Ideally news journalism should act a little differently than business journalism. Its role in the public sphere is to act as a skeptical medium that checks and verifies facts and provides balanced arguments on pressing issues of the day. Good journalism should take into account all different points of view so the public can be better informed when making decisions. Ideally journalism is supposed to fact-check and verify claims made by governments and business so voters and consumers can be knowledgeable about the everyday issues that help make up public opinion.

Habermas argues that everyday lifeworlds and institutional subsystems like media uncouple when the task of producing the binding effects between them is transferred from communicative actions to other spheres of society. In modern societies, creation of the public sphere relies on increased rationalization of conflicting lifeworlds in order to maintain a unity that is protected from economics, law, and politics. The 'cultural autonomy' of lifeworlds also increases pressure back on the public sphere, which must also absorb other forces. For example, the modern discourse on rights sets up a cascading effect so that claims of autonomy for a lifeworld are repeated across distinct lifeworlds as a plea that seeks constantly to redraw boundaries or achieve more equitable representation within the public sphere itself or that reaches into the economic, legal, or political spheres for a more equal share of goods and services.

Habermas follows Mead's definition of society as a regime of communication going a long way to situate a critical sociology of mediated society. Being members of mediated society means we are socialized to understand what normal ways of acting and feelings are. We are always in a position where norms can be contested from the point of view of conflicting lifeworlds even though mediated society operates across the trilogy of basic sociological categories at the most basic levels. Mediated society organizes us around values or the things and ideas we think are desirable and reassures us about what we want regarding 'the good', the beautiful, and the 'ugly'. We learn roles or expectations about how to act and, most importantly, how to differentiate our increasingly complex roles according to the levels of status to which we achieve or aspire. Yet both learning and contesting norms are possible in a decentred definition of mediated society.

Negations: Jacques Derrida, Michel Foucault, and Judith Butler

Deconstruction helps us challenge how mediated society creates a sense of normalness rather than mapping out the functions media should play in society, as we just saw with Habermas. For Derrida, society is always what 'remains to come which must include the possibility of a future that cannot be predicted from the past'. For deconstruction any statement that defines who or what the subject of mediated society is needs to be put into question so as to 'dislocate, displace, disarticulate, put out of the joint of authority' (Derrida, as cited in Lucy, 2004: 12). Only by finding out the **undecidables** within a given context can we find ways to question the normal, natural way of doing things and point to both alternative strategies and the possibility of what is yet to come.

This suggests that once again we also need to think about how media discourse is presented toward both an imaginary and real audience. As we discussed earlier, an implied audience is the one that media imagines it is addressing, whereas the real audience is the one that experiences the program. Although it is impossible to ever see or meet all the other members of a mass audience, it is possible to imagine oneself within the mass. It is also possible to imagine an image about who that mass audience is in terms of how they might feel about what is right or what are normal values. For example, when we watch Tina Fey on *Saturday Night Live* imitate Sarah Palin, we may watch it alone or with friends but we know there is at least a good chance we share the same laughter with many others we do not know personally but who we can assume watched the same program. We call this the imaginary audience, as opposed to the real or empirical audience. The imaginary audience is not made up or fictional but it is not real either. Without any knowledge about who the others are we still have a common idea about what they would find funny. These generalized attitudes are inscribed in the media, which also houses an assumption about what is the normal way to feel about things and what is not.

Deconstruction means questioning this 'normal' meaning of the 'real'. It studies *how* something means and not *what* it means (Derrida, 1992; 2002). If we ask an audience what a red light at a street corner means, for example, we can say it is a sign that means all possible members of the audience should stop their forward progress when they approach it. But if we ask how the red light is constructed as a meaning, the first thing we want to know is how is this a 'normal' meaning and not an ambiguous one, and how is the audience for this meaning real or simply potential? How is it that the green light means we should move forward and not simply stop and think about it or stop and talk it over (Powell, 2007)? When we ask how images, sounds, and words mean things and see that they can mean many opposite things, we know we can always call into question their normal meanings.

The goal of deconstruction is to seize upon a meaning that is undecidable so it calls into question how origins, centres, and binary oppositions like green and red, male and female, or right and wrong are used to make up meaning in the first place. In other words, creating undecidables defers meaning. To capture both the sense of deferral and the sense of a constant difference Derrida coins the term '*differance*'—spelling it with an *a* rather than an *e*. No strong decision about anything important should be made without undecidables or without differance. Hence, for deconstruction, how to represent something begins with tracing its origin and undoing that to which it refers.

Undoing Gender Norms

Mass media play with undecidables all the time. For example, can we know for sure whether the image of Hillary Clinton's tears during her speech to the

Democratic presidential primary in 2008 was telling us that her feelings were hurt or was it more about manipulating public opinion? Or both? If we ask *what* the image means and to whom we get a different answer than if we ask *how* it means and to whom it is implied. How is the picture of Hillary Clinton's tears a mediated experience and not an immediate and real one? We all know that when we view her image we are not immediately experiencing her act as if we were standing next to her. And yet, we do get a real experience about society's order because of her image—a sense of its patriarchal past and sexism against women, of what is yet to come (the first woman president?), or what some might hope against (not another Clinton?) or hope for (that she wins? that Obama wins?).

In deconstruction meanings are governed by binary opposites whose genesis vastly extends back and beyond our individual capacities to touch, sense, and grasp all of what is going on. In other words, even Ms Clinton's tears extend into both the past and the future. This disruption of the past through the possibility of a future is why society is always becoming itself and can never be an exact copy of what it was before. If Hillary Clinton is not simply a copy, it follows that media are very much involved with old questions about who we have been and who we might become with them and through them. Once again we find ourselves with the problem of norms but here it is more about their symbolic implication than either their imaginary representation or real practice.

Michel Foucault's genealogical method, like Derrida's deconstruction, looks to upset claims about what is 'normal' or 'natural' by tracing the origins of discourse, disciplines, and institutions or regimes of knowledge that struggle to shape the body, mind, and emotions (Foucault, 2003). Key to Foucault's analysis is a new concept of power. What he calls the 'spiral of power and pleasure' occurs whenever institutions and technologies try to repress or correct abnormality. The more power seeks to define an abnormality then the more the abnormality resists definition. There is pleasure in the application of the technologies of power and there is pleasure in hiding the abnormality, going underground, and resisting. Power in this sense is not a force of domination but a force that is everywhere while at the same time being a force that is resisted everywhere.

The poststructural way of thinking about power means looking at events as creating subjects. These subjects, in turn, resist discipline rather than examining subjects or selves that act against or create structures, as we saw with classical sociology and other modern theorists. The discourse of mediated society would be seen by Foucault as a contemporary form of bio power that helps make bodies more docile. More docile bodies can be governable and, in the process, produce subjects. In mediated society we can say that discourse means everything that is said, and everything that can be said, written, filmed, or transmitted through communication technologies that subjects us to normalization. Poststructuralist approaches in line with Derrida and Foucault examine the subjection of the self or subjects to discourse, power, and knowledge. In other words they ask how subjects emerge from events or acts and not how the self creates an event or act.

In this same approach, Judith Butler, the popular American feminist and queer studies scholar, understands gender norms not so much as rules or laws that guide how we should perform our gender but as 'implicit standards of normalization' that shape us as subjects and, in the process, set the standard for what it means to be human or non-human. As Fred Evans points out, Butler 'replaces Derrida's notion of text with the Foucauldian idea of power . . . power precedes and constitutes our recognizability as gendered bodies, and it also exceeds the identity of subjects it has created' (Evans, 2008: 132). However, Butler is not entirely satisfied with Foucault's theory. She sees that Foucault has understood how subjects are created by regimes of power but she wants to also know who those subjects are and what definition they have been given regarding the possibility of recognition as being human subjects. For Butler, the significance of Hillary Clinton's tears would not simply be a question about performing a certain kind of femininity in politics but also about how *gender is subjected to a compulsory norm* and how the gendered subject gains recognition of its norm from others. Gender is not what one is 'nor what one has, it is the apparatus by which the production and normalization of masculine and feminine takes place'. Gender is a performance of an idealized form or one that 'acts to approximate it' (Butler, 2004: 42). Butler asks us to consider more carefully and more critically the history of gender ideals in order to undo what they imply will be and will not be a recognizable form of 'normal' human existence.

Butler's more active and interventionist stand avoids the approach to understanding norms as products of communicative action or any neutral regime of communication. Butler would define society more as a regime of discourse, power, and knowledge than a regime of communication. For Butler, norms are not fixed laws or rules because they can also be overturned, ruptured, or transformed. Rather than approaching the self as looking to join a generalized other, she would want us to examine how the regime of communication that makes up the generalized other excludes all those who do not fit the norm. She asks what norms govern my being as a recognizable person and where and who is the other that recognizes me (Butler, 2006).

At first glance deconstruction, genealogy, and performance theory appear to contradict the approach of communicative action where we seek understanding together in society understood as a regime of communication. Yet if we can agree that communication discourse refers not only to everything that is said in mediated society but also everything that is sayable in a given context, then both approaches are clearly needed. Critical sociology works toward uncovering the processes in mutual understanding but also considers these processes in light of undecidables and the critique of norms. It asks not only the question about what something in the media means but also *how and toward whom is it performed*. Otherwise we risk falling back into the negative media centred thesis according to which no emancipatory form of communication is possible.

Summary

In this chapter we introduced the sources needed to develop a critical sociology of mediated society. Sources were drawn from classical sociology and from both media centred and decentred sociological and philosophical principles. Critical sociology looks to understand the tension between how a discourse imagines it is addressing itself, what is the subject being represented, how the subject is being subjected, and who is being recognized in the message. It asks how the meaning is framed by seizing upon undecidables in the image. It also distinguishes between good and bad uses of media. A television program, a newspaper report, a film, and a YouTube video are all ways of inferring how a set of norms and values accepts, rejects, or holds alternative views. Finding the tensions between whose views are addressed by the program producers or authors; how the subjects of the stories, images, or reports are given meaning; and who actually watches the program or reads the magazine are what the critical sociology of mediated society is all about.

In many ways mass media of communication communicate with us at the interpersonal level in the same way Mead, Innis, and McLuhan saw that we communicate with each other. In other ways, through culture industries or simulations, for example, they do not work at all the way we communicate together. On the one hand, Adorno, Horkheimer, and Baudrillard argue that the social that sociologists refer to has actually lead us into mystification, or even disappeared into the mass, which, in turn, is an effect of new media as they become more and more sophisticated and able to copy human intelligence. We are in this sense subjected to the mediated society even when we are unaware of how much media are simply representing or informing us about others' experiences. On the other hand, critical sociology also understands, along with deconstruction, that challenging what is normal is always happening in culture. The pull against certitudes is there whenever we challenge an 'is' with a 'maybe'. As such, it is important to look at the audience from the point of view of the discourse, the said and the sayable, or the language of gestures that carries the sense of truth and its link to power and discipline. We become men and women—and maybe both men and women at once. We become parents but were once children, teachers but were once students. Sometimes our friends can become our enemies or our enemies can become our friends. Feeling and desires are disciplined within and across a variety of institutions but feeling and desire are never reduced to these institutions or to the disciplines that may have named them. Even when they are, we can call those disciplines into question; we can get rid of them for better ones, or we can pretend to go on without discipline.

Enhanced Learning Activities

1. Explain the concepts of norms, values, and roles as they are presented in an episode from the HBO series *Mad Men*. Explain how the series is both an instituted and instituting representation of gender, family, and social life in mediated society.
2. Compare the differences between negative and positive media centred approaches discussed in the chapter. Which one do you see as more relevant to understanding your experience of mediated society?
3. Compare and contrast the differences between positive and negative media decentred approaches. Which one do you see as more relevant to understanding your experience of mediated society?
4. Discuss the family in the television series *Weeds* and how the series is an example of deconstruction and of undoing gender norms. Explain Derrida's and Butler's definitions of these concepts.
5. Choose a film or television series you like that illustrates Habermas's concept of communicative action and Mead's theory of the 'I', 'me', and 'generalized other'.

Annotated Further Reading

Jean Baudrillard, *Simulations*. Trans. P. Foss et al. New York: Semiotext, 1983. *Simulations* is a very accessible presentation of the critique of stages of media, culture, and societal development from feudalism to the present.

James Gordon Finlayson, *Habermas: A Very Short Introduction*. New York: Oxford UP, 2005. This text is an accessible introduction to Habermas's theories of the public sphere, the discourse principle of democracy, and communicative action.

Amy Goodman and David Goodman, *Static: Government Liars, Media Cheerleaders, and the People Who Fight Back*. New York: Hyperion Books, 2006. This work is a basic resource for mounting a critique of contemporary media. Amy Goodman is a tireless advocate for making mediated society into a better world.

Jim Powell, *Deconstruction for Beginners*. Writers and Readers Documentary Comic Books, 2007. This is good background reading for understanding the way deconstruction is used in critical sociology; it is also one of the clearest introductions to Derrida's deconstruction.

Niklas Luhmann, *The Reality of the Mass Media*. Stanford, CA.: University of Stanford Press, 2000. This is a rare outline for a general sociology of mass media by the late German sociologist, and it is very helpful for understanding the mass media as a system and as an environment for mediated society.

Judith Butler, *Undoing Gender*. New York: Routledge, 2004. This is a collection of essays that provide a critical sociology of contemporary norms of gender and sexual orientation.

Useful Media

Concision: No Time for New Ideas **(1994; 14 min, 37s)**
http://onf-nfb.gc.ca/eng/collection/film/?id=31896

This video considers the implications of the structure and format of television, especially how the consequences of these elements can shape the messages of the medium. The media construct reality, and in the conclusion we see the author participating in that very process.

Constructing Reality: Exploring Media Issues in Documentary—The Politics of Truth **(1993; 72 min, 40s)**
http://onf-nfb.gc./eng/collection/film/?id=29925

Constructing Reality is designed to stimulate critical examinations of documentary filmmaking, television, and culture. This film—one of a series—deals with conventions of authenticity, the creation of propaganda, the status of docudramas with their mix of fact and fiction, and the biases involved in the construction of television news programs.

2

The Public Sphere

Learning Objectives

- To learn the meaning of discourse, dialogue, and dialogic
- To consider publics, public opinion, and public spaces
- To assess the strength of media-produced public spaces
- To consider the role of gender in the creation and use of public spaces
- To review state control of media in relation to public spaces
- To review commercial control in relation to public spaces
- To consider the commodification of audiences

Introduction

In this chapter we continue the main theme of **mediated citizenship** through an exploration of media-constructed public spaces and the tensions arising as citizen, state, and corporate worlds collide over issues of content, control of, and participation in the media. We explore the media as a public space in which dialogue and debate are either encouraged or restrained. We look at both the state and private enterprise from a perspective of encouragement and restraint. Following a discussion of Jürgen Habermas's concept of the public sphere, initially referred to in the previous chapter, and Charles Taylor's work on **public spaces**, we note that mass media is, among other things, a vehicle of public opinion—both carrier and creator. Even the most passive listening (radio) or watching (TV) carries a level of interactivity and public **discourse**.

For the last 25 years the press, the academy, government policy debates, and innumerable other sources have informed us that we are in the midst of a great transformation brought about by new, and, yet again, newer technologies of communication, earlier referred to as 'the information highway' and now as the new media or 'Web 2.0' technology. Claims are made regarding the expansion of dialogue, social networks, community, and public spaces and an enhancement of democracy and citizenship (Mosco, 2004; Carey, 1989: 113–41). Consider that during the summer of 2008 customers lined up at stores around the world to buy an iPhone; in Canadian cities, customers lined up at 3:00 PM on a Thursday afternoon in order to be first in line the next morning! Following sea, rail, and air transport; the press; telegraph, telephone, radio, and television; and now the Internet and the iPhone, have we arrived at the zenith of human communication? Have we now reached the summit of our communications capability? Maybe, but some caution is required. The distinction between **agency** (the power of self-determination) and **structure** (the exercise of power and authority—interests and social relations that regulate actors) draws attention to everyday discourse and public spaces as potentially dialogical and active—as interactively communicating ideas, hopes, and fears in contrast with interests as organized status and power (Archer, 1988; Habermas, 1987). The new media, specifically the Internet, are inclined to invite open discourse (agency) but within the confines of the marketplace (structure and power relations).

Accordingly, taking into account the social and economic organization of the Internet, it has been pointed out that although one might posit Internet sites as public spaces, one must also 'take into consideration the extent to which it is now a commercial space in which the logics of promotion and consumption organize and order all social dynamics, including those of community and self' (Cavanagh, 2007: 133). Note, too, that as early as 1995 one researcher concluded that 'the convergence of technologies are [*sic*] structurally transforming our economy, with three results: privatization, deregulation and globalization' (Johnston, Johnston, and Handa, 1995: 211). Indeed, the very process of individualization—the breakdown of community and common interests—accompanying much of the new technologies would appear to preclude genuine dialogue in the sense that each party to a conversation fully recognizes and respects the other and positions taken are not subject to authoritarian judgment. In contrast, promises are made: promises concerning the potential for dialogue and the potential for amplifying citizen participation in community, regional, and national decision making.

Considering these issues, the objective of this chapter is twofold. We will explore, on the one hand, the tension between the promise of dialogue and the commercial forces of privatization, regulation, and control and, on the other hand, the tension between the process of individualization and the compelling drive toward community inherent in the means of communication. We must recognize as well that the very concept of community is fragmented along ethnic, racial, linguistic, and gender lines. In the course of pursuing this line of inquiry we will examine the impediments to and opportunities for creating public spaces open to the new media. We begin with an examination of the concepts of the public sphere and public space. This will be followed with a look at the way in which radio in the past has made use of its potential in this regard, a consideration of television as public space, and the Internet and related technologies. Finally, we will revisit state control and commercial dominance.

Public Spaces

The concept of the 'public sphere' was advanced by Jürgen Habermas, specifically referring to the eighteenth-century development of a 'sphere of private people coming together as a public . . . to engage [authority] in a debate over the general rules governing . . . commodity exchange and social labour' (1991: 27). The public sphere is a concept that has come to mean a place where discussion is carried out about what goods and services should be transformed or kept, regulated or deregulated, about what laws should be changed or reinforced, about what languages should be encouraged, about what religious practices should be accommodated, and about where schools should be built, among any other number of subjects concerning the common good. In principle, anyone may enter this sphere and challenge the 'normal' way of doing things in society but, in practice, the ability to enter the public sphere has always been constrained and highly regulated. The modern public in mediated societies like ours is made up of multiple 'imaginary communities' of individuals who are addressed through the media. It is therefore important to consider not only the time in which people are 'listening' or 'watching' programs together but also the places from which the programs are produced and the kind of access the audiences have to participation in the production of public space. From a parallel perspective and with contemporary media in mind, Charles Taylor elaborated on the concept, describing the public sphere 'as a *common space* in which the members of society meet, through a variety of media (print, radio, TV, the Internet) and also in face-to-face encounters, to discuss matters of common interest; and thus be able to form a common mind about those matters' (1995: 259).

The key to understanding the relevance of public spaces in relation to the media lies in Habermas's reference to 'private people coming together as a public'. People, as individuals—free from the constraints of family, kinship, the state, and their occupations—gather to 'discuss matters of common interest'. Habermas's work was an historical and sociological analysis of public gatherings during the seventeenth and eighteenth centuries and their impact on the political life of the time. Habermas, as we discussed in Chapter 1, is criticized for both his optimism regarding the ideal possibility of dialogue in democratic societies and for his pessimism about the **commodification** of media (Goode, 2005).

Taylor expanded on the possibilities inherent in the work, pointing to contemporary media as a venue for public debate; that is, as a public sphere or, to use his later concept, the media as *public space*. Public space is equated with civil society as 'elaborated entirely outside of . . . any authority whatever . . . [and] through no official, established hierarchical organs of definition' (1995: 217). This perspective, as Charles Taylor noted, emerged from seventeenth- and eighteenth-century debates on the role of free associations (including communities) and association (including interactive networks) as a political force. These debates generated the notion of an autonomous public and, later, a conceptualization of 'public opinion' (1995: 216–17). Before proceeding further we must stop to consider the concepts of *the public* or ***publics*** and ***public opinion***, concepts which in their use imply the opposite, *private space* or *opinion*.

Publics

We begin with reference to Vincent Mosco's discussion in *The Political Economy of Communication*. He noted that *public* life draws attention to 'social processes that carry out democracy . . . advancing equality and the fullest possible participation in the complete range of economic, political, social, and cultural decision-making' (1996: 170). These processes differ from the individual's *private* life and from the marketplace. This straightforward public/private distinction is further complicated by the several referents used when we speak about 'publics'. Consider the following uses:

1. 'Public' as government activity, as in 'public service broadcasting' (e.g., CBC in Canada, ZDF in Germany, BBC in the UK, or PBS in the United States). In this sense 'private' refers to commercial broadcasting (e.g., CTV or Global in Canada, or CBS or NBC in the United States);

2. 'Public' as something available to all, such as a 'public park', or that which we hold in common, in contrast with 'private property' and the market-place; and,
3. 'Public' as in town hall meetings, community gatherings, or a pickup hockey game on an outside rink, in contrast with the 'privacy' of family or personal life.

The second and third uses of 'public' convey a sense of private individuals participating in public domains and, as pointed out by Thompson, 'the nature of what is public and what is private, and the demarcation between these domains, are transformed in certain ways by the development of mass communication . . .' (1990: 238). Images and thoughts which were considered private but which are becoming public as they are loaded onto Facebook and YouTube is an example of this. Between broadcasting and the Internet the boundary between public and private is weakened.

Media as a public space and as the creator and mediator of publics is somewhat akin to Castells' 'network society': a social structure composed of virtual 'networks powered by microelectronics-based information and communication technologies' (2004: 3). As Castells so clearly pointed out, current Internet communication in a multimedia system is no longer 'characterized by one-way messages to a mass audience' (2004: 3). There are always other radio and TV stations and other new media that can deliver the message. When critical sociology asks who are the audiences for these messages it is not only referring to the publics that are listening or seeing them. It is important to also know who the audiences are which the senders of the messages imagine they are addressing. This is complicated because multiple channels of communication increase interactivity between senders and receivers. The implication is that public spaces have multiplied, as have their real and imagined audiences. It would appear that media no longer constructs public space as a single space held in common, but as a plurality of spaces built around a variety of interests. But what of the public good, free of the authority of the marketplace and the state? What are the implications of a plurality of decentred spaces for any attempt on the part of the media to create dialogical and deliberative spaces? Is there always the danger that media-created public space will turn into commercial and marketplace traps, thus ensuring that participants revert to the role of highly individualized commodities? Can we assume the possibility that market-driven publics are counter-public? We will return to these questions.

Public Opinion

'Public' in the sense of the second and third uses described in the previous section, especially the third use, implies discussion, debate, and negotiation over the issues of the day. This, in turn, implies the formulation of agreements, of consensus, and of opinion held in common or public opinion. In this use, 'opinion' is understood to be a statement of an individual or a collective thought on a particular topic or question, such as an upcoming election, the effect of copyright law on the Internet, or crime and punishment. These are both real and imaginary processes in mediated societies. Here we find not just the sum of individual opinions, as is found in public opinion polling, but a position which has been elaborated through discussion and so recognized, and a position which has been elaborated outside of official, hierarchical, and established structures (Taylor, 1995: 216–17). In this sense public opinion is not a marketing or political device presented as public opinion by the press and electronic media. Nevertheless, there is a very strong movement to present the results of polling as though they represented public deliberation and argument; that is, true public opinion. Polling presents the reader/listener with no more than the sum of individual, private opinions classified according to common demographic variables. Our question is, to what extent does the media, if at all, create and communicate collective and deliberative public opinion? To answer this we turn to an assessment of media-created spaces.

Media and Public Spaces

To assess past and existing practices of media-constructed public spaces, where citizens will find opportunities for deliberation and decision making elaborated entirely outside of any authority whatsoever and through no official and established hierarchical organs of definition, we advance the following evaluative criteria. Media-constructed public-spaces must be:

- *Dialogic and active* in the sense of facilitating reasonable discussion and argument or discursive relationships between organizations, groups, and individuals ordered through dialogue rather than through existing patterns of authority (Slevin, 2000: 5). Dialogical discourse presupposes intersubjectivity such that the speaker and addressee recognize, respect, and enter each other's space of authority. It is in this space that exchange, agreement, and disagreement become a creative process (Nielsen, 2002: 49–65). More than a decade ago Niklas Luhmann drew attention to a crucial difference between interaction among those '*co-present*' and the 'interposition of technology' by media institutions (Luhmann, 2000: 2). The potential for a media-constructed space to be dialogic is thus, for the time being, limited.
- *Free from the organizational thrust of promotion and consumption in the marketplace.* Commercial control of public spaces may unduly influence free discussion. Once participants are subjected to commercial spin and become commodities for sale to advertisers, free discussion is severely limited;

limited because the commercial imperative takes over the design and intent of the site.

- *Free of hierarchical organs of definition.* 'How might . . . [broadcasters] allow organizations, groups and individuals to make things happen rather than to have things happen to them, in the context of overall social goals' (Nielsen, 2002: 49–65). To what extent does state control of radio, television, and Internet outlets discourage or unduly influence free discussion? Who selects the topics for discussion, the authority vested in the site, or the participants?
- *Respond to the problem of a plurality of spaces.* Is it possible 'for interlocutors to bracket status differentials and to deliberate *as if* they were social equals' (Fraser, 1992: 117)? Variations in age, gender, race, language, and income will tend to create, at the level of everyday life, a multiplicity of publics and public spaces. Can this plurality of spaces be temporarily put aside in response to an inclusive definition of the citizen? Perhaps, but to assume that a plurality of sources can simply and without negotiation be put aside risks ignoring the fact that societal inequality, including gender, is indeed a fact of everyday political life.
- *Respond to the question 'who are the publics implied by the media address?'* What is the relation between media institutions, the subjects they discuss, and the publics they imagine they are addressing? Are there gaps between the publics they imagine and the subjects they discuss? Can these gaps help us understand the relations of order in the public sphere as well as the potential for disrupting order?

Keeping these criteria in mind, we will examine: (1) early radio programming designed to create public debate; (2) the interlocutor role of radio in a **multicultural** setting; (3) current press, radio, and television links to the new media; and (4) the new social media.

CBC Radio's Early Experiments with Public Spaces[1]

Beginning in the 1930s and through to the 1950s the Canadian Broadcasting Corporation (CBC) broadcast various discussion programs focusing on national, regional, and local community political issues. Two test series, *Inquiry into Co-operation* and *Community Clinic*, were broadcast during the late 1930s. These depression-era programs involving community organizations in discussion sessions predated the later *National Farm Radio Forum* (known to its listeners as simply the *Farm Forum*). Once launched, *Farm Forum*—a listener discussion program devoted to political and agricultural issues—was supported by the CBC, the Canadian Association for Adult Education (CAAE), the Canadian Federation of Agriculture, the United Farmers of Ontario Co-operative, and Montreal's Macdonald College. Incidentally, apart from the CBC itself, these and many similar associations were the backbone of the Canadian Radio League, which pressured the federal government into nationalizing broadcasting in 1932. Listeners, mainly rural residents, gathered around the radio to hear and discuss the latest agricultural news and political issues relevant to farming. The broadcaster encouraged and received letters supporting or rejecting positions taken over the air.

Following the success of *Farm Forum* as a discussion program, the CBC and the CAAE began experiments in Western Canada in 1940, leading to *Farm Forum*'s urban cousin, *Citizens' Forum*, which was described as 'Canada's national platform for the exchange of views' (*CBC Times*, 16 Oct. 1949: 5). With one program oriented toward agricultural interests and the other toward general social issues, the two programs adopted a similar format. With the exception of regular dramatic presentations on *Farm Forum*, each program invited listeners to form discussion groups in their *communities and associations*. At the conclusion of each day's program the group's secretary would mail in a report on their deliberations to a *Farm Forum* or *Citizens' Forum* provincial office. These reports, in turn, would be summarized on a subsequent broadcast. Groups were invited to suggest topics for programs and 'weekly bulletins for background reading in connection with the broadcasts [were] sent regularly to those listeners who [registered] with their provincial office.' In addition, *Farm Forum* held annual conferences. One such, held in 1950 in Brandon, Manitoba, 'included provincial *Farm Forum* secretaries, representatives of listening groups, and [representatives from the CBC and farm organizations]' (*CBC Times*, 16 July 1950: 4). In 1948 it was reported that 'more than twenty-seven thousand persons met regularly in sixteen hundred groups on farms and in towns to listen to the National Farm Radio Forum broadcasts' (*CBC Times*, 23 Oct. 1949: 5).

The newer *Citizens' Forum* reported more than 400 groups participating in 1947 (*CBC Times*, 24 Oct. 1948: 5). *Citizens' Forum* also used a variety of formats, ranging from single speakers to panel discussions and broadcasts from community group settings. This latter format included the Edmonton Home and School Council, the Ottawa Branch of the Community Planning Association, the Regina Chamber of Commerce, the Hamilton Film Council, and Montreal's NDG Community Council (*CBC Times*, 15 Oct. 1950: 10). At the suggestion of participants, 'How to use farm credit', 'What will the St Lawrence Seaway mean to us?', and 'Compensation for farm workers' were examples of topics addressed on *Farm Forum*. 'Has NATO supplanted the UN in Canadian Foreign Policy?', 'Is it a case of quality versus quantity in education?' and 'Has parliament become a rubber stamp for cabinet?' were among the issues considered on *Citizens' Forum*.

Yet another attempt at participant programming during the 1950s, *The Ways of Mankind*, was linked to these earlier designs through the use of much improved recording technologies and the presence in almost every household and community group of a 'hi-fi' turntable, amplifier, and speakers. In 1954 the series was remastered on 33.3 RPM vinyl discs and distributed with an instruction manual and readings by the CAAE to community groups across the country. The recordings, distributed as a discussion package with manuals, and an invitation by the CAAE to share discussion conclusions linked the *Ways of Mankind* series with the earlier *Forums*.

The first segment of this series comprised 13 one-hour dramatizations designed to 'explore the origin and development of cultures, customs and folkways in various parts of the world' (*CBC Times*, 5 April 1953: 2). In effect, this was an introductory anthropology course written by several regular contributors to CBC drama productions. The series was 'produced at the broadcaster's Toronto studios as part of a project arranged by the (American) National Association of Educational Broadcasters (NAEB) under a grant from the Fund for Adult Education established by the Ford Foundation' (*CBC Times*, 5 April 1953: 2). Walter Goldschmidt, then Professor of Anthropology at the University of California, Los Angeles, was the director of the project. Covering the topics of language, culture, education, values, ethics, religion, authority, groups, status and role, family, technology, and the arts, the series was first made available to 70 member stations of the NAEB (the forerunner to National Public Radio) and later broadcast as a CBC drama department production over its Trans-Canada Network.

The material received critical acclaim in the United States, from *The New York Times*: 'Some of the best radio programming on this side of the Atlantic has been produced in the studios of the Canadian Broadcasting Corporation' and from *Variety*: 'Mr. Allen [the producer] and his colleagues are not the ones to be overwhelmed by the word "education". They believe in bringing the real professional know-how of entertainment to their task and they did this superbly . . . a little more radio like this and it will be television's turn to start worrying' (*CBC Times*, 5 April 1953: 2). The reference here was to the first episode in a series titled 'A Word in Your Ear', as announced on the opening recording:

> This is the first of a series of ten discussion programs offered by the Fund for Adult Education to help you achieve a better understanding of the basic principles that govern human behavior. The programs have been constructed around ten radio dramas selected from the series *Ways of Mankind*, prepared under the supervision of Dr. Walter Goldschmidt, of the Department of Anthropology & Sociology, the University of California at Los Angeles. These dramas, designed to show how people live in different times and places, were done under the auspices of the National Association of Educational Broadcasters; they were produced in the studios of the Canadian Broadcasting Corporation, Toronto. The ten recordings selected for this series have been adapted for discussion by Dr. Goldschmidt in collaboration with the staff of the Fund for Adult Education. (Jackson, 2002: 95–107)

Small groups of people gathered in communities across Canada in homes, schools, churches, and other venues to cover the accompanying readings, listen to the recordings, and debate their conclusions. For example, in 1957 one such program took place in an Ontario paper-mill town in a local YMCA. The group comprised two mill workers and their wives, a mill supervisor, a physician and his wife, an office secretary, a clergyman, and a moderator and held two-to-three-hour sessions once weekly for 13 weeks. Reports of discussions were mailed in and comments received in turn.

James Slevin, in his search for a social theory of the Internet, asked the following question: 'To what extent might the Internet facilitate an advance in intelligent relationships between organizations, groups and individuals which are ordered through dialogue rather than through existing patterns of domination' (Slevin, 2000: 5)? These series, two broadcast six decades ago and one five decades ago, would seem to answer the question, but via radio and not the Internet! This was, perhaps, radio and mass media in general at their best, most especially as a constructed public space free from constraints imposed by the marketplace, seeking and encouraging face-to-face dialogue over political and community issues and, in the case of *Farm Forum* and *Citizens' Forum*, designed to allow for decision making and feedback. Adding *Ways of Mankind*, the three series depended on local community groups: audiences which received, processed, and interacted minus commercial interference and as collectivities rather than one-on-one. Additionally, each series was created in the context of cooperative actions involving state-controlled media and national and local associations in the fields of education, agriculture, recreation, and labour unionism. More to the point, civil society and a plurality of persons—men and women, labourers, farmers and professionals—were involved. The technology was not interposed between the co-present but was instead used by them as an aid.

Radio as Interlocutor[2]

Contrary to these earlier CBC attempts at creating public spaces, James Slevin, referring to Thompson (1995), has noted that 'media such as radio and television . . . create a fundamental break between the producers and recipients of information.' Furthermore, it is noted that the '*non-dialogical mediated publicness*' characteristic of radio and TV should not be taken as a simple extension of the traditional model of the public. Rather, a new kind of public is posited: a 'non-localized, non-dialogical, open-ended space . . . in which mediated symbolic forms can be expressed and received by a plurality of non-present others' (Slevin, 2000: 183). The research to which we now refer followed this model, viewing radio as the interlocutor, meeting young people on the 'public stage' of radio, encouraging interaction across diversity, giving opportunities free from institutional restraints, and permitting experimentation with identities. To be able to analyze the idea of radio as interlocutor in an ongoing dialogue with young people, it was first necessary to document and classify radio listeners according to birthplace of parents and the broader culture of which they were a part. For the young people in this study radio was viewed as taking on the role of the 'other' in a dialogue between the audience and the broadcaster. Accordingly, the listener is, in his or her mind, taking part in a conversation with the instrument occupying centre stage as the interlocutor engaging the others listeners in dialogue. The conversation may be through words or music. Whatever it is, radio engages the listener's mind and imagination. Radio use creates, temporarily at least, a public space within which a variety of people participate, *linking with each other in an awareness of that public space*, albeit a non-dialogical, non-localized space.

The study queried university and college students aged 18–24 on their patterns of radio use and how those patterns, in turn, stimulated interaction around the subject matter of selected programming (usually music and talk-radio). A total of 155 students were selected, 75 taking part in 11 focus groups addressing programming preferences and reactions to selected talk-radio shows, and, in addition, 80 were interviewed with questions designed to tap patterns of radio use. Though the principal research question revolved around the issue of radio use patterns of second-generation young people, of interest here is that, by far, the majority of the sample discussed the merits of various radio programs and music with their friends. Much of this discussion took place in various associations and clubs—two-thirds of those interviewed belonged to one or more school-based or community-based groups.

Here was evidence of a public space—a 'cultural commons'—where young people from a variety of ethnic and national backgrounds met, principally around interests common to their generation, through the medium of radio. Though public spaces like this created by radio are limited dialogically and controlled in the main by the marketplace, they are, from a young person's perspective, free from parental guidance and the boundaries set by formal ethno-cultural institutions (churches, schools, associations). As listeners interact with each other discussing music preferences and the merits of various radio stations they discover a commonality which overrides linguistic, ethnic, and cultural differences.

Figure 2.1 illustrates the manner in which radio constructs an interactive space. A radio program (music, talk, or news) is received by listener A and listener B. Listener A and B, friends perhaps, meet later and talk about the program content. A similar model would hold for television.

The three programs referred to in the previous section, *Farm Forum*, *Citizens' Forum*, and *Ways of Mankind* created limited public spaces. They were limited in the sense that the space created was not completely free of hierarchical organs of definition; in all three cases the CBC, a **Crown corporation**, designed the output and controlled input. In the fourth case, radio does

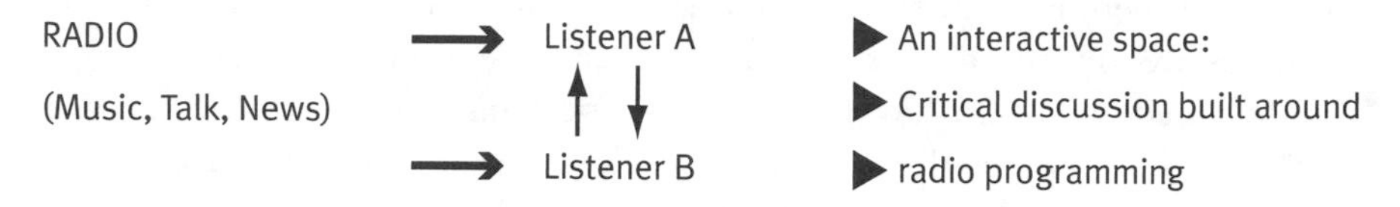

FIGURE 2.1 Radio as Interlocutor

indeed act as an interlocutor, but its imagined audience is designed by commercial interests, preventing a truly public space.

However, interactivity at a much stronger but nonetheless limited level may be found in the Internet services made available by radio stations, newspapers, and television. These services provide a more complete interactive space.

The Press, Radio, Television, and Interactivity

Listening to radio and watching television, followed by discussions over the content with friends, constitutes a very weak public. According to Fraser, *weak* publics are those 'whose deliberative practice consists exclusively in opinion formation and does not encompass decision making' (Fraser, 1996: 109–42; Fossum and Schlesinger, 2007: 4). Weak publics are more monologic than dialogic because opinions look for their imagined audience to agree with them. *Strong* publics imply some level of decision making and tend to engage more in disputes over opinions and so are more dialogic. Or, again in Fraser's words, 'publics whose discourse encompasses both opinion forming and decision making' (Fraser, 1996: 4). Another look at the CBC's early discussion programs suggests that from the perspective of the participant there existed a feeling of belonging to a socially constructed enterprise in which dialogue took place among the discussants and between them and the broadcaster. The next step early on taken by radio was the talk/call-in show. There was, and continues to be, a reasonably consistent audience for these shows. However, for the most part, contact is limited to one-on-one conversations; that is, conversations between individual listeners and the show's host. Dialogue in the sense of debate and conclusion is absent and little effort is made to bracket status and cultural differences.

The possibility of stronger publics appeared when newspapers, radio, and television adopted the Internet. In the first instance, this gave a wider set of readers and listeners/viewers an avenue through which to respond to news, editorial comments, and opinions. Most newspapers now have a website and many deliver a digital edition to their subscribers via the Internet. Most are familiar with the invitation to respond to news items and editorial writers. Journalists publish blogs on the paper's website and readers are invited to respond. But note that the frequency of responses on many sites is very low and seldom are there respondent-to-respondent debates. In other words, though responses are invited, the rate at which readers respond to comments entered by other readers is very low. A few newspapers have introduced discussion windows around selected news items. *The Globe and Mail*, one of Canada's two English-language cross-country newspapers (*Le Devoir* is the French-language cross-country newspaper), is a good example. Recently, the *Globe and Mail*'s website opened a discussion (one among several) on a poll reporting possible outcomes of the October 2008 federal election. Readers were invited to respond to the pollster who, in turn, responded to comments entered. The story was published on 3 September 2008. By 1:30 PM that afternoon 40 comments had been posted. Though low in an absolute sense, this was a higher level of participation than found in most of the websites that particular day. The cross-discussion—reader to pollster and pollster to reader combined with reader-to-reader comments—pointed to an emerging strong public.

Radio and television stations present similar Internet protocols. With most, as with the press, interactivity is limited to one-on-one. Three public service, state-controlled broadcasters—the CBC, Television Ontario (TVO), and Télé-Québec—are the exception. As do the private stations, they invite responses to news and editorial items. Editorial items, for the most part, are limited to one-on-one with very few comments; news items draw considerably more comments and comments on comments. For example, on 31 August 2009 the CBC's website invited comments on a news item reporting a meeting between the federal parliament's Liberal leader of the opposition and the Conservative prime minister. A total of 392 comments were received during a very short time period. As was the case with the *Globe and Mail*, comments on comments were posted, suggesting the presence of a rather strong public. Additional links were provided to Facebook, with the comment 'see what your friends think', and to bloggers writing about this and related issues outside of the purview of the CBC via the website www.technorati.com. (Technorati.com is a website that collects a variety of blogs organized according to a set of topical categories.) TVO, too, has created reasonably strong publics.

The websites allowed for the bracketing of social and cultural inequalities. A respondent entered the space free of ascriptive and acquired characteristics; only his or her input was recognized and considered. Negatively, this type of interaction blocks the possibility of genuine cultural and social interchange by ignoring difference, a step removed from the early CBC discussion groups which combined farmers with unionized workers and mill workers with professionals. Dialogic, to a point, but the websites tend to fall short of dialogical discourse. Nor are the sites totally free of marketplace forces or authoritarian control. On the latter point, the broadcasters—private and public alike—and the press select the items to be discussed. There is greater flexibility in several Internet websites independent of the press or broadcastersstart-up websites now referred to as 'social media'.

Social Media

Sites like technocrati.com and commoncraft.com, although both commercial websites, open the door far more widely to the creation of publics through links and blogs. However, even here interaction remains one-on-one; that is, questions are posted to the website and viewers read the website with little cross-interactivity. Social media sites, such as Twitter.com. Linkedin.com, MySpace.com, Facebook.com, YouTube.com, and Wikipedia.org, encourage the creation of network development and interaction. The level of connectivity among users is high. Each site is organized around the concept of social networks, encouraging viewers to join and to create networks of friends, family, and co-workers as a means for the development of ideas, businesses, finding jobs, finding partners, etc. However, with the exception of Twitter.com and Wikipedia.org (for the time being at least), these and other sites are commercially driven. For example, comScore, a marketing research company, reported that social networking sites in the UK 'accounted for 13.8 billion display ad impressions in August 2009, representing more than 25 per cent of all display ads viewed online' (comScore, 2009). Social media companies are easily able to solicit advertising by promising the delivery of niche audiences at a cost. The user is transformed from citizen-user into customer/commodity.

Twitter and Wikipedia are different in this respect. Neither seeks advertising nor attempts to turn users into commodities. Twitter is a privately funded company located in San Francisco, CA. Founded in 2006, it serves as a real-time short messaging service—'microblogging'—operating over multiple networks and devices. The user joins or creates networks, communicating in 140-character bursts (or 'tweets'). A user may subscribe to a feed where comments are exchanged in an active and rapid comment-and-reply protocol. In countries all around the world, people follow the sources most relevant to them and access information via 'Twitter as it happens'—from breaking world news to updates from friends.

Wikipedia, a non-profit organization also located in San Francisco, is financed by volunteer fundraising and operates under volunteer units around the world; outside of North America there are chapters active in 17 different countries. Volunteers collaborate in the writing and editing of material. Discussion pages are created around a number of categories and sub-categories (e.g., in the 'media commons' division the following string may be followed: Society & Culture > Politics > Elections by country). Users are invited to create discussion pages according to selected categories and sub-categories. This yields very active discussions locally or worldwide around any number of issues. Wikipedia is very popular, currently ranking fifth after Google, Microsoft, Yahoo, and AOL in the number of users and second after YouTube in the number of unique visitors monthly (Gardiner, 2008).

Social networking sites come close to constructing public spaces but, for the most part, fall short on at least three of the evaluative criteria proposed earlier. Again with the exception of Twitter and Wikipedia, these sites are not free of commercial control and the commodification of their users. Indeed, they are ensnared in a web of advertising and commercial spin. The main thrust of broadcasting and websites—commercial and state controlled alike—is competitively oriented toward capturing audiences. Via various rating instruments audiences are perceived and recorded as commodities to be sold to advertisers, if advertising is used, or to justify the cost of state-controlled broadcasting to governments of the day. The 'commercial imperative' is readily acknowledged in programming and website design. An interesting instance of this imperative appeared in a recent advertisement for a conference on the new media published in a Canadian daily under the title 'What happens online pays offline'. Potential delegates were informed:

> Used to its full potential, social media can be an important component in your *marketing mix*, enlarging your online footprint and engaging your audience in meaningful conversations . . . choosing the right media forums; the role of blogs and podcasts in *marketing*; and how to establish goals and measure the success of your social media *marketing efforts*. (*Ottawa Citizen*, 6 Sept. 2008a: H3, emphasis added)

Evidence of the controlling presence of the market is not difficult to find. In February 2010 the Canadian Recording Industry Association expressed considerable concern over the Songwriters Association of Canada's request for a $5.00 levy on Internet usage to cover the cost of downloading practices (*Ottawa Citizen*, 23 Feb. 2008b: D2). And, a month later, the National Union of Public and General Employees (Canada) expressed alarm at the 'traffic shaping' practices of Internet service providers Bell Canada Inc. and Rogers Communication Inc., both of which limit the download speed on such file-sharing protocols as BitTorrent, which is used by many to share large video files (CBC News, 28 March 2008).

The marketplace has control of the Internet and most of its uses. Is there any possibility of escaping the commercial imperative, at least in part, in order to create interacting publics responding to each other around local, regional, national, and global issues? Of all the contemporary sites examined, Twitter and Wikipedia are free of the commercial imperative, encourage dialogically active participation, and encourage a plurality of sites. Table 2.1 presents an assessment of the sites and broadcasters discussed. Unexpectedly, the oldest and the newest—CBC radio programming broadcasts from almost seven decades ago and two new social media sites, Twitter and Wikipedia, with Wikipedia ahead—appear to meet the criteria for reasonably strong publics!

TABLE 2.1 **Weak to Strong Publics**

Criteria	Early CBC Experiments	Internet Press	Social Media Sites	Internet Radio/TV	Radio	Twitter & Wikipedia
Dialogic and Active	Yes, combined with community & collective involvement	Yes, but very limited.	Yes	Yes, but limited. Much less limited on CBC and TVO	Yes, but very limited	Yes, & in Wikipedia community & collective involvement
Free from Marketplace	Yes	No	No	No	No	Yes
Free from Hierarchy	Yes, but fairly limited	No	Not totally	No	No	For the most part
Difference Recognized	Yes, community differences bracketed	Probably, though limited by access	Yes	Probably, but limited by access	Unknown except in special cases	Yes

The State and the Commercial Imperative

To this point we have given some thought to state and commercial control of broadcasting and the Internet. Although the two modes of control do sit side by side and, in Canada, have evolved side by side, the relationship is testy. Public spaces, weak and strong alike, are *highly contested*, not only by various groupings of citizens defined according to social class, gender, and nationality but also by governments and corporations. The issue of gender is especially important here. As Nancy Fraser so comprehensively pointed out in her critique of the concept of a public sphere, gender is a 'key axis of exclusion' (Fraser, 1992: 113), and must be taken into consideration in any assessment of the quality of public spaces. Governments and corporations most certainly compete to control the media.

The State

The role of governments in this respect is variable. Those states which are democratically inclined tend to apply a minimum of controls on the media and are disposed to own and operate broadcasting channels and Internet services as a public service. Additionally, state-controlled broadcasting, especially via radio and television, has played a major part in nation building. The role of state radio and television as a national tool is well recognized in the literature (Hobsbawm, 1990; Innis, 1956; Leys, 2001).

Most countries, the US being an exception, possess and operate a national broadcasting unit. Canada's CBC/SRC, the UK's BBC, Australia's ABC, Finland's YLE, Japan's NHK, and Germany's ARD and ZDF are among the many public broadcasters which, though owned by national governments, operate at an 'arm's length' from state controls. PBS and NPR are public broadcasters operating in the United States with a minimum of government support; they

On Nation Building and Communications

Government and subject citizen were inevitably linked by daily bonds, as never before. And the nineteenth century revolutions in transport and communications typified by the railway and the telegraph tightened and routinized the links between central authority and its remotest outposts. (Hobsbawm, 1990: 81)

From R.B. Bennett, Prime Minister of Canada, 1930–35: This country must be assured of complete Canadian control of broadcasting from Canadian sources. Without such control, broadcasting can never be the agency by which national consciousness may be fostered and sustained and national unity still further strengthened. (Canada, 'Report of the Task Force on Broadcasting Policy', Ottawa: Minister of Supply and Services, 1986: 6)

The conflict between the two systems [an economic system linking Canada to Europe and one linking it to the United States] has cumulative effects. Nationalism becomes more intense. The influence of radio is canalized through the Canadian Broadcasting Corporation and interest in national culture is intensified. (Innis, 1956: 236)

are dependent on private donations. PBS and NPR are structurally similar to Ontario's TVO/TFO, Québec's Télé-Québec, and British Columbia's Knowledge Network, all provincially owned and operated.

As noted above, these 'arm's length' public broadcasters have progressed considerably in providing interactive public spaces through Internet services, podcasting, and blogging. A convergence of platforms is inherent in this compounding of services as the Internet moves into a dominant position. Measuring use according to number of unique visitors monthly, seven state-controlled broadcasting Internet sites are in positions 10 to 16. The UK's BBC is in position #7 and, as already noted, Wikipedia—neither state nor commercially supported—is in position #2.

State broadcasters provide geographically universal coverage and envision their mission as one of strengthening national identity and promoting national culture in the form of drama, comedy, music, and talk shows. Although generally free of political and government influence, state broadcasters tend to operate in the interests of the state's central authority, ignoring regional interests and promoting the dominant culture. Political and government influence over and control of state broadcasters are much more prevalent in those countries which discourage democratic institutions. One might visualize a scale from point '1' (very little government and political control of state broadcasters) to

From Frantz Fanon, *A Dying Colonialism*

During the Algerian crisis Voice of Free Algeria, an independent radio station, carried the news of the revolution to the revolutionaries, frustrating the broadcasting objectives of Radio-Alger, the official French-language broadcaster. Toward the end of 1956 'tracts were distributed announcing the existence of [the] Voice of Free Algeria. The broadcasting and the wave-lengths were given.' (Fanon, 1965: 72–73) Thus did the acquisition of a small radio set become the major means of linking with the Revolution and its cadre.

'10' (complete control). Broadcasters like Canada's CBC and Finland's YLE, to name but two, would fall very close to '2', perhaps '3' or '4' on the scale. State broadcasters in Burma, Pakistan, and North Korea would come very close to '10'. Such governments will and do quickly move to close all media sources except the state broadcaster during periods of political crisis.

In spite of state and commercial domination of radio, the Internet, and television, these channels of communication are frequently used as tools in political protest, organizing resistance, and calling for demonstrations. In oppressive states, radio takes on considerable importance because of its low cost and easy availability. For example, during the Algerian revolution in the mid-1960s a low-frequency independent radio station, the Voice of Free Algeria, free from the constraints of official authority and the state, provided an opportunity for the revolutionary forces of the time to communicate and organize.

A half-century later and in spite of advanced communications technology, radio continued to play a significant role as a channel of communication under circumstances of political turmoil. Consider the following headlines: 'On the weekend of August 11, 2007 one of the three founders and an employee of an independent radio station (Hornafrik) in Somalia were assassinated'

Pakistan Suspends Constitution

In early November 2007 the president of Pakistan, General Musharraf, declared martial law, suspended the constitution, and placed the country's chief justice and six other Supreme Court justices under house arrest. In response to the ensuing protests the government kept independent news stations, the BBC and CNN off air. (*Ottawa Citizen*, 6 Nov. 2007)

(Thomson and Andrew, 2007), 'Somali debates return to war-torn land' (*Ottawa Citizen*, 14 Aug. 2007). HornAfrik had managed to broadcast to people under attack from their government. Because of its very low cost and availability, radio tends to trump other means of communication in traumatic situations.

Given the knowledge and resources needed to own and operate desktop and laptop computers, the Internet has also become a space for protest, in which citizens may exchange political views relatively free of the limitations placed on communications by authority. States are well aware of the dangers of a free and open press as a venue for citizen participation. Recently, the government in Pakistan suspended all independent broadcasting as well as the major international news media to control information which could possibly aid protest groups.

The Commercial Imperative

The more independent of government, the more likely are media to promote free exchange over crucial political and economic issues in public spaces. What are the alternatives? Commercial control of media outlets appears to be the dominant alternative. With this alternative the bottom line is neither public service nor public space but profit—broadcasting is a commodity. As we have noted, commercial broadcasters' audiences are sold to advertisers as commodities; the role of citizen is diminished. John Porter drew our attention to commercial control of the means of communication over 40 years ago in his classic publication, *The Vertical Mosaic*. Accompanied with extensive charts plotting corporate connections in media ownership, he noted that 'Canada's mass media are operated as big business', exhibiting a complex web of ownership of newspapers and radio and television stations by 'media elites' (Porter, 1966: 457–90). A decade later, Wallace Clement reviewed and updated the complex ties of media ownership, referring to mass media as a social technique for the conduction of dominant ideologies (Clement, 1975).

The concentration of media ownership in the hands of a few corporations continues. A look at the scope of four of the major media corporations in 2008—CanWest, TorStar, Québecor, and BCE—reveals the extent of commercial domination. The 2008–09 recession bore down on CanWest, which went under credit protection and began restructuring in the fall of 2009. Québecor emerged from bankruptcy protection during the spring of 2009.

CanWest (recently under bankruptcy protection and selling several of its major assets)

- GlobalTV network and 28 specialty channels
- Radio: 4 FM stations in Turkey
- 6 speciality channels including HGTV, HistoryTV, and Showcase
- Digital services including BBC Canada, BBC Kids, National Geographic

- Newspapers: *The National Post* plus 10 large city dailies and several community newspapers
- Magazines in Canada and the USA
- TV in Ireland and New Zealand
- 10 Network Holding Limited in Australia
- Advertising services in Canada and Australia

BCE

- Bell Canada telephone, wireless, Internet, digital TV, Voice over IP
- *Globe and Mail* newspaper
- CTV Network
- TorStar (In March 2010, expressed an interest in acquiring CanWest newspaper assets)

Star Media Group

- *Toronto Star* newspaper
- Digital properties
- Metroland Media Group
- Community and daily newspapers in Ontario
- Harlequin Enterprises

Québecor

- Sun Media Corporation
- 20 city dailies in Ontario, 8 major dailies in Ontario and Québec
- 35 community newspapers in four provinces
- Vidéotron cable services
- Illico digital services
- Internet and telephone services
- TVA, the largest French-language TV service in North America
- 22 French-language magazines

Here we have a very heavy concentration of ownership of major communication outlets in print, television, telecommunications, Internet and digital services, and publishing. There is a tendency for each major media corporation to absorb its competitors. In March 2010 Torstar and Shaw Communications (a cable, satellite, and digital phone company) went after the bankrupt CanWest Corporation. Monopoly control is not an uncommon conclusion to this process. Later in 2010 Postmedia Network Inc. acquired CanWest's print section. Postmedia now publishes twelve daily newspapers across Canada as well several community papers and Internet sites. This is the commercial imperative. These major holding companies control the output of much of the ideas and information Canadians hear, watch, and read on a daily basis. Commercial control enters at two points in the production process. The first is where the driving energy behind product design and programming is advertising, an almost desperate search for revenue and profit to be acquired through the sale of audiences to advertisers. Count the number of minutes of advertising in a one-hour-long program on Global, CTV, or CBC. Based on program ratings to set the price, you are the commodity up for sale during the time allocated to advertising. This issue will be examined in more detail in Chapter 3. 'Commodification fundamentally changes social relations—relations previously based on reciprocity and expressivities are transformed into relations resting on instrumentality and private gain' (Jackson and Vipond, 2003). In effect, commodification tends to reduce the role of citizen and maximize the role of consumer. Agency is diminished while structures capture and confine more and more everyday activity.

The second point is more complicated. In states favouring democratic institutions the commercial hold on broadcasting and Internet services does not completely strangle critical ideas and freedom of expression. Journalists, writers, and producers jealously guard their freedom. What does occur is much more insidious. The established commercial world view is subtly transmitted in such a way that critical and opposing perspectives are negatively affected (Abercrombie, Hill, and Turner, 1980). An example of this process may be found in a research report by Martha Lauzen and others who, after an analysis of 124 prime-time US television drama programs during the 2005–06 season, demonstrated that 'female characters continue to inhabit interpersonal roles involved with romance, family and friends' while male roles are work-related roles. Female roles tended to change in drama written by women (Lauzen, Dozier, and Horan, 2008: 200–14). This is only one instance of the extent to which established norms overshadow attempts at establishing new social avenues. Broadcasters, state and commercial alike, and newspapers are beamed toward implied audiences, a topic we will address in a later chapter.

Are there other routes or spaces where the possibility of **establishing** overcomes the **established**? One route is through comedy and satire. In a recent analysis of the CBC television show *This Hour Has 22 Minutes*, Tammy Saxton and others noted that the program clearly threatened closed systems, most especially systems circumscribing gender and regionalism (Saxton, Rocher, and Jackson, 2004: 182–98). References to gender exclusion abound in this satirical take on contemporary political issues. Another route, but one rarely followed, may be found in the formation of independent broadcasting and print outlets which are audience (citizen) supported, without either state or commercial support. 'Community radio' (licensed low-frequency broadcasters) as well as some Web 2.0 sites meet this requirement. The 1960's Voice of Free Algeria and the recent HornAfrik radio stations referred to above are both examples. WBAI of Radio Pacifica is another example of listener-supported broadcasting. Internet websites such as YouTube and Facebook were potentially public spaces until commercial interests moved in. Bloggers set up spaces open for exchange free of authority. Wikipedia and Twitter are also excellent examples.

A Note on Regulation

The Western European, American, and Canadian experiences with broadcasting have been somewhat dissimilar. In Western Europe broadcasting began as a state-supported public service. It was not until the mid-1950s that commercial broadcasting began to intrude. In Canada and the United States broadcasting began as a commercial enterprise. By the 1930s Canada had succeeded in setting up a public service, state-supported broadcaster, CBC/SRC. Now CBC/SRC television, though retaining a public service model, behaves very much like a commercial broadcaster, with advertising and ratings controlling its programming. The United States has shied away from a central government-supported, public service radio/TV outlet similar to those found in Canada and Western Europe. In the US, PBS and NPR are partially listener supported and partially government supported.

In addition to state control of broadcasting, the use of the airwaves and wireless and wired communications are regulated by the state (Raboy, 1990). The regulation of commercial broadcasting and telecommunications corporations is a fiercely contested site. Regulations may serve to enlarge or reduce the profit margins of media corporations.

It is significant that the Canadian Broadcasting Act of 1991 considers broadcasters, public and private alike, as a *single system* to which the Act and all subsequent regulations apply. The Act is based on the premise that the airwaves are *public property*, but it allows for the existence of a private sector within the whole. Article 3.1.b of the Act reads as follows:

> The Canadian broadcasting system, operating primarily in the English and French languages and comprising public, private and community elements, makes use of radio frequencies that are public property and provides, through its programming, a public service essential to the maintenance and enhancement of national identity and cultural sovereignty. (Canada,1991)

Thus the Act signals: (1) the tension between the public good and private gain; (2) the fact of a particular relation between private and public broadcasting in Canada; and (3) the possibility that the relationship may simultaneously address issues of national sovereignty and also be beneficial to capital accumulation. Private and public broadcasters fall under the regulatory control of the Canadian Radio-television and Telecommunications Commission (CRTC). The CRTC is the state regulator covering all modes of electronic communication. Given that major commercial media outlets such as CTV (Bell Canada Enterprises) and Québecor also control print media, the convergence has caused a quandary for the CRTC. In the early spring of 2010 the CRTC announced that it would require cable and satellite providers and TV broadcasters to negotiate broadcast fees. This will be a new source of revenue for broadcasters and, undoubtedly, will result in increased fees for household users.

Summary

In this chapter we continued the main theme of mediated citizenship through an exploration of media-constructed public spaces. We examined four examples in which tensions arise as citizens, state, and corporate worlds collide over issues of content in, control of, and participation in the media. The concept of 'public space' as a media construction was advanced not as a geographic space but, following the work of Charles Taylor, as a discursive space. A discursive space designates both real and imaginary coming together of citizens to discuss, debate, and seek conclusions to issues which interest them. We have suggested that the media provide such opportunities, but they are opportunities which may limit the exercise of agency in favour of imposed structures and the power arrangements of the day. In order to assess the potential of various media to open public spaces we proposed the following criteria—a public space must be:

- dialogic and active,
- free from the organizational thrust of promotion and consumption in the marketplace,
- free of hierarchical organs of definition, and
- responsive to the problem of a plurality of spaces.

Apart from a very early experiment by CBC radio, we have explored how, for the most part, the press, radio, television, and Internet offer only partial or 'weak' public spaces. *The Globe and Mail*, CBC television, and TVO/TFO construct reasonably strong public spaces. The strongest public spaces are provided by Twitter and, especially, Wikipedia.

The control of broadcasting, either by the state or by market-driven forces, was presented as problematic. Commercially owned broadcasting, which accounts for the majority of media outlets, tends to limit the extent to which forces seeking to undermine established structures can form public spaces and tends to maintain an ideological status quo. State broadcasting is highly limited in those states which do not champion democratic institutions. In states favouring democratic institutions state-owned broadcasting is frequently more open and discursive. However, over the last three decades these latter broadcasters have themselves been overwhelmed by the commercial imperative.

Enhanced Learning Activities

1. Using the proposed criteria for assessing the strength of public spaces, compare CBC TV (www.cbc.ca), GlobalTV (www.globaltv.com), CTV (www.ctv.ca), and TVO (www.tvo.org). Which of the four, if any, comes close to the strength exhibited by Wikipedia (www.wikipedia.org)?
2. Google the term 'community broadcasting'. You will find a number of sites and articles on the subject. Does community broadcasting escape the commercial imperative?
3. Compare the Australian (www.abc.net.au), British (www.bbc.co.uk), and German (www.zdf.com) public broadcasters with the Canadian (www.cbc.ca) public broadcaster with respect to the strength of public spaces created and the extent to which the commercial imperative appears to have penetrated each.
4. Using www.oreilly.com as an example, contrast and compare Web 1.0 and 2.0 technologies.

Annotated Further Reading

Craig Calhoun, ed., *Habermas and the Public Sphere*. Cambridge, MA: MIT Press, 1996. This book is a collection of readings critically addressing concepts of the public sphere. Nancy Fraser's article dealing with weak and strong publics and specifically dealing with gender is in this collection.

Manuel Castells, ed., *The Network Society: A Cross-Cultural Perspective*. Cheltenham, UK: Edward Elgar Publishing Ltd., 2004. Manuel Castells has written extensively on the Internet and its uses. This book is accepted as a major work in the field of Internet communications. A collection of articles provides a contemporary look at the Internet as a creator of social networks.

Allison Cavanagh, *Sociology in the Age of the Internet*. Berkshire, UK: Open University Press, 2007. This book investigates the Internet as both a sociological and historical phenomena. It is most suitable for anyone with an interest in the relationship between the Internet and society.

John Eric Fossum and Philip Schlesinger. *The European Union and the Public Sphere*. New York: Routledge, 2007. This is an excellent examination of Habermas's concept of the public sphere and a consideration of its influence on the debates surrounding the contemporary public sphere in the European Union.

Vincent Mosco, *The Political Economy of Communication*. London: Sage Publications Ltd., 1996. Published 12 years ago, this book remains a major work addressing the political economy of communications. It will give the reader an opportunity to explore the commercial imperative bearing upon communications.

Charles Taylor, *Philosophical Arguments*. Cambridge, MA: Harvard University Press, 1995. This is a philosophical examination of human interaction and discourse. Chapter 12, 'The Politics of Recognition', and Chapter 13, 'Liberal Politics and the Public Sphere', are both referred to in this chapter.

James Slevin, *The Internet and Society*. Cambridge, UK: Polity Press, 2000. Here you will find an historical and sociological treatment of the Internet. Professor Slevin explores the impact of the Internet on contemporary society and culture.

Notes

1. This section is adapted from Jackson, John D. Jackson, 'From Cultural Relativity to Multiculturalism: The CBC's *Ways of Mankind Series*, 1953', *Fréquence/Frequency* 9/10 (2002): 95–107.

2. This section is adapted from John D. Jackson and Michael Rosenberg, *Recognition and Mis-Recognition: Radio as Interlocutor*, Montreal: Centre for Broadcasting Studies, Concordia University, 2004.

3 Citizenship and Audiences

Learning Objectives

- To reflect on the media system as a system of social relations
- To consider the participants in media systems and the distribution of power
- To explore the role of the audience as a social actor within the system
- To review corporate media definitions of audiences: the audience as target; the audience as commodity; and the audience as participant
- To review audience research definitions: the passive audience; the mass persuasion audience; audiences as users seeking gratification; and audiences as decoders of messages
- To consider democratic responsibility and the audience as citizen

Introduction

Listening to radio, watching television, and surfing the Internet capture the bulk of people's leisure time and provide the major source of music, information, and images. Moreover, given the increasing popularity of interactive Internet sites, the communications industry is rapidly becoming a primary channel of social interaction. Needless to say, communications industries are different from other industries because of the excessive amount of time and money the public spends on media consumption. In addition the media can have a 'profound social and political influence . . . affecting political and cultural attitudes, voting behaviors, and a propensity toward violence' (Napoli, 2003: 15–16). It is our objective to pursue the question of audiences, a pursuit which can be complicated. Audiences are consumers in an industry dominated by very large corporations located in complex systems where the role of audience members varies; audiences may be participants, have influence, or be totally powerless. Moreover, given the potential social, cultural, and political influence of these corporations, both corporation and consumer carry a responsibility as citizens.

Accordingly, it should not seem too odd to ask if media producers and advertisers see a real audience out there or is their 'audience' a consequence of audience ratings, demographic segments, and statistical artifacts? Audience ratings yield numbers, averages, and demographic constructs—not the real you. We will begin with a look at the way in which the audience, as a social role, is linked to the media as a system of social relations. This demands that we consider several participants as the building blocks of mass-media systems:

- the creators (writers and producers);
- the performers (actors, hosts, newscasters, etc.);
- the carriers and transmitters (broadcasters, cable companies, webcasters, podcasters, newspapers, etc.) of information and entertainment;
- the advertising agencies and related corporations; and
- the audiences.

A brief examination of the concept of 'social systems'—a fairly common concept in sociological analysis—will be helpful.

Following this we will turn our attention to the way in which media construct their audiences, and the variety of research traditions addressing the concept of audiences. Finally, and grounded in this research, we turn our attention to citizen interaction with media and media responsibilities as a part of the larger society.

Mediated Society as a Social System

It may be helpful to begin by asking what you think about when you use the word 'system'. Perhaps you think about a collection or an arrangement of things related or connected in such a way as to form a unified whole, such as a solar system, a supply system, or a school system. This suggests that viewing a system as a collection of things indicates that we have observed elements or individual entities which appeared to be related in such a way as to hint at the presence of a unified whole. It is in this sense that a social system is understood to be a set of related and interacting elements, the elements being roles, statuses, groups, or institutions. The emphasis is on *interaction*: who is interacting with whom or what is interacting with what and to what end? Thus a **social system** is a set of interacting elements moving in some discernable direction or exhibiting some function. Furthermore, systems are always open, linking in one way or another with other systems in their environs.

We can think of media systems in the same way, but a cautionary note is required. The notion of 'system' is a useful metaphorical device enhancing our ability to analyze and understand social phenomena. A glance at the *Canadian Oxford Dictionary* tells us that a metaphor is 'the application of a name or descriptive term to something to which it is imaginatively but not literally applicable'. For example, we have heard references to a 'troop surge' to describe US military strategy in the Middle East or 'a mortgage meltdown' to describe the rapid decrease in property values. Or, Pizza Hut's '3 Cheese Explosion: aim away from face'. *Surge, meltdown* and *explosion* are used as metaphors. This is the sense in which 'social system' is used as a metaphor. The concept is 'imaginatively but not literally applicable'; that is, we can observe *only* interacting actors which appear to operate in consort, we do not observe a 'social system'. True enough, some systems theorists such as Luhmann (1995) and Parsons (1951) would object to calling a system a metaphor; they prefer to see the concept of system as a theoretical construct. What is important to understand is that the notion of a social system is not literally present in everyday social life. The concept of a social system helps us to understand and talk about linkages, relationships, and power.

Journalists, writers, and performers as well as government and corporate agents provide the material for broadcasting. Broadcasters, in turn, beam the messages to audiences. Audience reaction indirectly feeds back to broadcasters in the form of ratings or assumptions made by broadcasters as to 'what the audience wants' or directly via invited telephone calls or Internet responses. Broadcasters also interact with creators by carrying feedback from audiences requesting revisions and new material. The system as a whole functions in a broad social context with linkages to other operating systems (industrial, educational, political, religious, etc.) and responds to established economic, political, and ideological directions active within the society as a whole.

Other elements and somewhat different arrangements may be observed pointing to various configurations of groups and institutions. For example, in *Measuring Media Audiences* Raymond Kent draws attention to 'advertising agencies, media consultants and specialists, and market research agencies' as

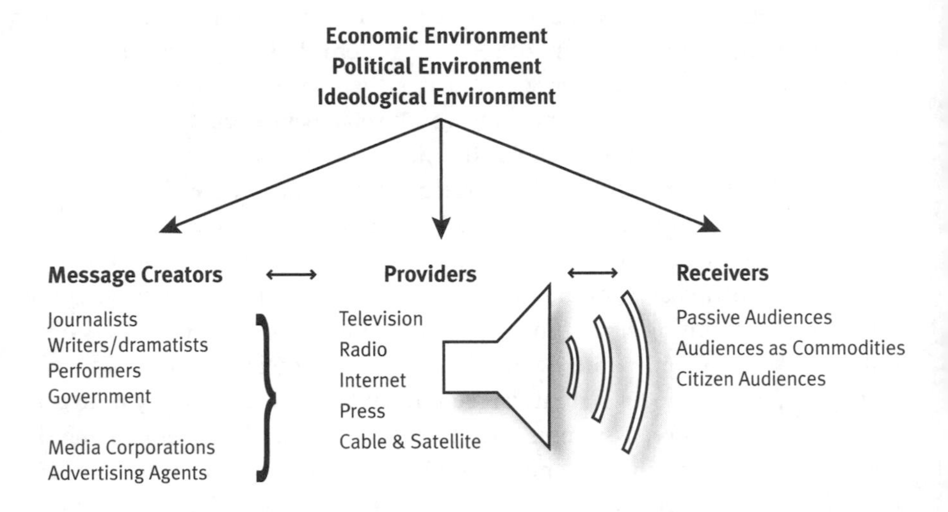

FIGURE 3.1 A Media System

a subsystem of sorts relating to audiences defined as rating statistics (1994: 3). In *Audience Economics*, Philip Napoli implies a media marketing system encompassing broadcaster (content), provider (cable, satellite), audience rating firms, advertising agencies, and the measured audience (2003: 15–35). Note that in this case the audience is defined as 'the measured audience', suggesting that particular configurations of elements yield varying audiences, not different people but varying role segments.

Two additional points should be noted regarding systems. First, Figure 3.1 implies the presence of an established, orderly, and predictable system. It is that, but only in a very limited way. Disorder accompanies order; the drive to rearrange the relations inherent in the parts and the drive to **institute** totally new relations is always present and constantly tears apart an **instituted** system. Providers compete for audiences defined as **commodities** in the advertising game. Journalists strive to control their output but are subjected to editorial constraint dictated by publishers and owners of electronic providers. Community radio undermines the hold of regular corporate and state broadcasters. Social Internet sites pop up and undermine established commercial sites. The system, though recognizable as a set of social relations operating in established economic, political, and ideological environments, is in a constant state of instability. Second, power tends to be uneven in social systems. In the case of media systems, the corporate and advertising elements tend to dominate. Audiences are defined according to the interests of the dominant elements.

We will continue to address parts of media systems in each chapter. In this chapter we draw attention to the multiple roles that comprise an audience, a major and, for the most part, the least powerful element of media systems. Identifying an audience is more complicated than one might at first assume. It has already been suggested that the audience is not the real you but a defined role segment—a demographic unit, the number of people watching a show on a given day in 15-minute segments, a particular number of potential viewers sold to an advertising agency, and so on. Even media research scholars define audiences differently. Some see the audience as a *passive recipient* of messages, others as a *commodity*; still others see the audience as an *active participant* interacting with broadcaster and message. Each of these 'audiences' has emerged from different research traditions.

We will examine these traditions and the role of the citizen as audience. Democracy is located within interacting networks of citizens, networks which, at times, coalesce into more or less predictable values and behaviour-forming institutions. The question posed in this chapter asks if media enhances or degrades citizenship. Returning to issues addressed in Chapter 2, is the citizen audience inclined to acquiesce to the audience as commodity? In considering citizenship and media, can we ignore the hegemony of corporate media and the state?

Audiences: Real or Imagined?

A key step in applying critical sociology to the analysis of mediated society, as we saw in Chapter 1, is to examine the gaps between subjects that media creators and providers report on and the audiences that are implied by their address. In this chapter we add the definition of the audience, or message receiver, as an element in a media social system that changes according to the location of power in various media systems and subsystems. There is a kind of kaleidoscopic effect. As the centre of power shifts, for example, from owners of providers to the creators and performers, the definition of the audience tends to change as well. Owners of providers see their audience as statistical objects for sale to another element in the system—advertisers. Creators and performers tend to see their audiences as individuals appreciative of drama or quality newscasting. Furthermore, it is difficult to untangle the audience constructs emerging from business practices and those emerging from research practices. We will attempt to unravel several images of audiences, concentrating in this section on audiences as viewed by the corporate world. Then we will turn our attention to images of audiences produced by media researchers.

As we will see, there is a long tradition of quantitative research into audiences that has delivered reliable aggregate data at both domestic and global levels regarding the consumers of media. Audiences have been studied as media commodities (Smythe, 1977). Some researchers go as far as to reject the category of audiences as anything more than an economic invention of media systems (Mosco and Kaye, 2000). Conversely, in feminist media studies, audiences continue to be studied as agents of resistance (Radway, 1984;

Gallagher, 2003) while the ethnographic turn in cultural studies has also theorized the audience in active rather than passive terms for more than 20 years (Ross and Nightingale, 2003). Additionally, critical discourse analysis and labelling theory demonstrate how entire segments of populations become stigmatized through normalizing linguistic practices (Chavez, 2001; Gans, 1995) while others have also discussed how media both criticize and reproduce values of citizenship and exclusion of audiences (Curran, 2005; Keane 2005). Our critical sociology of the relationship between media and an implied audience helps pinpoint the sense of citizenship that media promotes in a way that complements each of these approaches.

We introduced the concept of the implied audience in Chapter 1 in order to better illustrate how media actively create conditions and gaps between the subjects reported on and the sense of citizenship implied in the framing of the address. The approach also provides a way of thinking about a triangular relation inside and outside the audience in a given media system, as seen in Figure 3.1. The relation is between (i) the message creators send, (ii) through a provider, toward (iii) an implied audience that creators assume is situated within a given environment. For example, when a journalist addresses a story about problems in democracy, she does so through the provider (the newspaper company), for whom the implied audience is its ideal citizenry or the common people of that democracy and not only the actual readers of the newspaper. We maintain that this triangulation is both an internal and external feature that can be distinguished in a given media system. For example, a polemic from a radio talk-show host may be directly addressed against a city official in the studio. The city official who is addressed is an instance of an interior audience. The exterior address to an implied audience is enacted through the tone and framing of the dialogue event itself. The implied audience is thus defined as the audience imagined by the creator of the message through the providers' media. It is an address that can reach far beyond the discussion directly occurring inside the media event.

The continuing argument around shifting definitions of media audiences can be attributed to several scholarly articles which appeared during the late 1980s and later, which, in one way or another, questioned the existence of a 'real' audience in the plans and schemes of media companies and researchers alike (Allor, 1988: 217–33; Grossberg, 1988: 377–92; Radway, 1988: 359–76). We will review three definitions of audiences commonly used by media companies and advertisers: (1) the audience as a target, (2) the audience as a commodity, and (3) the audience as a participant.

The Audience as a Target

The audience is the object toward which broadcasters and Internet providers direct their information and entertainment. This sense of audience was best expressed by Raymond Kent:

> Those to whom the communication is addressed will normally be called the 'audience', although for the print media the audience may be referred to as its 'readership' . . . [A]udiences . . . need to be addressed with a suitable marketing mix . . . product design and specification. (1994: 1–2)

Kent went on to note that, in addition to product design and specifications, pricing, promotion coverage, and distribution had to be matched with the 'organization's particular capabilities'. It is in this framework that the audience is viewed as simply a passive receiver. The product design, promotion, advertising formats, and distribution are administrative problems for the media corporation; the audience is seen as a faceless mass waiting for information and entertainment. Likewise, from the perspective of associated writers, producers, hosts, etc., material is to be created and distributed to audiences passively waiting to be informed or entertained. The audience appears to be a target anxiously awaiting the speeding bullet from various elements in the system. In this system the audience, as one of the elements—a crucial element at that—possesses the least power, if any. The audience as citizen is absent.

The Audience as a Commodity

Simply put, a commodity is an economic good, a product carrying an exchange value, or an article which can be bought and sold. Commodification is a process whereby something is turned into a commodity or treated as a commodity. The notion of media audiences as commodities has its origin in the work of media scholar Dallas W. Smyth. Professor Smyth pointed to media companies as producing audiences and selling them to advertisers (Smyth, 1977: 1–7). Implied was a system which linked media companies, advertising agencies, corporations, and audiences. In this system media companies create audiences by measuring the number of people 'tuned in' to their programs in 15-minute segments. They then sell the resulting 'measured audience' to advertising agencies who, in turn, sell time to corporations ranging from automobile manufacturers to pizza vendors (Mosco, 1996: 148).

Table 3.1 is a sample of audience ratings provided to broadcasters by the audience rating firm the Bureau of Broadcasting Measurement. Note that audience measurements are made available in quarter-hour segments. The table is merely an excerpt from a much larger table provided to clients showing data for men and women in several age categories in the 'Montreal Anglo Central Area' (BBM, 2000). Additional time block data was also provided in the original table. The data refers to radio station CJFM in Montreal during the summer of 2000; television data is presented in much the same format. During the summer of 2000 CJFM— known as Mix 96—broadcasted contemporary hits and was very popular with 18-to-24-year-olds. Data was gathered

TABLE 3.1 Excerpt from an Audience Rating Table (BUREAU OF BROADCAST MEASUREMENT, 2000: 50)

Bureau of Broadcast Measurement: Montreal Anglo-Central Area

Time Blocks for Radio, Summer 2000

	Total			Women				
Station CJFM	12+	18+	18–49	18–44	18–34	18–24	25–24	25–49
1. Standard	Average Quarter-Hour Audience in Hundreds (00)							
500A–100A MO–FR	261	118	112	106	74	39	77	73
500A–100A SA–SU	160	76	73	67	51	30	45	43
700A–700P MO–FR	353	158	150	143	98	48	108	102
700A–700P SAT	235	119	116	105	79	42	77	74
700A–700P SUN	176	81	75	69	47	31	50	44
Weekly cume (00)	2575.0	1151.0	1070.0	970.0	672.0	317.0	803.0	753.0
Weekly cume (%)	36.3	34.4	54.0	57.4	65.1	76.9	43.9	48.0
Total hours (000)	3254.0	1481.0	1412.0	1327.0	941.0	513.0	950.0	899.0
Share Wkly Hours	19.9	18.0	31.1	33.9	41.3	48.3	23.3	25.8
Avg. Weekly Hours	12.6	12.9	13.2	13.7	14.0	16.2	11.8	11.9

through the use of one-week listening diaries given to a representative sample of listeners over 12 years of age.

The first part of the table presents the *average* quarter-hour audience for the station. Note that for the 18-to-24-year-old grouping, the smallest age interval in the table, 4,800 was the average number of female listeners over quarter-hour periods from 7:00 AM to 7:00 PM, Monday to Friday. As you might expect, the numbers drop during the weekend period. Note the total number of hours—513,000—reported for the 18-to-24-year-olds relative to other age intervals and the share of weekly hours—48.3 per cent. This table, presented as an example, addresses a female audience. The total database provides distributions of listening habits according to age, gender, first language, and location. These variables make a difference with respect to listening habits, and broadcasters and advertisers take full advantage of the differences.

These are the data sold to broadcasters by media rating firms. In turn, broadcasters sell time periods containing specified audiences by gender, age, first language, geographic location, etc., to advertisers. In this system it is your listening preferences and social status which are the commodities circulating in the media system. Enter a cable or a satellite company into the mix and the commodity route becomes more complex. For example, cable companies seek broadcasters as clients selling advertising slots to local, regional, and national advertisers. According to Napoli, 'Broadcasters compete with content to attract [measured] audiences' (2003: 4). Content providers (cable, satellite, and broadcasters) deliver demographic groups (audience measurements) available in varying quarter-hour segments to advertisers. Thus do audience size, demographic composition, and patterns of use become the primary commodity exchanged in a media system (Meehan, 1984: 216–25).

The Audience as a Participant

A participant is someone who takes part in a project. It is difficult to think of the corporate practice of defining audiences as passive targets yielding a framework for participation. Broadcasters have tried to do so, first through the introduction of the radio talk show and, later, through providing a means for receiving telephone and email comments and suggestions on various programs and, finally, through the provision of Internet sites and blogs. In Chapter 2 we considered the extent to which commercial media creates public spaces. We noted that there were very few, according to our criteria for public spaces. We also noted minor exceptions in some public broadcasting, community radio and television, and some social networks, though many of these latter have fallen to purely commercial interests. The overwhelming commercial orientation and values built into media systems almost preclude recognizing audiences as participants. Blog or Internet audiences remain either targets or commodities. Commodified audiences, albeit elements of a system, are not participants. Persons are indeed statistical artefacts.

Audiences through the Lens of Social Research

On the one hand, individual listeners, readers, viewers, and users of media are social creatures interacting with others and within communities and carrying identities that have emerged from such interaction. Media use is simply one more system of action within which the individual assumes a particular role—that of audience member. On the other hand, the research problem under investigation and the theoretical orientation of the researcher will yield particular definitions of media audiences. One researcher may be interested in the way in which the creators in the system envision their potential audience; another may focus on the way in which listeners and readers process news and information; yet another might research the reception of entertainment programming. Most certainly there is overlap between the ways in which the corporate world and social researchers define audiences. We will try to capture the variations in audience definitions appearing in the research literature under the following four categories:

- the passive receiving audience;
- the mass persuasion audience;
- the users and gratification approach to audiences; and
- reception studies and encoding/decoding.

The Passive Receiving Audience

This view of audiences is similar to the 'audience as target' definition assumed by media companies. According to an entry in the archives of the Museum of Broadcast Communications,

> [M]edia are seen to have the power to inject their audiences with particular 'messages' which will cause them to behave in particular ways. This has involved . . . perspectives which see the media as causing the breakdown of 'traditional values' and . . . perspectives which see their audiences [acquiring consumer values] as some form of false consciousness. (www.museum.tv/archives/etv/A/htm/A)

The notion of a passive audience receiving messages without judgment, sometimes referred to as the 'hypodermic model' of media influence, follows two lines of thought. The first is a critical view of popular culture that has its origin in the works of Theodor Adorno and Max Horkheimer. In addition to introducing a concept somewhat akin to audience as target, the perspective opened the door to the audience as commodity designation. Cultural industries, including the mass media, were assumed to carry sufficient authority to block out the critical thinking of mass audiences and, thus, to succeed in feeding the users the dominant ideologies of consumerism, lack of civility, and violence. It was believed that children watching violence in TV cartoons become violent children; young people watching violence on TV and playing computer games become violent young people; and sexual messages, direct and subliminal, cause sexually abnormal media users. In Adorno's words, 'the concepts of order which it hammers into human beings are always those of the status quo' (1991: 90). He elaborates by stating: 'It proclaims: you shall conform, without instruction as to what; conform to what exists anyway . . . [t]he power of the culture industry's ideology is such that conformity has replaced consciousness' (1991: 90).

The second line of thought, media effects research, is much more closely allied to the 'audience as target' definition. It emerged from a critique of the pessimism inherent in the work of Adorno and others. Effects research, associated with samples and measurements of audience reaction to media content, assumed that the power in the message/sender/receiver relation rested with the sender. You, the audience member, simply sat back and passively absorbed the message. In rebuttal one media scholar noted:

> Research shows that viewing is almost never passive. People interpret, evaluate, dismiss, and argue back at the screen on the basis of their social experience and their involvement in other media. . . . The problem is that cultural forms that were previously separated from the television system are being increasingly tugged towards it, reinforcing its command over experiencing and debate. (Murdock, 1990: 77)

It is generally accepted that well-crafted messages of an informative, entertaining, or advertising nature can affect or persuade audience members. At the same time it is accepted that audiences are selective and pay attention to critiques of media content offered by friends and neighbours—television and press content are discussed and argued. Thus did scholarly arguments circulating around the level of passivity of audience members lead to a new set of research orientations championed by such sociologists as Robert Merton (1946) and Elihu Katz and Paul Lazarsfeld (1955).

The Sociology of Mass Persuasion

The empirically oriented works of Merton, Lazarsfeld, and Katz were labelled the 'sociology of mass persuasion'. In the early 1940s Lazarsfeld and his team at Columbia University presented evidence that audiences were much more active than previously suspected. The concept of audience communities was introduced. Discussion, critiques, and opinions among friends and neighbours regarding the information and entertainment flow through media sources was observed as having an influence on the manner in which media users selected and interpreted programming. Lee Becker (1998), a major 'media effects' researcher, noted that, following a set of classic studies on voting behaviour, researchers took a new direction. 'Rather than asking what effect a message had on audience members, researchers were encouraged to ask what uses audience members made of the media and what gratifications they obtained from this use' (Becker, 1998: 60).

Research focusing on *use* rather than *effects* clearly demonstrates audience selectivity, audience evaluation of programming, and the operation of group values on usage. As previously discussed, gender, age, and ethno-cultural background have considerable impact on listening and watching decisions. For example, recent research has demonstrated that women and men view and perceive news differently (Kamhawi and Grabe, 2008).

Considering 'audience communities' as a perspective on audiences, we might also consider the research conducted in Montreal between 1999 and 2002 that examined radio usage among 18-to-24-year-olds that was discussed earlier. The first phase of the project used focus groups in order to acquire some knowledge of radio use (Jackson and Rosenberg, 2004).[1]

A total of seventy-five 18-to-24-year-olds selected from two colleges and one university took part in 11 focus groups, an average of 6.8 per group. With respect to parentage, a major variable in the larger study, 32 reported Canadian-born parents; 14 reported one parent born abroad; and 24 reported both parents born abroad. In addition, five were themselves born abroad. Participants discussed their radio listening preferences, their reactions to various radio formats, and their use of Internet radio. The discussion was built around three taped selections from regular broadcasting: an excerpt from an 'ethnic' station, playing Greek music, the DJ speaking in Greek; an excerpt from a regularly scheduled Montreal English-language talk show; and an excerpt from *The Howard Stern Show*. The objective was to measure reactions not to these specific programs but to the formats and to elicit a general discussion on radio use.

Regarding radio use in general:

- Radio was for music; 'pop' stations (Mix 96, CHOM, CFQR, CKOI) prevailed
- Minor interest, increasing with age, in 'alternative music' (rap, hip hop, reggae). In this respect stations selected were CKUT (McGill University); K103 (CKRK, the station of the Mohawk Nation); WBTZ (The Buzz, Vermont)
- A tendency for respondents of West Indian origin to tune in to CKUT and K103, but not to the neglect of 'pop' stations
- Minimum use, but some, of radio for news and talk shows
- Most listening time was during the morning wake-up call, in the car, and at work
- Rare, but present, listening to CBC and SRC (English- and French-language public broadcasters), usually older group

Regardless of ethnic background, North American 'pop' culture monopolized radio listening interests, although much more so for women than men. Apart from 'alternative music' interests, Mix 96 and CHOM dominated. First-language French speakers listened to French-language popular stations as well as the English-language stations. The very few unilingual Anglophones in the sample remained with English-language stations while bilinguals (French and English) and trilinguals (French, English, and parents' language) used both French and English stations. There was a reluctance to admit to radio listening, either because it is so pervasive that respondents were not aware of its presence or because radio was not 'with it'; however, respondents were very knowledgeable about radio and the musical programming of Montreal stations. Radio is tuned in for the morning wake-up call, is used in the car while commuting, and is ever-present in some work situations, although the listener does not control frequencies in this situation.

Regarding discussion around the taped selections, the participants indicated that 'ethnic' stations were for parents and grandparents. As one reported, 'This music is associated with my grandmother's generation, the kind of music you hear at weddings—folk music.' Participants were not inclined to tune in 'ethnic' stations, regardless of parentage. Age was a far more salient social category than ethnicity or language with respect to radio listening in general and culturally specific programming in particular.

On the standard talk-show format there was a *general* rejection of this type of show—again, major rejection in the context of generational interests—'talk shows like this are for opinionated older people in their 50s.'

With respect to *The Howard Stern Show*, participants were offended at racist and sexist remarks, but attracted by the outrageous nature of the presentation. Freedom of speech and freedom of the airwaves were highly valued in the discussions. Generally, the position taken was that the show ought not to have been removed. One respondent reported that the show would not appeal to their parents' generation; 'they are inclined to take it literally, they just don't get it.'

In sum, age and to a lesser extent gender appeared to control radio listening habits. It is well known that age is a major independent variable with respect to music preferences. What is of interest in the framework of this study was that age was a prime mover with respect to radio formats. These respondents placed their priority on music formats with a minimum of DJ interference. News, talk, and sports were secondary and of little interest. The structured talk-show format was uniformly rejected. The often aggressively presented opinions expressed by callers and hosts alike angered participants, as one reported, accompanied with much nodding of heads, 'it's like listening to my mother.' Age also played a role in the discussion of *The Howard Stern Show* excerpt. First, there was a general acceptance of the format and a preference for satire over the opinionated talk-show format. The older generations, according to the participants, take the material literally, missing the irony, satire, and sheer outrageous comedy. The outrageousness and impertinence of it all seemed to appeal as a kind of carnivalesque liberation from older adult constraints.

Nevertheless, the responses were not uniform in the study. A few participants found the material offensive. More women than men expressed this thought, suggesting gender as an influencing variable. A feeling of offensiveness did not follow parentage. However, one participant, whose parents were both born in Jamaica, reported that he found Stern's show quite amusing, 'especially', he added, the 'ethnic slurs'. Yet to another young woman, both parents born in Canada, 'he's mostly about sex and body parts, he bugs me, five minutes is enough, why do people like it?' The particular focus group in which this woman participated was composed solely of women, all of whom rejected Stern's show as offensive. But these, as well as most other participants in all groups, condemned the removal of the show from the Montreal station CHOM.

Reception Studies and Encoding/Decoding

This research orientation has its origin in the work of Stuart Hall and the Birmingham Centre for Contemporary Cultural Studies during the mid-1970s (Hall, 1974). Looking back at the 'passive, receiving audience'—where the emphasis in the message/sender/receiver link was on the sender—in reception studies the encoded message remains a key element but the emphasis shifts to the receiver as a decoder of messages. Rather than a speeding bullet sent to the receiver, the message is **encoded** by the sender and **decoded** by the receiver. The receiver makes sense of the message, an understanding which is by no means identical to the encoded meaning. Thus, various audiences will attribute various meanings to a single message. This, by the way, incorporates the view that audience members are influenced by the social group in which they are located.

There is no denial that messages have an effect, but the effect is complicated by the perceptual, cognitive, emotional, and ideological influences present in the receivers' socio-cultural location. Meaning as encoded and decoded takes on an importance not found in other audience-research orientations. Put another way, the emphasis in this research orientation shifts from the measurement of audiences' viewing and listening to a semiotic emphasis (Alasuutari, 1999: 3–4).

One media scholar introduced the approach in the following way: '[Hall] challenges the idea that it is possible to determine the nature of communication and meaning by the application of measurement techniques. [He] insists that meaning is multi-layered [and] multi-referential . . .' (Gray, 1999: 27). With layers of meaning and multiple references, messages are bound to be differentially received. Effects, however, will persist. In the media system as portrayed above, both power and authority are on the side of the creators and providers as encoders. The writers, performers, financial backers, and providers comprise powerful political and cultural institutions. Accordingly, the process of encoding is the product of institutional activity working under the umbrella of the prevailing ideologies. However, decoding will occur within this system. As noted earlier, the system, as a set of social relations operating in established economic, political, and ideological environments, is in a constant state of instability; the system can be undermined. Taking from the 'uses and gratification' approach, the question is, 'how are the messages used?' Michel de Certeau, when highlighting the manner in which messages are *used*, put it this way:

> [T]he analysis of the images broadcast [the reference is to analyses of the content and structure of messages] by television and of the time watching television should be complimented by a study of what the cultural consumer 'makes' or 'does' during this time and with these images. (1984: 31)

How the messages are interpreted is the crucial question. The decoding process may occur within the domain of the dominant ideology, consistent with that of the encoding process. The extent to which audiences simply accept the dominant ideology in their interpretation of a media message is always an open question subject to inquiry; they may or may not. Nevertheless, audiences make do with what they receive, rearranging the meanings to suit their collective vision. Codes may be negotiated in the sense that receivers employ tactics to weave in and out of and around the official encoded meanings, or they may be oppositional in the sense that receivers reverse the meanings encoded to their advantage. Neither the message nor the receiver is static. Two projects will serve to illustrate the decoding process. For the first example we will return to the research addressing 18-to-24-year-old radio users. For the second example we will consider research reported by John Fiske (1994: 189–208) on television use.

During the focus group sessions in the radio usage study referred to earlier a tape was played of a standard talk show with a phone-in format broadcast over Montreal station CJAD. These shows were based on selected news or editorial items of the day. The host commented and listeners were invited to phone in to discuss the issue of the day with the host. The selected news item on the taped excerpt was the reported desecration of a Roman Catholic cathedral in Montreal in the name of the pro-choice movement. The issue gave the show's host an opportunity to raise the question of hate crimes, a violation of the Canadian criminal code.

Among the sample subjects there was a general rejection of this type of talk show and that rejection was in the context of generational interests—'talk shows like this are for opinionated older people in their 50s.' To summarize the responses,

- Aggressively expressed opinions by host and phone-in audience members angered the focus group participants. As mentioned earlier in this chapter, they appeared to be reacting to the authority of their parents' generation—'its like listening to my mother', stated one participant.
- References were made to French-language talk shows as more relaxing and funny. Other talk shows were mentioned as perhaps more entertaining but nevertheless too opinionated and outdated.
- In the excerpt played, respondents were more captured by the issue of abortion and pro-choice than by the raid on and desecration of a church, described as a 'hate crime' by the show's host.

In sum, the structured talk-show format was uniformly rejected. Nor did the issue raised in the excerpt draw out the reactions one might expect, given the ethnic mix of the participants. These 18-to-24-year-olds simply didn't respond to the issue, overcome as they were by their anger with the format itself. What response to the issue did occur was an occasional expression in favour of the pro-choice movement. The young men and women in these groups rejected a highly popular radio format and local show and sympathized with the demonstrators' cause rather than with the opinion of the show's host and audience members. Here we have an example of oppositional decoding based on affiliations with differing social groups.

Another example of decoding can be seen by considering television. In his work John Fiske changes 'audience', a noun, to 'audiencing', a verb, in order to emphasize active usage of media. Consistent with this emphasis others have noted that 'several interpretations coexist as potentials in any one [media] text, and may be actualized or decoded differently by different audiences, depending on their interpretive conventions and cultural backgrounds (Jensen, 1990: 57–8). Here audience inquiries place the accent on sociology—on social groups and social formations. Members of the audience become social actors; that is, subjects acting in relation to other subjects and within particular cultural contexts.

The project monitored a small group of first- and second-year university students through one season (1989) of the TV sitcom *Married . . . with Children* on the then new Fox television network. Each session was closely observed, recording comments in process and discussions of the program. The comedy was somewhat outrageous or carnivalesque, with action circulating around bodies, bodily functions, and sexuality. From an adult point of view, the viewers' parents' generation, the program was considered offensive and to be sending the wrong message to young people. From the perspective of the young audience, the view was different. The program allowed them to mock the differences between their parents as teenagers and themselves, and between their parents now and themselves. In Fiske's words,

> Watching the program involved a series of interactive comments that took every opportunity the show offered to draw disrespectful parallels between it and the families the teenagers had so recently left. The comments ranged from delight in representations . . . ('My Dad does that') . . . to more engaged family politics . . . ('I wish my Mom had seen that'). (1994: 191)

The program gave the audience—that particular audience—a route through which to engage in age and gender politics.

The impact of age on interpretation reported here is similar to the research on radio listening reported above. This does not mean that you can automatically read the direction an interpretation of a particular program will take from age or gender alone. In the two cases reported, age and gender affiliations were rooted in particular social groups collectively communicating values and attitudes. We could perhaps speak of an 'interpretive community' bringing about shared interpretations of the surrounding social and cultural environment (Tompkins, 1980: xxi). 'Social formation' (or social groups) is the concept used by Fiske to draw our attention to the fact that audience members belong to more than one social formation and, therefore, to more than one interpretive framework. In other words audiences are not only active but fluid as well.

This insight appears to run counter to the commercial vision where, as noted above, audiences are either a likely target for received wisdom, a commodity for sale to advertising agencies, or, and much less likely, a participant. Even when audience members are defined as participants, they remain subjected to commercial interests. Media researchers, while recognizing the influential and authoritative impact of encoded messages received from a variety of media sources, allow for decoding variations rooted in social group membership. Since any one individual is likely to be affiliated with several social groups, media selection, program selection, and interpretive codes will vary considerably for any one person. The question remains, do and can people react to media as complete persons? To respond requires a consideration of media practice and citizenship.

The Media System and Responsibility

The notion of citizenship introduces a rather complex set of ideas. The commonly accepted meaning associates citizenship with a legally defined membership in a polity; that is, a nation state or a particular city or town. Another, broader definition has recently gained acceptance. Membership in a polity entails 'sharing and participating in a common project or identity' (Nielsen, 2002: 143). Thus is sharing, participation, interaction, and debate around common political, social, and cultural projects a part of the practice of citizenship. Media present us with opportunities for such activity and, for most citizens, attachment to media sources appears to be extensive and intense. Are we not constantly watching, listening, linking, texting, and talking over or on radio, television, the Internet, cell phones, and land phones?

The questions to be considered are varied. Does this intensive activity

- link us with the political community of which we are a part?
- involve us in sharing common projects and identities?
- encourage us to interact across the diversity of people and ideas in our environment?
- encourage media creators and providers to act as interlocutors opening opportunities for interaction across diversity and to experiment with identities and belonging?

If the answer to these questions is affirmative, then the media system (citizens and producers alike) is meeting its responsibilities as a democratically oriented system. If the answer is negative, then the system is not meeting its responsibilities. In reality there are several flaws in the system that curtail a successful execution of the responsibilities of citizenship:

- For the most part media providers are businesses; the objective is commercial success, not the development and encouragement of citizenship.
- To the extent that media creators and providers are *committed* to news and political evaluation and information, the emphasis is on journalism as the established authority rather than on citizenship as an interactive element

within the system. In the media system, democratic responsibility requires at least a minor shift of power and authority to citizens (i.e., the audience).

- As the authority, the authors of news and current affairs are inclined to view newscasts, current affairs programming, and discussions dominated by experts as the only source of civic information and thought. That entertainment, blogging, tweeting, and so on may encourage citizen interaction is scoffed at and ignored.
- The citizen, as an audience member, all too frequently succumbs to the consumer role. Consumerism tends to define personal identities, blocking the encouragement of civic action.

In spite of these flaws, the media system as an institution not only carries opportunities for the exercise of citizenship but also has potential for further development. As noted in Chapter 2, there is potential for developing broad interactive relations within the system, relations which acknowledge the input of a citizen audience. This potential rests principally with social network sites and the use of these sites by conventional media outlets. Whether used or not, these are the sites to which users (audiences) are migrating. Conventional broadcasters and newspapers are aware of the migration but appear to be trapped in their old models of transferring information and entertainment. In Canada, CanWest Global Media, CTV, and the *Toronto Star* have all reported serious economic problems, some of which are related to the 2008–09 economic recession, but they have also acknowledged audience loss as a result of people increasing their use of Web 2.0 technologies at the expense of traditional sources.

Professor Jeffrey Jones (2006: 367) made the following observation in the journal *Social Semiotics*:

The news media are therefore seen as the most important players in the creation and/or representation of political reality.

To be sure, these functions are vital to successful self-governance. Nevertheless, this persistent focus on news media has weaknesses. It leads to dismissals of other, more popular sources of political information and content as illegitimate. Entertainment media are seen as distractions from the serious duty of the informed citizen.

Furthermore, news stories are simply one type of narrative, while entertainment media provide yet another. Thus, it is important to recognize that different media can, and often do, present different narratives about politics.

There is some movement across the barrier wedged between conventional methods and Web 2.0 opportunities. In November 2008 YouTube, purchased by Google Inc. in 2006, announced a plan to display its videos on TV screens. In the United States CBS launched a YouTube channel. In Canada the CBC and TVO (both public broadcasters) announced their YouTube channels. During the 2008 election campaign in the United States both political parties demonstrated the value in engaging citizens via Web 2.0 technology. In many ways the election was an 'Internet election' with sophisticated websites, active blogging, YouTube videos, Facebook groups, and rapid-fire Twitter postings. The citizenry used the many opportunities for participation—small communities, university campuses, and local meetings all made use of the sites provided. In contrast, in the recent Canadian election the parties fenced themselves in with sites 'dismissed as juvenile that did more harm than good' and 'a model of top down messaging with even local candidates required to follow a common' script (Geist, 2008b: B1–B6).

The extent to which the political parties in the United States made use of Web 2.0 technology hints at the potential for citizen engagement within the media system if traditional media providers are prepared to take the risk. And there is risk involved. With the exception of public broadcasters (though they too carry a certain amount of risk), media outlets, including the press, are losing their main sources of revenue—audiences which can be sold to advertisers. They are losing this source not only because of migration to new technologies but also because advertisers are concerned about the lack of response from Web 2.0 users. This is the dilemma, a dilemma resulting from a major contradiction within the media system if providers are to assume their

> Facebook has been riding a tidal wave of momentum behind an exploding user base and increasing mainstream acceptance for more than a year, but financial realities are threatening to bring the social network and its peers back to Earth in 2009.
>
> In 2007, the ascension of Facebook, MySpace, and other social networks [became] mainstream staples of online communication. . . . Micro-blogging site Twitter enjoyed a similar coming-out party in 2008.
>
> Marketers salivated over the technology these sites boasted that allowed them to tailor advertising to reach individual users and niche audiences. That was all before the collapse of the global credit markets and before marketing experts began to fret that 2009 could be a rough one for industries that rely on advertising. (M. Hartley, 2009: A10)

democratic responsibilities. The contradiction is this: to pursue democratic responsibility requires that audiences be defined as citizens, but to remain viable economically, providers must define their audiences as commodities.

Citizenship implies membership in a polity. Membership grounds a person in a social role implying participation, interaction, and sharing. We have posed the question as to whether or not the media as a social system is capable of defining its audiences and readers as citizens and, accordingly, encouraging participation, interaction, and sharing. To some extent media providers have made opportunities available for the exercise of citizenship via the use of Web 1.0 and Web 2.0 technologies. However, as commercial enterprises they have little choice but to define their audiences as targets and commodities. With the exception of public broadcasters, at least to some extent, the audience/reader as citizen will remain a low priority. Working against this trend is the fact that audiences are rapidly and in significant numbers migrating to Web 2.0 technologies—to social networks, iPods, and texting. This migration signals the possibility that more and more audiences will *define themselves* as citizens and thus reorder the relations within the media system.

Summary

We began with an examination of the concept of 'social systems', defined as a set of interacting roles, social categories, groups, and institutions. This enabled us to view the multiple parts of the media industry as a system encompassing creators, performers, carriers and transmitters, advertising corporations, and audiences. Media system relations, though neither fixed nor stable, tend to be hierarchical; that is, authority and power relations are built into the system. The focus of this chapter was on audiences, the element with very little, if any, authority but the potential, *as citizens*, to exercise power within the system.

In examining the various roles assigned to audiences it became clear that identifying an audience is more complicated than one might at first assume. Within a system dominated by media corporations, the audience is not the real you but a defined role segment—a demographic unit, the number of people watching a show on a given day in 15-minute segments, a particular number of potential viewers sold to an advertising agency, and so on. Several definitions of audiences as seen by media-related corporations and by media scholars were noted. Media corporations view their audiences as targets, as commodities, and, within limits, as active participants. The principal roles assigned audiences by corporations are those of commodities and targets, roles which dehumanize audience members and severely limit their ability to act as citizens.

Media scholars have carefully examined these various corporate role definitions within another framework set according to their research objectives.

Here audiences were defined as passive receivers, the subjects of mass persuasion, users seeking enjoyment and satisfaction, and users decoding received messages according to their social locations.

Finally we considered audiences as citizens seeking to meet their democratic responsibilities through participation and sharing. We noted that it is difficult to act out the role of citizen within a system dominated by conventional broadcasting, much more so where private broadcasters dominate over public broadcasters. However the media landscape appears to be in flux as audiences migrate to social networks while avoiding conventional outlets. It is in the domain of Web 2.0 sites where audiences readily and easily participate and share as citizens. The economic downturn of 2008–09 and perhaps beyond will, ironically perhaps, enhance the role of media citizenship as conventional providers suffer extreme economic difficulties.

Enhanced Learning Activities

1. Watch the late-night news (the 10 PM and 11 PM broadcasts) on CBS, CTV, and CBC. Using a stopwatch, compare the amount of time devoted to advertising on each channel. Compare US and Canadian channels (CBS for US, CTV and CBC for Canada) and private (CBS, CTV) with public channels (CBC).
2. Compare the advertising time on CNN and CBC News Network late-night newscasts.
3. Compare the interactive tools made available by TVO and CBC with those made available by GlobalMedia and CTV.
4. From the perspective of citizenship responsibilities, compare and evaluate the interactive tools made available by your closest daily newspaper with those made available by *The Globe and Mail* (www.globeandmail.com) and *The New York Times* (www.nytimes.com).
5. Select a one-hour drama presentation on TVO (Ontario public), PBS (US public), and CTV (Canadian private) and compare advertising time.

Annotated Further Reading

Theodor W. Adorno, *The Culture Industry: Selected Essays on Mass Culture*, J.M Bernstein, ed. London: Routledge, 1991. This is an excellent collection of Adorno's essays introducing the reader to the 'Frankfurt School'. The reader is introduced to Adorno's essays on cultural industries and the arts and the media, specifically music, film, and television. The introduction opens the contemporary debate on Adorno's work.

Pertii Alasuutari, ed., *Rethinking the Media Audience*. London: Sage Publications, 1999. Viewing the audience as, most of all, a theoretical construct produced by a particular analytic gaze, this is a collection of articles addressing media audiences' shifting according to particular analytical frameworks. The reader is asked to consider that the 'real' audience in its totality is never quite grasped. Articles address audience research through sociological and cultural perspectives.

Raymond Kent, *Measuring Media Audiences*. London: Routledge, 1994. Viewing the media as primarily vehicles for the provision of information or entertainment including advertising and sponsorship as a source of revenue, this book addresses the need for audience measurement. The reader is able to gain considerable understanding of the behaviour of the dominant actors in the media system, which views the audience as a potential market requiring a suitable marketing mix of product design and specification, pricing, promotion, coverage, and distribution, all matched with the organization's capabilities and opportunities in the marketplace.

Philip M. Napoli, *Audience Economics: Media Institutions and the Marketplace*. New York: Columbia University Press, 2003. This book addresses the media as a large-scale corporate industry, investigating the economics of audiences and various ways of looking at audiences from a marketing point of view. Measured audiences and actual audiences are considered. A useful picture of the media system is provided as a 'marketing system' comprising broadcaster, provider, audience, rating firms, and advertising agencies.

Social Semiotics, Vol. 16, No. 2 (June 2006). This is an issue of *Social Semiotics* worth examining. Responding to the question 'what does it mean to be a citizen in contemporary societies and what role do mass media play in the construction and practice of citizenship?', the issue carries several articles on 'Mediated Citizenship(s)'. Among the selected pieces are articles on Chinese citizenship and the media, citizenship and national identity, and citizenship and public broadcasting.

Useful Media

Museum of Broadcast Communications

www.museum.tv

The website of the Museum of Broadcast Communications presents a very comprehensive coverage of broadcasting. Among others, special links to the Radio Hall of Fame, the Encyclopedia of Television, Docufest, and the MBC blog are all worth further exploration.

Bureau of Broadcast Management

www.bbm.ca

The Bureau of Broadcast Management is the leading provider of TV, radio, and consumer information to Canadian broadcasters, advertisers, and agencies. It provides broadcast measurement and consumer behaviour data, as well as industry-leading intelligence. Although the main data bank is available only to members, the website is very informative regarding the broadcasting audience measurement industry.

The Corporation (2004). Directors: Jennifer Abbott and Mark Achbar. Starring: Jane Akre and Ray Anderson.

This is a very well-produced critique of the corporation as an historical institution. It is not directly related to media, but the theories discussed in this chapter are easily applied.

Note

1. This section is adapted from John D. Jackson and Michael Rosenberg. *Recognition and Mis-Recognition: Radio as Interlocutor*. Montreal: Centre for Broadcasting Studies, Concordia University, 2004.

4 Consumption and Advertising

Learning Objectives

- To consider the paradox of consumption
- To review classical sociology on consumption through the work of Marx, Simmel, and Veblen
- To question the limitations of classical sociology
- To review contemporary sociology on 'cultural capital' through the work of Bourdieu, Baudrillard, and de Certeau
- To consider feminist critiques on gender, political economy, and consumption
- To discuss advertising as mass communication

Introduction

Mediated society is also consumer society. Advertising, promotional materials, leisure activities, and commodities of various brands and logos prevail and tempt us to consume. Different forms of media are saturated with advertisements designed as simple factual statements, sophisticated narrative developments, or complex symbolic **undertones**. Moreover, social practices and relationships are interwoven with shopping and consumption. This results in making everyday life ordinary, or particularly rendering holiday celebrations or vacations into something special. However, what seems to be familiar and omnipresent is by no means a simple matter. For instance, is consumption simply about purchasing in an economic sense? Why do we choose one brand over the other? Why do we replace a perfectly functioning commodity with something newer, more advanced, or more fashionable? How does advertising work in the making of the image culture? We know advertising's explicit and implicit goals are to promote, stimulate, sell, and make profits. But how else does it impact the consumer?

The learning objective of this chapter is to unpack the complexity and paradox of consumption. A reading from classical to contemporary theories in this field helps develop the necessary conceptual tools while also demonstrating the contrasting perspectives of social structure and agency throughout an analysis of the intertwinement of production, advertising, and consumption in contemporary society. We also consider how social class and gender are configured in the debates, and whether advertising is a deceiving sign system of communication or if it is open to interpretation. We balance the theoretical arguments with concrete examples including sweatshop production, advertising for bottled water, and the wearing of jeans.

Consumption: The Paradoxical Phenomenon

Consumption touches upon many aspects of contemporary life. Many of our everyday practices are organized around consumption—grocery shopping, participating in leisure activities, comparing prices and searching for the best deal, daydreaming about a commodity, and shopping for all sorts of special occasions, among others. To a less visible extent, consumption is also integral to policy making. Sales taxes are the most obvious example, and luxury items, tobacco, and alcohol are heavily taxed. Urban planners might consider whether a development project entails potentials for consumption and sales. National governments might also stimulate the economy through encouraging consumption. For instance, President George W. Bush urged Americans to return to normal life after the 9/11 attack by encouraging them to go back to work, *to go shopping*, and to take in ball games; President Obama considered a 'Buy American' clause as a part of his plan for economic recovery.

Consumption is, therefore, more than style, and it broadly includes leisure, arts, sports activities, and industries. It can be ordinary, special, personal, collective, direct, mediated, structural, policy-oriented, and transnational. This is also to say that consumption can be social, cultural, psychological, economic, political, and historical, depending on which aspect of consumption we address and how we interpret it. More importantly, contemporary society is increasingly caught up in commodification as the most personal of issues: self-esteem, emotions, values, and relationships can be commodified, advertised, and sold.

Consumption is also treated in moral terms, as something good for self-expression, individual development, or a reward for hard work. On the other hand, it can be regarded as something wasteful, unethical, or a bottomless desire for objects; material ownership can be seen as a sign of greed, superficiality, and insensitivity to social justice. This is especially the case when it comes to luxury items such as tobacco and alcohol, where high sales taxes have become the embodiment of moral punishment. The recent economic crisis was partially regarded as a moral deficit, as consumers shopped and bought based on a credit system that actually went beyond personal financial limits. This is the reason why US President Barack Obama has emphasized the need to sacrifice consumption as a way of taking collective responsibility. The question is: how do we make a moral judgment with regard to consumption? Wearing perfume and jewellery can be luxurious and unnecessary for students; yet, it can be ordinary and essential for those in the media production industry. Greed can be the cause of the economic crisis, but who is greedy exactly? Do we blame the ordinary consumer who buys beyond financial limits, or do we point the finger to those who deregulated the credit system and encouraged consumption through marketing and advertising? Contrary to being something morally questionable, consumption can also be considered a process of victimization. The consumer easily falls for the advertiser's allure, temptation, persuasion, and trap. If marketing and advertising aim to sell, they can package a product into the solution to personal problems or create commodity images in association with personal emotions, values, and relationships that camouflage the real demand for commercial interests.

So far, our exploration shows that consumption is a multi-faceted and often contradictory phenomenon which also evokes diversified interpretations from classical to contemporary social theories. The following discussion focuses on concepts and practices of consumption in order to ground our further discussion about advertising and marketing.

The Marxist Perspective on Production and Consumption

Taking a Marxist perspective, we start by analyzing consumption from a structural point of view and in terms of class relations. Consumption, for

Marx, was not about individual taste, purchasing power, or freedom. Marx saw the inseparable relations between consumption and production at three levels: first, '[p]roduction is . . . also immediately consumption, consumption is also immediately production' (Marx, 1978: 229). This immediacy concerns both productive consumption and consumptive production. The former refers to consuming raw materials in production. As an example Marx points to the making of a wool coat. A producer needs to consume wool, water, and coal, the most immediate raw materials required at the time. The latter is the necessity of consumption for subsistence: 'It is clear that in taking in food, for example, which is a form of consumption, the human being produces his own body' (Marx, 1978: 228).

At the second level, production and consumption constitute a mediated relation because of their mutual dependence. No matter how production and consumption are directly identified together, they remain distinctive. This mutual mediation is described by Marx as the relation in which '[p]roduction creates the material, as an external object, for consumption; consumption creates the need, as an internal object . . . for production (Marx, 1978: 230). Simply put, production is a means for consumption and consumption the purpose of production. For instance, a wool coat becomes a wool coat only by being worn, consumed, or used. In turn, the need and the purpose of wearing a wool coat drive the production and reproduction of this particular material object.

At the third level, each of consumption and production completes and creates itself as the other, and each feeds off the other as an expression of supply and demand. Production is not finished and the purpose of supply can become useless if the material object is not used or consumed. This is not simply about the relations between production materials and consumption acts. It is also about the relations between the producer and the consumer. That is, consumption makes production meaningful. In turn, production validates and creates the specific manner, use, and stimulus of consumption. The inseparable connection between consumption and production at three different levels points out that consumption is not an individual, subjective behaviour detached from greater socio-economic structural forces. Consumption, for Marx, is not about individual tastes, an expression of individual achievement, or individualism rewarded by material substances.

Consumption is far from politically neutral once it is only understood in relation to production. 'The incessant reproduction, the perpetuation of the worker, is the absolutely necessary condition for capitalist production' (Marx, 1990: 716). Use value, functions, or utilities of products are overridden by exchange value, which turns products into commodities in the process of monetary exchange for the accumulation of capital. At the same time, workers are caught up in the process of commodified, and thus alienated, exchanges of their own labour in terms of production. Labour becomes a commodity to be bought and sold. In addition, the worker is alienated from her or his own products as the products become a part of the capitalist wealth and 'an alien power that dominates and exploits him[/her]' (Marx, 1990: 716).

Meanwhile, consumption becomes the modern form of justification for running and maintaining capitalism in order to seek endless profits through satisfying the unsatisfied material needs. It also functions as an ideological apparatus that creates a double false consciousness in due course. Consumption for the worker is understood at two levels: first, it is productive consumption that turns labour purchased by capital into the process of production; second, it is individual consumption, an offering to the workers as rewards for their work. However, individual consumption in turn is converted into means of subsistence to ensure the continuation of productive consumption for the capitalist.

Horkheimer and Adorno follow Marx's critique and focus on consumption, especially in its *mass media form*, as the embodiment of propaganda and ideology in maintaining industrial capitalist society. The culture of the commodity, including mass media, film, radio, and television, functions to control the lives of workers in a seemingly ever-improving living standard saturated with an endless desire for commodities. Consumption, consequently, creates the first false consciousness that misrecognizes the meanings of commodities. When consumption appears to reward the worker's labour, it creates the second false consciousness that material goods can provide satisfaction. Further subject to the wider analysis of commodity fetishism, the hidden value of owning properties and commodities is mediated in social relations because the worker sees consumption as the motivation for the otherwise exploitative yet hypnotic conditions. In short, the worker becomes a passive victim of consumption when the exchange values of money and commodities are offered as rewards.

Example: Sweatshops and Consumption

For those who follow the argument in the Marxist tradition, the relations between production and consumption are fundamentally unchanged despite the expansion and complication of capitalism in the global age. This is especially the case when it comes to global sweatshop conditions. Sweatshops are the places where many labour-intensive commodities, such as garments, shoes, electronic gadgets, and other small consumer items, are manufactured. These places are at the bottom of a myriad of supply and demand chains that can easily involve hundreds of independent companies seeking profits and pushing the exchange value to exceed the use value. To use a pair of sneakers as an example, the production cost can be less than $15 USD while the retail price, as the embodiment of exchange value, can be $200 USD. Furthermore, while sweatshops continue to exist in ethnic enclaves of major Western cities like New York and Los Angeles, the majority can be found in less developed countries where human rights are questionable. Sweatshops are therefore characterized by domineering, abusive conditions brought about by poor manufacturing facilities, low, piece wages, long working hours, and inhuman administrative rules and regulations (Young, 2007).

It is common that the manufacturing labour cost is no more than one per cent of the retail price (Ross, 2004). Workers, who are usually from rural regions in search of a better life in the city, work between 10 and 16 hours a day during the peak seasons from May to December in order to meet the Western demand for Christmas shopping. There is minimum social security for those who are sick or injured at work. Factories can be excessively noisy and uncomfortable, without sufficient lighting, adequate ventilation, or temperature control. Poor work conditions and low wages are a means to minimize the cost of consumptive production and maximize profit. For the worker, the wage earned from manufacturing labour can be more rewarding than what could be gained as a peasant, and the material life consumptive ability improves. For instance, a Chinese industrial worker can potentially earn four times more than his or her counterpart in the rural area, and the salary can become remittance back home or a source for consuming items, such as electronic gadgets or fashionable clothing. However, if we consider the substantial gap between their hard labour and rewards, and between use and exchange values of products they produce, empowerment through purchasing and owning commodities is actually a false consciousness. The labour power in the commodities no longer belongs to the worker; however, the worker does not know the problems built into commodities and consumption.

Georg Simmel on Fashion and Urban Life

While considering consumption as a structural problem, you might be puzzled because, according to our own experiences, shopping can be fun, finding a good bargain can be enjoyable, advertising can be creative, and purchasing can be empowering. You might ask: is consumption only determined by the structural forces of domination and exploitation outlined by Marx and his followers? Why do we seek one style over the other? Where are agency and individuality in this case? Where does media and advertising fit? To answer this set of questions, we turn to the work of Georg Simmel for some possible explanation.

It is a common concern for classical social theorists to consider where capitalism characterized by mass production and consumption leads us. While Marxists term it **alienation** and critical theorists emphasize **false consciousness**, Georg Simmel sees fashion, commodities, and consumption as the sites where modern individuals strive to stay autonomous against universal social forces, and where individualism takes shape in urban life. Consumption, as a result, is the constant process of negotiation between subjective and objective cultures, and between the individual and the social.

GEORG SIMMEL ON AGENCY AND STRUCTURE AND FASHION

The DEEPEST PROBLEMS of modern life flow from the attempt of the individual to maintain the independence and individuality of his existence against the sovereign powers of society, against the weight of the historical heritage and the external culture and technique of life. (Simmel, 1971: 324; original emphasis)

Fashion is the imitation of a given example and satisfies the demand for social adaptation . . . . At the same time it satisfies in no less degree the need of differentiation, the tendency towards dissimilarity, the desire for change and contrast . . . . (Simmel, 1971: 296)

Simmel suggests fashion gives satisfaction as one moves between individuality and conformity. There are two aspects to this satisfaction arising from the mediation between the social and the individual. First, a constant change is the universal source of uniqueness. What is in style today is in itself distinctive from what used to be in style yesterday. Cities thus provide the spatial opportunity for a fashionable individual to be the temporal carrier and embodiment of the objective social transformation. Fashion, in addition, is a phenomenon of social class that stratifies and distinguishes individuals, although the boundary manifested through the leading trend constantly needs to be redrawn, once imitation occurs. For instance, when the haute couture runway fashions become popular market items which can be easily copied and consumed by ordinary people, then there is a demand for a new runway design. As another example, because an iPhone is not an affordable item, the copycat version—the so-called Hi phone—sold for one-third of the price of an iPhone, has become popular in China. Imitation, however, is not simply a copycat act, and pirating leaves room for interpretation before moral condemnation.

For Simmel, imitation has its charm in that it allows the ordinary person to feel representative of mainstream culture. In other words, imitation gives both a sense of satisfaction and a sense security by allowing a person to not be singled out in society. To put it in another way, imitation which spreads and eventually annihilates one particular fashionable consumption not only expands and extends the practical demand for creative activity but also takes away the individual responsibility for making decisions about what to wear, buy, or use. In short, it seems paradoxical and contradictory that fashionable consumption makes an individual unique on the one hand; yet it renders one into a creature of the social group or the carrier of social contents. However, the paradox and contradiction arise precisely because of the mediating process between the individual and the social.

For Simmel, consumption as mediation between the social and the individual is also manifested in urban life itself. Cities host the money economy; that is, money becomes the value in itself and it denominates all else. Consumption by the wealthy can receive considerable recognition in the public, and it boundlessly sets benchmarks of values in both material and psychological terms. Consuming material goods is, at the same time, an important source of emotional stimuli. It agitates the individual's nervous energy while seeking more stimuli, and the senses of individual autonomy and freedom, on the one hand. On the other hand, emotional stimuli largely derived from consumption also result in the blasé attitude typical in cities. Urban life, saturated by the money economy and an endless pursuit of pleasure through consumption, also makes one indifferent because it stimulates one's emotional reactivity too strongly and for too long to allow any further reaction. From this perspective, it is therefore unsurprising that city dwellers might no longer feel sympathy for the poor in the land of plenty. It is disheartening but normal that subway riders who are busy using hand-held electronic devices might be indifferent to a beggar's demand at the same time.

Leisure Class, Gender, and Conspicuous Consumption

Thorstein Veblen's work *The Theory of the Leisure Class* has been regarded as the forerunner of consumption studies. He introduced several concepts that remain crucial to our contemporary analysis. First, similar to Simmel, Veblen also considers consumption as the social force that makes social class possible, and as the site of struggle for individualism. Second, with regard to social class, what comes to Veblen's attention is not the working class or proletariat in the Marxist tradition, nor the interaction and imitation between social classes outlined by Simmel. Rather, Veblen argues that the advancement of modern society, propelled by capitalist expansion, technological invention, and mass production—and we might now add mass media—is accompanied by the rise of a middle or leisure class defined by the practices of consumption as opposed to those of production. By invoking the non-productive aspect of modern life, '[t]he **leisure class** as a whole comprises the noble and the priestly classes, together with much of their retinue. The occupations of the class are correspondingly diversified; but they have the common economic characteristic of being non-industrial' (Veblen, 1994: 2). Veblen takes into account the importance of ownership and the wider processes of industrialization and commodification, which result in the luxury and comforts of life for the leisure class.

Veblen suggested that the rising leisure class usually manifested social status with accumulated wealth and **conspicuous consumption**. Conspicuous consumption broadly refers to consumption patterns prompted by symbolic significance more than material utility. For instance, when someone replaces a perfectly functioning but traditional and bulky TV with a new flat-screen model, when fixed-gear track bikes without brakes burgeon and roam across major North American cities, or when fashion overrides function, much of it has to do with the pursuit for social status and lifestyle embedded in the material goods or leisure activities. Consequently, conspicuous consumption entails a pejorative slant toward wastefulness and idleness. The sense of extravagance or uselessness is invoked in the pursuit of social status through unnecessary material goods or lavish entertaining.

Veblen also explores the question of oppression in relation to consumption. Unlike Marx, who connected the issue with social class, Veblen observed the social practices toward the end of the nineteenth century, directed attention to gender, and discussed how women are owned and commodified, while production and consumption divided along gender lines. Consumption was regarded as explicitly gendered work because women gained their own 'separate sphere' and undertook shopping tasks. Men in this case, it was believed, could not spend time on consumption as a way of maintaining a serious, masculine, and noble image. This was vested in the idea that consumption is an indulging way of life that cannot be taken seriously. Meanwhile, the wife's buying power demonstrated the wealth and status of the male counterparts, and 'the performance of conspicuous leisure and consumption came to be part of the services required of them' (Veblen, 1994: c.7).

Classical Sociology of Consumption: The Limitation

We might find the above classic writings on consumption oversimplified when viewed in our contemporary context. For instance, Simmel's analysis of consumption and urban life is ambiguous because the struggle and reconciliation between the objective and the subjective paradoxically can result in either neurosis or individual freedom. His analysis of fashion and imitation is limited to class relations materialized in a trickling-down process from dominant to dominated social classes. However, consumption and fashion can also be a trickling-up effect. That which once belonged to the underclass can be appropriated by the dominant, upper classes. For instance, in 2007 Louis Vuitton designed a new line of leather bags honouring the French tricolor of red, blue, and white. However, this new fashionable bag was regarded as an imitation of the bag commonly used by the Chinese working class. To use Marx as another example, his account of consumption as the source of oppression for the working class assumes a structural approach; nonetheless, it leaves no room for the role of agency. In other words, it remains unclear about the individual's capacity to make a difference and to change social norms and regulations by drawing resources from within the structure. Finally, Veblen is suspicious of sexism, and his sensitivity to gender and consumption remains ambivalent from today's viewpoint. The role advertising plays in normalizing gender and consumption is also missing in his account.

Despite the rough edges of these conceptual tools and the limits of their specific historical circumstance, these classical social theorists remain influential in our contemporary analysis of consumption and the role played by media advertising to further consumption. We will trace the conceptual linkage and transformation in contemporary work about gender, identity, and social class in relation to consumption, and will discuss how the socio-political transformation since the 1960s has made our investigation more complex and dynamic.

Cultural Capital and Social Class

Pierre Bourdieu, a contemporary French sociologist, provides a detailed tabulation of the routines and lifestyles of Parisians with a particular focus on habitual practices including dress, hairstyles, dining, choices of educational institutions, and magazine reading among others. By grounding his theory in consumers' empirical experiences, Bourdieu echoes Simmel's concern for both subjectivity and objectivity, and considers consumption as the mechanism of forming and sustaining personal identities and social status. His central argument starts with the recognition of taste as both personal and social, because '[t]aste classifies, and it classifies the classifier' (Bourdieu, 1984: 6). In other words, taste facilitates individual distinction within a broader context of social conformity, and it allows the recognition of social class and stratification. This further echoes Simmel's concern with imitation and differentiation among social classes, although Bourdieu's theorization of the inextricable interplay among social classes is formulated through introducing the idea of cultural intermediaries.

Cultural intermediaries are defined as experts who give consultation to the middle classes about correct styles, appropriate images, and standard ways of living. This not only defines the middle classes' social role through habitual practices of consumption, but also maintains their status and position by cultivating specific knowledge, expertise, contacts, and networks, or Bourdieu's influential concept of 'cultural capital'. There is a strong connection between economic and cultural capital in that how one cultivates taste and how one consumes correspond to how one spends and accumulates wealth. For instance, paying for education in private high schools or Ivy League universities is not simply because of a naive decision about seeking better education. Rather, it is a choice of cultivating suitable manners, correct accents, competent second or third languages, class-fitting tastes and leisure activities, and valuable networks and networking. Cultural capital, as such, is accumulated and educational choice is tapped into a wider social status and economic systems that prepare and ensure the spot in the workforce of the middle classes in the future. In addition, cultural capital can turn itself into economic capital, as those of multilingual capacities can turn themselves into cultural intermediaries across national boundaries by taking up the roles of diplomats or corporate expatriates.

This also turns patterns of consumption into a political question. First, magazine editors and advertisers as well as radio, television, and Internet advertisers play a significant role in the creation and choice of appropriate tastes, habits, leisure activities, and lifestyles. They decide the 'ins' and 'outs', assign values and significance to commodities, and create what Bourdieu calls 'symbolic violence'. The maintenance and accumulation of cultural capital are therefore connected to the structural role of cultural intermediaries who act as gatekeepers, and to the social mechanism of consumption, which is also the site of social struggles for defining and controlling taste and lifestyles.

Feminist Critiques: Gender, Political Economy, and Consumption

Since Veblen, gender continues to be a crucial issue in the study of consumption, and the inquiry often dwells on three key aspects: gendering products, practices, and production. We examine different feminist arguments to unlock the interconnectedness between the role of women and the practices of consumption to see if they lead away from the ambiguous stance manifested by Veblen, with regard to the nature of consumption as emancipation or oppression for women.

First we pay attention to sex-specific commodities associated with either masculinity or femininity. Most commodities entail no intrinsic gendered nature: they can be designed, produced, advertised, and used by one gender or the other. For instance, except for very few exclusively gendered products (e.g., feminine hygiene products), there is no substantial differentiation for most commodities. That is, the substance stays more or less the same from one brand of cigarettes to the other. However, Marlboro was strongly associated with the sign values of cowboys and masculinity, while Virginia Slims were considered to be cigarettes for women and femininity. In addition, pink has long been the colour for a baby girl in contrast to blue for a baby boy; a fast car is gendered into the symbolic power of masculinity, while jewellery is associated with the glamour of femininity.

Corresponding to gendered commodities and advertising, consumption is also about gendered practices. While Veblen's division between female shoppers/consumers and male workers/producers is an outdated stereotype, advertising for consumption has developed along with another line of gendered practices and stigma interconnected with the types of labour or productive work women or men do. For instance, shopping at a hardware store for tools and construction materials is something masculine, while shopping on the first floor of department stores for perfume and cosmetics is something feminine. While men are the major audiences of hockey or other sports events, women make up a significant portion of the audiences for soap operas and talk shows seen on afternoon television. This not only suggests that the actual and implied audiences for producers and advertisers are gendered, but also that social, physical spaces and mediascapes are tied to consumption through gendering processes. In these processes, stereotypical concepts, images, and commodities appear in a complex package of marketing and advertising to reinforce, maintain, and normalize gendered practices of consumption.

Finally, the production of consumption itself is a gendered process. This is evident by the division of design for men and women. In addition, it also occurs in various divisions of production. For instance, a T-shirt can be sold as a unisex item; nevertheless, gender differences that manifest body contours for a better fit and demands for masculinity and femininity are usually considered in design and advertising. In the process of producing T-shirts, men are usually in charge of tailoring and ironing the final product, while women are in front of the sewing machines, doing quality control and final product packaging. This division is based on the arguable belief and gendered stereotypes that men meet the physical demands of tailoring and ironing while women provide agility and meticulousness in sewing, inspection, and packaging.

Regardless of products, practices, and production, consumption and advertising continue to be divided and saturated with gendered stigma, and gender stands out as one of the most crucial and omnipresent aspects in advertising. For some feminist critiques, gendered consumption and advertising are the source of oppression precisely because they encourage and perpetuate stereotypes with the pretension that shopping is a source of happiness or gratification. Ann Oakley, Betty Friedan, and Christine Delphy respectively provide strong condemnation of housewifery, middle-class femininity, and the roles of women in Western capitalist households (Edwards, 2000). In contrast, consumption and advertising can also be a source of empowerment, according to Janice Winship, who examines women's reading of women's magazines and emphasizes the interactive nature of the construction of feminine consumption. Janice Radway's *Reading the Romance* (1984) is another classic research volume that analyzes reading and consuming popular fiction as a complex and necessary act of declaring independence and a source of pleasurable experiences for women in the given social and material structure.

The contrasting set of feminist perspectives on the relation between consumption and gender is in a sense a continual debate between a more Marxist, structural approach emphasizing political economy and a more cultural and textual approach emphasizing psychoanalytic critiques and possibilities of agency. Iris Young's work on female clothing and fashion imageries best brings together the seemingly contradictory arguments as she bridges aspects of both structure and agency. On the one hand, Young argues that '[o]ne of the privileges of femininity in rationalized instrumental culture is an aesthetic freedom, the freedom to play with shape and color on the body, to do various styles and looks, and through them exhibit and imagine unreal possibilities . . . . such female imagination has liberating possibilities because it subverts, unsettles the order of respectable, functional rationality in a world where that rationality supports domination' (Young, 2005: 74). Simply put, gendering consumption is the process through which stereotypes and sustaining social norms can be challenged by the active consumer's imagination, which further creates a space of negotiation for possible alternatives. On the other hand, gendering consumption through fashion fantasy entails specific exploitative and oppressing aspects, when it draws resources from many places and time for production and contributes to 'the commodification of an exotic Third World at the same time that they obscure the real imperialism and exploitation that both the fantasies and realities of clothes enact' (Young, 2005: 74). In other words, the contradiction of consumption occurs because the possibility of liberation through fashion imagery takes place *within* the structural constraints and political economy of global production.

Young's arguments serve as a reminder that no matter how consumption and advertising in general are gradually discussed in the wake of individualism and pluralism in identity, it is still a collective experience inseparable from the study of production at a global scale. This point will be further developed when we consider consumer citizenship at the end of the chapter. In the next section, we focus on advertising—the epitome of contemporary concepts and practices of consumption—for a further understanding of mediated society as consumption society.

Advertising as Mass Communication

Advertising actively seeks to market and sell by stimulating demand for consumption. Ideally, advertising generates profits while satisfying consumer needs. However, there is less consensus over what advertising is and how it reaches the consumers. For instance, we occasionally see creative advertising challenging our perceptions or touching our emotions, but the majority of advertising tends to normalize social practices, reinforce stereotypes, and serve the dominant interests. We often think that particular needs can be met by certain commodities, although these needs are often created by advertising.

Advertising also ties to the earlier debates over consumption between a macro, structural approach of political economy and a micro, textual approach of culture, identity, and agency. Advertising normalizes and creates social norms and practices at the same time. We will deepen the discussion by considering more general theorization of advertising and individual cases of advertisements. We therefore discuss how advertising on the one hand facilitates a legitimate form of identity and self-realization in the increasing importance of the consumer's subjectivity in association with sign value over the utility value of commodities, leisure activities, or services. On the other hand, advertising is interlinked with the rise of mass consumption and mass market, and it is integral to the structural development of media industries specifically and industrial capitalism in general. Advertising, composed of images and texts, becomes mass messages with wider social, cultural, and political ramifications. We will first discuss advertising as mass communication before exploring the two major perspectives with regards to advertising as either ideology or interpretation.

Advertising is ubiquitous and is intertwined with the saturation of media in everyday life. We immediately recognize that advertising fuels media institutions. Even today's public broadcasters need advertising and the associated promotional culture. This is especially the case in Canada and the United States, where governmental financial support has, over the years, been considerably cut. In other words, advertising is a financial prerequisite of mass communication, and its absence or reduction can be an immediate threat to media institutions. Nevertheless, we are concerned less with the political economy and institutional relations between advertising and media institutions than advertising as *de facto* mass communication. We will examine the phenomenon first.

Advertising: The Phenomenon

We can barely imagine a society without advertising, or a contemporary city without signs or neon lights among other advertising forms. Cities transforming from socialist to capitalist society are often characterized by the mushrooming of advertisements in every corner of everyday life. For instance, advertisements are practically everywhere in Chinese cities: multimedia panels and screens of small to gigantic size broadcasting advertisements nonstop are seen in public transportation, elevators, and landmark urban landscapes. In Canada and the United States, advertising occurs during the intervals of a television or radio program and pops out of the Internet browser with great regularity, and corporate logos are printed or engraved on all kinds of everyday commodities which we seem to wear with pride. Therefore, living in the world of advertising, we tend to take it for granted or even treat it as a natural phenomenon. We can even proclaim that advertising crystallizes capitalist consumer society and urban life. To follow Simmel, advertising is a source of emotional stimuli in cities where commerce aggregates and constantly needs reinvention for more intriguing, surprising, or even shocking effects. Nevertheless, urbanites may develop a blasé attitude toward the constant bombardment of advertising. In addition, while the primary function is to provide information about a given commodity, service, or activity, advertising can appear as a neutral conduit of communication that varies from one form to the other, from the physical site of the shop floor to the virtual space of the Internet, and from depicting facts and specifications to symbols of meanings and associations.

Furthermore, different commodities usually opt for different forms of advertisements. For instance, advertising used cars usually resorts to plain textual description, with or without images, in newspaper or online classifieds. In contrast, new cars are likely advertised in the most exaggerated and surreal scenarios. Advertising, therefore, can be either as simple and straightforward as classified ads, shop signs, and brand logos or as complicated and grand as developing a narrative in a cross-media campaign which mobilizes various existing media technologies in promoting the objects of consumption. Consequently, the advertiser has both actual and virtual consumers in mind, and the modes of communication used by the advertiser range from direct, interpersonal encounters to indirect textual and image mediation.

Questions do remain, though. The omnipresence of advertising in contemporary society might make it appear to be a natural phenomenon, but is it neutral? What is advertising and what does it do to the consumer? What does advertising mediate or communicate in addition to information about commodities? We will explore this set of questions from angles of both structure and agency.

Signs, Ideology, and Manipulation

Advertising is indispensable and seemingly natural in the capitalist consumer society. However, from what we learned in the previous section, if consumption is never politically or culturally neutral, neither is advertising. From a Marxist perspective advertising may be viewed as ideology. It is much simpler just to note that the main objective of advertising is profit making. Nevertheless, along with the advancement in media technologies, the complexity of production and consumption and the intricate intertwinement between the social and the individual—how advertising becomes ideology—deserves further exploration. We first introduce Jean Baudrillard, a French post-Marxist thinker, for this section of the discussion.

For Baudrillard, the analysis of contemporary society centrally lies in the system of material objects and its promotional messages comprising both image and discourse. This is because consumption is increasingly significant as a way of life and as an organizing mechanism of society. Simultaneously, the commodification of everyday life, the proliferation, diversification, and fragmentation of commodities, and the endless escalation of material demand are all caught up in the visual cultures of marketing and advertising in and through the media. Therefore, Baudrillard makes a clear remark that 'there is no such thing as advertising strictly confined to the supplying of information' (2005: 178).

Through advertising, the creation and re-creation of mutually referred and recycled images and signs mediate not only the myriad networks of social interaction but also individual personality and personified commodities. Advertising, vested in symbols and signs, gives meaning not only to commodities but also to the consumer. Simply put, the consumer is defined by means of the commodities. As a result, the function of advertising is more than supplying information. It endows minor or insignificant commodities with stereotypical characteristics in order to provide a system of meanings through which differentiation from one consumer to the other is imposed. This does not mean that advertising functions in a totalitarian manner forcing acceptance. On the contrary, advertising for differences gives a double sense of affluence and freedom because it provides choices and dreaming opportunities in everyday life. For Baudrillard, 'the consumer society . . . offers the individual the possibility, for the first time in history, of total liberation and self-realization' (2005: 2001). Different choices offered by advertising in a sense mediate the idea that one is free to be oneself and also free to project one's desires onto commodities.

Advertising therefore functions more like hidden persuasion, with the supply of the ideal object that gives the consumer imaginary potentiality and a sense of gratification and protection from the void in real life. For instance, comparison is always made on shopping channels in order to give the audience the feeling that the advertised commodity can do what the existing ones cannot. In addition, advertising, according to Baudrillard, gives 'communicational warmth' to the consumer in the sense that the 'ideal' object is being produced and promoted for the sake of the consumer's well-being. It might sound exaggerated but a familiar promise is that 'buying one specific item can immediately solve your problem' or that 'owning this particular object will bring happiness to your life in no time.' In other words, the commodity loves and cares for the consumer, and the industrial consumer society adapts itself to the demands and desires of the individual. Baudrillard therefore argues that '[t]he abundance of products puts an end to scarcity; the abundance of advertising puts an end to *insecurity*' (2005: 189).

The problem is that the imperative of advertising is *ideological*: it replaces morality and politics as the symbolic system of manipulation. Advertising consists of a communicative regime of meaning and understanding arousing emotions and deteriorating contemporary consciousness by conveying images of satisfaction. These images, in turn, only evoke other images that do not resolve personal problems or conflicts in reality. This is ideological manipulation because 'advertising will assume moral responsibility for society as a body, replacing puritanical morality with a hedonism founded purely on satisfaction and introducing a new state of nature, so to speak, into the bosom of hypercivilization' (Baudrillard, 2005: 202). In other words, as a system of *seduction*, rather than of production, advertising generates increasingly self-referential imaginary signs detached from material production. The mixing of the real and the imaginary, or the sign-object, constructs not only a complex and wide landscape of social and cultural meanings but also confusion constructed and manipulated around commodities and social relations.

Simply put, advertising is problematic because any human value or emotion can be turned into a symbol, metaphor, or narrative in advertising. This is the reflexive process of advertising that can turn anything to its own objectives of profit making.

Example: Water

One of the best examples is water. Water is no longer simply about satisfying thirst. It is increasingly bottled, branded, and sold as a pervasive global business, especially in developed countries where clean, safe tap water is already available at minimum cost. Richard Wilk (2006) argues that the insignificant difference between tap and bottled water is hardly a secret in industrial practice. Coca Cola's Dasani water was discovered to be no more than filtered London tap water. However, when water is taken from the nature and being marketed as scientifically filtered for safer and healthier intake or technologically treated for better taste, nature ironically becomes an artificial device for advertising, and is simultaneously destroyed and rendered into the sign of 'the natural'.

Water, the most essential component of survival, is advertised as something essential with a twist: it is good to drink bottled water because it is convenient and safe. Bottled water from exotic sources is also advertised as something of good taste in both literal and symbolic senses. Ordering a bottle of exotic water further adds signs of social status and prestige to the consumer. Water in this case becomes a sign-object in Baudrillard's term. At the same time, it seems obscure when one small bottle of water is sold for $20 USD in the upscale Chelsea market in New York City.

Advertising as Cultural Parasitism?

Advertising could be 'a form of cultural parasitism, so that every attempt to find non-commercial moral meaning in the world just becomes more grist for communication . . . to the point where even anti-consumption rhetoric becomes a kind of marketing' (Wilk, 2006: 320). In short, advertising can absorb and transform criticism of advertising to form its meta-message, as long as it helps to reach the end goal of designating a product through emotional connotations. Thus, it does not adhere to any specific ideology, as what helps to sell can be manipulated into *the* ideology of the moment.

If advertising is ideological and manipulative through appropriating and circulating signs and symbols out of a greater context of social codes, emotions, and values, it dupes and controls the consumer. As a result, advertising gives meaning not only to commodities but also to the consumer. In addition, advertising sheds light on consumption as bottomless demands for material fulfillment camouflaged by the false promise of consumer democracy and freedom. This theoretical perspective holds its validity to a certain degree, but it is equally problematic: it mainly derives meaning from within advertising; yet there is no guarantee of advertising as a successful and effective apparatus for self-promotion.

More importantly, it gives little room for resistance, negotiation, or opposition from the consumer. In other words, when advertising is discussed as ideology, the focus is often on its theoretical or political ramification projected from a rather pessimistic viewpoint, omitting interpretation and meanings given by the consumer. In the following section, we consider the other camp of scholars who discuss advertising as interpretation and who emphasize agency and creativity from the consumer or the user.

De Certeau on Agency, Interpretation, and Advertising

In this part of the discussion, we draw insights from Michel de Certeau for an interpretive approach toward advertising. We consider how the significance of advertising is not derived from within advertising itself or as an ideological component in capitalist societies, but from the consumer's use, reading, interpretation, and interaction in the process of consumption. De Certeau's work on the practice of everyday life has been inspirational, with a wide theoretical implication and application for those interested in studying consumption, advertising, and popular culture. With a class division between elites and the mass in mind, de Certeau sheds light on the latter's resistance and active participation in transforming a given social setting/institution or a cultural artefact and developing social relationships around specific social or cultural sites. His work thus concerns the empowerment of the 'weak', the user, and the consumer. He does so by questioning the dichotomy separating the elite, the producer, the gatekeeper, or cultural intermediaries in Bourdieu's view, from the mass, the user, the audience, the reader, the consumer, or the weak. De Certeau negates the idea that those who are in the categories of the weak are inactively shaped by the powerful in absorbing given information or ideology.

In the case of advertising and consumption, there is no doubt that the consumer is engulfed by consumption as a way of life and lives in an environment of effervescent advertising. In other words, the consumer is structurally confined to what is given by the advertiser. This structural confinement, be it a commodity or its promotional material in advertising, operates with the guidance of formal rules, rational schema, and coercive power. They are employed in order to formulate official knowledge and total discourse exercised or reinforced as ideology for influence over the consumer or the audience.

The forces of 'proper' knowledge, rules, and power can never overpower the consumer. Instead, using various tactics the consumer exhibits individual knowledge and interpretation by assuming a level of anti-ideological and anti-disciplinary practices in the wake of the seemingly persuasive force of advertising. Empowerment is a tactical act which entails no intention to destroy or tear down the structural formulation of advertising, commodities, or services for consumption. Rather, it is the calculation of manoeuvring within the given system as a way to fit in without compromising the consumer's own interests.

The consumer, therefore, is equally active and productive in a sense that he or she is able to develop different interpretations and multidimensional social relationships around the practices of consumption. Beyond the producer's and the advertiser's imagination, the process of making do is central to the consumer's practices. As de Certeau holds, 'we mustn't take people for fools' (1984: 176). He also argues against Baudrillard's pessimistic views of the silent, powerless, and manipulated consumer by stating that '[t]he only freedom supposed to be left to the masses is that of grazing on the ration of [images] the system distributes to each individual. That is precisely the idea I oppose: such an image of consumers is unacceptable' (de Certeau, 1988: 166).

Accordingly, de Certeau legitimizes possibilities and creativities opened up by the consumers' tactical acts and interpretations. In other words, they take advantage of a given moment to transform the established system according to their own rules and interests. These chances occur when the power of the 'proper' is absent and when fragments of the given commodity or advertising are used for the sake of the consumer. The consumer's tactics, as a result, are not only creative but also oppositional to the given instituted systematic structure, without calling forth revolution. Their tactics might not be preplanned, nor might they possess the chance to form another totalizing system of knowledge and discourse. In other words, the consumer's tactical operations do not form power, nor do they construct an autonomous place despite their creativity. Advertising in this sense is open to interpretation, while consumption is the social site where struggles over meanings take place.

Example: Jeans

Advertisers can promote jeans with discourse about sexual attraction, feminist empowerment, leisure comfort, individual freedom, social conformity, or anything that might help the promotional purpose. Nevertheless, as John Fiske in 'The Jeaning of America' shows, every respondent, despite being a member of fairly homogeneous groups based on social class, ethnicity, gender, or age, can still give very different reasons and interpretations for wearing jeans (Fiske, 1989). In addition, tearing a pair of jeans can be a way to show individual differences as a tactic against the uniformity provided by producers or retailers. Fiske further argues with de Certeau that torn jeans, which were once seen as the consumer's tactic of making do, gradually transformed the system by changing the way designers and manufacturers now make so-called 'junk chic' a fashion statement.

Structural Approaches to Consumption and Advertising

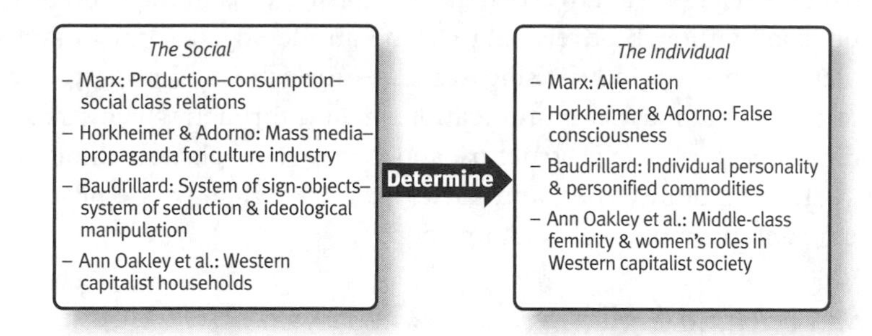

Interactive Approaches to Consumption and Advertising

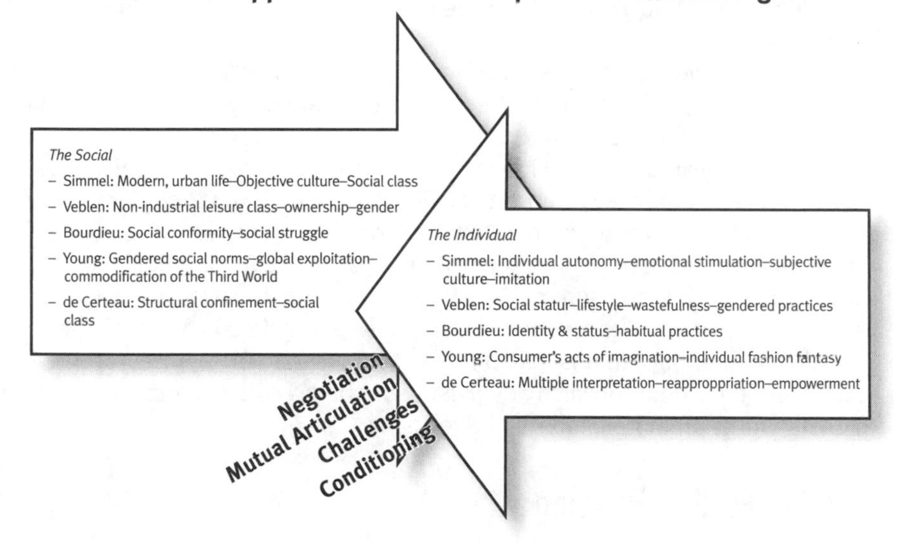

FIGURE 4.1 Structural Approaches Toward Consumption and Advertising

Summary

In this chapter, we discussed the ways in which production, consumption, and advertising triangulate consumer society. We drew insights from both classical and contemporary social theories and paid attention to the ways in which social class and gender are configured and mediated into consumption and advertising. We also juxtaposed the opposing perspectives of structure and agency in our analysis. This juxtaposition demonstrated that it is not sufficient to explain consumption in relation to capitalist production, nor is it satisfactory to associate it with personal taste and individualism.

It is only through reading both perspectives that we can have a better understanding of the paradoxical or contradictory phenomenon of consumption. In the same sense, we articulated advertising from two distinctive frameworks and reached the understanding that there is a mutual perpetuation of producer–consumer relations in advertising. The consumer is not a dupe or victim of capitalism, although advertising can be an ideological or sign system of manipulation. In short, advertising saturates the mediated society, and it is a significant form of mass communications in and through which struggles and negotiation between social structure and agency take place. Behind all of this exist radio, TV, the Internet, and social networking, all prime producers of advertising and promoters of consumption.

Enhanced Learning Activities

1. Compare and contrast Marx, Simmel, and Veblen on consumption. What are their differences? How do they see the individual and social class in consumption?
2. Summarize Baudrillard's work on advertising. Explain his work through an example of green advertising that emphasizes health and safety for both the environment and the consumer.
3. Explain the key arguments by Iris M. Young, Pierre Bourdieu, and Michel de Certeau. How would they interpret the film *The Devil Wears Prada*?
4. Divide the class into two groups: Distinguish the perspectives of social structure from those of social agency with regards to consumption and advertising. Each group summarizes the main points from classical to contemporary work. Debate the reasons why Apple's iPod is one of the most popular commodities in this decade.
5. Document the extent to which advertising on the CTV, Global, and Fox television networks promote gendered advertising.

Annotated Further Reading

Georg Simmel, 'Fashion', in *On Individuality and Social Forms*. Chicago: Chicago University Press, 1971. In this text Simmel demonstrates how fashion is a social site in which objective and subjective cultures come across, the individual and the social negotiate, and social class and status are prominent.

John Fiske, 'The Jeaning of America', in *Understanding Popular Culture*. New York: Routledge, 1989. John Fiske analyzes one of the most common commodities, jeans, as a way to provide an easy access to understanding Micheal de Certeau's work. In this article, we see how consumption as an everyday practice is a source of empowerment for the consumer without calling forth revolution against capitalist functions.

Iris M. Young, 'Women Recovering Our Clothes', in *On Female Body Experience: 'Throwing Like a Girl' and Other Essays*. New York: Oxford University Press, 2005. Iris M. Young explores the significance of fashion as a gender issue. She discusses how clothing and femininity are constructed by patriarchal norms while, on the other hand, she considers whether the submissive positions revealed in female clothing can be a subversive and alternative source of criticizing the given norms and structure.

Jean Baudrillard, 'Advertising', in *The System of Objects*. London: Verso, 2005. Baudrillard provides us with a cultural critique of consumption, commodity, and advertising. From a neo-Marxist perspective, he emphasizes the omnipresence of signs and images in the mediation between individuals and society. He also considers the deceiving functions of advertising as feeding the consumer's desires without real empowerment.

Thorstein Veblen, *The Theory of the Leisure Class*. New York: Dover, 1994. Veblen explains how modern society is reorganized around the practices of consumption, how the gender difference is significant in the process, and how the leisure class and conspicuous consumption characterize modern society. This is considered to be the pioneering work of consumption study by combining interests in both economy and sociology.

Useful Media

Malls R Us (2009). Director: Helene Klodawsky.
Through exploring architectural design, technological spectacles, and natural landscape, this film leads us to rethink how shopping malls epitomize consumerism, and how the good life can be confused with the world of goods.

Art & Copy (2009). Director: Doug Pray.
This film takes on the perspectives of the advertising industry by showing us the creations of some influential popular culture. While being integrated with new media, advertising is often considered to be the culprit of capitalist manipulation. This film nevertheless indicates the complexity of the phenomenon as advertising at times rebels against the mainstream, and at times defines popular culture.

Cover Girl Culture (2008). Diirector: Nicole Clark.
Through interviews with supermodels, magazine editors, and celebrities, this documentary provides a critique of magazine culture, singles out the responsibility and liability of the culture industry, and reflects upon girls' empowerment.

The Social Network (2010). Director: David Fincher.
In light of the creation and development of the social network site Facebook, this film not only helps us understand how our contemporary time is defined in the digital age, but also how Facebook exemplifies powerful banality in everyday practices.

5 New Media, New World?

Learning Objectives

- To consider new media and the social imagination
- To explore new media in the 'global north' and the 'global south'
- To understand new media as an historical event
- To explore the fear and hope accompanying the introduction of new media
- To examine the positions taken by Benjamin and Adorno regarding media advancement
- To critically examine new media as a force for good or for bad

Introduction

Emerging or **new media** are often endowed with magical, revolutionary properties. New media announce hope: a sense of hope carried by images, stories, and legends integral to sustaining and expanding the instituted social order. Consider, for example, that the internal code name for the Nintendo Wii was 'Revolution'. This gaming console is praised by the popular online gadget guide *CNet Review* for its 'revolutionary controller design' that 'offers unique motion-sensitive gameplay options' (http://reviews.cnet.com/consoles/nintendo-wii/4505-10109_7-31355104.html). The Wii is considered to be magical because the mediation itself allows a gamer physical engagement in the interactive process of virtual space. A similar endowment was also given to another popular device, the iPhone. Steve Jobs, Apple's CEO, promotes the iPhone (and now the iPad) as a revolutionary and magical product that is literally five years ahead of any other mobile phone . . . 'We are all born with the ultimate pointing device—our fingers—and iPhone uses them to create the most revolutionary user interface since the mouse' (http://www.apple.com/pr/library/2007/01/09iphone.html). While the Wii leaps beyond thumbing, the iPhone celebrates the simplicity of using fingers for a hand-held device. Both popular media at the beginning of the twenty-first century give us a hint that the social imaginary of media revolutions evolves from our desire to expand the capacity and freedom of our sensory systems and the promise of a better world.

The prospects for new media are not always rosy. New technologies can also bring about a sense of fear and uncertainty regarding the social order and legitimacy established through existing, familiar media practices. For instance, struggling with parents over the amount of time spent or gaming choices might be a familiar experience among young gamers. In an extreme case, gaming has been blamed for the tragic death of Brandon Crisp, an Ontario teenager who ran away and was eventually found dead after arguments with his parents and being grounded from playing the Internet-based military game *Call of Duty*. In addition to some video games of a violent nature, certain genres of films, popular music, TV shows, and comic books are also condemned for their negative effects on the user's world view and behaviour. This gives rise to a fear that an irrationality stimulated by images takes over the rational intellect based on textual logic, thereby, it is believed, deforming rational and critical thinking abilities, endangering security, and eventually obstructing liberty and democracy. When new media's importance and implication in reordering social practices remain uncertain, they are far from promising a brave new world.

Before we enter the central focus of this chapter—the hope and fear generated by new media—we may well ask: What are new media? What new is new? Is new automatically revolutionary? These are valid questions as soon as we consider that what is innovative today can be obsolete tomorrow. For instance, the Wii's capacity to extend or integrate physical movements into the game itself has brought gaming to a different level. This makes previous generations of consoles antiquated, no matter how much they were a source of stimulation and excitement. Nevertheless, since its introduction to the market in the mid-1980s, the Mario Brothers (Mario and Luigi) continue to be iconic figures and the focus of several popular Nintendo games. Despite evolution in graphic design and interactive processes, the original game's structure and goals have stayed more or less intact. More importantly, the strong desire for new technologies and the progress of new media in the social imaginary continue to fuel the maintenance and expansion of the commercial capital.

By the time you read this paragraph, the Wii and iPhone might not be obsolete, but it is doubtful that either device will continue to top the dream gift list. In addition, what your parents might consider new and difficult to navigate, such as using an MP3 player, uploading a clip to YouTube, or reading Japanese manga, may be something ordinary for you. We soon realize that the rapid transformation and the short lifespan of new media technologies make the sense of novelty ephemeral. When we see the traces of older media in the design and functions of newer ones, what seems to be revolutionary might, at best, be evolutionary. The task remains: how do we make sense of the hope and fear accompanying new media?

We will take two approaches to explore the above questions. One approach is empirical, focusing on a discussion of contemporary media practices. The other is retrospective, reflecting on older media when they were new. These two approaches are complementary because looking back into history helps us articulate continuity in the transient transformation of media technologies. We also take on the theoretical interpretation of critical theory tied to a Marxist understanding of new media and popular culture at the juncture of political violence and rapid social transformation, not only in the interwar period during the 1920s but also our own time. Through juxtaposing the historical approach, the contemporary inquiry leads us back to rethink the magic or revolution permeating our everyday practices. In addition, we also explore the idea that what often appears as banal is indeed magical when the hype for one particular medium no longer exists, and when it becomes indispensable in everyday life.

New Media: A Contemporary Phenomenon

The term 'new media' came to prominence in the mid-1990s, although new media has been around since the 1960s. In the first issue of the journal *New Media and Sociology* in 1999, Roger Silverstone pinpointed the centrality of digital technologies as something new. They enhance our capacities and pave our way to a different future (Silverstone, 1999: 10). A decade ago, the research on new media mainly concentrated on the rising popularity of the Internet and the virtuality of cyberspace traversing time and space. Nevertheless, it was rather vague and unclear about what was new exactly, because the discussion hinged on the uncertain, fluid, rapid innovation, adaptation, and potential of new media. To explore this issue further, we will distinguish the dominant characteristics of new media in the **global north** from those in the **global south**.

New Media in the Global North

Over the past decade, new media have been widely practised and accepted by the public, and researchers have gained some detachment from the transformation of individual subjectivity and mediated society in and through new media. For instance, researchers including Wendy Hui Kyong Chun (2005) and Robert Hassan and Julian Thomas (2006) continue to stress the centrality of computation and digital technologies with more certitude. However, new media are beyond adding new digital devices to the existing list. The Internet is not simply an invention that occupies a different channel of mediation. Nor is the significance of new media limited to the digitalization of older textual, image, and video material. New media instead entail the ability to converge other existing media into an interconnected mediascape.

Chun sees new media as 'fluid, individualized connectivity, a medium to distribute control and freedom' (2005: 1). Compared to the predecessor, what is considered to be new is thus the networkable capacity of different forms of media in structure and practice. Institutions (e.g., government and private companies), devices (e.g., cellular phones, personal computers, digital cameras, and MP3 players), and practices (e.g., online billing and payments, Facebooking, and text messaging) all have their places in our consideration of new media. As Robert Hassan and Julian Thomas argue, 'new media technologies are above all connectable, compatible with others, creating in their plurality a highly mediated context which connects to numberless other mediated contexts that users create in their day-to-day life' (2006: xxiv). Furthermore, in contrast to the older media of *broadcasting* for wide, public dissemination, new media are characterized by individualized, focused dissemination, or *narrowcasting*. New media with an individuality and fluidity cut across once separated channels of mass media found in telephones, radio, TV, films, books and newspapers, among others.

To illustrate the above point, let's compare and contrast traditional and digital photography. After developing traditional images, we usually store and circulate pictures in print form. In contrast, we can produce a digital image in print and store it in a photo album as if it were a digitalized version of the traditional photography. Nevertheless, an image from a digital camera or a camera phone is more often stored on a personal computer, a DVD, a portable hard drive, or an online photo album. It can be displayed in a digital photo frame or on a TV screen, circulated through instant messengers, like Skype or MSN Messenger or as an attachment to an email, or uploaded to photo-sharing sites, like Flickr or Snapfish, with the print option left up to the viewer. The same picture can also be uploaded to Facebook and its status is announced in the news feed of this virtual social network. In addition, members appearing in the same picture can be tagged and viewed by more members of other Facebook networks as long as the privacy setting allows.

Let's take online news sites as another example. Because we can acquire information from watching video clips or a podcast, listening to live broadcasts or archival recordings, reviewing photos, and reading texts, online news sites structurally integrate the defining characteristics of the older media. They also serve as an extension or supplement of the older media. Television and radio hosts often encourage the user to log on to their websites for further information or in-depth discussion about particular subjects. This encourages active participation or interactivity between the user and the producer, either through leaving comments or through recommending and forwarding an article/video clip/photo to another user. Digitalization allows entrenchment and individualization across both physical and virtual platforms of communication. We further understand that new media create compounded networks of mediation.

New Media in the Global South

We nevertheless hesitate to announce that the Internet is *the* new media or that our mediated society is cyberspace. This medium has certainly played a central role in facilitating, circulating, and converging with other existing, emerging media in the global north. However, mobile telephony, without doubt, is the digital opportunity in the global south. As a result of the lack of extensive landlines and transportation infrastructure, there is already evidence that African mobile penetration doubled from 6.5 per 100 inhabitants in 2003 to 13.1 per 100 inhabitants in 2005. As a region, Africa's mobile market has been the fastest-growing market in the world, averaging 50 per cent growth per year since 2000 (ITU, 2007).

The fluidity and individualization of new media are primarily a phenomenon of the global north. Different degrees of media interactivity are evident when we compare the ways cellular phones are used in the global south and north. In contrast to the individualized multimedia devices for telephoning, emailing, photographing, music listening, text messaging, and Web browsing in the global north, cellular phones in Africa reflect a different reality in usage and ownership. They are shared and communal more than individualized. For instance, household surveys in Botswana reveal that 62.1 per cent of cell phone owners share their devices with family members, 43.8 per cent with friends, and 20 per cent with neighbours. Only 2.2 per cent of phone owners charge for the sharing of their handsets (Sebusang et al., 2005). Alison Gillwald (2005) explains that, depending on accessibility and disposable income at the time, African users employ a creative 'multiple communications strategy' to save cost and to stay connected with contacts working in town. Therefore the beeping of a missed call can serve as notification to recipients for a call back. A costless single beep can be a signal of greeting without anticipation of the recipient's call back.

Cell phones play a central role not only in Africa but also in the Middle East. Because political censorship continues to be an issue and because the popularity of the Internet remains relatively low in the Middle East (18 computers per 1,000 people in Arab countries, compared to 78 per 1,000 globally in 2003), creative acts of citizenship in and through cell phones attract attention to socio-political transformation in the region (2005: 5). As Philip Seib argues, text messaging fosters expansion of speech because it 'allows people to send messages that they would not say in public' (Seib, 2005: 8). In 2005 text messages, along with emails, were sent in Lebanon to rally anti-Syrian demonstrators. In the same year, women in Kuwait organized protests about voting rights and employed text messaging as an effective tool to mobilize young school women. Nevertheless, in light of the personal attack on an organizer of the Kuwait women's rights demonstrations, text messaging can also be a negative tool of rumour and anonymous discredit. This also makes us cautious; whether or not new media technologies are beneficial or threatening to social and political transformation largely depends on how they are used for particular purposes. We will continue to explore this viewpoint in the section on new media and political violence.

How New Is New?

New media pose different degrees of threat to their predecessors with regard to communication form and content. The floppy disc for data storage, as a medium, was extinguished and replaced by the CD, the DVD, and then by Blu-Ray. Newspapers in print, as another form of communication medium, are declining in the face of increased online versions. The American Audit Bureau of Circulations reported that during the six months that ended on 30 September 2008 more than 500 newspapers across the industry had gone through a decline of 4.6 per cent for weekday circulation, and of 4.8 per cent for Sunday circulation (*The New York Times* Online, 28 October 2008). New channels of communication, such as satellite, that traverse national boundaries can also bring challenges to older media confined to rules, structure, and specific local contexts. For example, in the Middle East state-based public broadcasters under strict political censorship face strong competition from Al Jazeera, the Arab news network, through satellite technology. This Qatar-based news agency is watched in the region as the most trustworthy voice of pan-Arab identity, and it has been regarded as a counterbalance against the hegemonic voice circulated through Western media like the BBC or CNN. Furthermore, Al Jazeera advocates social and political reforms within the Middle East and has posed a threat to political dictatorship and oppression expressed through the state-based channels of broadcasting. In short, Al Jazeera relies on new satellite technologies to form the media content of competing discourses within and beyond the region (Powers and Gilboa, 2007).

The threat of new media nevertheless is far from a total break from the past or a complete overthrow of the form and content of traditional media. In other words, new media do not yield an unrecognizable world. New ways of mediation in both form and content can only be worked out or negotiated on the basis of the instituted order. It is rather naive to think that new media heralds a new social order, as if what emerges from new media is something completely unknown. Despite the tendency to erase history, ignore the linkage between the old and the new, or forget the fascination of the old in the face of the new, there are persistent patterns in new media. In other words, new media evolved from their own past, and the challenges they pose also have an historical trace. Grappling with these patterns in new media is, therefore, an effort to capture what stays constant underneath the rapid, fluid, and ephemeral transformation and uncertain outcomes that dazzle, surprise, confuse, and overwhelm us. In the next section, we explore the continuation of hopes and fears for emerging media in the languages of utopia and dystopia.

New Media: An Historical Phenomenon

If we compare and contrast the emergence of media since the end of the nineteenth century, we are struck by persistent hopes and fears for personal and social transformation. New media, in one form or another, have been with us throughout different times and spaces. On the one hand, each new medium and its social implications carry hope for emancipation, advancement, and empowerment. New media have been considered to be the force that ends politics and social struggles. New media can bring excitement for existing media organizations looking for newsworthy stories. They can bring a certain aura to politicians who want to align themselves with the next new thing. New media are also the content and conduit for commercial enterprises in association with the latest promise for a better world. On the other hand, uncertainty, anxiety, and mistrust equally prevail in antipathy to oppression, alienation, and catastrophe.

As a result, new media are, as a force, bringing us to either **utopia** or **dystopia**. The presence of both utopia and dystopia accompanying the emergence of media is by no means pure fantasy; their formation departs from a perceived reality that reflects the specific contexts of the time. They also delineate our boundaries and the particularities of the **social imaginary**. Hopes and fears for new media further guide our ways of imagining and exploring the possible shifts in the social order.

In the previous section, we discussed new media as a contemporary issue specific to our epoch. In this part of the discussion, we consider new media as an historical phenomenon, since *everything new still carries a history* and since history gives insights into problems and challenges in something new. New media here broadly include the use of new communication technologies for familiar or novel reasons, and creative ways of using existing channels and devices. We simultaneously examine the challenges from emerging to existing media and consider the processes as such to be particular historical moments when institutions, social relations, habitual practices, and individual subjectivity anchored in older communication technologies are under scrutiny. The discussion in retrospect is less concerned with the revolution or evolution of technical efficiencies in speed, capacity, and performance. It rather goes underneath the surface of the impermanent yet recurring hype and angst in social imaginaries. In other words, we are less interested in the historical record of cumulative advancement or technological breakthroughs than in the continuous imagining of new media as the forces of reordering socio-political relationships.

In juxtaposing the examples of electricity and animation with critical theory, as we do below, the objective of this section is to reach an understanding that the debates around old media as they emerged are as familiar as the current debates around the Internet or cellular phones.

Electricity

It is rare these days to consider electricity as a form of media technology. Its prevalence and sheer banality hardly excite us. Nevertheless, all debates about electronic media start with the invention, application, and popularization of electricity. As Carolyn Marvin argues, 'the ambivalence that so much characterizes contemporary regard for electronic media did not originate with twentieth-century radio and television, but in threats to social interaction set up by their nineteenth-century prototypes' (1988: 7). First, we do not need much explanation that electricity allows the communicative possibilities of five modern prototypes of mass media, including the telephone, phonograph, incandescent light, wireless, and cinema.

Second, electricity itself enabled experimental possibilities and new messages in the form of mass spectacles that promoted the encouragement of consumption. The capacity of electric light as a communicative conduit survives today in commercial neon signs and the landscape of urban streetlights. In addition, spectacles of incandescent light pioneered dramatic ritualistic events for the public. They allowed public gatherings, on a small or large scale, to move from indoors to outdoors. Mass entertainment, popular culture, and political rallies were made possible with electricity. Electric light is the predecessor of the advanced, sophisticated design of current spectacles in the Olympics, rock concerts, and massive political gatherings. Electricity also created the legacy of glittering audio-visual effects, more commonly attributed to TV, appealing to our senses and altering our ways of imagining the social with concrete images, sounds, and illuminated textual messages.

Third, as the most technically and socially developed media device in the late nineteenth century, electrification benchmarked the social imaginary of the future in the reflection of limits and possibilities of specific historical moments. Consider that spotlights and short flashes projected on the surface of the sky and clouds were in use for figures, words, advertisements, and election results in New York in the 1890s. The enabling capacity of electricity further enlarged the scope of imagination and anticipation, as some imagined casting powerful flashlights onto the moon's surface in order to project English (as though English were the only language) messages to be viewed by everyone around the globe. In a plan described by an American named Hawkins in *Science Siftings* in 1895, '[i]f a flash of sufficient strength could be thrown upon the moon to be visible to the naked eye, every man, woman and child in all the world within its range could read its messages, as the code is simple and can be quickly committed to memory' ('A Message from the Moon', quoted in Marvin, 1987: 187).

Discussion as such showed confidence in technologically driven transformations which maximized the scale of electric spectacles and of the audience through new modes of global communication. The conviction was also expressed that modern people, with the aid of electricity, could reach the height of civilization through relaying messages to outer space, overcoming geographical boundaries. The assumed extended capacity and thus intercultural comprehension was the social imagination of the time, one that simultaneously singled out a collective desire for defying and compressing the time–space distance with instantiated signals. While exploring the possible future of intercultural and international communication, dreamers of the time did recognize the impossibility of extending a transmission cable to outer space. The proposition of spotlight signals as the wireless solution thus received wider public acceptance. This also suggests that hopes and fantasies for new media work within acknowledged technological constraints.

With little interest in unravelling cultural puzzles, the above example about international communication via outer space was nevertheless culturally bounded by English sensitivity. English letters and vocabularies were dreamed to be cast on the moon with the expectation that everyone around the globe would understand. It reflected the colonial context that English provincialism and Anglo hegemony were automatically assumed to be the universal governing language of communication around the globe. Contacts afar awaited the technological linkage in order to conform to the assumed norm. Intercultural communication via outer space eventually would make cultural differences redundant. In short, '[l]ife in utopia, [was] always the Caucasian standard' (Marvin, 1988: 202).

In addition to the hopes for technological and cultural transformation which influenced the limits and opportunities in the ways people imagined themselves and society in the late nineteenth century, there were also prospects for material affluence and consequently social equality. The abundance and popularity of electricity would be unprecedentedly revolutionary because it could bring sufficiency to everyone, regardless of social class. If everyone had the ability to possess electrical devices and consume freely, it would end politics, that is, the struggle over scarce resources. It would also end the duality of the **have** and the **have-not**. More importantly, social equality as such is the ultimate utopia where differentiation in itself would no longer exist.

As T.C. Mendenhall, a retiring president of the American Association for the Advancement of Science, stated in 1890, 'With this spark, thanks to science, the whole world is now aflame. Time and space are practically annihilated: night is turned into day; social life is almost revolutionalized, and scores of things which only a few years ago would have been pronounced impossible are being accomplished daily' (quoted in Marvin, 1988: 206). Revolution brought by the popularity of electricity and the association between consumption and prosperity in a sense would eliminate political upheaval. The distributive power of electrical amplitude was perceived as distributive justice.

Electrification was also a dream of the early Soviet regime in the 1920s. As a measure of socialist development, industrial modernization, and cultural sophistication, electrification was both a technological and political program. Developing power grids would redress rural backwardness. The state electrification commission promised that 'electrification would accelerate economic reconstruction while simultaneously transforming the country from a poor cousin of Western Europe into a modern, cultured society saturated with electric light and radios.' As a result, the production and consumption of kilowatt-hours were proposed as 'an index of culture and progress' (quoted in Buck-Morss, 2002: 140).

The transformation in media patterns is also a threat to familiar structures of communicative association. We witness how electrical communication devices made people of the late nineteenth century fearful. For instance, the telephone was a new mode of communication that threatened direct face-to-face encounters as the habitual social exchange of daily life. An early comment on telephones captures this particular fear: 'When a man tells you a story face to face . . . he can see by the expression on your face, if he has the least knowledge of physiognomy, how the story strikes you, and it is an easy matter to cut a man off by a look or a gesture. But where are you when the storyteller is 10 miles away? He has you cornered and you must listen' (quoted in

Marvin, 1988: 86). The use of telephones thus challenged the customary proprieties of social relations concretized in proper distance, intimacy, and trust between individuals. An 1889 record entailed a similar fear and anxiety about telephones: 'when the telephone was put into commercial use, being sometimes addressed by an unseen and often unknown speaker, in language such as a man would rarely use face to face with another man' (quoted in Marvin, 1988: 89). Telephones thus were worrisome because their usage could be potentially abused by loosening standards of social interactions or by trespassing the given norms and boundaries governing social class and status, especially when visible social identifiers, such as clothing and gesture in face-to-face encounters, became invisible.

On the one hand, fears of electrification and the most common and convenient electrical devices, such as telephones, puzzle us. Fear as such is derived from hesitation and mistrust about the uncertainty of reordering social norms, practices, and structure around new media. At the same time, new media are perceived to be threatening to the circulation and distribution of power and resources through the older, familiar mediation processes. On the other hand, our hindsight quickly tells us that the hope for electricity was naive, as if technological transformation itself can create magic alone. Intercultural mis- or non-communication prevails even when technological advancement has brought people onto the moon's surface. The discrepancy between the have and the have-not more than a century later only accentuates social inequality. To put it another way, we may be living in the dream world of energy and material abundance for which the people of early modernity longed. However, to ensure continuous material prosperity, this utopia is also a dystopia where environmental damage and the global division of production contribute to social inequality at an unprecedented scale.

The Sociological Imagination of New Media

Walter Benjamin and Theodor Adorno of the Frankfurt School of critical theory took on the issue of new media and popular culture during the interwar period of the 1920s. Their debates pioneered competing discourses on media's roles in modern society. They engaged each other in direct correspondence, explicitly in Benjamin's writings about Disney and implicitly in Adorno's later work on jazz. They took modern cinema, early Disney, and Mickey Mouse seriously because they considered the signifying importance of media and popular culture at the juncture of technological advancement, social transformation, and political instability. Both Benjamin and Adorno discussed the early Mickey Mouse in the Marxist language of **emancipation** and **alienation**. Their ideal society was not liberal democracy characterized by universal suffrage, political liberties, the rule of law, and political competitions, because they considered it the conduit and platform of bourgeois ideology, an ideology that hijacked the real emancipation of the majority of have-nots. Liberal democracy was therefore not the final solution in their view. They furthered their arguments by observing and interpreting the particular historical contexts of rapid urban and industrial development, sweeping fascism in Europe and the counterforce of socialism in Russia, and the rising capitalist mode of production in America.

Both noticed the sense of excitement new media evoked. In addition, they both agreed that the relentless pursuit of more excitement through technological progress was repetitive and symptomatic of modern industrialization and the source of alienation. As a result, what seems new is nothing special. However, Benjamin and Adorno disagreed over the potential of new media and popular culture; Benjamin saw a source of emancipation but Adorno considered them as a further embodiment of alienation. Let's explore these ideas with some of the key classical sociological concepts used by Benjamin and Adorno.

In contrast to Weber's **disenchantment**, Benjamin considered modernity as a ***re*-enchanted** social world where modern people are under the euphoric spell of the desire and excitement of consumerism while being pushed deeper into an individual, isolated state of alienation. For Weber, modern society is demythified and disenchanted because abstract, formal reason—the brainchild of the enlightenment of the eighteenth century—ushered in and broke the mythical ground of religion. Reason itself had become the organizing principle of the political (**bureaucracy**), the economic (capitalism), and the cultural (music and law). As Susan Buck-Morss (2002) argues, Benjamin would not have objected to the rationalization of modern structures and institutions. However, it is precisely through the systematic processes of rationalization and in the rationalized social and cultural institutions that modern people are re-enchanted into a dream-like state.

Re-enchantment is evident in the glamour of an urban landscape, the charm of commercial advertisements, the allure of commodities, the desirability of new media technologies, and the incoherent dreams of advancement and fulfillment that popular culture creates. The almighty, mythical power of God in the pre-modern time is reactivated and transferred to technological progress. This re-enchantment is played out through the endless supply of newness and is driven by the ideology of industrial modernization. In other words, a ceaseless demand for changes and newness underlines the modern dream world. However, this utopia of material newness and prosperity only camouflages the interests and ideologies of the dominant class by keeping the mass asleep in isolation without a sense of collective empowerment.

Based on an analysis of economic relations, Marx once used the term ***phantasmagoria*** to describe the deceptive appearances of commodities, or commodity fetishism. Phantasmagoria for Marx is about how the exchange value of commodities depreciates the value of productive labour. For instance, the value of an iPhone reflects no amount of capital paid to the faceless, nameless Chinese pieceworkers who earn less than $1.00 USD per hour. The value of this popular communication device corresponds to the generated hype and desire for its novelty in the market. As a result, commodity phantasmagoria serves to maximize profits. Phantasmagoria refers to the commodity acting according to its own rules, animating its own life, and dictating human desire. For Marx, phantasmagoria alienates because it is the process through which consumers identify themselves with commodities—material objects become humans and humans turn into material objects.

Phantasmagoria, for Benjamin, was less about certain conferred characteristics of social and economic relations in material objects. He takes on a philosophical understanding of the newness manifested in urban–industrial transformation in general and in new media specifically. This transformative characteristic of modern society is progress fetishism. Newness regenerates its own life and importance through relentless urban planning, world fairs, commodity invention, and media forms. Regardless of the urban–industrial form progress reincarnates, it keeps pushing and extending the limits of our sensory experiences. For Benjamin, the dazzling effects of technological advancement create phantasmagoria as 'a magic-lantern show of optical illusions, rapidly changing size and blending into one another' (Buck-Morss, 1989: 81).

Progress consequently gives rise to a reified utopia of a thing-filled abundance at the cost of a genuine revolution waking the mass from the spell of phantasmagoria and challenging the dominant capitalist mode of exploitation. Democracy is problematic here precisely because it is often promoted under the banner of liberty; however, liberal democracy is conflated with the freedom of consumer choice and a desire for newness that gives a temporary sense of instant gratification. Phantasmagoria produces the 'wow' effect that anesthetizes or enchants with a mythical belief in progress as freedom and with the illusion of newness as emancipation. Phantasmagoria alienates in a second sense, as it results in a failed perception of and a fatal hope for constant change and a better future. For instance, we can argue that iPods, regardless of changing generations' size, thickness, colour, capacity, and interface, have given us a false consciousness of phantasmagoria. The production of the new as always the same simultaneously marks history in the manifestation of the commodity form.

By now we understand that new media are not simply conduits of information and communication. They also entail aesthetic and sensorial terms that challenge, expand, and redefine individual subjects' relations with material commodity cultures in a modern society. This transformation simultaneously gives Benjamin and Adorno different modes of reflexivity over hopes and fears for new media. This is also the point where the two theorists depart from each other. We explore their views of early Mickey Mouse to explain.

Debates about Early Mickey Mouse

Mickey Mouse has been a Hollywood and international star since 1930, but the early Mickey Mouse was not the comic children's character of the last 40 years or the children of the 'Mickey Mouse Club'. For Benjamin, Disney created a marginal subject: Mickey Mouse was an uninhibited, ratty, low-life creature that made trouble, played tricks on friends, got into fistfights, and indulged in mass entertainment. Being insubordinate and disrespectful, he refused to be a diligent worker. Mickey Mouse's life was surrounded with jazz rhythms, which were considered to be rather frivolous at the time. This creature always displayed grotesque images of the body, including acts like spitting and vomiting, tail wagging, and buttock swinging. His lower-body language often singled out the magic he could make easily without complicated machinery or technological design. Mickey Mouse's body thus expressed not only his free spirit and creativity but also his nonconformist character against the given **bourgeois** values of the industrial-capitalist society represented by Tom Cat, the cartoon character that disciplined, commented, punished, and competed against the mischievous. In short, Mickey Mouse was rebellious and, at times, barbaric.

For Benjamin, Mickey Mouse was more than an anti-bourgeois subject. This cartoon creature visually and audibly reflected the reality of alienation, conditions of production, and technological domination over individual subjects. Benjamin claims that in the Mickey Mouse films, 'for the first time . . . it is possible to have one's own arm, even one's own body, stolen' (2008: 338). Our own bodies no longer simply belong to us in the capitalist-industrial world because they are alienated from us in exchange for money or for lifeless material objects. Early Mickey Mouse films challenged civilization and turned it around with the criticism that modern society is barbaric. The early Mickey Mouse enjoyed a huge popularity, not due to the mechanization or form of the animated cartoon as a new medium, but due to the fact that 'the public recognizes its own life in them' (Benjamin, 2008: 338).

Mickey Mouse, in Benjamin's view, not only outsmarted but also mocked the dazzling effects of technical advancement. No complicated machine was needed to impress. Magic was easily and smoothly performed out of Mickey Mouse's body parts. His pocket was an arsenal of handy instruments and efficient machines. For the majority of the working-class audience who worked with machines and were conditioned by a mechanical urban-industrial life, the delivery of Mickey Mouse's humour in gags and stunts based on either technical or natural objects acknowledged, taunted, and reworked the myriad of technology used in daily practices. The audience was confronted with technological progress as their second nature, and their collective laughter also made individuals realize their common social problems and potential as participants of an awakened, emancipated mass.

Adorno agreed with Benjamin on the particular mode of subjection in modern mediated society: the inability to recognize one's own interests and mortal enemies in two modes of self-alienation—the identification with the commodity propelled by the enchantment of progress and the anesthetic reception of technology numbing individual subjects with sensory effects. However, while Benjamin celebrated the great merit of the industrial cinema, animation, and popular culture figures, Adorno expressed a rather passive view of the deformation of the individual psyches as new media facilitated by American capitalism sugar-coated the bourgeois ideology even in its most progressive outlook. He was suspicious of the therapeutic power of collective laughter provoked by films, in which Benjamin had faith. For Adorno, it was a flagrant romanticism which distracted the attention of the working class from an emancipating imagination and sensibility directed toward a new formulation of social relations.

In the same vein, Adorno cautioned against the sense of emancipation and liberation promised by jazz. The association between Mickey Mouse and jazz was common; jazz was usually the synchronizing rhythm of Mickey Mouse's movements. Jazz conveyed an individual, anarchic, and ecstatic protest against social authority. For Adorno, when the culture industry took over the traditional forms of culture, alienation deepened. Mass cultural production had become dependent on mass consumption predicated on mass communication in turn.

TV: A Continued Debate

So far we have seen how the promise of novelty in media functions as a demand for attention and mobilization on the one hand, and how the fear of novelty functions as a request for scrutiny and resources on the other hand. These demands are not only created and sustained in the commercially and politically driven world of media industries, in ordinary people's social imaginaries, but also in the commentaries of media scholars. We see a continuation in similar arguments about whether we are either saved or doomed by TV. For instance, Marshall McLuhan (1994) celebrated '**the medium is the message**.' Media change the world through their fundamental characteristics as carriers. These characteristics include extensions of our sensory perceptions and capacities, which allow us to develop networked associations beyond political and social boundaries. McLuhan refers back to the ways the light bulb and electrification function as a conduit without content itself; yet they have dramatically transformed the world simply with their presence as media that illuminate and enable different forms of communications. TV and multimedia thus are celebrated because they extend our sensory systems across boundaries to an even larger extent. In other words, what is more important is the form, rather than the content, of the media.

Table 5.1 Hopes and Fears Associated with New Technologies

	Electricity	Radio	Internet
HOPES	The [Niagara] Falls were of a beauty that their daylight . . . never equaled. For the first time since a factory was erected to draw its power from the rushing water the garish outlines of the bleak brick buildings were gone (*The New York Tribune*, 1907, quoted in Nye, 1992: 58).	Radio represents not only a more advanced technical stage, but also one in which technology is more evident. The masses it grips are much larger . . . its programming is . . . closely intertwined in the interests of its audience (Benjamin, 2008: 394).	In fact, one of the most remarkable aspects of this new communications technology is that it will eliminate distance . . . (Gates, 1995: 6).
FEARS	In 1885, Yale students who were getting "more light than they relished" chopped down an electric light pole erected at the corner of the campus. Student threats to dismantle the re-erected pole occasioned special police protection (Marvin, 1990: 164).	If most of the radio stations and movie theatres are closed down, the consumers would probably not lose so very much . . . this bloated pleasure apparatus adds no dignity to man's lives (Adorno, 1944).	The [www] superhighway is a lot of hype and fantasy, promising services that most people do not want, nor are willing to pay for . . . (Noll, 1997, quoted in Mosco, 2004: 25).

Other scholars follow Adorno's more pessimistic view in analyzing the negative effects of TV on subject transformation and social order. For instance, moving away from the Marxist theory and inching closer to liberal democratic ideas of the social order, Neil Postman (1986) argues that the utopia of a mass democratic society lies in the hands of citizens' discerning and debating capacities for the best political judgment and results. Thus, Postman argues against TV as the source of entertainment that eventually amuses us, the audience, to death. TV's appeal to the emotional and the sensational is the mortal enemy of individuals in particular and democracy in general, because the emotional stimulation and excitement TV offers hinder the development of the intellect and the rational. TV deprives a person of rigorous and linear thinking capacity usually developed through textual reading. Contrary to McLuhan, Postman sees TV as technologically detrimental in modern mediated society.

It has become an ongoing debate about pros and cons of new media with regard to its alluring and transforming effects on individual subjects and society. New media thus reincarnate old theories, revive dreams, and revitalize hopes and fears for emancipation, democracy, the public sphere, and capitalism. What seems relentlessly new in fact has and leaves an historical trace. We therefore considered mediated society as a result of the mutual articulation between the modern culture that thrives on a belief in novelty and the progress of industrial capitalism and its political agenda. We return to our contemporary era to consider how the magic of new media is played out when it becomes ordinary in everyday life.

New Media and Political Violence

While Benjamin and Adorno debated about Mickey Mouse, Disney productions headed toward an increasing commercialization and were gradually stripped of their revolutionary promise. At the same time, both critical theorists expressed their concern about the sophisticated technique of re-enchantment being appropriated not only by capitalist commodity culture but also by fascism. Benjamin (2008) cautioned against fascism's aestheticizing politics in weaving a dream state of political phantasmagoria. He argues that '[t]he logical outcome of fascism is an **aestheticising of political life**' (Benjamin, 2008: 41). Nazi Germany was skillful as a populist mass dictatorship which used entertainment leaning toward popular tastes as a progressive means of gaining emotional identification with the Nazi movement. It then further won a sense of community among German citizens by propagating a belief in a superior Aryan, blue-eyed, blond race while simultaneously generating fear and eventually terror among Jews, homosexuals, gypsies, and any others considered to be unfit or threatening to the Nazi nationalist and racist core values.

The aestheticizing of politics during the Nazi regime was evident in the mobilization of media technologies. To take Leni Riefenstahl's documentaries as an example: the German filmmaker was commissioned to document the now notorious 1934 Nazi Party Congress in Nuremberg and the 1936 Berlin Olympics. Rienenstahl's documentaries, *Triumph of the Will* and *Olympia*, were in themselves a manifestation of progress because they showcased new filming techniques, established the genre of documentary, and benchmarked the aesthetic standards of propaganda. With regard to film language, content, composition, and dramatic repertoire, both *Triumph of the Will* and *Olympia* were also a manifestation of aestheticized politics that conveyed not only the message of the grandeur of the Olympics as the communal experience of a superhuman race, but also that of Nazism's core values of nationalism, anti-Semitism, and anti-Modernism.

As Christoph Classen rightly stated, Nazi mass media entailed the 'performance side of politics' and 'virtually lived off communication *with* it' (2007: 558). This is to say that Nazi Germany relied on the intertwined appearance of and promise for progress in new media to facilitate 'seemingly "apolitical," aesthetically and emotionally appealing formats' (Classen, 2007: 556). Light musical entertainment, radio shows, films, newsreels, or animation that attracted individual subjects' sensory experiences thus were produced and circulated as propaganda for growing political affinity within the Third Reich.

This is not the only occasion when media were in the service of a destructive force against humanity. As Allan Thomson and his colleagues (2007) demonstrated, in the 1994 Rwanda genocide, local radio and print—the most common of media—were used as instruments of ethnic hatred and antagonism against neighbours. At the same time, international media turned their back on the massacre out of an apathy engendered by a political–economic calculation of newsworthiness. This is to say that local media in Rwanda facilitated the genocide through capitalizing on media's insinuating and agitating impacts on the sensory, emotional systems on the one hand. On the other hand, emotional indifference, that is, shutting down the media impacts on sensory systems as a way of ignoring the ethical demands of vulnerable others, on an international scale, equally contributed to the catastrophe. Media, at the juncture of political violence in Rwanda and international geopolitical marginalization, failed millions of lives.

What Is Banal Is Magical

Let's return to our earlier example of the iPhone. Walt Mossberg, a *Wall Street Journal* columnist, explained on his popular blog why the iPhone is going to revolutionize the advanced industrial society of global north. He praised the iPhone as the 'first hand-held computer with a PC-class operating system', which makes it more than simply a cell phone. It allows the expanding capacity of a personal computer in a pocket-size device, and it further permits the user to carry around the Internet all day. It thus allows the user to stay on the Internet grid of spatial-temporal connectedness and instant information availability, the two quintessential wonders of the Internet. Does this excitement about newness sound familiar by now? We have learned that new technologies praised in previous generations suggested a radical outlook and hopes for a better life.

Mossberg nevertheless emphasizes that the revolution is just at its beginning, and it will be complete only when nobody finds the iPhonc and the Internet special: 'The less often you hear about the word "the Internet," the more important and intergrowing to your life [it] will be.' This seems to be an oxymoron, but Mossberg uses an allegory of electricity: we feel the importance of electricity only during a blackout. Otherwise, we do not proclaim that we are on the electrical grid every time we plug something into an outlet. Similarly, the new world can be made only when smart phones like the iPhone and their potential implication of popularizing the Internet become as banal but as powerful as electricity.

Media technologies are therefore revolutionary and magical only when they become banal and popularized. Mosco (2004) considers them as a '**powerful banality**'. In other words, it is a paradox that the indispensible is also the transformative. Media technologies make magic once they are habitual in everyday practices, without the awe and aura of the earlier age, and once they are integral to social functioning without being the source of visions of either utopia or dystopia. This also includes the devastating opportunity of political dystopia, like the Holocaust and the Rwanda genocide, taking place. That is, myths and beliefs about new media of an earlier time have evolved into sustaining social practices, relations, and institutions with creative or destructive consequences.

This is far from implying that the powerful banality of media technologies makes hopes and fears of the past generation come true. Such a statement can easily lead us to **technological determinism**, against which we caution. Technological determinism, exemplified by McLuhan's and Postman's arguments, considers technology as the independent variable in cause–effect relations with other social factors. As a result, social changes are simplified into something driven by technologies, the dynamic processes of social transformation become static, and media are regarded as fixed objects with natural edges which revolutionize the world with their sheer presence. Stressing the powerful banality of media technologies thus helps us to avoid the pitfall of technological determinism because it keeps the overestimation of media effects at bay, and because it requires us to contextualize technologies in the given social order. Simply put, no media in themselves can create change. Their power of transformation is possible only when they are creatively embedded in other social structures and practices and their transformative power is considered within social contexts. Media become powerful only through their integration into other aspects of social life.

What does a powerful banality imply concerning political emancipation, to which the utopia and dystopia of new media technologies point? This line of argument makes us skeptical about the ambitious claims regarding new media's individual power of political transformation, especially its liberating or democratizing potential or threat. Democracy does not emanate simply from the media, nor does emancipation occur without substantial transformation in habits, process, and institutions. The examples of the Nazi Germany and Rwanda have showed that media technologies can work as lethal political weapons in catastrophe. The move is toward dystopia, mobilized as an instrument of force that turns against the very people who were supposed to gain the benefit of utopia. Nonetheless, if we recall the examples of the Al Jazeera network and text messaging in the Middle East, we also understand that media can work as a catalyst for political solidarity or justice. They, in the same manner, rely on speed, extension, and expansion across time and space, everyday entrenchment and banality, and audio-video effectiveness to carry and work out the ideals of emancipation or democracy.

Summary

In this chapter, we explored how media are imagined in both hopes and fears for a new world. Our inquiries started with the new media of our time and considered how the interconnectedness of various media technologies catches our attention in the global north while cellular phone and/or satellite technologies become the denominator of the new world in the global south. We shifted our exploration to the time when old or older media were once new as a way to introduce a historical dimension to new media. With the examples of electricity, Mickey Mouse, and TV, and with the theoretical arguments from Benjamin, Adorno, McLuhan, and Postman, we learned about similar praises and blame for emerging media's roles in social transformation. The discussion helps us to grapple with ordinary people's persistent social imaginaries and theorists' sociological imagination about socio-political changes in the face of emerging media technologies. We then considered media as a double-edged sword: media can play a central role in dystopia when they are used as a destructive weapon in political violence. Media can also be a positive force in reorganizing social structure and everyday practices. We discussed the powerful banality of media technologies as a way to challenge technological determinism and to address the importance of understanding media in given social contexts. To conclude, despite all the dazzling or puzzling emergence of new media technologies, we learned from this chapter that new media only make a new world when they are entrenched in social practices, and that the entrenchment itself is banal yet magical.

Enhanced Learning Activities

1. Review the early Mickey Mouse in *Steamboat Willie*. Summarize Benjamin's ideas about new media, and explain how the early Mickey Mouse was considered as the hope for a new world.
2. Find advertisements for the traditional telephone device in the late nineteenth century. Compare and contrast the ads for the traditional phone and the iPhone. What are the differences and similarities in terms of hopes for these media?
3. Review either the film *Olympia* or *The Triumph of the Will*. Explain how Benjamin and Adorno consider the relations between new media and dystopia. Explain how they serve as an aestheticizing of political life.
4. Review the film *The Matrix*. Summarize the main arguments formulated by McLuhan, Postman, and Mosco. How would each thinker interpret *The Matrix*?

Annotated Further Reading

Walter Benjamin, *The Work of Art in the Age of Its Technological Reproduction and Other Writings on Media*. Cambridge, MA: Belknap-Harvard, 2008. This is a collection of Benjamin's essays on various forms of media, ranging from script, image, painting and graphics, photography and film to the publishing industry and radio.

Susan Buck-Morss, *Dreamworld and Catastrophe*. Cambridge, MA.: MIT, 2002. Buck-Morss compares and contrasts visual images, such as *King Kong* versus the project for the Palace of the Soviets, as a means to explore the construction of utopia and the dream world of the twentieth century. Fears of political enemies and hopes of awakening, mass sovereignty, revolution, and mass culture were a driving ideological force of technological advancement and urban-industrial modernization in both capitalist and socialist worlds.

Vincent Mosco, *The Digital Sublime: Myth, Power, and Cyberspace*. Cambridge, MA MIT Press. Vincent Mosco critically examines the promises of the digital era in comparison with other technological developments, such as radio and cable TV, in the past century. While considering the dazzling and puzzling effects of digital technologies, Mosco discusses the myths constructed around media technologies and their persuasiveness and implication in lifting us from mundane daily practices.

Useful Media

Walt Disney's Mickey Mouse Steamboat Willie
http://www.youtube.com/watch?v=AEEaT_UQnVM
Benjamin praises early Mickey Mouse for its revolutionary power.

The Triumph of the Will (1935) **and *Olympia*** (1938). Director: Leni Riefenstahl.
Leni Riefenstahl's two ground-breaking documentaries commissioned by the Nazi regime help us understand emerging media and the socio-political background in the 1930s against which Benjamin and Adorno worked on a critical social theory of media.

The Matrix (1999). Directors: Andy Wachowski and Lana Wachowski.
This popular science fiction film about how a simulated reality created by sentient machines creates both dream world and catastrophe explores the concepts of technological myth and powerful banality and how they are played out in conjunction with hacker subcultures, religious ideas, and the sociology of the self.

McLuhan's Wake (2002). Director: Kevin McLuhan.
This 94-minute DVD produced about Marshall McLuhan by The Disinformation Company Ltd., New York (www.disinfo.com), is an interesting take on McLuhan's view of media based on his *Laws of Media*.

Part 2

Media Events and the Sociological Imagination

In this section we explore global, national, and urban media events. We argue that media events are a crucial and complex social phenomenon that require linking theories from sociology and discourse analyses with media and cultural studies for a thorough understanding. The following chapters include different kinds of media events ranging from celebrations, like the Radio Canada program *Le Bye Bye* on New Year's Eve; debates in newspapers over urban amalgamation; rituals, such as Remembrance Day ceremonies; spectacles, like the Vancouver Olympics; natural disasters, such as the earthquakes in China's Szechuan province in 2008; conflicts and violence, including the September 11th, 2001, attacks; and historical memories mediated through events, such as the CBC program *A People's History*. Regardless of the type or scope, media events tend to interrupt our everyday routines, occupy several channels, intensively capture the attention of a vast population within a specific period of time, and forge an historical sense of significance through participating and witnessing the unfolding of live, staged, or mediatized events.

Why is the study of media events important? Media events are a crucial aspect of national culture. More importantly, these events are a force for social integration or cohesion—they are sources for imagining a homogeneous community to which everyone belongs. A central proposition in sociology suggests that social cohesion is needed when members are highly dispersed, when the centrifugal forces of fragmented social groups threaten social order, and when creating a shared sense of 'we' is believed to hold the society together. In this section we challenge the association between media events and social order/cohesion by considering how the former are in fact constructed or framed as a means of establishing certain discursive, mythical, and ideological positions and maintaining power and hegemony over populations. This challenge is mainly derived from the observation that a thematic core of media events always generates multiple centres of framing and interpretation. In other words, centripetal and centrifugal forces are formed around media events. For instance, there have been multiple readings of the United States and the Middle East since 9/11, each depending on how the framing positions are situated. Nevertheless, the readings all refer to the same repetitive set of mediated images, notably the attack and collapse of the World Trade Center. To comprehend media events as multi-centred constructions, we introduce the concept of **dialogism**; that is, how equally weighted discourses clash, intersect, challenge, or collapse by pointing to the same reference. We also resort to poststructuralist views to explore what are and are not constructed as media events in relation to power and hegemony. We equally provide an analysis of media events taking a feminist approach to questions of visibility and invisibility.

Andreas Hepp and Nick Couldry define media events as 'certain situated, thickened, centring performances of mediated communication that are focused on a specific thematic core, cross different media products, and reach a wide and diverse multiplicity of audiences and participants' (Hepp and Couldry, 2009: 12). Although we separate global, national, and urban media events into three chapters, the arguments in each are co-dependent. In fact, nation-states and national cultures are the overarching themes in this section for two reasons. First, national interests continue to be the framing sources, the hegemonic concerns, and the thematic core of media events. In other words, national elements continue to define various communication channels and contents. Second, we recognize that communication networks and flows are no longer nationally or territorially bound. The imagined enclosure of national communities is constantly challenged from within urban centres and from outside of the national boundaries. Furthermore, a concern for social conflicts and political economy becomes a key inquiry into the global economy, over which national sovereignty and welfare states no longer exercise full control while the autonomy and importance of cities is, at the same time, on the rise. Therefore, it is equally important to see how the social imaginaries of our time are triangulated by the specifics of global, national, and urban life, and how global and urban forces in and through media events transform our sense of the national within a mediated society.

6 Global Media Events

Learning Objectives

- To explore the meaning of globalization
- To consider channels and networks of global communication
- To examine examples of events attracting global media attention
- To assess the way in which global media events are represented
- To examine global media events in relation to justice and citizenship
- To learn about ways in which news is framed for particular audiences

Introduction

In this chapter, we explore global media events as contesting sites and processes of visual imaging and textual discourse in the construction and circulation of cultural materials and news information. We start with the buzzword **globalization** in order to demythologize some common ideas before gaining a better grasp of the transformation we are experiencing. We challenge the common belief rooted in neo-liberalism that the communication processes of globalization facilitated by new media technologies allow easy, transparent, and instant linkages around the globe without barriers. We also challenge the misconception that globalization replaces nation-states as a result of worldwide exchanges and movement. We examine how global communication is uneven with regard to the power structures of global media institutions, the asymmetrical access and flow of information and communication products, and the framing of media discourses and representations. We will consider that what is presented to us as global media events are subject not only to the economic logic of transnational media institutions but also to the nationalist prism of framing and interpretation. We will also look at how the systematic filtering of international affairs results in many crucial affairs turning into *absent* global media events. This chapter not only inquires into the exercise of geopolitics in parallel with the construction of media spectacles but also calls for a consideration of justice and citizenship in the light of global media events.

What Is Globalization?

Globalization has been characterized by accelerated, intensified connections and networks in both physical and virtual senses. It is commonly understood that globalization consists of constant and rapid movements of all sorts across national boundaries, from the financial, cultural, and social to the exchange of information. Made possible by new media technologies, it flattens barriers of time and space and contributes to the growing interconnectedness of different parts of the world. As a result, globalization is conceived of as a utopia of free movement or as something supranational challenging national sovereignty or eroding boundaries between nation-states. To cite Marshall McLuhan's vision in the 1960s, this interconnectedness, based on new technologies, leads to a cooperative global village that dramatically improves intercultural communication. Globalization is also seen as the result of new media technologies forging a global culture beyond particular national or local interests. Based on the belief in free trade, exchanges, or communication from various local points, it nevertheless simplifies the complex and contested nature of the temporal–spatial transformation we are experiencing. First, unlike neatly nesting Russian dolls, the local, the national, and the global intermingle and interpenetrate. In other words, globalization occurs and transforms on different temporal and spatial scales and originates in and impacts widely dispersed places or networks of places and in a presumably long-lasting manner. It is a misconception that globalization is a homogeneous, uni-directional, bottom-up, or top-down movement. Simply put, globalization is more uneven and undetermined than fair and systematic in reordering time and space. It is uneven because globalization and its implied sense of freedom give rise to an economic citizenship that gives advantage to those who have already been advantaged the most. We witness a continuing domination of the north over the south, a post-colonial legacy, and the ever-expanding gap between rich and poor in the global economy on the one hand. On the other hand, we also witness a questioning of and challenges against global capitalist development, geopolitical hegemony led by the global north, and the functioning of global capitalism in both violent and non-violent manners.

Secondly, while greater global interdependence through the constant and instant flow of exchanges makes national boundaries more porous, we must consider the misconception that downplays the importance of nation-states. This misconception is based on the pursuit of profit through lowering the global threshold of withdrawal from the market and the movement of goods and services. The ideal of free economic exchange becomes a weapon disarming national boundaries. However, national sovereignty is equally questioned as a barrier to the implementation of universal human rights. No matter how these two strains clash, they simultaneously question nation-states as the imagined community sustained and reconstructed by national cultures. In Benedict Anderson's work (1983), national cultures, composed of narratives, legends, and images, and facilitated by mass media, are the sources of social imaginaries that enable large groups of people to have common understandings of their surroundings, confinements, and practices. Nation-states, therefore, are imaginative mappings of social spaces constantly created and regenerated throughout history in order to establish a coherent unit of culture permitting its members to cultivate a sense of belonging in contrast to other units. In our discussion later, we will find out, contrary to the forecasts of globalization adherents, that nation-states and national cultures from where people draw their social imaginaries from are far from obsolete.

Thirdly, there is no doubt that new media technologies, such as satellites and the Internet, play a key role in global transformation as they allow communication to uncouple from land and air transportation. One of the salient features of globalization, therefore, is the massive transmission of messages and information across wide spaces with relative ease. However, it is another misconception to simply claim global communication networks to be the cause of globalization. Media technologies alone do not and cannot determine the structure and strategies of social changes and practices. As Roger Silverstone argues, 'media technologies have to be seen through the single, albeit kaleidoscopically single, lens of social practice. And what we do with them is a function of our skills, competence, social positions, symbolic and material resources, and our hopes and fears' (2004: 587). The existence of media and communication are usually intertwined with other factors that require us to link media and communication practices to specific social, economic, political, or even military concerns.

Identifying misconceptions also establishes a framework for the discussion of three interlaced working principles of the globalization of communication. We first examine the uneven yet undermining structuring and patterns of global communication channels and networks. This concerns the emergence of transnational media conglomerates as key players in controlling and diffusing information and turning communication into a major sector of global business. Furthermore, through analyzing the specific media representation of global events, including the 9/11 attack, the war on Iraq, and the 2008 Beijing Olympic Games, we consider how national cultures continue to play a key role in our ways of imagining, making sense of, and participating in globalization. This chapter will consider the intertwinement of media, the control of symbolic powers, and geopolitical interests in determining what counts as a global media event in whose interests.

Global Media Domination and Resistance

Prior to the 1990s, the ownership of media systems was predominately national. While newspaper publishing, to a degree, remains domestically owned, television has transformed drastically. Along with movies, music, and print publishing, TV and radio systems have, in most parts of the world, succumbed to deregulation and privatization. New communication technologies have also enabled media conglomerates to establish powerful channels of production and distribution across national boundaries. During the last decade or more, global media systems have fallen under the control of ten transnational corporations (TNCs) mostly based in the United States, including General Electric, AT&T, Liberty, Media, Disney, Time Warner, Sony, News Corporation, Viacom, Seagram, and Bertelsmann (McChesney, 2000). The concentration of media ownership at the national level is equally evident. For instance, before bankruptcy protection in the fall of 2009, CanWest Global Communications Corporation owned 37 of Canada's daily newspapers and reached 4.9 million readers per week through the Global Television network and E! and 26 specialty broadcasting networks which covered 30.1 per cent of commercial specialty channels. It also owned the Web network canada.com, which complemented its print publication and which received 4.5 million visits on average per month. CanWest also branched out to Australia, New Zealand, Asia, Europe, and Turkey.

The concentration of global media ownership pursues open markets and is tied in to the mantra of the global economy: expand or die. That is, staying in the domestic market does not guarantee maximized potential growth. Expanding the scale of ownership abroad is the only way to stay competitive. Nevertheless, as Robert McChesney (2000) points out, the global media market is characterized less by a competitive marketplace than by a cartel where cross-ownership, joint ventures, or mergers among media organizations have made the global media system complex and interdependent. As a result, global conglomerates reduce competition and risk among themselves in order to ensure profitability. In addition, the process of global media concentration is through both vertical and horizontal integration. The former refers to the control and synergy of specific but related sectors from production and circulation to consumption of media contents, while the latter refers to the mergers or joint ventures of the same media sector. CanWest serves as a good example of vertical integration. Taylor and Francis, a leading international academic publisher, is an example of horizontal integration. It has expanded rapidly in the past two decades through the acquisition of other publishers, including Routledge, Spon, Press and Carfax. Its horizontal integration continues as it consumes more established but less competitive publishers. With offices in major cities in Europe, North America, and Asia, this academic publisher produces and circulates more than 1,000 journals and around 1,800 new books per year.

There has been a growing and legitimate concern that global media concentration will respect no local cultures, traditions, or customs as long as these factors stand in the way of profits. In addition, global media giants are politically conservative because they benefit from existing socio-political relations, resist any challenge or upheaval in property or economic relations, and execute soft censorship over media content. Unlike explicit censorship exercised in authoritarian regimes, censorship in the 'free world' is implicit and self-imposed by automatically skipping touchy issues, silencing marginal voices, ignoring inconvenient facts, and a framing which would leave out the oppositional or the ambiguous. Furthermore, because dominant global media forces are mainly from the United States, there is an equally growing concern about Americanization or American cultural imperialism facilitated by the strong presence of American media content, viewpoints, and ideologies. These concerns are underlined by the fear of cultural homogenization or 'the Hollywood juggernaut'. There is no doubt that the global conglomerates' strong impact on the diversity of local cultures is visible, especially in places where media systems are corrupted and particularly when profits are the final concern for global commercial media. As a result, it equally gives rise to the forces of resistance and alternative views.

One of the best examples of resistance against media conglomerates in the global north has been the establishment of Al Jazeera. Since 1996, the Qatar-based satellite station has played a significant role as the counterforce against the dominant global media (e.g., CNN and the BBC). These Western channels were once the major source of international news in the Middle East. American and European policy makers tend to see Al Jazeera as a rogue broadcaster, especially considering its unique positioning and relations with terrorist groups or states, including al Qaeda and the Taliban. It is also considered a rival because it does not follow the same logic of media framing. What is easily edited out by dominant global media can be found in Al Jazeera's media content. For instance, graphic coverage of the damage and destruction done by American's invasion to Iraq was transmitted through live broadcast across the Arab world.

Al Jazeera's role and significance have to be considered from the viewpoint of Arab audiences. Among the tightly state-controlled and relatively morbid media environment in the region, Al Jazeera stands for the access to a public space in which Arab audiences from different countries can express viewpoints on international issues, engage in debates, question the status quo, and form pan-Arab identities through shared anger, frustration, and aspirations. According to a report by the US Institute of Peace, Al Jazeera's programming allows Arabs 'to vent, formulate, and discuss public affairs. They bring Arabs closer together, breaking taboos and generally competing with each other and their respective governments for the news agenda' (Seib, 2008: 142). Compared to the state-owned media channels under the heavy shadow of political censorship, Al Jazeera, according to Bernard Lewis, 'brings to the peoples of the Middle East a previously unknown spectacle—that of lively and vigorous public disagreement and debate' (Seib, 2008: 143). Finally, Al Jazeera has been regarded by the Arab population as a trustworthy source of news and information. This transnational media channel reaching both Muslim countries and countries of Muslim immigrants is credited as serving the interests of Arabs and Muslims. In other words, its most important attribute has been about gathering news independently and witnessing events through their own eyes for Arabs and by Arabs.

In this section we understand that global media channels are conglomerates such that the globalization of communication yields an uneven power structure in controlling information flow. However, media like Al Jazeera exist as the voices of Arabs in challenging the hegemonic domination of the global north and in establishing channels of public diplomacy to leverage pan-Arab concerns. These counterforces of alternative or opposing viewpoints and content not only make the Americanized tendency of global media unstable, but also question homogenized information flow. In the following discussion, we continue to consider the uneven yet undetermined nature of globalization of media through a consideration of the nationalization of global media events.

Global Media Events, National Views

The 2003 Iraq War was a major media event constructed very differently by broadcasting networks in different parts of the world. While the US networks framed the event as 'Operation Iraqi Freedom' (the Pentagon concept) or 'War in Iraq', the Canadian CBC used the term 'War on Iraq', and various Arab networks presented it as an 'invasion' and 'occupation' (Kellner, 2004: 69). Olivier Boyd-Barrett (1977) had already argued in the 1970s that there was a heavy flow of exported media products from the US to the rest of the world but very limited media products entering the US. This statement remains valid more than three decades later but it does not lead to an overwhelming Americanization or cultural homogenization of cultures, views, and practices. Indeed, the world seems to be flatter or we seem to be closer to each other. As we learned from the previous section, this is partially due to the counterforces at the level of media structures that provide different channels, views, and interpretations of the same event. Moreover, the domesticated understanding of global media events makes the complete Americanization or cultural homogenization impossible. Thus, '[i]n the shadow of cultural and technological globalization', Chin-Chuan Lee and his colleagues strongly argue that 'international newsmaking remains inherently ethnocentric, nationalistic, and even state-centered' (Lee et al., 2002: 2). Before working on this statement as the central argument of this part of the discussion, we consider how news is presented as an event.

When something catches journalists' attention and hits news headlines around the globe, it usually carries the sensationalism of the extraordinary, the unexpected, and even the inconceivable. This partially responds to the demands of the profit-making nature of global media organizations. News is about something new and global news is usually presented as events or spectacles that blur the boundaries between consumption and information. News about global mega-sport events, like the 2008 Beijing Olympics, serves as a good example. It has been the common agenda for these events to celebrate humanity forging a global unity, fostering international friendship, and creating cosmopolitan identities. Following the same humanitarian ideals, it was claimed that the Beijing Olympics was held 'to promote the spread of human rights and democracy and improve inter-cultural understanding, and such processes are claimed to be reinforced by the IOC's [International Olympic Committee's] "Celebrate Humanity" campaign' (Maguire et al., 2008: 64). Joseph Maguire and his colleagues argue that spinning around these ideals in fact helps to build circuits of promotion in the media–sports complex where the concept of global citizenship becomes a selling point. The IOC's 'Celebrate Humanity' campaign, which incorporates the mechanisms of marketing, advertising, and sponsorship at different levels of global media structure and representation, is thus a branding effort. Nevertheless, while global cosmopolitanism is turned into an overt commercialism in packaging the Olympics, it does not mean that nationalism and competing national interests are hidden in encouraging Olympics viewership.

Ironically, hosting the Olympics is an act designed to flex national power. The Olympics are in themselves a global media event glorifying national strength, progress, and success, and enhancing or confirming the international status of the host country. For the Chinese, the summer Olympics in 2008 was not only a recognition of their rising economic power as a global player, but also a sign of the country's moving away from the political turmoil and the shameful sense of backwardness characteristic of the past century. Chinese nationalism, as a result, climaxed during the global broadcasting of the opening ceremony, where staging the humanitarian theme of 'One World, One Dream' was rendered secondary by Chinese achievements from the past (the inventions of paper, typesetting, gunpowder, and the compass) to the present (the world-class pianist Lang Lang, etc.).

The fireworks at the opening ceremony of the Beijing Olympics literally put the spotlight on China in front of a global audience. However, the splendid fireworks also temporarily blinded the audience to the domestic challenges of unbalanced economic development between coastal and inner provinces, the gap between the rich and the poor, and political oppression of dissidents. The unfair treatment of ethno-cultural groups, notably Tibetans and Muslims in the Western regions, was certainly left out while Chinese multiculturalism was showcased in the ceremony.

In addition, when athletes represent their respective countries and stand for excellence by setting benchmarks or winning the competitions, national identities are built and rebuilt around the attention to and the celebration of their performance of excellence. Mega sports–media events are paradoxically occasions for waving national flags, patriotic acts, encouraging national conflicts, and expressing national sentiments in a legitimate manner. The acts of national citizenship intertwined with the acts of sports–media consumption reinforce the sense of national membership through identifying with the heroic acts of the athletes, creating the 'we' feeling of community, and idealizing certain visions of the national culture, while at the same time developing a temporary amnesia about the complexity of conflicts, challenges, and problems within a nation-state. Despite the rhetorical objective of global humanism and imagery of international friendship, sports–media events, and especially the associated ceremonies, are 'a stylized introduction to metaphorical war between nation states' (Bernstein and Blain, 2003: 14).

How do we make sense of actual wars between nation-states mediated into global events from our own mostly remote immediate settings? For instance, 'Why do they hate us?' was a common question among mainstream Americans after the 9/11 event in 2001. This event was important not simply because it was the first major attack on the American mainland. It was also a decisive moment in contemporary history, one that marked the new century with a more assertive, conservative, and aggressive US foreign policy. As a result, it redefined US relations with other countries by ending the ambiguous transitory diplomacy that existed following the Cold War period, when the definite imaginary enemies or the post-Soviet threat was firmly reconstructed as the primarily Islamic 'Other'. Then–US President George W. Bush's famous statement that dichotomized countries as being 'either with us or against us' in the war on terrorism in particular became the central theme of media representations of the 9/11 events and the wars in Afghanistan and Iraq.

When mainstream Americans turned to mass media for answers, newsmakers were required to draw concepts, vocabularies, and explanations from the repertoire of the ordinary, the expected, and the familiar in order for average readers or viewers to make sense of the mediated collective experience, as puzzling and inconceivable as it was. In other words, what happens, no matter how important, spectacular, or shocking, has to be comprehensible and relevant to domestic audiences. As Murray Edelman (1988) argues, news is more than facts because it offers familiarity and reaffirms the sense of shared communities, while establishing credibility and confidence in explanations of complex issues. This is also where news framing from the national angle comes in to construct or reinforce interpretations in the languages with which we are familiar.

Framing the News

What is **framing**? If we follow the work of Robert Entman, '[t]o frame is to select some aspect of a perceived reality and make them more salient in a communicating text, in such a way as to promote a particular problem definition, causal interpretation, moral evaluation, and/or treatment recommendation for the item described' (1993: 52). There can be considerable variation in the way in which a national press reports on global events, as each tends to frame the observed news in a light favourable to its national objectives. We might, for example, consider an incident which occurred at the 2010 Vancouver Olympics, in which Georgian luge competitor Nodar Kumaritashvili died during a training run. Table 6.1 below compares reporting from four national sources about the event: Canada reported the event as an unfortunate accident, the US reported the event as a result of Canadian authorities not allowing full access to its facilities, Georgia reported the event as an accident which

TABLE 6.1 Variations on Reporting Global Mega-sports Events

Canada Reporting	USA Reporting	Georgia Reporting	China Reporting
'The death of Georgian [L.N.] Kumaritashvili was a result of the athlete losing control of his sled and not an unsafe track, The International Luge Federation said Friday night in a statement' (*Globe and Mail*, 12 Feb. 2010).	'Canadian Sports officials will face criticism for giving athletes from other countries relatively little access to most Olympic venues in an effort to give Canadians a competitive advantage for the games' (*New York Times*, 13 Feb. 2010).	'Mr. Saakashvili [the Georgian President] said, "I don't claim to know all the technical details, but one thing I know for sure: No sports mistake is supposed to lead to a death"' (*Georgian Times*, 15 Feb. 2010).	'The German got his, Gonzales said. It totally changed the whole race. It use to be Armin Zoeggeler of Italy and Albert Demtschenko of Russia . . . But now it's a German race' (*People's Daily*, 15 Feb. 2010).

should not have happened, and China reported the event in terms of a change in the chances of certain competitors.

Nevertheless, as Karim Karim argues, it is 'not a deliberate plan by the mass media to portray certain issues in particular ways, but a "naturalized" hegemonic process through which they adhere to a common field of meanings' (2000: 5). In short, what seems to be abnormal has to be normalized through framing.

The mainstream American news, which is available via the four major networks ABC, CBS, NBC, and Fox, as well as the news network CNN, has given answers to their audiences about the 9/11 attack by defining the problem as a terrorist act and morally evaluating the terrorists as evil people. The causal interpretation is that these evil people hate democracy and freedom—the American way of life. Finally, the treatment recommended, aligned with the American administration's responses, is for the whole world to declare a war on terrorism in order to guard the universal values of democracy and freedom. The framing for the wars in Afghanistan and Iraq also followed the US administration's foreign policy agenda, couching imperial military actions in the name of humanitarian interventions, for liberating Afghanistan from the authoritarian Taliban regime and al Qaeda, and for democratizing Iraq and replacing its dictator Saddam Hussein. In addition, the world was dichotomized into two camps: (1) friends aligned with the American administration and (2) enemies. For instance, circulated in both traditional and new media, there was great antagonism against France, a country sharing 'our way of life' of democracy and liberty, for its refusal to send troops to Iraq. As a result, France was morally evaluated as betraying the free world, and one of the treatments called for—no matter how irrational—was to boycott French baguettes and to rename french fries as 'liberty fries'.

A similar interpretation of the 9/11 events and the Iraq war can be found in Canadian media, especially in the news outlets owned by CanWest Global Communications, a firm supporter of Israel in the Middle East. In Ross Perigoe's (2007) analysis of the *Montreal Gazette*, the English daily owned by CanWest, misrepresentation and misunderstanding of Muslims and the Middle East are perpetuated in racist rhetoric and discourse. For example, while the Taliban were debased as 'ignorant psychotics', and 'living in a rat's nest of international thugs', bin Laden was compared to Hitler (Perigoe, 2007: 331). Perigoe states that the '*Gazette* participated in the construction of a reading of the 9/11 attacks as worthy of retribution, violence and deaths of others who were as innocent as those who died in the World Trade Center, the Pentagon, and a field in Stoney Creek Township in Pennsylvania' (2007: 333). It echoed the persistent lack of historical and cultural understanding of violence and conflicts involving Muslims and the Middle East. As Karim Karim (2000) argues, this misunderstanding and misrepresentation, as such, has its roots in the recurring stereotyping of Muslims for over a millennium in Europe. Daya Thussu (2005) holds that the mainstream American framing facilitated by the US-dominated global news networks followed the American administration's foreign policy in general, and became the main news source of the 9/11 events.

For a strong presence, main news sources usually appear to be global. Nevertheless, as Lee and his colleagues argue, '[i]nternational news represents the global production of the local and local production of the global. The mediating mechanism of the global–local linkage is domestication' (2002: 61). To put it in another way, globalization is a process of **glocalization** (Featherstone, 1995). If we compare and contrast news representation from different countries, once again, we see how different national interests play a key role in interpreting and interlocuting with main news sources fed by the dominant American framing, which tends to present itself as the 'global'. The approach we take in juxtaposing different media framing around the globe makes it important to single out the domestication of global media events by national concerns.

Inspired by Bakhtin's ideas of dialogism (1984), it also helps us to understand how equally weighted, simple, or complex voices address the same event in such a way that they cannot help but gravitate toward one another. They might confirm, support, contradict, or challenge each other, but overall they assure the impossibility of monologic discourse in homogenizing the globe. Putting them side by side as comparison is an important step in international communication.

To start with an example of a strong challenge against the hegemonic discourse circulated by the mainstream US media, Qustandi Shomali shows that the political reality of Palestine played a significant role in its press response toward the United States after 9/11. Palestine loathed the US support for Israel and for invoking its veto power in the UN Security Council. However, this did not suggest a single voice on the subject of the 9/11 attack. Media representations ranged from support of the United States to opposition to the US policies, and from rational analysis of the attack in relation to international law to irrational criticism of the United States and Israel. One end of the spectrum was represented by political caricatures or cartoons. Cartoons are powerful images underlined by the public discourse and emotional sentiments of specific social and cultural contexts. While caricatures entail the potential to push the boundaries of sociological imagination and social norms, they can be equally limiting by reinforcing stereotypes and encouraging violence. For instance, satirical criticism and strongly offensive language targeted at American and Israeli leaders were vividly expressed in political caricatures. George W. Bush and Israel's Prime Minister Ariel Sharon were often paired together as the bulldozers against Palestinians. In many caricatures, Israel was portrayed as reaping political and financial gains from 9/11 and the sequential wars on terrorism. This is to say that Palestinian reactions toward 9/11 were mediated by their antagonism against the occupation conducted by Israel and backed by the United States. At the same time, emotional hatred, fear, grief, and anxiety, fused with the sarcastic attitudes in caricatures, continued to be central to Palestine's struggles for statehood and nationalism.

At the other end of the spectrum, support and sympathy for the United States could be found in two major newspapers. All of the Palestinian political organizations, including the Palestine Legislative Council, unions, committees, and human rights agencies, condemned the 9/11 attacks and expressed their sympathy for the victims and their families. Nevertheless, the support itself revolved around and referred back to its own concern about national statelessness. While condemning what happened in the United States, the Legislative Council warned Israel against using 9/11 as a pretext to escalate attacks on Palestinians, as well as continuing its advocacy for equity in ending the occupation. At the same time, by pointing to what it considered to be Israel's state terrorism, it subverted the typical stereotyping of Palestinians as suicide bombers and the geographical grouping and racial profiling of terrorism in the northern media representation.

In India, an audience that had been previously dependent on CNN or BBC for international news was disappointed by the pro-Western coverage filled with perceived state propaganda of the United States and Britain. Accompanied by an increasing demand for India's own voices, the major global channels, including CNN and BBC, dropped two per cent of their Indian viewership, while 38 per cent tuned in to the Hindi news channel, Aai Tak. Janet Fine (2007) argues that the Indian media reportage on the 9/11 attack overall provided an acceptable alternative viewpoint with a critical reflection of the American framing and of the issues Indians were most concerned with most. For instance, Mani Subramanian, a Mumbai wire service editor at the time, described how the focus of Indian media was primarily on how Indian families were affected by the death of near and dear ones at the World Trade Center and how tightening of security measures at airports in the United Sates would affect Indian travellers. The usual eyewitness accounts of how the aircrafts crashed into the twin towers were used by Indian television and pictures displayed by Indian newspapers were lifted from US media sources like CNN and NBC or published by arrangement with Western media. Indian newspapers carried cartoons of Osama bin Laden together with the president of the United States. Indian media also assessed the threats from terrorists on Indian soil and there were calls for more Indo–US cooperation in the war against terrorism (Fine, 2007: 217).

We have shown the ambivalent relationship between India and the United States. India's rising economic power in the global economy, strong presence, and independent position in the region allow for less coercion by the American administration. This encourages journalists to form alternative views and to use materials censored in the US-dominated networks. At the collective level, despite being wary of American moral values, Indians' ultimate dream is to immigrate travel to, travel to, or study in the United States. The tightening of security measures at US airports and the long passport queue crowding the American Consulate in Mumbai have become a central concern for Indians. Nonetheless, the 'American dream' persevered even after the 9/11 actions taken by the US administration in the subcontinent region were reported by Indian news with a collective sense of unease for both racial and religious reasons.

Sreeni Sreenivasan, president and co-founder of the South Asian Journalists Association in New York and the Dean of Students at Columbia University Graduate School of Journalism, noticed the unfolding of another tragedy following 9/11. There were reprisal attacks against South Asians across the United States and Canada because of their 'brown' colour: '[O]ne Sikh had been killed in Arizona and others injured, obviously in what was a clear case of mistaken identity' (Fine, 2007: 220). In addition, since conflicts of religion have always been a domestic issue in India, where the world's third largest Muslim population resides, the Indian media was critical of the mainstream American media representation. For instance, Sevanti Ninan, an Indian journalist, reported that

> when the projected villain is Islamic fundamentalism, the Muslim community worldwide, as innocent as the victims of terrorist attacks, ends up bearing the brunt . . . there were occasional references on television to the disappearance of New York cab drivers . . . substantially West Asian in origin. Eight million Muslims in the US would have instantly begun to feel vulnerable. So what can the media do about it? (Fine 2007: 221)

This is the concern over the inability to distinguish diversity within Muslim societies while a global, monolithic, and static Islamic entity is constructed in the northern media imaginary for the general public. This common concern expressed by the Indian journalist echoes Karim's argument that '[w]hereas the followers of Islam adhere to a set of beliefs in common, there remains a plurality that exists not only in cultural but also religious behaviour among the billion Muslims living around the world' (2000: 7). In addition, 'Muslim' can be a source of cultural identity detached from religious practices; the novelist Salman Rushdie has notably been the case here.

Global Media Events as Spectacles

We continue to probe into the making of global media events in order to understand what events make their way into the circulation of seemingly rapidly increasing channels of global communication. Why do certain events hit global media headlines? Why do certain crises escape global media attention? For some, the explanation lies in whether an event is entertaining or spectacular enough or not. In other words, 'the logic of making news is hijacked by the logic of staging a media spectacle' (Lee et al., 2002: 6). For Guy de Board, '[t]he spectacle is not a collection of images; rather, it is a social relationship between people that is mediated by images' (1995: 12). This is to say that the 'logic of staging a media spectacle' cannot be considered without the commercial objective of media production: profit making and consumption. Mega sports–media events like the Olympics are the immediate and obvious examples. In a less evident manner, global media channels are filled with 'lifestyle' stories and reports, such as travelling, cooking, fashion, etc. For instance, this genre made up 18 per cent of total network news stories on the big three US television networks and their global branches. It dropped only one per cent in October 2001, the month immediately after 9/11. It climbed back to 19 per cent during the first three months of 2002 (Seib, 2004: 76).

We can further push the argument by considering that the images and representations mediated between social relationships are in fact the separation of reality and hyper-reality in meeting the demands for sensational experiences. Jean Baudrillard equally singles out the importance of understanding media in terms of simulating signs and stimulating consumption, as we have discussed in Chapter 4. At the same time, he directs our attention to the spectacular nature of wars and political violence, which evoke our sensory experiences in a different manner. During the 1993 Gulf War, he compared and contrasted the violence of the old and the contemporary: the former was enthusiastic and sacrificial, whereas the latter was hyper or virtual. For Baudrillard, political terror in our time is a simulacrum of violence emerging from the screen, and violence is in the nature of images. It is as if the Gulf War did not happen in reality (Baudrillard, 1995). Echoing de Board, the production and mediation of spectacles are not about accumulating representation or bombarding us with images. Rather, considering media representation of wars and political violence, there is a strong relationship between acts of terrorism and growing media fascination. In this relationship, consumption and entertainment are created in the capital's logic of production for sensationalism; yet the feelings of fear, anxiety, and paranoia, produced by the logic of political violence, are reproduced with a safety mechanism in place. We will explain this point step by step.

For Jacques Derrida, this relationship between media and violence is also evident when he rhetorically asks, 'What would "September 11" have been without television?' He asserts that 'maximum media coverage was in the *common* interest of the perpetrators of "September 11", the terrorists, and those who, in the name of the victims, wanted to declare "war on terrorism"' (Borradori, 2003: 108). Derrida continues by proposing that the socio-political relationship mediated by images of global media events, like 9/11, is in the exploitation and repetition of the images, beyond the horror residing in the actual acts of attack and killing at the twin towers and the Pentagon. Perhaps the terror lies in the fact that '[t]here is quite clearly a widespread public acquiescence to the enjoyment of war as a spectacle, especially if it is safe for the spectators', as Denis McQuail argues (2006: 117).

The mediatization of wars and political violence into global media spectacles, to follow this argument, presents safe events for consumption. Joanna Zylinska rightly states that 'mediation functions as a safety mechanism: the physicality of a TV screen (in the case of 9/11), but also the numerous projection screens put up by our unconscious, allow us to observe and simultaneously consolidate the "polluting or contaminating other", seen as "an impurity or stain", from a distance' (2004: 236). In other words, watching or reading the global coverage of wars and political violence is a paradoxical experience: on the one hand, audiences or readers as spectators experience media events filled with heartbreaking stories and sensational events with demands for sympathy and caring. On the other hand, an imaginative enemy is constructed, creating considerable distance between reading/watching and experiencing political violence. Global media events of wars and political violence become theatrical spectacles.

Mediating Citizenship Through Global Media Events

The paradoxical participation in the theatrical spectacles of wars and political violence or the consumption of related news becomes a patriotic act of citizenship. While sympathy is dispensed, anger is vented, the enemies are identified, 'the polluting and contradicting other' is imagined, fear is evoked, a sense of solidarity is built, and the **imagined political community** is constructed and reconstructed. This does not simply intensify and simplify the paradoxical nature of national citizenship that it includes and excludes at the same time. It also questions what a patriotic citizen can do beyond the mediating experience. To further consider 9/11 as an example, many Americans have never visited or known anybody in New York or Washington, DC. Their national sense of belonging is largely imaginative, but participating in the theatrical spectacles of the crashing twin towers and the Pentagon through repetitively viewing the same images, seeking explanations, and experiencing moral panic has tied them to their now fellow New Yorkers. The global media spectacle of wars and political violence then opens up another paradoxical question concerning patriotic acts of citizenship: when the violence targets the imagined political community populated by citizens separated by great distances and viewing positions, what counts as a patriotic act of citizenship often requires the application or circulation of national symbols and images, such as raising a flag outside of the house or affixing a patriotic slogan sticker on a car bumper. These powerful national images at a specific time then become a spectacle themselves that express an imaginative sense of togetherness through weaving an intimate relation between a patriotic citizen with victims of political violence whom he or she never met or knew before.

Missing Global Media Events

The third myth holds that globalization of communication has resulted from new media technologies and creates a utopia of intercultural communication through which people around the globe can understand each other easily, information freely flows, and a new global order becomes possible. From the previous discussion, we already understand that channels of new media technologies are controlled and distributed unevenly, and that national interests still weigh in heavily news reportage and the (re)construction of an imagined political community. In this part of the discussion, we look at missing global media events to further understand that new media technologies guarantee neither a utopia of intercultural communication nor free access to and flows of information. Rather, the interests of journalistic practices tied to geopolitical calculations often determine the presence of global media events. Understanding what is left out of global media framing is as important as interpreting what is kept inside. We start with the dehumanization and effacement of victims in the recent war against terrorism as one void in global media coverage. We continue with examination of the ignorance about and indifference to the 1994 Rwanda genocide as another type of missing global media event. Both exemplify the paradoxical relationship between the increase in media technological capacities in news production and the decrease in international news circulation and consumption. They further point to the failed acts of global journalism in striving for justice.

Dehumanization and Effacement

Mannika Chopra, a columnist, criticized the framing processes of the war against terrorism by pointing out the undertones of American ethnocentrism. Chopra's message clearly questioned the missing news about what happened to civilians during the US bombardment in Afghanistan. The US military took a 'shock and awe' strategy by producing a global visual spectacle of bombing that simultaneously numbed the sensory systems and blinded our ability to see the mass destruction of infrastructure, houses and homes, sources of water and habitable spaces, and lives themselves. When wars become virtual, when the images of bombardment are taken from a macro perspective where no close shots of what is actually destroyed and injured are taken, when the casualty news is dominantly framed around the soldiers' heroic and patriotic acts of citizenship, and when we do not see the suffering of Afghani or Iraqi, the framing of these global media events becomes the source of global injustice.

In Judith Butler's words, this is mediation characterized by 'the derealization of loss—the insensitivity to human suffering and death. . . . This derealization takes place neither inside nor outside the image, but through the very framing by which the image is contained' (2006: 148). For instance,

William Hart and Fran Hassencahl (2002) analyzed over 1,300 caricatures and cartoons about war between January and March 2003 in US newspapers. A significant amount portray the Iraqis as faceless and voiceless by representing them as an abstraction. This is a process of **media effacement**. That is, coupled with the derealization of the loss, we do not see the victims' faces, nor do we hear their agony. Victims are un-nameable and un-grieveable, because the framing erases the presence of the other's face by rendering their sufferings, demands, lives, and deaths non-existent.

Hart and Hassencahl also show that a great many caricatures and cartoons dehumanized Iraq and Iraqis. As Butler argues, derealization and effacement go hand in hand with dehumanization. The pictorial portraits of the imagined enemies are animals, barbarians, criminals, devils, and torturers. The political images resonated with the rhetoric of the American administration and international allies in their moral dichotomy between the good (us) and the bad (the other). Or, simply put, '[t]hese are media portraits that are often marshaled in the service of war, as if bin Laden's face were the face of terror itself, as if Arafat were the face of deception, as if Hussein's face were the face of contemporary tyranny' (Butler, 2006: 141). As Philip Seib argues, '[i]n news coverage, as in politics, a vacuum exists if there is no "enemy"' (2004: 76). However, what remain vacuumed out in the global media event where the enemy is demonized without a recognizable human face are the articulation of the historical complexity and the investigation into geopolitical interests and conflicts in the Middle East.

Missing News from the Global South

What is missing in the dominant global media framing of wars and political violence are not only the other's suffering and an in-depth analysis of geopolitical conflicts, but also conflicts and violence at the margins of global power dynamics. For example, terrorism in India is almost a missing global media focus in the 9/11 discourses, although India has been a target of international terrorism for decades and has its share of painful experiences with political violence and conflicts. As K.K. Katyal, in India's influential newspaper *The Hindu*, mentioned:

> The sweep of the media coverage and the intensity of the discussions [on 9/11] was not a surprise. What was a matter of surprise was that India did not figure or was insignificantly mentioned . . . [India has been] in the forefront of struggle against terrorism. But now it was conspicuously absent—so it seemed from London and, perhaps, most other European capitals—in the global discourse on terrorism. 'It seems India does not exist on the globe,' remarked an irate NRI [non resident Indian] in an informal conversation in what seemed a representative comment. (quoted in Fine, 2007: 222)

In the Indian media, there has been a general analysis that the missing global news about terrorist attacks in India has resulted from the United States' geopolitical interest in Pakistan's role in capturing Osama bin Laden and the al Qaeda hiding near its borders, while India and Pakistan remain antagonistic on the sub-continent. When a terrorist attack in India finally seized global attention in 2008, it was largely due to the fact that many tourists from the North were trapped and victimized by the siege in a Mumbai hotel. Global media attention was centred on tourists' safety. Once the siege was over, attention on the global scale was shifted to elsewhere immediately.

Missing global news about humanitarian crises epitomizes the uneven processes of the globalization of communication, compounded by geopolitical interests in controlling the flows and framing of information. Seib notes that while the global media focus had been on 9/11 and wars in Iraq and Afghanistan in 2003, it 'virtually ignored humanitarian crises from Chad to Chechnya to Colombia and beyond that were identified by Doctors Without Borders in the organization's annual list of the ten most under-reported stories' (2004: 76). Conflict and drama certainly sell, but when the coverage is about difficult, complex, and foreign issues, journalists are constantly engaged in editing out ambiguity as a way to maintain and create drama in an instant response, while chaos, crisis, and anarchy continue to strike at different dark corners of the globe. As the International Federation of Red Cross and Red Crescent Societies points out in *World Disasters Report 2005*, '[e]ditors sort stories by death tolls. Disasters that are unusual yet explicable, and that cause considerable death or destruction in accessible places which the audience is believed to care about, get covered. Baffling stories get less attention' (quoted in Thompson, 2007: 438–9).

Driven by ratings and framed into half news and half entertainment, dramatic natural disasters like the tsunami in Southeast Asia in 2005 and earthquakes in Sichuan, China, in 2008 are newsworthy. In contrast, long-lasting crises that are difficult to describe, explain, witness, and record are easily left out in the abyss of missing global news. In addition, one global media event is usually turned into *the* big event at the expense of another. As a result, global media channels are overwhelmed by what Allan Thompson describes as the Cyclops of monocular gaze through which the 'media glare of the big story casts a deep shadow on its fringes'. The editorial framing process of international news proceeds hand in hand with the paradoxical phenomenon of global media events: the more advanced the global media technologies, the less diversified news is channelled through to viewers. Claude Moisy, former chairman and general manager of Agence France-Presse, notes that 'the amazing increase in the capacity to produce and distribute news from distant lands has been met by an obvious decrease in its consumption' (Thompson, 2007: 436).

One of the darkest examples has been the 1994 Rwanda genocide. Two weeks after Rwandan president Juvénal Habyarimana was killed in a plane crash on 6 April 1994, the ethnic conflict between the majority Hutu population and the minority Tutsi turned to genocide. Hutu extremists disagreed with the power-sharing agreement signed in 1993, and the fatal plane accident, blamed to be caused by the Tutsi, was immediately used to mobilize extreme hatred and massive, systematic killing of the Tutsi. When the Hutu extremist newspaper and the radio were used as extensively, explicitly, and relentlessly as weapons like machetes in destroying the Tutsi population, the global media first mistook the massive killing for tribal warfare, and then turned its back on the genocide after the coverage on evacuating expatriates was done. While the killing, intensified by domestic hate media, continued, most international journalists had left the country. This tiny central African country did not seem to matter to politicians of the North because of its lack of economic and geopolitical strategic importance. Not only political but also media intervention failed at the international level. As the UN peacekeeper, Canadian General Roméo Dallaire remarked: 'The media, like so many others in Rwanda, failed. The world powers failed. Individually we failed' (2007: 14). As a result, 'the massacres were being perpetrated silently yet systematically' (Roskis, 2007: 238), as 800,000 people were killed in six weeks.

While the killing went on in Rwanda, global airwaves were occupied by O.J. Simpson, a former American professional football star, who was on trial for murdering his wife; Nelson Mandela's election in South Africa; conflicts in Yugoslavia; and Tonya Harding, a US figure skater who attacked a competitor. International journalists finally responded to Rwanda when the plight of refugees in Goma led to a '"safe humanitarian zone" created by the French military . . . and gave the photo stylists and other photo award hunters one compact, convenient location where they could instantly access an inexhaustible supply of the raw materials they need to produce images of Africa for Western consumption . . .' (Roskis, 2007: 240). The UN was reluctant to make the necessary political intervention as the killing was ignored and misconstructed as barbaric tribal conflicts, in contrast to the 'ethnic cleansing' of religious and ethnic antagonism in Yugoslavia. At the same time, global media intervention also failed Rwanda because media coverage does matter in changing the course of foreign policy decisions. For instance, the so-called **CNN effect** is characterized by the intensive 'cyclops of monocular gaze' in providing information directly (Canada's CBC has recently adopted this method of delivering news) and shaping the directions of public discourses and opinion indirectly, especially when policy makers are uncertain about their next move. In the case of Rwanda, when there were only two journalists left and when there was almost no visual witnessing and recording circulated in the global channels of communication in the course of the massacre, there was no ethical outcry in the name of the weak or the suffering other.

It is strongly believed that more media coverage and exposure of the Rwanda genocide could have minimized the scale and intensity of killing and saved hundreds of thousands of lives. This is also to say that media intervention is crucial in global justice. For instance, the images of a young man who attempted to stop tanks en route to Tiananmen Square for a crackdown on the 1989 Chinese student movement allowed the global audience to experience feelings of awe related to the man's courage and his safety. The image of the 'Tank Man', standing in front of the column of tanks, not only became a symbolic figure of democracy but also brought China's human rights into the global spotlight. Also, the image of a running burnt girl in tears disturbed the public sense of security, infiltrated the hegemonic field of media representation in the North, and questioned US citizens' moral consciousness about participation in the Vietnam War. Therefore, it is important to measure the impacts of global media events framed in certain ways, and it is equally important to dig into missing global news that has been systematically downplayed.

Summary

In this chapter, we started with the conceptual framework of globalization by pointing out three common myths or misunderstandings of this popular term. We used concrete examples including mega sports–media events (the Olympics), the 9/11 attack, and the Iraq/Afghanistan wars to illustrate the ways in which a global mediascape is constructed as an uneven but undetermined field due to the competing forces between the centripetal, dominant media from the global north and the centrifugal, opposing, or alternative media from the global south. These examples also give us an idea of the entrenchment of global media channels across national boundaries. Nevertheless, a careful reading of these global media events equally gives us an idea that nation-states and national prisms are far from obsolete. They continue to serve as the conceptual frameworks through which news makers or media producers define newsworthiness and provide meaningful or relevant explanation to the national audience. In other words, global media events mediate national interests and geopolitical policies at the same time.

We also examined the construction of global media events as spectacles of both entertainment and information. When the concept of spectacles was introduced, we aimed at emphasizing the aspects of social relations between the spectacle (the media event) and the spectator (the audience), as well as the danger of desensitizing, amplifying, or manipulating the problems of political violence in the ways media events are presented. While we continued to investigate the framing of national interests in global media events, we equally considered the mediation of citizenship via imagining participation in the given political community.

In the third part of the chapter, we shifted the spotlight to missing global events and considered two dimensions of their absence: first, we examined the framing strategies of the northern global media that derealize, dehumanize, and efface those who are considered to be the enemy or the unimportant. In other words, we problematized what is left behind in the dark and what is rendered into non-existence in global media events. Second, we exemplified missing voices and the complete absence of crucial events such as the Rwanda genocide. As a result, the lack of global media attention to places of less geo-political importance and the exaggeration of rather trivial media events not only results in the inability to present human disasters, but also reflects the failure of international journalism in terms of global responsibility.

Enhanced Learning Activities

1. What is globalization? What is not globalization? In considering global media events, ask yourself how the analysis of global media events helps to clarify some misconceptions of globalization. Use one current news source to illustrate your points.
2. What is framing? Compare and contrast news reportage on the 2010 Vancouver Olympics in American, Canadian, Brazilian, and/or Chinese news sources. What differences and similarities do you detect in their discourses? Evaluate how the national concerns and interests of each country are a part of global media events.
3. Why are certain crucial issues absent in global media channels? Search for three events concerning human rights that deserve immediate attention in dominant media products and communication channels. Note to what extent they are absent from mainstream media and explain why they deserve more attention.
4. What are derealization and dehumanization? Describe and analyze how they are mobilized in news about Canadian troops in Afghanistan.

Annotated Further Reading

Judith Butler, *Frames of War: When Is Life Grievable?* New York: Verso, 2009. Butler reflects upon the US-led wars and provides a critical evaluation of media framing. The analysis balances a theoretical concern based on norms, power, and violence with empirical examples of media representation, policy making, and public debates.

Chin-Chuan Lee, Joseph Man Chan, Zhongdang Pan, and Clement Y.K. So, *Global Media Spectacle: News War over Hong Kong*. New York: State University of New York, 2002. This book explores the concept of media events as staging spectacles through examining news reportage on the return of Hong Kong from Great Britain to China in 1997.

Karim Karim, *Islamic Peril: Media and Global Violence*. Montreal: Black Rose, 2002. By studying media coverage and framing of conflicts involving Muslims prior to the 9/11 event, Karim not only points out the lack of historical and cultural understanding in the Northern media but also challenges the myths about

Muslims in their own media discourses. He calls for stronger journalistic ethics to improve intercultural communication and to mitigate global violence.

Useful Media

Opening Ceremonies of the Vancouver or Beijing Olympics

Various video clips of this event can be found on YouTube. Comparing and contrasting commentaries from narrators of different countries give us an idea of how a global media event is nationally framed.

Hotel Rwanda (2004). Director: Terry George.

This film gives us an idea of how the withdrawal of the international media was partially liable for the genocide, and how the powerful banality of radio was as fatal as the machete.

Reporters Without Borders website

http://en.rsf.org

This website sheds light on missing media events and on the grey zone of human rights obscured by specific political and economic interests.

English *Al Azeri* and CNN on American troops in Iraq

The two channels make a sharp contrast between perspectives from two continents on one of the defining media events of the twenty-first century. The comparison itself is also a Bakhtinian exercise of dialogical engagement through which we learn to listen to voices of difference and conflicts and to trace sources of contrasting ideas accented by similar emotional tones and orientations.

7 National Media Events

Learning Objectives

- To explore the role of national public media in Canada
- To think about the response of public broadcasting to French/ English duality
- To think about national media events in the context of the struggle for national cohesion
- To examine public broadcasting as a creator of public space and instrument of public dialogue
- To consider English Canada as the 'Absent Nation'
- To understand multicultural issues as national media events

Introduction

We have discussed how a national prism deflects global media events. In this chapter, we consider the role of national media institutions in framing, facilitating, and creating platforms for national media events. National media institutions tend to produce a collective identity in order to mobilize citizens for large-scale projects and to distinguish peoples and practices. They are an important part of these processes because they can make national identity, projects, and distinction possible beyond the immediate spatial and temporal contexts. In other words, by creating mediated centres of the nation-state, national media tend to integrate relatively impersonal agencies and institutions, form mass societies, and bridge shared social values and understandings (Dayan and Katz, 1992).

In this chapter, we focus on public broadcasting, although we consider both public and private nation-wide institutions and draw examples from various media platforms including TV and newspapers. This focus allows us to explore the sociological significance of media events in relation to the construction of and struggle for national cohesion. We start the discussion with the mandates of the CBC and La Société Radio-Canada (SRC) in relation to a multicultural Canadian-ness as a unified national identity. Out of this public mandate, Canadian media events become the mediated centre of Canada countering the centrifugal forces of diversity, threat, or disintegration. These forces are either external—coming through porous national borders—or internal—coming from within national boundaries.

We further explore how constructing and maintaining the nation-state via national media events cannot help but create perpetual tensions or paradoxes. In light of the work by Mikhail Bakhtin and Jacques Derrida, the example of the Remembrance Day ceremony broadcasted live across Canada, and that of the Kanehsatake/Oka crisis help us to understand how national media events provide mediated centres in the struggle for national cohesion. In conjunction with Will Kymlicka's work, we also consider how the interests of nation-states and national discourse embedded in national media events can be both positive and negative.

We deepen our understanding of the paradox inherent in national media events by showing how English Canada is defined through its non-relation to external and internal others. An analysis of the CBC program *Little Mosque on the Prairie* is coupled with an examination of news reportage on the popular singer Céline Dion in the context of Canada–Québec tensions in the 1990s. The first example helps us to see how English Canada is defined against the global dominant force of the United States, and how its existence as a homogeneous country paradoxically resides in the tensions between the mediated centre (Toronto) and the Prairie region. The second example shows how Canada is defined through a dialogical relation with Québec, and how the multi-nation reality is ignored by nation-wide media.

The last part of this chapter addresses the role of multicultural framing in making history and common memories. Using the examples of the CBC programs *A People's History* and the *Heritage Minutes*, we consider **docudrama** as a genre of media events that relies on turning histories and memories into historical media events in an entertaining way. This prompts us to examine the limitations and failure of multicultural framing in public broadcasting.

Multinational Canada and Public Broadcasting

A good example of the key role played by public broadcasters in defining national identity is seen in the history of the CBC and SRC. As key producers of mediated Canadian and Québec societies, the CBC (est. 1936) and SRC (est. 1938) have served as important forces in the democratization of each society and as organizations that have had a prominent role in reproducing the narratives of a variety of life worlds through music, drama, entertainment, and news. In order to trace the path of multicultural policies in broadcasting, it is necessary to bring four institutions into play: (1) the Broadcasting Act and the Canadian Broadcasting system, (2) the Canadian Radio-television and Telecommunications Commission, (3) the Canadian Association of Broadcasters, and (4) the Canadian Broadcasting Standards Council. Each of these is the locus of policies and regulations governing the recognition of diversity in broadcasting (See Table 7.1 below).

Although there have been several versions of the Broadcasting Act since 1932, we refer here to the most recent, passed in 1991. It is significant that the Act considers Canadian broadcasters, public and private alike, as a *single system*—the Canadian broadcasting system—to which the Act and all subsequent regulations apply. Furthermore, the intrusion of the Act into the private sector is based on the premise that the airwaves are public property. According to the 1991 Broadcasting Act,

> the Canadian broadcasting system should through its programming and the employment opportunities arising out of its operations, serve the needs and interests, and reflect the circumstances and aspirations, of Canadian men, women and children, including equal rights, the linguistic duality and multicultural and multiracial nature of Canadian society and the special place of aboriginal peoples within that society.

The priorities, as they emerged from a variety of legislative and institutional actions between 1960 and 1990, are summarized in Table 7.1. They may be described in abbreviated form as requiring programming that is

- to be typically Canadian,
- to serve the special needs of regions and be in the national interest,

TABLE 7.1 Legislation and Policies Bearing on Multiculturalism in Broadcasting

1960s	1970s	1980s	1990s
Bilingualism & Biculturalism	The Multiculturalism Act	The Constitutional Act	The Broadcasting Act
Recommendation		The Charter of Rights and Freedoms	
The Official Languages Act	The Canadian Human Rights Act	The Canadian Association of Broadcasters Code of Ethics	
		Formation of the Canadian Broadcasting Standards Council	

- to be broad in its diversity, and
- to be provided in both the French and English languages and serve the minority language of each of the official language groups. (It is notable that the mandate requiring it to reflect the multicultural and multiracial character of Canada, a seventh priority today, was added after the 1991 Act).

The official mandate absorbs a balance of historical conflicts and external contradictions over interests that originate in (1) the opposition between systems of private and public broadcasting organizations; (2) the inherent geopolitical contradiction between central and peripheral regions in Canada; and (3) the often opposite interests of cultures whose memberships are notoriously difficult to define sociologically—Anglophone, Francophone, First Nations, and a growing number of diasporas and transnational groups (Nielsen, 1995). Bringing the complex demands of diversity together in a unified communications subsystem of the public sphere has been a long political process that has shaped national media events for more than 75 years in Canadian society.

If we ask how public broadcasting gets the 'Canada' into the Canadian Broadcasting Corporation, we take the first step toward deconstructing the CBC and SRC. Perhaps if one thinks of the programs as the caramel and the CBC/SRC as the chocolate bar, one gets an image of the autonomy of cultures, as if the various regions and distinctions between Québec and the rest of the country were pieces from the same chocolate bar—and all of this regulated under one state authority.

To begin with, nothing from the federal mandate actually indicates that either network seeks to produce a multinational project that would reflect inner tensions or contradictions. Each network absorbs a reference to its 'other' (national) audience so that Radio-Canada is simply the French network of the CBC, as the CBC is the English network of Radio-Canada. Québec and English Canada are not trapped in a contradiction. But the two definitions of 'Canada' and 'Québec' do require a binary or opposite discourse of themselves, and it is in this opposition that we can see that in any final definition the networks need to be left somewhat undecided. The absorption of the one into the other demands an absence of a strong sense of regional 'we' identity, given that Radio-Canada's majority French-speaking Québec audience for the most part does not easily imagine itself as just another Canadian region or province like the others.

While Québec is an absent region for English Canada, the CBC is careful to maintain an absence of reference to any strong sense of an English-speaking national 'we'. In other words, English Canada doesn't usually understand itself as a nation on its own. Although it is a society in the sense that it has a system of institutional structures (legislature, economics, education, arts, etc.) as well as a unique culture that could be seen as societal, it has not cultivated the capacity to imagine itself as one of two, three, or more nations. The impetus for defining Canada as a multinational federation has almost always been derived from Québec or Aboriginal sources (Gagnon et al., 2008). On the other hand, Québec tends to see 'the rest of Canada' as a unified 'we' and so the stronger regional 'we's' (the West, Ontario, the Maritimes, the North, etc.) are less known among *les Québécois* than among English Canadians. This is easily heard by just listening to national news broadcasts from the CBC and SRC. It is clear that the CBC addresses a distinctly English-speaking Canadian audience on all kinds of national events, and although there has been much historical lip service paid to addressing regional drama, news, and multicultural programming, the product has, for the most part, been directly or indirectly issued from Toronto. In a parallel sense, while SRC provides services to the tiny number of French-speaking minorities across the federation through its programs and its policies almost exclusively produced or defined in Montreal, it addresses a distinctly French-speaking Québec national audience that has the historical capacity to imagine itself as a people without the rest of Canada. Ironically, neither network comes close to representing the growing multicultural populations in either city where the main productions take place—a point we return to in Chapter 8.

A Double-Faced Janus: National Media, Social Order, and Disorder

Janus was the Roman god of gates and doors, thought to have two heads that faced opposite directions. National discourse and media, epitomized by public broadcasting, can act as a double-faced Janus in building social order. Public broadcasting counters the erosion of local democratic practices and public participation by global commercial media. National media products and communication channels carry the potential of safeguarding a public space for dialogical exchanges. Exchanges as such are important for preserving and appreciating differences, interpreting multiple sources of national integration, and negotiating collective identities. Dialogues through national media mean that publics anticipate rejoinders from one another which do not preclude the possibility of confrontation or antagonism. Nor is the attainment of agreement between two differently situated views suggested. For instance, neither the Canadian nor Québec governments took up each other's positions during past referenda, but they still enter a dialogical relation in that both anticipate and address each other's responses in a way so that neither can finalize or give closure to or impose dominance. Consequently, this conception of dialogue deepens the interpretation of the Canada–Québec relation because it requires that viewpoints of both sides are treated with equal seriousness, intended or weighted. Without such an articulation in national media, we would fail to see how one's particularities are developed out of the other, and how they intersect, overlap, reconcile, contradict, or avoid each other. But public broadcasters can also be implicated in disreputable societal forces, as we will see in the following sections. National media and its discourse can be negative in the sense that what is national for some in a given time and place can simultaneously be a reason for exclusion or oppression for many others. There are various examples of past national media events that give pause in that both media forms and content become tools for a form of **state violence**. For example, during the Rwandan genocide, one of the worst scenarios in recent history, radio was used in the organized massacre of Tutsis (see Chapter 6). The world also witnessed how the 1936 Berlin Olympics during the German Nazi regime was planned, staged, and mobilized to promote racial superiority through constructing a celebratory national media event. In other words, regardless of the types of national media events, they become mediated centres facilitating state violence.

To bring out this two-sided effect of national media more fully we set aside our discussion of the two nations embedded in Canadian broadcasting and borrow conceptual tools from Jacques Derrida and Mikhail Bakhtin to help reveal the ambiguous and thus arguable foundations behind the discourse that normalizes a just or natural sense of social order or national cohesion within national media events.

National public media are faced with the daunting task of framing media events while coping with the centrifugal forces of internal differences and simultaneously insisting on a **grand narrative** about national unity. As described above, the pursuit of balance within multinational federations, or between the centripetal and centrifugal forces in mediated society, remains a challenge. One dimension of nationalism is the production of a cultural understanding and **rhetoric** to enable people to think about and cultivate their aspirations for national identity. This production is tightly connected with national projects, social movements, and state policies as attempts to advance national autonomy, independence, territorial amalgamation, or increased participation within an existing state. National discourse is also central to cultural politics and ideologies that claim uniqueness or even superiority of one particular nation. At the same time, they entail an imperative to ensure the correspondence of national and state boundaries. Under the suggestion of individualism, it is also an ethical imperative that a nation-state ought to be an internally unified entity yet independent from others, as if it were an autonomous person.

For Derrida (2002), the state establishes and relies on mechanisms of both physical and symbolic violence. The former refers to the exercise of police or military force against internal outlaws and the mobilization of wars against external intruders. The latter refers to the symbolic means of disciplining, educating, classifying, and stigmatizing domestic populations through media, educational systems, statistics, criminal records, primordial ethnic or religious categorization, etc. By exercising state violence in both the physical and symbolic sense, the nation-state aims to reinforce national solidarity and guard against 'foreigners in our midst'. In short, state violence is there to found, support, and maintain the social order and thus the interests of state or governing authority.

It is in the interest of state authority to stigmatize 'internal foreigners' through, for example, media treatment of Aboriginal issues and recounting the colonial past. The national threats from the foreignness of others comes from within. The term 'internal foreigner' indicates a third space for those who are both insiders and outsiders in the nation: they are insiders in the legal sense of belonging, on the one hand, yet they are outsiders because they do not fully or substantially belong to the nation in terms of ethnicity, political ideologies, cultural experiences, or religious and historical backgrounds. As Wendy Brown argues, national security as a right and freedom is historically ingrained in the demand for protection from both external and internal enemies. However, this demand for national security also camouflages the need for building 'a national consensus behind state violence' (Brown, 2006: 106). It further serves to internally distinguish good, law-abiding citizens from bad, law-breaking citizens, and to establish a link between what is a national threat—internal foreigners and non-legal citizens. In other words, law does not guarantee justice and the internal foreigners' demand for justice challenges the legal boundaries of national citizenship.

By keeping the above contesting arguments in mind, we demonstrate how discourse generated in national media events provides a centripetal force in time and space against centrifugal forces of internal differences. We start with the 1990 Kanehsatake/Oka crisis. This crisis was a conflicted national media event or mediatized public crisis that hit news headlines and caught public attention intensively within a direct confrontation between the state authority and indigenous people just outside the Montreal area.

The Kanehsatake/Oka Crisis

In March 1990, Oka—a Québec municipality—proposed to build a golf course and condominiums on indigenous ancient and sacred burial grounds. Land disputes have been a consistent problem between the indigenous and the colonial, and this particular failed negotiation lead to the establishment of a barricade by Mohawks. Perceiving them as internal foreigners threatening national security, the mayor of Oka requested the Sûreté du Québec, the provincial law enforcement agency, to intervene. The consequent shooting death of a Sûreté officer considerably increased the anger directed toward the Mohawk people. The death of a law officer symbolizes one of the most serious offences against social order, and the most severe challenge against the foundation of governing authority. More confrontations occurred when Mohawks blocked the Mercier Bridge, and the solidarity among Mohawks and other indigenous peoples across Canada and the United States fuelled and intensified the fear of a disintegrated or fragmented nationhood. Another failed series of negotiations between Mohawks and the provincial and federal governments in August resulted in the deployment of 2,500 Canadian soldiers to four locations near the Kanehsatake/Oka region. A 78-day stand-off ended after several military raids. The 34 arrested Mohawks were acquitted on all charges ranging from weapons possession and assault to participating in a riot.

When national integration is threatened and social order is disturbed, the dominant communication channels become the mediated centre exercising centripetal forces. While invoking the fear of social disorder, a sense of foreignness based on racial stigmatization is also reinforced. 'They', the Mohawks, were no longer part of the Canadian 'us' because 'they' threatened 'our' security and became outlaws. In addition, 'they', the barbaric, posed a violent threat to national identity (peaceful and tolerant Canadians), territorial integrity (denial of the national boundary), and economic prosperity (the proposed golf course and condominiums).

In Donna Goodleaf's analysis of the Kanehsatake/Oka crisis, one of the centripetal forces in use was to racialize Mohawks as savage extremists. We read headlines in the *Montreal Gazette* informing us that 'Warriors Hold 6,000 Guns, $30 Million in Coffers'; 'Homes behind Barricades Looted: Mohawk'; 'Police Union Warns Quebec: Let Us Act or We'll Put Out: Fed-Up Sûreté Officers Want Army to Move in and Arrest "Terrorist" Mohawks and Rioters' (Goodleaf, 1995: 67). In this context a national media event re-invoked the colonial legacy of racial fear and governing violence against an indigenous people, and legitimated the expropriation of indigenous land.

To reinforce the centripetal forces, the textual discourse regarding the dangerous, centrifugal Mohawks was buttressed by visual images of 'radicals' in army-like uniforms. This is in contrast to images of harmonious and spiritual native Canadians in other national images about a benevolent, united Canada. Overall, linking the Aboriginal with violence and criminality is not something new. It has been a pattern used repeatedly to discredit Aboriginal people and their demands in national media events for some time. This journalistic tactic serves the national interests by reinforcing 'old and deeply imbedded notions of "Indians" as alien, unknowable and ultimately a threat to civil order' (*Royal Commission on Aboriginal Peoples*, 1996: 5).

For Bakhtin, the above discourse framing the event is **monological**. It is the manner in which one 'does not recognize someone else's thought, someone else's idea, as an object of representation. In such a world everything ideological falls into two categories . . . a thought is either affirmed or repudiated; otherwise it ceases to be a fully valid thought' (Bakhtin, 1984b: 80). Monological discourse, propelled by a centripetal force around a homogeneous void, seeks to shut down any possible response from the receiver. Simply put, in monological discourse, one refuses to see oneself in the light of the other. One assumes the possession of a fully valid thought that gives finality without anticipating rejoinders. This leaves national media events open to dispute, given that the immediate interest in social order and integration through shared values and norms may well be overshadowed by coercion and domination.

As Robert Harding (2006) points out, Canadian media in the past decade has had a tendency to report on Aboriginal issues from the viewpoint of dominant national interests, although the news reportage is not totally homogeneous. Though mainstream journalists show some sympathy for indigenous rights, there were some dissenting views in national newscasts, alternative channels were set up for Aboriginal voices, and the public showed a certain resistance against racist and stereotypical media framings and interpretations. To follow Bakhtin, these factors are the centrifugal forces of differences spinning away from the centre of national discourses and representations. It thus becomes a constant struggle between two forces over the definition of who belongs, whose history counts, and how national memory is invoked. Before considering how national media respond to centrifugal forces, notably the multicultural reality, we continue to examine how pan-Canadian nationalism is imaged and constructed out of an **absent nation** against American imperial encroachment.

English Canada: A Mediated Absent Nation

In this part of the discussion, we consider how the centripetal force of English-Canadian national media creates an absent nation. That Canada shares a border and common language and culture with the United States challenges the sense of Canadian-ness and makes its claim to national distinctiveness somewhat confusing when examined in the context of the approach we have developed so far. We have argued elsewhere that English Canadians have little or no sense of national identity as a separate community. In the official culture of English Canada, there has been a struggle to develop 'a symbolic order that would allow an imaginary sense of "the Canada". . . [which] has yet to achieve that goal in any homogeneous sense. The base continues to reside in anti-Americanism, a kind of identity by default of what one is not . . .' (Nielsen and Jackson, 1991: 283). To put it another way, if there is any communal sense of an English Canada, we argue that it is 'almost always defined negatively and almost always measured against the United States, as in earlier years it was measured against British culture' (Nielsen and Jackson, 1991: 283). For instance, it might be a shared personal experience among English-Canadian travellers to attach a Canadian flag to luggage. This is most likely motivated by the need to signal a non-American identity, given minor or indistinguishable differences in the accent and the similar values and lifestyles of English Canadians and Americans. If we understand this lived personal experience it is not difficult to understand the same demand in Canadian culture industries' search for national identity. In this case, if national identity is categorical, it is established by social actions as struggles against others.

As mentioned, when media function as a state project of nation building, they become the engine of official policies and institutionalize a social imaginary that potentially brings peoples together. Media establish a common societal culture, build solidarity, and generate political cohesion. The idea of *one* Canada or *one* Canadian national culture is thus constructed and perceived to be an entity above differentiations of peoples, multiple nations, and various regional differences.

Will Kymlicka (1998) argues that despite the fiction of a one Canada, there is an advantage in lacking a strong sense of what English Canada is: for example, by not resorting to primordial elements, it avoids ethnocultural nationalism in association with xenophobia, exclusion, war, and hatred against external and internal foreigners. To put it another way, English Canada does not perceive itself as one linguistic or ethnic nation reproduced through a particular ethnonational culture and identity. It bypasses bloody internal conflicts in the pursuit of ethnic purity, and it avoids eradicating minorities in the search for totality. If we follow Arjun Appadurai's ideas (2006), an absent nation is not a likely source of frustration or enragement leading to a complete exclusiveness or predatory nationalism to ease the anxiety of incompleteness or about achieving 100 per cent ethnic purity. Pan-Canadian nationhood is not based on blood or descent, nor is it based on some heroic or glorious national character.

The pan-Canadian nationalist discourse, produced, institutionalized, and essentialized out of a void, is problematic. It over-centralizes common interests for English Canadians, such as by using English everywhere, maximizing

During the very early years of broadcasting in Canada the national mandate was clearly stated by Prime Minister R.B. Bennett upon the formation of the Canadian Radio Broadcasting Commission, the precursor to the CBC/SRC, in 1932: 'This country must be assured of complete Canadian control of broadcasting from Canadian Sources. Without such control, broadcasting can never be the agency by which national consciousness may be fostered and sustained and national unity still further strengthened.' (*Report of the Task Force on Broadcasting Policy*, 1986: 6) employment opportunities, and exercising political power coast-to-coast at the expense of recognizing other national aspirations, notably those of Québec and Aboriginal peoples. 'Because of their numerical superiority, English-speaking Canadians can afford to focus on a pan-Canadian community, forsaking any direct institutional expression of their linguistic community' (Webber, 1994, quoted in Kymlicka, 1998: 158). In other words, it tends to reduce multiplicity in the Canadian population to some single criterion as if they were the most crucial characters, overriding differences among national or regional aspirations. We turn to an example from the CBC program *Little Mosque on the Prairie*, to demonstrate this negligence or imbalance.

Little Mosque on the Prairie

The federal policy of *one Canada* allows no alternative imagination of another nation created or mediated by cultural institutions. Out of this national imagination, as we already saw at the beginning of the chapter, Radio-Canada is, after all, the French-language network of the CBC, and the CBC is the English network of Radio-Canada. This is especially evident in the imbalanced media representation between the central and the regional. More importantly, the national discourse centralized around the void is politically defined against the United States. For instance, the official discourse distinguishes Canada from the United States by its assumed greater tolerance for racial and ethnic differences, and there are indeed fewer gated communities, less racial segregation, and less discrimination against visible minorities. Television programs like *Little Mosque on the Prairie*, which is aired on CBC, are produced to showcase Canadian differences from Americans in terms of race and ethnicity. The show was picked up for a second season at the last minute after it received attention and interest from the United States. It was unique for Americans at the time to make fun of Muslims, and it consequently meant a huge success for the CBC production. The survival and success of this show is symptomatic of English Canada's acting and defining itself as an absent nation against the United States. To put it another way, such programs are produced and continue to thrive on American attention and the internal demand to distinguish Canada from the United States.

It should be noted that, after a short first season, the production unit was pulled away from the barely 10-year-old Regina studios and from its proximity to the fictional Saskatchewan town in which the comedy was set. Like most of the CBC programs, *Little Mosque on the Prairie* is now produced in Toronto. The actors have no prairie accents and the Muslims look more like folks from central Ontario. Even if one of the CBC mandates is to represent different regions and to fulfill regional demands, this type of programming is created out of a national discourse that only imagines what the differences are in the peripheral regions and simulates an image of multicultural integration.

Simply put, this CBC program exemplifies the imbalance between the central and the regional in the national media. In response to the strong cultural and political American presence and the negation of what Americans are not, the act of promoting a Canadian official culture *qua* multiculturalism is a way of defining what national sovereignty is, but it ironically subsumes, absorbs, excludes, or represses lived multicultural experiences. As a result, the public here, which the public broadcaster serves, is constructed in the service of a nation-building project. Simultaneously, the very diversity and fluidity of local cultures are lost in the official reproduction.

Céline Dion

Céline Dion, a Francophone singer from Québec, serves as a good example of how pan-Canadian discourse for an absent nation is constructed in English-Canadian media. Dion emerged as an international pop icon in the 1990s, and has frequently been in the media focus ever since. It was the same decade in when the failed constitutional negotiations at Meech Lake would have fulfilled majority wishes in Québec, and when the 1995 Québec referendum threatened Canadian unity.

While the centripetal construction of one homogeneous Canada was no longer sustainable due to a mutual sense of discontent in Québec and the rest of Canada, the English-Canadian press took a strong federal approach, reporting events in ways that affirmed unity and favoured centralization, calling for more authority to be vested in the federal government. This tendency was evident in the framing of personal stories about public figures like Céline Dion. Simultaneously, in 1990, Dion's album *Unison* was released and went double platinum in a short period of time. She then quickly became a pop diva following a successful packaging on the international stage. Her popularity gained considerable media attention and presented a perfect occasion for advocacy of national unification. In other words, Dion's popular media events were compounded by the conflicted media events around Canada-Québec relations.

We can read passages of a binary pro-unity framing of sovereignty versus federalism in the following passage: 'While it might be a bit much to lay on the young lady's shoulders, she's just what this pained country needs right now' (North, 1991, quoted in Young, 2001: 650–1). Dion's concert performances and political statements about her personal political preference for Canadian federalism were appropriated by the English press for the advantage of the existing political arrangement in Canada. In contrast, her political stance in favour of federalism was a source of upset for Québec nationalism, because it seemed that the favoured daughter of the nation was ignoring Québec's aspiration for societal distinctiveness and sovereignty association

Dion refused to be Anglophone artist of the year with respect to the Félix awards from the Association québécoise de l'industrie du disque, du spectacle et de la vidéo in 1992, and claimed to be both Canadian and Québécoise. In response to her identity claims, 'A Vocal Appeal for Unity', an article in the widely circulated English-language magazine *Maclean's*, failed to articulate the multiple interpretations of the Québécois identity or the complex double identifications of both Canada and Québec. The article framed and simplified Dion's statement by insisting 'but now . . . Dion favours a "united Canada"' (*Maclean's*, 13 July 1992, quoted in Young, 2001: 653). When Dion collaborated with the Anglophone singer Bryan Adams, it was interpreted by the Canadian Press as 'sing[ing] the praises of Canadian unity' or 'doing her bit for national unity'. Examples such as this were abundant in the 1990s, although Dion had publicly refused to associate her work and performances with any political intent (Canadian Press, 1992: A3, quoted in Young, 2001: 652).

Multicultural Framing: Common Memories and National Histories

To this point we have focused on how framing national media events inevitably is a struggle and negotiation between centripetal and centrifugal forces. To ensure social order and national cohesion, we discussed how a dominant national discourse plays out in national media events that either conceal the governing violence or distinguish external/internal others out of the nation-building exercise. This might already challenge our impression of Canada as an open, peaceful country that welcomes immigrants, pioneers multicultural policy, and promotes strong integration. Indeed, the official policy, the 1988 Multiculturalism Act, entails four general objectives: (1) to support the cultural development of ethnocultural communities, (2) to help members of ethnocultural communities to fully participate in Canadian society, (3) to encourage and promote creative and meaningful exchanges among members of all ethnocultural communities, and (4) to assist new Canadians in acquiring one of the official languages (English and French). Multiculturalism is considered by the Canadian government to be 'a sociological fact of Canadian life' (http://www.parl.gc.ca/information/library).

Canada has been one of the leading countries in the world with regard to multicultural policy. It has also avoided the xenophobic wars and conflicts witnessed elsewhere in the world. As a response to the pressures of and demands for immigration, Canada made the multicultural policy official to ensure integration into common institutions, participation in common societal cultures, and the cultivation of common identities and solidarity. Multiculturalism thus is a distinctive state project and is considered by the federal government to be a cornerstone of social equality, political cohesion, and democratic participation. This is particularly important to balance the centrifugal forces of existing differences driven by involuntary national minorities, including

Québécois and Aboriginals, and by voluntary or semi-voluntary groups with no significant institutional power to refuse integration, including refugees and immigrants. To achieve multiculturalism, national media institutions, especially public broadcasters, are also required to revise the framing of national history and the invocation of public memory because they traditionally entail racist or colonialist overtones.

The problem is that multiculturalism still advantages the dominant group and exercises exclusion when attacks are made on the 'building *one* Canada' project. The extent to which the Canadian state does not officially recognize multi-nationhood, by respecting the demands of national minorities for their distinctive cultural and linguistic differences from English Canada, means that multiculturalism is problematic. As Kymlicka puts it ,'[n]ational identity is something that people feel, and if some people do not feel that they belong to an English-speaking nation within Canada, then there's no point in telling them that they should' (1998: 165). If the integration into Canadian society is at the cost of members of the ethnocultural groups' capacity to reproduce specific cultural, religious, and linguistic practices after one or two generations, cultural differences will be stripped of multiculturalism. Simply put, we risk creating multiculturalism without cultures.

The construction of public media under the official guideline of multiculturalism shows the above problems as another dilemma of national media in Canada: *the dilemma of building one Canada couched in the language of diversity and integration*. We might see more media representation of Aboriginals or ethnic minorities, or we might even start to have some journalists on TV who speak English or French with foreign accents. Nevertheless, it continues to be problematic when the inclusion of differences and minorities is routinely undertaken through the framing techniques of racialization, misrepresentation, deflection, de-contextualization, and tokenism. In other words, simply gaining more visibility in national media does not guarantee an understanding and respect for differences.

National history, as a source of collective identity, is bound to discourses of national memory and is rewritten and organized by the media and other public institutions. The demand for national history responds not only to the need for nation (re)building but also to the demands for deeper cultural and psychological nourishment. In other words, history and tradition are to be not only found or inherited but also constructed or reproduced. Public television is one of the most important cultural institutions for recreating the lost link and mediating new ties among historical events, current policy orientations, and future national development. In other words, re-enacting an historical event is not only a way of responding to contemporary problems regarding the claims of nationhood, but is also a means to express hopes and fears for the future. In addition, memories can only be brought alive through communication. Without dissemination and communication in words, images, or sounds, past events cannot be remembered and stored in the public memory through which identities are articulated and contested.

The special live broadcast of Remembrance Day ceremonies in Ottawa every 11 November is not simply about remembering Canadian soldiers in past wars. It responds to current demands, seeks national support for Canadian soldiers overseas, and gives an interpretation of history that is contemporary as a result. Dominant discourses about remembrance and history determine the cultural expression and narrative of the past in national media events. Therefore, Canadian participation in the Second World War is honoured on Remembrance Day as a particular yet repetitive occasion to integrate heroism into Canadian nationalism. Remembrance Day as a media event includes broadcasting special ceremonies and recounting war stories, interwoven with living or fallen Canadian soldiers and their contribution to world peace. These are ways of constructing pan-Canadian identity around the ideal of a just and peace-loving nation. They therefore serve as centripetal forces of Canadian nationalism in seeking national pride and solidarity. National media events as such become a symbolic representation of a special community and a foundation for collective identity through conveying certain implicit or explicit messages and values. To follow Simon Cottle (2006), ceremonies broadcasted nation-wide are mediatized rituals that intend to serve, sustain, and mobilize collective sentiments and solidarities. However, whether the purposes of social order and integration succeed depends on whether the audiences voluntarily participate and share the same sentiments and solidarities at the same time. It should be noted that national discourse built around the invocation of shared memories and facilitated by historical media events does not guarantee the success of a homogeneous national consensus or unity. For instance, Remembrance Day is not a history of pride or glory but a reminder of pain and injustice for Japanese Canadians. Because of their ethnic origins, despite generations of immigration history, Japanese Canadians' full citizenship was denied, and they were rendered into internal foreigners and enemies under strict surveillance during that same war in the name of national security. November 11 is a day to remember not only heroism but also the racialization of Japanese Canadians.

We also use docudrama to deepen our understanding of the struggles and debates inherent in mediated historical events. As Tobias Ebbrecht (2007) argues, a recent form of recounting history in television is the docudrama. It combines documentary and feature film narratives to reformulate historical events and to replace the classical historical television documentary. In a ritualistic and event-specific mode, the docudrama produces, organizes, stores, and, to a large extent, homogenizes public memory. Consequently, it serves as a vehicle to shape historical consciousness in a less dogmatic or pedagogical manner and is fashionably considered to be an ideal facilitator of national memory. History in the docudrama is no longer something frozen in the past, but animated as both entertainment and an 'historical event-television'

(Ebbrecht, 2007: 221). In other words, unlike media events that have happened to us, such as natural disasters or political events, the preplanned program/media event is organized by the media institutions themselves. Unlike ceremonial media events, historical event television is less formal or ritualistic. Unlike conflicted media events that have to mediate moral panic or public crises in an immediate fashion, the manufactured historical media event already enjoys the hindsight of how panic or crises could be resolved.

It is, however, problematic that designing audio-visual events of public memory can easily create an uneasiness when memories are recreated, reanimated, and circulated constantly and repeatedly. Collectively shared versions of history in the docudrama can be easily reified between the real and the imaginary, between factual knowledge and subjective memories, between history and its simulation, and between memory and national appropriation. It especially becomes problematic when media mix stereotypes and second-hand historical materials with cultural policy. In part, reification or stereotyping is inevitable because television and the docudrama reduce complexity and ambiguity in history and memories in order to assure the entertaining component and to captivate audiences' emotional resonances through intensified, sensual viewing experiences. Storytelling of national history as such also needs the emotional effects of dramatization, given the limited amount of show time. Ebbrecht argues that 'these broadcasting events work with a kind of popular history-telling, and use aesthetic and dramatic methods intended to guarantee audience ratings' (2007: 224). The docudrama thus relies on 'an attractive combination of fast cuts, dialectics of color and black-and-white footage, dramatic music, an aura of authenticity, and a compelling narrative framework delivered in short, distinguished sound bites' (Ebbrecht, 2007: 226). In short, history is revived through a combination of fiction, personal stories, experiences, and testimonies and is set in a larger historical event method of historical authentication and visual and audio conventions of images and imagination.

Two CBC docudrama series show us how history and memories can be turned into media events by writing a national history through the invocation of public memories. In the following section, we demonstrate a recent normalizing effort presented in national public media by rewriting the official memory and history of Canada in the language of multiculturalism and in the context of a search for a new Canadian identity following the 1995 Québec referendum.

The *Heritage Minutes* and *A People's History*

The CBC and SRC productions of *Heritage Minutes* and *Canada: A People's History* exemplify the docudrama as a genre of national discourse on television. The former refers to a collection of 60-second short films produced and broadcast since 1991. Each short film introduces an important moment in Canadian history. The latter refers to two seasons of docudrama about Canadian people broadcast between 2000 and 2001. As Emily West argues, these programs take on 'an undeniable ideological and political position—that Canada is one nation, sea to shining sea, and it ought to stay that way' (2002: 213). Nevertheless, while the public broadcasters follow the official policy of multiculturalism, '[t]he balance act in these productions is between the representations of diversity and unity—not a challenge unique perhaps to Canada—but one that seems particularly precarious in a nation where the future shape of the country is an issue never far from the top of the political agenda' (West, 2002: 213). In other words, these programs are the site where the representations of the past, the selection of national memories, and the current federalist agenda are carefully crafted and interwoven in order to avoid alienating viewers of different backgrounds and to show that diversity is possible in a unified Canada. On the one hand, these programs are made as both history and entertainment without giving the impression that a homogeneous national history is being fabricated or imposed on viewers. On the other hand, they are explicitly produced in a defence of *one Canada* against various internal and external threats from the tensions between Canada and America, Canada and Québec, and the federal and provincial governments, or simply from globalization. 'While political negotiations, dialogues and agreements fall apart, constructing national, collective memory provides a solution for holding a nation-state together' (Quill, 1995, quoted in West, 2002: 217).

The producers of *Canada: A People's History* intended to fill the gap in collective memories and to ensure that Canadian history can also be exciting (West, 2002: 215). To redress the impression that Canadian history is dull and banal, or to satisfy the hunger for 'our' stories, the program producers point the finger at educators and historians in the past who failed to do their jobs properly in telling how Canadian history can be full of powerful stories with 'vibrancy, surprises and humanity' (West, 2002: 215).

Aiming at linking historical events, public memory, and national identity through a conventional mode of storytelling that guarantees the excitement of Canadian history, Patrick Watson, the producer of the *Heritage Minutes*, claims it is necessary to engage viewers, especially the younger ones, by producing Canadian history in the mode of drama-like movies. This mode of presenting national history and public memory is simultaneously an effort to dilute the intention of the program objectives while continuing to emphasize the possibility of seeing Canada as more than the sum of different parts. Stereotyping and historical distortion take place when the historians' participation is minimized in favour of the maximized journalistic approach toward the docudrama. These programs claim to construct an authoritative account of Canadian history, but emphasize a form of journalism while working with historical materials.

Summary

In this chapter, we examined the framing of national media events and the process of creating a mediated centre of national cohesion in nation-wide media, notably public broadcasting. With various Canadian examples and different genres of media events, we pointed to national media events as the sites of struggle and negotiation between the centripetal forces of homogeneity and the centrifugal forces of heterogeneity within and beyond national boundaries.

Through juxtaposing theoretical arguments with empirical examples from the conflicted media event of the Oka crisis to the media creation of historical memories in *Heritage Minutes* and *A People's History*, we further discussed that the inevitable struggles and negotiation in national media events generate paradox and ambiguity. On the one hand, they meet the demands for national identity and integration and entail the possibility of democratic dialogical exchanges. On the other hand, the governing violence of state authority or the need to fill the void of an absent nationhood through exercising centripetal forces can bring negative results. Here we referred to the imbalance between the national centre and the periphery, and the non- or mis-recognition of multinational and multicultural lifeworlds. In other words, the interests of state authority are equally present in the construction of media events as reality in maintaining the interests of the status quo and power relations.

Enhanced Learning Activities

1. Consider the 'Canadian Broadcasting Mandate' and multicultural policy. In this context, what are ritual media events? Consider how they are implicated in the framing of the Canada Day ceremony in Ottawa.
2. Explain the sources of paradox and ambiguity in national media events. What are centrifugal and centripetal forces in national media events? Use the media reportage on the Vancouver Olympics as an example to distinguish the paradox and centripetal/centrifugal forces to elaborate your points.
3. What is an absent nation? What are advantages and disadvantages of an absent nation? Select three or four Canadian personalities and examine the way in which the media presents them through the conceptual tool of an absent nation.
4. Explain how national history and public memory are made into historical media events. How would you interpret an episode of *A People's History* through the understanding of docudrama and media-created history?

Annotated Further Reading

Daniel Dayan and Elihu Katz, *Media Events: The Live Broadcasting of History*. Cambridge, MA: Harvard University Press, 1992. This book pioneers the study of media events and establishes media events as an important genre of mass communication. By resorting to theoretical traditions of sociology and discourse analysis, Dayan and Katz analyze important, 'historic' events such as John F. Kennedy's funeral, the moon landing, and the Olympic Games. From today's perspective, this book continues to be instructive in examining the character of **ritual media events** and their roles as a force of social integration.

Will Kymlicka, *Finding Our Way: Rethinking Ethnocultural Relations in Canada*. Toronto: Oxford University Press Canada, 1998. Following his influential work *Multicultural Citizenship*, Kymlicka provides a balanced analysis of the advantages, problems, and potentials of Canadian multicultural policy. He also considers the Québec–Canada, First Nations–Canada questions along with various ethnocultural differences as a positive challenge to pioneer an advanced model of the liberal nation-state. The concepts and examples provide useful sociological tools for the critique of multinational framing in Canadian communication channels and media products.

Greg M. Nielsen and John D. Jackson, 'Cultural Studies, a Sociological Poetics: Institutions of the Canadian Imaginary', *Canadian Review of Sociology and Anthropology* 28, no. 2 (1991): 280–2. In this article, Nielsen and Jackson make a forceful argument about the Canadian imaginary out of English Canada as an absent nation. They discuss how such a national imaginary shapes public broadcasting mandates, and in turn is shaped by public broadcasting products. This article provides insights into the inherent paradox and ambiguity in the multicultural framing of Canadian media events.

Simon Cottle, 'Mediatized Rituals: Beyond Manufacturing Consent', *Media, Culture & Society* 28, no. 2: 411–32. In this article, Cottle challenges the common assumption that the framing and outcomes of media events successfully serve national cohesion or social collectivity. Through a detailed classification, Cottle argues that media events of rituals and ceremonies are less consensual and less unifying, and open up the space of political subversion and enactment. He also pinpoints 'the ritual paradox' that it only serves the purpose of cohesion and integration when the audiences volunteer themselves for the making of collective identities, sentiments, and aspirations within the mediatized rituals.

Useful Media

A People's History (CBC)

This CBC series exemplifies national docudrama and its specific goal for Canadian unity under the framework of multiculturalism. It also helps us consider the dramatization and eventization of history.

Remembrance Day and the Canada Day Ceremonies in Ottawa (videos can be found on YouTube)
These video clips epitomize the intertwined relations among broadcasting, patriotism, and nation (re)building in a ritualized setting of the media event.

Myths for Profit: Canada's Role in Industries of War and Peace (2009). Director: Amy Miller.
This documentary shows how the Canadian reputation in foreign affairs is questionable and how we can take a critical approach toward Canadian identity as an international peacemaker.

Little Mosque on the Prairie (CBC)
This television series demonstrates the unbalanced representations and relations between the central and the peripheral, and between Toronto, the Canadian media centre, and the Prairies, a marginalized media zone.

8

Urban Media Events: Toronto and Montreal Case Studies[1]

Learning Objectives

- To identify the intersection between global, national, and urban levels of mediated society
- To define roles of urban newspapers and seriocomedy mediums
- To learn how national media in Canada and Québec shape cities like Montreal and Toronto, and how urban media help shape national cultures
- To understand the deconstruction of the 'normal' sense of the nation in urban case studies
- To consider newspaper coverage of forced mergers in Toronto and Montreal through seriocomedy in both cities

Introduction

Whereas global and national media events are often situated in cities, both their real and implied audiences are situated beyond the urban region. Many urban media events don't imply audiences beyond the local and yet are often framed by national divisions and global forces. This chapter provides a deconstruction of how local *urban media events* in Toronto and Montreal intersect with global forces and national divisions. We focus on a comparative social and cultural analysis of two archival case studies. The first includes a study of debate in newspapers from both cities over pleas for greater urban democratic participation versus more economic efficiency and global competitiveness. The second case includes a study of how popular national seriocomedies in English and French refer to the two cities and how each contradicts what the other perceives as 'normal' for the nation. These are drawn from the long-running radio series *The Royal Canadian Air Farce* (1972–96) and the celebrated year-end Radio-Canada television review *Le Bye Bye* (1968–98). Comparison of the two cities through the case studies helps reveal how media events provide a sense of order and disorder in the city out of the intersection with global forces and internal national divisions.

We first place the sense of order and disorder in the two cities within the larger contexts of English-speaking Canada and French-speaking Québec. Second, we situate the seriocomic differences between Montreal and Toronto in the national institutions of public broadcasting. Each step reveals that each city has a way of imagining the other that is mutually supportive and negating. As in all binary oppositions, one side cannot help but refer to the other for its own definition. For example, as discussed in Chapter 7, the simple naming of 'Canada' and 'Québec' can be understood as a binary opposition that puts into question the sense of a 'normal' imaginary nation when one is examined from the point of view of the other. A similar sense of the undecidable can also be heard in naming Toronto and Montreal and comparing their oppositions.

The difficulty of comparing the two cities is added to by constructing them out of two case studies that draw on different media and languages. Thus, before proceeding, we offer some definitions of each medium and provide further context for the selection of examples. Discourse analysis of the radio and television seriocomedies is then presented in the sections 'Toronto and the Absent Nation' and 'Montreal and the Absent Region'. The following sections, 'Amalgamation Debates' and 'Crossover Voices', provide a similar reading of letters to the editor and feature articles from newspapers concerning national and local urban democracy references in each city. After comparing representations of urban media events from the two cities as well as their different ways of imagining themselves and each other, we conclude that deconstructing urban media events means finding out a level of undesirability that refuses each side's claim to any singular sense of belonging.

Seriocomedy, Newspapers, and the Well-Ordered City

Seriocomedy provides countries around the world with relatively inexpensive entertainment in a voice and accent that expresses cultures of laughter in local communities, and often in ways that confirm or transgress complex political and moral issues. The seriocomedy genre includes a variety of poetic devices that converge or bring into collision the serious and the comic; critique the traditional from the point of view of the contemporary; ironically reverse social, linguistic, and bodily hierarchies; clash and fuse accents, different vernaculars, and speech genres; and address aspects of the human condition that range from the darkest, most cynical, and acerbic to the most light-hearted, mindless, and silly (Bakhtin, 1984a, 1984b). Examples of seriocomedy with a global range of audiences can be seen in the earliest feature-length slapstick stick comedies of Charlie Chaplin and the Marx Brothers to current farce like Borat, from the late-night talk show format to YouTube and accessible television magazines like *Saturday Night Live* or *The Daily Show*. Seriocomedies typically employ satirical treatments of current popular icons that both reproduce and sometimes create cultures of laughter. A culture of laughter is defined here as a set of values and norms that shape a strong sense of 'we' that anticipates a response from all those who belong or do not belong in an image associated with a particular emotional attitude.

While radio, television, film, and Internet-accessible seriocomedies are more recent media, seriocomedy has its origins in the oldest urban genres in the history of the culture of laughter (Frye, 1962). Newspapers perform many of the same tasks as seriocomedies without the poetic devices, and in so doing provide other kinds of outlets for deliberation over disputes about the common sense of the 'we' within democratic publics. Democracy comes from the Greek word *demos* and means rule by the 'people'. Newspapers are among the oldest urban mass media and are also considered to have played a major part in the production of the modern imaginary nation and its citizenship. Yet newspapers are often overlooked in urban studies, which tend to focus more on concrete spaces, policy issues of governance and regulation, leadership and resource mobilization, or the impact of new transmission technologies.

Today, newspaper industries are enjoying robust growth in India, China, and Latin America, while in post-industrial areas such as Canada, the US, and Europe, a pessimism about the future economic viability and civic role of newspapers has been spreading at the same time as overall revenues have actually had modest increases (WAN, 2008). The lack of consensus about the future viability of the newspaper and its role in providing outlets for debate on public issues about citizenship is rooted in pressures that include deregulation and increased corporate media concentration, convergence of different media platforms (e.g., Internet, television, other print media), shifting advertising revenue streams toward new media, audience fragmentation, citizen journalism (blogging without editorial control), the fusion of news and entertainment, the disproportionate role that the public relations industry plays in the generation of news stories, and the still limited range of voices granted the opportunity to speak through mainstream media (Deuze, 2007; Silverstone, 2007; Palmer, 2000; Bird, 1997).

As we saw in Chapter 1, well-known media activists have long charged mainstream journalism with the facile 'exchange of truth for access to power' (Goodman and Goodman, 2006), but today even mainstream journalists question the ability of the press to fulfill its public service ideal and articulate the multiple and often contradictory voices of citizenship in **civil society** (Kovach and Rosenstiel, 2007). As we also saw in the chapter on new media, the question is not only what are the economic and political forces that drive new media, but also how old media adapt to new environments. The figures in the table below on US and Canadian circulation 'join a list of indicators . . . that, after years of slipping, have accelerated sharply downward. Through the 1990s and into this decade, newspaper circulation was sliding, but by less than 1 percent a year. Then the rate of decline topped 2 percent in 2005, 3 percent in 2007 and 4 percent in 2008' (Perez-Pena, 2009: B3).

Newspapers as well as radio and television seriocomedies have nonetheless endured as fields of urban cultural reproduction, partly because of their capacity to adapt themselves to any city and form of governance and partly because their basic ingredient, the critique of the traditional from the point of view of the contemporary (or vice versa), remains intact as their own institutions continue to evolve. By studying radio and television seriocomedies that discuss or satirize global forces and the sense of the nation in the city, and by examining debates over local democracy in newspapers side by side in Toronto and Montreal, we can see how mediated society sociologically actively establishes varying levels of ordered normality.

National Public Broadcasting of the Cultures of Urban Laughter

Given that the CBC and Radio-Canada (SRC) have been centred in Toronto and Montreal, the question becomes: what are some of the media events that have most exemplified the urban culture of laughter provided by the seriocomedy genre? The distinction between serious and popular radio comedy has its origins in ancient forms, as noted above. However, it should be pointed out that the carnival or rural influences on seriocomic laughter are heavily concentrated on grotesque elements and on reference to the lower bodily stratum. Urban comedy also begins in this corporal region, but the emergence of mass audiences and electronic media would initially at least become more focused on the 'upper bodily stratum'.

From the 1930s through the 1940s and 1950s, CBC radio satire presented a light version of seriocomic laughter in the sense that there remained words

TABLE 8.1 Top 25 U.S. Newspapers' Average Weekday Paid Circulation

Rank	Newspaper	Circulation as of March '09	% Change (Year over Year)
1	USA Today	2,113,725	-7.5
2	Wall Street Journal	2,082,189	0.6
3	New York Times	1,039,031	-3.6
4	Los Angeles Times	723,181	-6.6
5	Washington Post	665,383	-1.2
6	New York Daily News	602,857	-14.3
7	New York Post	558,140	-20.6
8	Chicago Tribune	501,202	-7.5
9	Houston Chronicle	425,138	-14.0
10	Arizona Republic	389,701	5.7
11	Denver Post	371,728	N/A
12	Newsday	368,194	-3.0
13	Dallas Morning News	331,907	-9.9
14	Minneapolis Star Tribune	320,076	-0.7
15	Chicago Sun-Times	312,141	-0.04
16	San Francisco Chronicle	312,118	-15.7
17	Boston Globe	302,638	-13.7
18	Cleveland Plain Dealer	291,630	-11.7
19	Detroit Free Press	290,730	-5.9
20	Philadelphia Inquirer	288,298	-13.7
21	Newark Star-Ledger	287,082	-16.8
22	St. Petersburg Times	283,093	-10.4
23	Oregonian	268,512	-11.8
24	Atlanta Journal-Constitution	261,828	-19.9
25	San Diego Union-Tribune	261,253	9.5

Canadian Total Circulation: Traditional

Average number of copies sold per publishing day			
2008 Total Circulation		2007 Total Circulation	
98 Newspapers	4,295,238	99 Newspapers	4,674,900

Percentage Difference -8.1%

Circulation in Competitive Markets: Traditional

	Average number of copies sold per publishing day		
	2008	2007	% Change
Toronto	1,031,601	1,203,235	-14. 2%
Montreal	620,640	661,900	-6.2%
Vancouver	342,528	318,255	+7.6%
Ottawa-Gatineau	203,762	215,674	-5.5%
Edmonton	177,225	193,164	-8.3%
Quebec	175,422	191,015	-8.2%
Calgary	171,433	185,029	-7.3%
Winnipeg	159,469	165,396	-3.6%
Sherbrooke	37,853	38,543	-1.8%

Source: Canadian Newspaper Association 2008 circulation data report

that could not be uttered, comic reversals that could not be achieved, and levels of laughter that could never be expressed. This atmosphere had changed somewhat by the 1960s, when conventions were expanded and became more permissive as a cultural shift began its transformation of the older order. By 1972 the main seriocomedy program for CBC radio in Toronto was the weekly half-hour series called the *Royal Canadian Air Farce* (Nielsen, 1999). Roger Abbott and Don Ferguson, two of the original members, were graduates of Montreal's Loyola College (later part of Concordia University) and came out of the late-1960s stand-up comedy scene in English-speaking Montreal—a background that would feed their political satires for 30 years. In its early years, the troupe was influenced by a mix of commercially orientated light comedies but also the more absurdist style of the very popular 1970s British comedy *Monty Python's Flying Circus*, as well as the American counterculture FM underground radio satire comedy *Firesign Theatre*. The *Air Farce* style grew from a wide mixture of the short sketch, stand-up comedy, English music hall, and theatre of the absurd.

Like the CBC in Toronto, Radio-Canada also came to take up a key symbolic national role in Montreal. As Germaine and Rose (2000) point out, a vision of Montreal as a media centre for French Québec and the Francophone world was conceived in the late 1950s by Jean Drapeau, then mayor of Montreal. He saw the development of a Cité des Ondes (City of the Airwaves) along with the new Place des Arts and Les Complexes Desjardins as a way to shift the centre of commerce eastward and away from the traditional westward-, English-leaning downtown core. The construction of the Radio-Canada Centre in Montreal was the first step in a futuristic vision that defined the city in terms of the new economies of telecommunications and, more recently, new media.

Québec's French-language urban laughter in a mass culture form also had its origins in radio during the 1930s (Pagé and Legris, 1979). Radio-Canada, headquartered in Montreal, has drawn talent from all over Québec and to a lesser extent from French-speaking regions across Canada since its birth in 1938, when the two networks first uncoupled (Nielsen, 1994). A standard theme across the history of Québec radio and television seriocomedy has to do with language. Social satires draw from the deep tension between traditional and modern culture through the ironic use of sub-dialects, local oral traditions, and regional accents. Language is stratified from top to bottom and is defined through a struggle between the peripheral forces of popular speech and the centralizing pull of literary correctness. Language stratification plays a key role in establishing a scale of satire that ranges from the serious to the light and that addresses audiences that are potentially both popular and scholarly. (Nielsen, 1999, 2008).

The *Le Bye Bye* year-end television series developed along the lines of earlier radio shows where the main cultural and political events of the year were treated to a seriocomic send-up. The two-hour year-end television review began in 1968 at the moment that the Quiet Revolution in Québec (a massive transference of power over civic welfare and education from the Church to the provincial government) became a *fait accompli*. The series stopped 20 years later in a context of Canadian constitutional malaise but was reborn shortly after and continues to cause controversy today. In its first decade, *Le Bye Bye* was considered as much political as cultural (Cusson, 2004).

We have been arguing that seriocomedies provide a culture of distinctly urban laughter that focuses on a stratification of languages and bodies, a critique of tradition from the point of view of the contemporary, and a mixture of language, accent, and dialect. In the next section, we continue to develop these formal characteristics through an analysis of various excerpts that directly refer to ways of imagining both Canada and Québec as distinct nations in the city. It is important to keep in mind that each city has served as metropolis for two different mediated societal cultures that have coexisted within one federal state. Here are two main points we have been making to keep in mind as we proceed:

- Public broadcasting organizations continue to produce complex national narratives about distinct cultures from within the vantage point of metropolitan centres.
- In mediated society the background tension of the nation in the city underlies overt disputes about local democracy and governance, even though such events do not always refer directly to the nation.

Toronto and the Absent Nation

Like prose and poetry, radio and television seriocomedy needs to be understood in terms of its place within the scale of possible comic expression that ranges from the serious to the light and whose reception often crosses the boundaries of the scholarly and the popular. Seriocomedy is a genre that pretends to expand the limits of what can be said or represented in a given imaginary structure at a given time through the use of irony, satire, and parody, but it is also a genre that can simply support popular prejudice. The structure for both *Le Bye Bye* and *Air Farce* are similar to that of other shows that stitch together four or five brief distinct skits in the form of fake reporting, talk or interview shows, dream or fantasy sequences, and any variety of satire on social or political situations. The genre is designed to reverse meanings and distance its author and listener from its subject through the use of irony or satire, which, along with parody, play on words, and jokes, institutes the mode in which laughter can be achieved.

A good example of the seriocomedy genre concerns how national representations of Toronto most often carry a negative image, reflecting how those from outside Toronto tend to perceive the city. Toronto is a city that Canadians love to hate. Does the negative national image of Toronto's chauvinism have anything to do with how Toronto imagines itself? Can such an image ever be completely mediated? Canada's view of Toronto and Toronto's view of its own diversity and cosmopolitan character can only ever be partially represented. Yet we can understand how Toronto is seen from the outside as both celebrated and debased and as though the city itself constitutes a culturally coherent whole in the following set of 1984 *Air Farce* fragments. The first one is a spoof on a rhyme recited before meetings of the Toronto City Council, while the second features a comic character familiar to Canadian audiences in the 1980s and 1990s:

> **December 9/84, Sketch B**: Toronto the beautiful / Toronto the great / Where piles of dough just grow and grow / For those who renovate / Toronto the Beautiful / A place that's full of freaks / Where most of the apartment blocks / Are owned by Arab Sheiks. . . .

> SERGENT RENFREW: When I got there the intersection was choked with traffic backed up for miles, and the people were insulting each other in seventeen languages. It was a perfectly normal Toronto afternoon.

We will have occasion to discuss the above example further in terms of interpreting the sense of chaos and loss of neighbourhood in the amalgamation debates, but first we want to consider another example of the seriocomic treatment of the relation of Toronto to Ontario and the rest of Canada and of the relation of Montreal to the province of Québec and the rest of North America. A slightly acerbic, rather than simply silly or ultra-light, definition of the two cities in relation to the larger societal cultures can be seen in this 1980 *Air Farce* sketch:

> **April 27/80, Sketch A**: Canada is divided . . . into ten wonderful provinces, loosely connected by fear. Quebec and Newfoundland do not seem Canadian: One has its own culture and a foreign language. The other is Quebec. Canada's population is composed of three main groups: native Canadians, naturalized citizens, and illegal immigrants. In some parts of Canada, the natives speak English, while in other parts the foreigners speak English. *Montreal* . . . Montreal has often been compared to Paris, although not favourably. It enjoys a reputation as an 'old world' city, but thanks to garbage strikes, municipal debt and criminal violence, it's quickly becoming known as a North American city. *Toronto* is quite different. The inhabitants are dedicated churchgoers, which is why every Sunday night all the topless bars and gay steam baths close at ten o'clock. Winnipeg is interesting because . . . uh . . . PAUSE.

The above was broadcast not long before the 1981 Québec referendum on sovereignty association. Imagining identities that can be recognized in both peripheral regions and metropoles like Montreal and Toronto creates ambiguous emotional tensions between the two. Part of the effect of producing narrative from metropolitan centres is the folklore image that is left on peripheral regions ('Winnipeg is interesting because . . . . uh . . . . '). At the same time, resentment from the regions fuels criticism against the cities of Toronto and Montreal, and this gets ironically absorbed in the bit. Similar kinds of stereotypical comedy that use reversed meanings to make fun of urban regions date back to the beginnings of radio. Although one does find examples that ironically present an image of Montreal as a French North American city, there are no examples before the 1970s that would use the image of Toronto as a city in transition from its staid Protestant past to its new, 'gay' future. Norms of sexual orientation were obviously as repressive in 1919 as they would be in 1950 (Marchessault, 2001). But in 1980 the deconstruction of these norms works and it works in part because cultures of laughter can, and often do, evolve in the city.

Comic deconstructions of identities like 'the Montrealer' and 'the Torontonian' are ways of answering the following questions: How does a collective identity get imagined in the first place and then how is it seen from different points of view? How far can we go in criticizing symbolic identities or how much of any identity can be contained within a symbol? And finally, what are the limits of what can be imagined and represented in an important sector of public life in the city, global region, and nation?

In reverse image from the French seriocomedy *Le Bye Bye*, *Air Farce* satirized the image of Montreal-French-Québécois from an English-speaking Toronto perspective for more than 30 years. On a world scale, we might say that Toronto sees itself as unique not only because of its actual existing cultural diversity, but for having achieved the transition toward a well-ordered multicultural city in record-breaking time. Montreal is also a multicultural city but is linguistically divided and a metropolis for a large national minority (Kymlicka, 1998; Legros, 2008). Canada's gaze on Montreal can easily be seen as a shared way of imagining largely because, despite regional differences within Canada, each region (excluding most of Québec and First Nations) has an ability to shape-shift, setting aside local differences to join in a consensus about a unified Canadian identity—especially if it is defined in its 'multiculturalness' and its difference from the American melting pot. The negative gaze on Montreal is embedded in the ethical and political collision over the individual rights defended by the Canadian Charter versus arguments for collective rights in Québec over language and access to schools and signage, and in a perceived rejection by Québec of Canadian multicultural policy (Angus, 1996).

The historical organization of national public institutions of radio and television also includes the development of **creative formations** and cultural audiences. It is interesting to note that while francophone Québec media audiences have been politically split over constitutional-type identity options for at least a generation (around 60 per cent for some version of political independence and 40 per cent for the status quo), in the main this has not been the case in English-speaking Montreal or the rest of Canada (Gagné and Langlois, 2002). The division over political options within the Francophone audience in part explains the relatively late arrival of similar kinds of seriocomedies like *Air Farce* and *This Hour Has 22 Minutes* in mainstream Québécois media (Robinson, 1998; Nielsen, 2004; Cusson and Nielsen, 2001; Saxon, Rocher, and Jackson, 2004). Much of English-speaking Montreal and most Canadian audiences outside Québec are united concerning constitutional identity options for Québec; thus political satire can count on a homogeneous audience response on a series of issues. *Air Farce* was among the first series to regularly show the serious negative political image that Montreal can have in 'English-speaking' Canada and to render comic the city at the centre of the controversy.

March 11/78, Sketch A: 'Moving from Montreal'

EDNA (whispered aside): Nicky, I thought you were going to get an English company to move us.

NICKY (whisper): There was only one left, and they were moving himself out. He even had to turn down Jean Chretien . . .

PIERRE: Hokay. Federstoneyhowz, we gonna move you, then. We thought you were maybe was one of those Anglaise rats leaving the sinking bateau.

NICKY/EDNA: Oh no! No!

NICKY: It's simply that I have to go where my job takes me. And by coincidence that happens to be Toronto.

PIERRE/GASTON: Oho! (FRENZIED MUMBLE, MILK AND EXTEND POSSIBLY. 'Welcome to Rosedale—kiss my ass.' ODD FRENCH WORD PUT-DOWN OF TORONTO.)

JAKE: (COMING ON) Hello! Hello! Oh hello, Nicky, Edna. In the midst of it I see. Finally getting out.

GASTON: (suspicious) Keep it up there, Pierre (REFERRING TO A BOX OF CHINA)

NICKY: Oh hello, Jake. (cautious) Well, you know how it is. When the company goes, you've got to go.

JAKE: Yes, well, you're fortunate being on the board of Sun Life.

GASTON: Hokay, Pierre! Let 'em go. SOUND: HORRENDOUS CRASH OF BOX OF CROCKERY BEING DASHED TO FLOOR.

EDNA: Oh no! —

JAKE: I knew it was coming of course, Nicky, the minute I heard you say, 'I've had this province right up to here.' It was where you put your hand that was significant . . . I say, the old drawers of wood and hewers of water are restless tonight. No, Nicky. I'd like to get out myself, but no matter how hard I try I can't budge the company . . . Hydro Québec are determined to stay and brazen it out. But we'll miss you, and your little tricks. Slashing René Lévesque's tires.

March 4/95, Sketch C: FRANCOPHONE

FRANCOPHONE: Oui, allo. I'm in favour of sovereignty. But it might hurt Quebec's economy. SOUND—TRAP DOOR CREAKS SLIGHTLY OPEN.

FRANCOPHONE: But it would ultimately be good for all Quebeckers. SOUND—DOOR CLOSES.

FRANCOPHONE: But it might cost us jobs. SOUND—CREAKS SLIGHTLY OPEN.

FRANCOPHONE: But it would preserve our culture. SOUND—SNAPS CLOSED.

FRANCOPHONE: But we might become isolated and inbred. SOUND—CREAKS OPEN.

FRANCOPHONE: But we wouldn't have federal government interference. SOUND—SNAPS CLOSED.

FRANCOPHONE: But we'd lose the benefit of federal social programs. SOUND—CREAKS OPEN.

FRANCOPHONE: But they could be replaced with our own social programs. SOUND—DOOR SNAPS CLOSED.

FRANCOPHONE: But then again. SOUND—TRAP DOOR SPRUNG OPEN.

FRANCOPHONE: (reverb going off) Ahhhhhhhhh!

CHAIRMAN: That guy was getting on my nerves. Who's next?

These *Air Farce* excerpts demonstrate a commonly held 'English-Canadian' way of imagining the nation in the city. 'English-speaking Canada' has not developed a capacity to imagine itself as a nation without Québec. It understands its profound difference from Montreal yet cannot see Québec as a nation on its own ('I've had this province right up to here'). As the Québec question shifted from 1978 to 1995, the argument was no longer the exodus from an intolerant Montreal to a very wealthy Toronto (Rosedale) but the contemporary background debate over individual ('But we might become isolated and inbred') and collective rights ('But it would ultimately be good for all') that continues to divide Quebeckers and Canadians. It is interesting to note that while the content of the representation shifts from the city to the national question, the normative horizon of expectation of the imaginary nation remains on the same even plane. Canadian radio and television seriocomedy provides examples of how two distinct societies look on one another's cities from within their own media. As they laugh at themselves and at each other, English- and French-language audiences are not aware of what it is the other is laughing about.

Amalgamation Debates: Normal Disorder of the City?

These are good seriocomic examples from which to step back and begin to interpret parallel references found in letters to the editor regarding serious political culture and how the cacophony of difference is interpreted concerning the opposition to legislated mergers or amalgamations in the two cities. Montreal is a city divided because of historical pulls and the tugs of forces that emerge from tensions between national majority and minority interests. While Toronto is not typically understood as a city at the historical centre of national politics, like Montreal, it is a city rich in cultural diversity and transnational diasporas and is defined by its own internal social divisions.

Although there is an important degree of similarity, most of the debates over amalgamation in Montreal (2001) and Toronto (1997) turned out to be over quite different issues. This indicates to us that legislated amalgamations in the two cities are not simply 'signs' of the globalization bulldozer's maximization of each city's economic efficiency at the risk of destroying distinct cultures. On the contrary, like the seriocomedy that we have just discussed, the debates over how to best govern the city are taken as emotional-volitional orientations within the city that clash over deep differences and struggles regarding the meaning of neighbourhood, community, and the 'common good'.

Most striking about newspaper reporting on the Toronto amalgamation as compared to the Montreal case is the extent to which the national gaze on Toronto is absent. This is in a sense opposite from the seriocomedy that we have just reviewed. Throughout the period of the amalgamation debate in Toronto, there is a palatable sense of being overrun by the wrong political world view. In the end, the debate is cast almost entirely between a neo-liberal discourse on practicality and efficiency, combined with an almost cynical mistrust of government, versus a gradually weaker plea for self-determination, local identity, and direct forms of social democracy.

Although several elements in the debates over amalgamation in Montreal and Toronto are similar, the difference in mediated societal cultures as well as the platforms of the political parties responsible for the legislation is in fact quite different. In Toronto the tension is not over a multinational quarrel about sovereignty but over traditional perceptions of left-leaning city politics that conflict with right-leaning provincial politics. The first indication of the Toronto amalgamation can be traced to the early trial balloons sent up through the press in the spring of 1996—two years before the first echoes were heard in Montreal and shortly after the election of a provincial Conservative government under the leadership of Mike Harris. The gap between rumour and legislation followed a pattern in Ontario similar to that seen later in Montreal.

Unlike in Montreal, large Toronto daily newspapers were not as unanimous in their opposition to the legislated amalgamation, but they were unanimous in their criticism of the downloading of debt and services to the level of the municipality (Boudreau, 2000; Sancton, 2000). The City of Toronto Act, Bill 103, was passed in February 1997 and became law in January 1998.

Opposition to the amalgamation in Toronto was more fragmented but no less emotional when it came to issues about local identity and democracy. As in Montreal, the former six municipal mayors were strong opponents of amalgamation. Michael Prue, mayor of East York, said at one point, 'We won't let them get away with it, East York is home to 102,000 people, many of them working to stop the megacity' (Talaga, 1996: A3).[2] However, unlike Montreal, the former mayors came under intense criticism for protecting the interests of their own office and territory against the interests of all. The popular press looks at the municipal arena as a truth that needs to be exposed and as a set of interests that need to be seen before the good of the city can be achieved. In a letter to the editor, Daniel Dostanich from Etobicoke wrote: 'My, how they whine when their jobs are on the line. Metro Council members, the six mayors and other municipal politicos, fearing job loss when Metro Toronto amalgamation comes to pass are crying that the process is undemocratic' (*Toronto Star*, 1996a: E3). 'Politicos' are obviously not actors who carry the good of the city in Mr Dostanich's view. Editorials are especially critical of the inability of the mayors to cooperate, as further proof of their redundancy, incompetence, and corruption: 'Six separate snow removal departments are gearing up to clear roads across Metro . . . In addition, the Metro government is in charge of arterial roads and expressways. Trucks can clear up one Toronto street, leaving a neighbouring street in York, Scarborough, North York or Etobicoke unplowed because it is in another city' (*Toronto Star*, 1996b: A46).

Opposition is also strongly voiced in terms of a sense of democratic betrayal. David Miller, mayor of Toronto at the time of writing, expressed his sense of disappointment in a letter to the *Toronto Star*, which took an editorial position against recognizing a referendum on the legislated amalgamation: 'The provincial government, which promised to preserve local municipalities and not amalgamate them without their consent, is doing the exact opposite. That is apparently okay . . . I once thought we were living in a democracy. Apparently, we are not' (*Toronto Star*, 1996c: A20). In another letter to the editor, Eric Colquhoun wrote: 'Would someone show me where the idea of Metro amalgamation was included in the manifesto for the Common Sense Revolution . . . It's one thing to live with all the ideological madness . . . It's quite another to have these little extras tossed in, without the chance to vote on them in an election' (*Toronto Star*, 1996: E3).

On the one hand, it is important to keep in mind that the initial announcement of the merger fuelled a large-scale opposition movement that responded to the shock waves set off by the new government's politics. Demonstrations, general strikes, popular referendums, legal challenges, and government opposition filibusters were launched. A largely middle-class citizens group, Citizens 4 Local Democracy (C4LD), came together in this context and organized regular events to block the government plans. In the end, however, opposition would fail to translate itself into an alternative political movement that could mobilize the majority of citizens to elect a mayor and council that would share the political vision of C4LD in the 1997 municipal election or help to defeat the Conservatives in the 1999 election (Isin, 2000). On the other hand, editorial positions in the main Toronto dailies remained divided. The *Toronto Sun*'s editorial opinion in particular favoured the merger and challenged opposition to consider the government's mandate:

> Time to change gears for a moment, from the teachers' strike to the megacity election. In many ways, of course, the two are similar. In 1995, when the Tories were elected, there was consensus among voters that: a) we had too many municipalities, too many bureaucrats and too many local politicians; and b) we had too many school boards, too many trustees and too many fat-cat school board honchos soaking up too many tax bucks on shrimp cocktails and junkets to Disney World. The Tories promised to end all that—and they did. There was the massive battle to rationalize government within Metro and now there is the huge offensive over education. On both counts, the government has immense communication problems. (*Toronto Sun*, 5 November 1997: 12)

While the *Sun*'s editorial approves of the government's agenda, it questions its public relations work. Criticism of the government's seriousness and even its resolve is dismissed in an early editorial comment from the *Toronto Star*:

> Conquerors of the debt? Leaders of a change so drastic they call it the 'Common Sense Revolution'? Inspirational role models for Bay St. and the captains of industry? Nuts. The suspicion is growing these guys couldn't order lunch . . . Leach [then minister of municipal affairs] still hasn't told us what the government's going to do—if it's going to do anything at all, except maybe keep sending out rumours and trial balloons. Meanwhile, the mayors are gearing up for a massive propaganda campaign designed to scare the daylights out of people. It's going to be expensive and it's going to be awful. It's also going to be effective. People are going to be rattled by the scare stories their mayors throw at them because there is nothing coming from the other side. (Stein, 1996: A8)

Emotional reactions to the merger were frequently interwoven with widespread protest against the Conservative government's massive cuts to Ontario public services, which were justified under the guise of fiscal responsibility and what the government called the 'common sense revolution'. The above quote from the *Star* puts the government ideology into a seriocomic light by further questioning the mayoral opposition while at the same time lamenting a lack of serious information for a full public discussion. The common good of the city here is about transparency and deliberation. But of course, the whole debate about local democracy and legislated amalgamation has to be thought through in terms not only of what is the common good, but also of what is the 'right' decision in terms of balancing complex urban problems of democratic communication, snow removal, the specialness of neighbourhoods, libraries, communities, and municipal management with all kinds of external pressures.

The wider picture that we want to recall as we shift back to the serio-comedy example in the next section is that the CBC, Radio-Canada, and newspapers are organizations that provide different points of view on a singular cultural continuum that serves two 'distinct' mediated societies. Thus they are organizations that reproduce the narratives of national majority and minority cultures in each of the cities. They are both objective producers of culture and receptacles for subjective expressions of identity. In other words, important self-perceptions about identity for each city are embedded in these narrative forms.

Montreal and the Absent Region

Citizens are emotionally and volitionally committed to their cities and feelings and are deeply implicated in a sense of belonging. An important issue to add when trying to reach understanding about the unique sense of belonging or wanting to belong is the issue of **two-sided answerability**. Mikhail Bakhtin argues the answerability of an act suggests a two-sided process in which a speaker anticipates a general or objective response (as in a culture of laughter) as well as a unique subjective rejoinder. An identity is answerable in the sense that its holder is responsible for it, but answerability lies beyond conventional responsibility. It lies in the capacity to evoke a response from others, to speak in a way that you can be responded to. Identity involves both a unique individual and general collective expectation of a response to a person's citizenship. Citizens inform one another about what makes them distinctive.

A representation of two-sided answerability is easily seen in a classic Radio-Canada television sketch on Montreal that starred the popular actor Olivier Guimont, who died only a few months after its broadcast. The text is from the *Le Bye Bye* New Year's Eve 1970 show. The show was recorded less than two months after the end of the October Crisis, which had seen the imposition of martial law (the War Measures Act) and hundreds of random arrests of intellectuals and artists without due process. The scene in Montreal was still tense at the time of the broadcast. The sketch that follows is an attempt both to make light of the situation and to offer a serious social commentary on the divisions between the English-speaking elite in Westmount (Montreal's, and one of Canada's, wealthiest municipalities) and the French-speaking working class, as represented by the neighbourhood of St Henri. A soldier from St Henri is assigned as a guard to a house party on

New Year's Eve where we see him on patrol walking back and forth in front of the house and up and down its stairs, which place it at the very top of the hill looking down on the city. The sketch is about the contact between the soldier and the bourgeois owner, Mr Thompson. The two first meet on the stairs as the owner opens the front door, dressed in formal evening wear. He is also a little drunk and carrying a glass of whisky in one hand and a bottle in the other. The sketch employs several elements of the seriocomedy genre. It especially plays on the reversal of hierarchy at both the physical and psychological levels through a set of politics that are simultaneously economic, linguistic, and ethnic. The municipality of Westmount sits at the top of the hill, whereas the neighbourhood of St Henri is situated at the bottom. Montrealers, like citizens of other linguistically divided cities, are used to living in one language at home and in another when they leave the house. The linguistic interference in the sketch (Mr Thompson's thick accent and state of inebriation limit his ability to grasp sarcasm in vernacular French) allows the soldier to communicate directly with the audience, which is in the know regarding how ignorant bourgeois Anglophones are of Francophone neighbourhoods. The bourgeois becomes the idiot, the soldier the savant. But the final word is given to recognition that the Anglophones boss and the Francophone soldier need each other, because in the face of violence, if one political will lets go, the other is likely to do the same.

The Scene in Westmount

MR THOMPSON: (speaking in French with a thick English accent) Could I possibly interest you in a drink, *mon ami*?

Soldier: No, no, thank you,. I really couldn't. Well, perhaps just one small one.

MR T.: No, no. To celebrate the New Year.

Soldier: Well (turns his walkie-talkie toward the ground).

MR T.: (in English) That's my boy! (Mr T. pours a drink and offers it to the soldier. As they talk they take turns drinking from the same glass while Mr T. holds the bottle in his other arm. They both continue to walk back and forth as if on patrol).

MR T.: (back to French with a thick English accent) It's so beautiful, the night before the next year. There is so much fun everywhere, eh soldier?

Soldier: Yes, a lot of fun everywhere (a bit sarcastically).

MR T.: Where are you from?

Soldier: I'm from St Henri, Mr Thompson.

MR T: I never been around there but heard a lot about it.

Soldier: Look, we can see it from here.

MR T.: Where? Where is it?

Soldier: Look way down there where there is almost nothing. We can see it from here.

MR T.: You are from St Henri and you are guarding Westmount.

Soldier: Yes. I joined the army so I could travel.

MR T.: Ha ha. That's very funny. Let's have another drink, to the health of St Henri.

Soldier: (speaking from the top of the steps now) It's true, from here it really is beautiful (he descends the stairs as if on patrol but slips and then barely recovers).

MR T.: Me, I like very much the whole province of Québec.

Soldier: You are really right (slurring his words now). A little drink to your province, Mr Thompson (he pours a drink for Mr T. and then descends the stairs again, now drinking straight from the bottle).

CHURCH BELLS RING.

MR T.: What's that?

Soldier: (completely drunk) Happy New Year, Mr Thompson. I wish your people a good year for 1971.

MR T.: Me too, I hope it will be a good year for your people as well. (They shake hands.) Well, I am going to go inside (Mr T starts up the stairs but after slipping takes hold of the soldier. Be careful, boy. Because if you fall, I fall!

HILARIOUS LAUGHTER, MUSIC, FADE OUT . . . SNOWFALL.

The second French-language extract that we discuss is also drawn from *Le Bye Bye* and was broadcast on New Year's Eve 1995, only two months after the narrow 'no' vote prevailed in a second Québec referendum for sovereignty and a new partnership with the rest of Canada. The sketch expresses the 'scene' in French-speaking Montreal at the time. Once again, this is a time when the city is intensely divided, again between the linguistic groups and again over the city's difference from the rest of Canada. The referendum vote was a period of high political drama, and the program adds to it through the satirical and ironic representations that it provides for a highly politicized audience. Whereas the soldier sketch reverses the hierarchy between class and ethnicity within Québec, this program, again authored from a Francophone Montreal perspective, looks to define Québec's difference from the rest of Canada. The sketch is a parody of a political rally in Montreal that brought around 100,000 Canadians to demonstrate for the 'no' side in the final days of the referendum campaign. It parodies a group of inebriated English Canadians who are flying to Montreal for the 'no' rally to tell the Québécois that they love them and that they should not break up the country by voting 'yes' in the upcoming referendum. Each of the actors in the sketch is a well-known Québec celebrity pretending to be an English-speaking Canadian. The sketch is titled 'We Love Quebec'.

[A rowdy and drunk partying group of Canadian Anglophones aboard an Air Canada flight en route to Montreal to join the unity rally.]

SERGE THÉRIAULT: Canada, Canada [. . .] when the Québécois see that us, the English, their superiors—we have come to Montreal from across the country to tell them that we love them—this is the best day of their lives, you see. Okay! Let's offer a toast to us, the saviours of Quebec!

ANDRÉ-PHILIPPE GAGNON: To love Quebec is like loving our women. It is easier when you are drunk. Ha ha ha!

DIANE LAVALLÉE: Hey! I brought a little piece of the Canadian Rockies to show why the Québécois should stay with us. It is just so beautiful! If the rock doesn't convince them I am going to throw it in their face!

S.T.: Look, look . . . it is really important that we come to your place before we burn the Quebec flags that we gave you last year! You Québécois don't find that hilarious? Ha ha ha!

D.L.: If Quebec separates there's a good side and a bad side. The good side is we will finally be rid of the goddamn frogs. The bad side is that the Québécois are all racists and all the ethnics are going to want to come and live with us. We are not racists, but dammit anyway, each one should live among his own ethnics!

S.T.: Are you ready to go? Chugalug! Chugalug! Chugalug! Cause if we are going to fix the vote we better fix it right. Have another beer!

A.P.G.: Eh, this referendum thing is a lot of fun! They should do this every year. I love Quebec!

DOMINIQUE MICHEL (disguised as an airline attendant): Quiet please. Shush! Please! Would the group of Canadians travelling to Montreal for the No side please leave by the side exit . . . [the Canadians cheer as they stumble out of their seats toward the exit of the aircraft] Meanwhile, everyone else please remain seated and please fasten your seatbelts; we will be landing in a few minutes. Bye-bye! Yuk yuk yuk![3]

This sketch shows how when Canadians from outside of Québec visited Montreal, they went hoping to be seen as loving '*les Québécois*', but they are satirized as being seen as wanting to be seen. Their intentions are ironically reversed. The tension here stems from a paradox in which the unfulfilled recognition of difference becomes a political condition. The 1995 sketches from *Le Bye Bye* and *Air Farce* demonstrate two very different desires to be answered to and two ways of imagining responsibility that demonstrate how difference and otherness might be understood between Québec and Canada. The *Air Farce* sketch against sovereignty association assumes an undivided audience that shares a common view of Montreal and the imaginary Canadian federation. *Le Bye Bye*'s ironic reversals assume a Québécois national way of imagining that is distinct from the rest of Canada, whether the Montreal audience favours a unified Canada or not. Whereas resentment in English-speaking Canada against Montreal is focused on Québec nationalism, cultural difference, and the inability to act as a region or province no more distinct or unique than the others, resentment in French-speaking Québec against Toronto has to do with its status as a centralized chauvinistic metropole.

Crossover Voices

At first glance the issue of municipal amalgamation does not seem to have much to do with imagining the city from the point of view of the nation in the comic way that we have seen so far. Indeed, public debates over the reorganization of municipal administrative and political structures in both Montreal and Toronto seem to be more about issues of local identity, taxes, garbage pick-up, snow removal, and dozens of other practical services. Yet the passionate defence of the local often employs the same logic as do the public media when justifying their role in nurturing national cultures. The municipal structure does have a constitutional reference and is implicated in a living set of cultural practices that often indirectly orientate themselves toward or against national identity. The fear of loss of community and the sense of a battle between civil society and the provincial state certainly provoked acerbic oppositional attacks against official positions for amalgamation in both cities. But it also disquieted some of the most personal kinds of objective cultural habits and subjective lifeworlds. Consider the following quotations, which were made in the period when debate was beginning in each city over the two amalgamations.

> **From Montreal**
> Every morning when the Côte St. Luc library opens at 10, Harry Greenberg hikes from his apartment across the street to begin his daily ritual. Dressed in a tweed jacket and sweater vest, the 79-year-old sits down in a sunny corner of the library and digests a daily helping of books and magazines. 'I spend six or seven hours here. I come in the morning, then I go home for lunch and come back,' said Greenberg, his owlish, bespectacled eyes rising from the inky pages of a newspaper. 'I'm retired, so I come every day, except when I go away on vacation, which isn't very often.' Greenberg can come every day because the doors of the Côte St. Luc Library are open 12 hours a day, seven days a week, 365 days a year. But that could soon change. (Hannes, 2000: A3)

A resident of the Montreal suburb of Côte St Luc (now a demerged municipality) expresses concern over possible changes to his daily routine should amalgamation occur. Similar sentiments regarding 'the local' were expressed by resident activists in the former North York suburb of Toronto. One of the activists, Joan King, a North York resident of 30 years, active in a community group in the Weston Road/Finch area, said she had trouble seeing how neighbourhoods would be able to protect themselves in the face of a larger and more distant municipal government.

Likewise members of a local residents' association in the Bayview area (between Highway 401 and York Mills Road) expressed dismay and anger over what appeared to be the pending destruction of local communities within

Metro. Considerable concern was voiced over the potential loss of local social patterns and cultural distinctiveness built up over the years.

The 'common good of the city' is not only about services, taxes, or governance but also about how objective culture has been built over time. 'The library caters to Côte St. Luc's many senior citizens, who come to socialize, read, play chess—even get information about medications they are prescribed. If the library was open less or not at all . . . many would spend long, lonely days cloistered at home' (Hannes, 2000: A3). The library developed locally with local input and as a result prospered as the municipality itself prospered. Like Mr Greenberg, David White and Joan King are concerned about the 'specialness' of their community and even evoke constitutional language ('distinct communities') to express a feeling of combativeness. Arguments for amalgamation hold that redistribution of resources is necessary to provide equity across the whole of the cities of Montreal and Toronto, which raises the broader question of the answerability of the whole of the city to its parts and, beyond that, of the answerability of the city to its larger societal culture.

Mr Greenberg from Côte St Luc in Montreal and Mr White and Ms King from North York in Toronto anticipate in fearful ways how amalgamations are likely to disturb their respective lifeworlds and potentially create chaos. But it is overstating the case to say that they share Sergeant Renfrew's comic view of the city that we saw in the *Air Farce* skit on the unbearable disorder of traffic, insult, and linguistic interference. What remains very interesting about the sense of difference and otherness that was raised at the end of the previous section on seriocomedies is the question of conflict and antagonism between different ways of seeing and the implications for thinking about political culture in each city. How is it that North Yorkers and Metro Torontonians or allophone Quebeckers and old-stock Franco-Québécois are able to gaze into each other's eyes without annihilating each other the way that they might do in seriocomedies? The tinge of violence hinted at here is pre-political, if we mean by the political the art of persuasion.

At the level of everyday political culture, this dimension of otherness suggests a degree of intimacy, whereas on the more abstract level of institutions, intimacy disappears into a more formal organization. On a macro level, the the cultural ***ethos*** or lifestyle of urban comedy and the political dimension of ***demos***, or the public administration of the people, can be considered interrelated to the extent that they divide citizens into various camps when public deliberations between distinct communities cannot be resolved (Anglo-Quebeckers move away from Montreal, as in the *Air Farce* skits, or soldiers guard affluent houses as in the Radio-Canada skit). For city governance, intersections between political parties, municipal policies, neighbourhoods, communities, and minorities can be contemplated through the processes of gaining understanding of the common good between groups. At the same time, the tension generated between groups seeking answerability can also be thought through in terms of reference points for new ways of posing questions as well as developing new kinds of solutions to problems that in turn require new responses.

For the Montreal amalgamation, opposition includes both Francophone and Anglophone municipalities and is expressed in voices that are found across an intense range of emotions that are not always measured against global forces or the background context of the nation. Unlike Toronto, suburban mayors in Montreal were not discredited in their bid to lead the most intense emotional reactions to Bill 170, which saw the restructuring of 28 municipalities on the island of Montreal into one municipal government, the formation of a new city of 1.8 million people, and the creation of an urban region of three million. Like the official voice, these opposition voices are not monologic. They respond to and anticipate rejoinders from the provincial government. When official voices continue to respond without answering to a sense of local democracy, opposition voices become increasingly accented with anger.

On the other hand, these mayors were located largely in the West Island, a predominantly federalist-leaning section of the city.[4] These mayors were not the only authors of the incensed verbal attacks in the anti-merger movement in Montreal, but they were often among the most vocal. They articulated a particularly biting anger toward Bill 170 before Christmas of 2000. The mayor of Baie d'Urfe said, 'I don't think you want to hear the rude words I have to describe how I'm feeling'; the mayor of Dorval said, 'There are no words in the English language to describe my disgust for the way this bill and this law came to be' (*The Gazette*, 2000: A6). Journalist Michel Vastel from *Le Soleil* points out that these suburban interlocutors are not angry at the principle of creating a Greater Montreal. What drove residents toward a mass public protest was 'the brutal autocratic nature of this reform from on high' (Chambers, 2000: B3).

The counterpoint between the legitimate differences of popular opposition toward and support for the amalgamation two years later in Montreal and five years later in Toronto is a good example of how the clash between opposed voices works in mediated society. A reading of the affirmation of each discourse means unravelling the tension between opponents over contradictory claims about the ultimate common good for the city. The following set of quotations clearly demonstrates how two ways of imagining the nation in Montreal confront each other (Nielsen, Hsu, and Jacob, 2002). The quotations are from Anthony Housefeather, then head of Alliance Quebec (a federally funded English-rights lobby group in Québec), and Louise Harel, former Parti Québécois (PQ) minister of urban affairs, who was responsible for the original legislation on Montreal's amalgamation. They concern reactions to the government's decision to fuse the cities on the island of Montreal into a new megacity.

> When reading the Québec Governments Bill 170, I began feeling physically ill. Nervous flutters, a sinking feeling in the pit of my stomach—symptoms I recognized from the weeks prior to the 1995 Québec referendum. The feeling I had when I felt I might lose my country was one that I will never forget. Now I feel the Parti Québécois government wants to take away my town, my home, my community and my way of life. Worse still, the government says that it will not even recognize votes held on the issue. How democratic. (Housefeather, 2000: B5)

> These are not republics, nor nations we are talking about! If this criticism were ever to be argued abroad we would become a laughingstock. It is absurd to compare the right of a people to self-determination with the right of cities to self-determination. Municipalities are an organizational form that needs to evolve . . . . This no longer has anything to do with ultra-local territoriality. (Harel, quoted in *Le Devoir*, 20 May 2000: F3)[5]

We have already seen examples of the negative reception of Québec's mediated societal culture as represented in the city of Montreal from the point of view of English-speaking Canadian seriocomedy. It is not hard to imagine what 'country' Mr Housefeather is referring to when describing his deepest fears of loss and absence. The 'Canadian' identity that he defends and how it is seen from outside Québec is well represented in the 1978 *Air Farce* skit on moving out of Québec. It is also the most embedded background identity for the majority of Montreal's West Island mayors. At the same time, thinking through Mr Housefeather's claims about the loss of his home and neighbourhood from inside the French-speaking Québec milieu, as in the *Le Bye Bye* sketches on the drunken Mr Thompson and the Canadians who came to Montreal to show their 'love of Québec', reverses this imaginary reference to the political culture of the province. From this vantage point, another 'country' (Québec) already exists right in Mr Housefeather's neighbourhood. This country has a strong sense of itself as a national minority within Canada and North America. The fear that comes from the absence of the other here is that if the national majority (Canada) were ever to recognize this existence of a national minority (Québec) in search of sovereignty, it would ultimately negate itself. On the other hand, reading Minister Harel's statement from the point of view of the 1995 *Air Farce* sketch on arguments for and against Québec independence reveals the slippery slope that Mr Housefeather and the West Island mayors have in mind. Minister Harel finds herself in an argument over sovereignty while the issue is about internal organization of urban governance. Here, the irreconcilable clash between the city and the multinational vision of its objective culture could not be made any clearer.

The two-sided politics of answerability is clearest in the above quotations in that neither Mr Housefeather nor Minister Harel have any interest in internalizing each other's ideal position, yet they each anticipate the subjective response of the other in striking ways. At one extreme, the example of Minister Harel's sarcasm proposes an accusatory sideward implication that suburban mayors opposing the merger maintain isolationist and anti-cosmopolitan tendencies (an accusation commonly levelled against her own political party because of its long-standing policy on national independence or shared sovereignty with the rest of Canada). At the other extreme, the much hotter tones of fear and moral indignation expressed in Housefeather's rejoinder argue for an absolutist individual autonomy and local democracy as the highest form of common good for the city. The impasse between the two discourses lies in the ultimate conclusion that the one will never quite 'get' the meaning of the other.

Summary

Comparison of serious debates over legislated amalgamations and of satirical caricatures that place the two cities within their societal cultures leads us finally to some surprising undecidables! Although the formal structures of debate over local democracy and the genre of seriocomedy are more or less the same in each city, through selected media both represent their cities in very original ways. Toronto and Montreal are cities that carry an ambiguous relation as metropoles to larger national cultures and global forces, and the imaginary horizons of expectation within each city in part accommodate this ambiguity. The cultures of laughter in Montreal and Toronto differentiate two very unique ways of imagining the nation in each city. English or French laugh at each other in a time and place that cannot happen anywhere else or in any other moment. At the same time, neither is aware of what the other is laughing about. We have also shown common forms between political statements on the amalgamation and governance of each city and interpreted them from the seriocomedies in several instances.

- Mr Housefeather's attack against the PQ government and the 1978 and 1995 *Air Farce* sketches about Québec share the same profound disdain for the Québécois national project.
- Another, much lighter, example of shared horizons was seen in Sergeant Renfrew's comic vision of urban sprawl and linguistic interference along with the lament over the imminent loss of 'neighbourhood' expressed by Mr Greenberg and others.
- On the other hand, the *Le Bye Bye* sketches share Minister Harel's vision of Québec as a distinct nation, one that can never really quite be grasped by Canadians who see Québec as a province or region no more different or distinct than any other.

The two case studies establish clearly defined limits between each city and, at the same time, demonstrate mutual support. Examining the interpretation of popular criticisms of political competence, the mayoral opposition to amalgamation, and pleas for local democracy found in the quotations from the Toronto and Montreal newspapers, all from the point of view of seriocomedy, one gets a larger sense of the extent to which popular culture holds any decision from the political class in contempt. As Mikhail Bakhtin notes, 'distrust of the serious tone and confidence in the truth of laughter has a spontaneous elemental character. Fear never lurks behind laughter and hypocrisy and lies never laugh but wear a serious mask.' The seriousness of politicians is 'elementally distrusted, while trust is placed in popular laughter' (1984b: 95).

While the newspapers report that Mr Greenberg and Ms White are worried about their neighbourhoods being disturbed by a new, distant and inhumane municipal government, the 1970 soldier sketch from *Le Bye Bye* brings the 'scenes' of terrorism and state violence directly into the view of mass media and turns them into a political truth about what happened to Montreal in the 1970 October Crisis. Preserving objective culture and social solidarity are ultimate goods in both scenarios. We get Toronto's counterpoint on Montreal's social solidarity in the 1978 *Air Farce* sketch on leaving Montreal: when the last moving company in Montreal itself has to move out, they are even forced to turn down Jean Chrétien's request for assistance (along with the other 'Anglaise rats leaving the sinking bateau'). By 1996 the 'common sense revolution' had hit Toronto like a rock, and for many it had gone way too far ('these guys couldn't order lunch'). In 2000 Minister Harel's political option for one city and one island leaves Mr Housefeather nauseous and suburban mayors apoplectic. In 1995, after another very tense moment in Montreal's political history, *Le Bye Bye* throws the drunken, amorous Anglophones off the plane, while *Air Farce* pulls the trapdoor on the Québécois contemplating voting 'yes'. In the end, argues Bakhtin, 'laughter is essentially not an external but an interior form of truth; it cannot be transformed into seriousness without distorting the very content of the truth which it unveils' (1984: 94).

Enhanced Learning Activities

1. Select your favourite seriocomedy and list examples that refer to serious and comic urban issues, that critique rural traditions from the point of view of the city, and that reverse meanings through the mixture of accents from different social classes or from jokes about bodies, genders, ethnicities, and corporal hierarchies.
2. Select five news articles from newspapers or other media on the 2010 Winter Olympics in Vancouver and describe how the city is framed through global forces and national identity. Do the articles imply an address toward a city, a national, or a global audience? Summarize the articles and explain your reasons.

3. Select five news items from newspapers or television on a conflict in a city. Do the articles imply an address toward the local, the national or a global audience? Describe the articles and explain your reasons.

Annotated Further Reading

Mark Abrahamson, *Global Cities*. New York: Oxford University Press, 2004.
This book combines urban sociology and communications studies to add the calculation of cultural industries into the more economic-centred definition of global cities (New York, London, and Tokyo) as strictly a handful of centres for world finance and service industries. While still considered second tier rather than global in this sense, Toronto and Montreal are included in the list of global cities of cultural production because of the importance of the English- and French-language television and film they produce and that are sold around the world.

Andrew Clark, *Stand and Deliver: Inside Canadian Comedy*. Toronto: Doubleday Canada, 1997. This is a surprising and lively history of English-Canadian comedy from vaudeville to stand-up and from radio to television and film. The history begins in the First World War and carries through to the Canadian invention of *Saturday Night Live* and the over-representation of its creative formation in the American scene well into the 1990s.

Harry H. Hiller, *Urban Canada: Sociological Perspectives*. Toronto: Oxford, 2005. An accessible collection of essays aimed at a general introduction to urban sociology with a focus on Canada, this book covers national and global aspects as well as issues of urbanization, rural–urban differences, urban communities, immigration, inequality, and political economy.

Joan Sloan, ed., *Urban Enigmas: Montreal, Toronto and the Problem of Comparing Cities*. Montreal: McGill-Queen's University Press, 2007. This text is an interdisciplinary collection of articles that provide theoretical strategies for comparing cities and a series of case studies that compare and contrast a variety of artistic, cultural, and political identities from Montreal and Toronto. This book also includes an earlier version of the present chapter.

Useful Media

Urban Studies
http://www.usj.sagepub.com
This site provides limited access to published articles on various aspects of urban life. Use its search engine for access to material on media and other subjects of interest.

Urban Justice
http://www.urbanjustice.org
A site on social justice with a focus on New York, sponsored by the Urban Justice Center.

Wikipedia—Urban Sociology
http://en.wikipedia.org/wiki/Urban_sociology
This site provides a general survey of urban sociology looking at a variety of research fields.

Notes

1. This chapter is in part derived from Nielsen (2007).
2. Thanks to Mircea Mandache for organizing the sample. The selection from the Toronto newspapers is taken from the *Toronto Star* and the *Toronto Sun*. Using a keyword search for 'amalgamation', 223 articles were selected in 1996 and 885 articles in 1997 from Canadian News Disc 2 for the *Toronto Star*. And 143 articles were selected in 1996 and 458 articles in 1997 from Canadian News Disc 3 for the *Toronto Sun*. After reading through the larger sample, a further sampling was done by selecting one article for each ten. For example, article 2 from articles 1–10; article 13 from 11–20; article 187 from 181–90, and so on. In this way, 22 articles were selected for a closer reading from the *Toronto Star* in 1996 and 88 articles from the *Toronto Star* in 1997. Fourteen articles were selected from the *Toronto Sun* for 1996 and 45 for 1997. From the remaining 169 articles, 20 were selected randomly, with preference being given to editorials and letters.
3. Stephan Laporte, 'We Love Quebec', 1, from *Bye Bye 95*, broadcast by Radio-Canada, 31 December, 11:00 PM, Société Radio-Canada Archives, Montreal. Assistant producer, Stephan Laporte. Producer, Jean-Jacques Sheitoyan. Principal actors, Dominique Michel, André-Philippe Gagnon, and Serge Thériault. My translation, based on broadcast tape and script.
4. Note that in the Montreal case, the focus of analysis is the merger debates, not the demerger debates that followed the 2001 legislation.
5. For a discussion of the selection process from the Montreal newspapers, see Nielsen, Hsu, and Jacob, 2002.

PART 3

Social Problems Through Journalism and Media

In this section of *Mediated Society* we turn our interest to the reporting of social problems. How are they presented by the media? Are particular problems emphasized over others? To whom are reports on social problems directed? You will recognize the source of these questions and the allusion that the very concept of 'social problems' requires scrutiny. Sociology, and most especially critical sociology, demands that we consider accepted ways of looking at the world in relation to established institutions. The construction and interpretation of certain behaviours as problematic and others as not is rooted in established interests, be they related to class, gender, ethnicity, social categories and groups, or economic, political, and ideological concerns. True, interests do not remain fixed. In practice their power or authority may decrease or increase; they may clash, overlap, be redefined. Behaviours and relationships negatively framed by media and journalists as social problems are generally received by readers and viewers as innocent statements of fact. Facts are reported, but they are constructed in particular ways. In this section we deconstruct the framing around social problems.

Chapter 9 addresses social problems in general. What makes a social problem? Are social problems mediated through media? Are they mediated through sociology itself? What role do journalists and social scientists play as observers? More importantly, how do the observers observing the observed come between the subjects of social problems as reported and the audiences their reports address? What about entertainment writing and programming? How is gender addressed on radio and television? What seems to be changing with respect to attitudes toward women, women's roles, and male–female power relations?

In Chapter 10 we examine how journalism and television comedies construct poverty as a social problem, by looking at the press and television in Montreal. This will be a lesson in the deconstruction of news reports and television programming. In order to do this we again bring into play the concept of the *implied audience* and we introduce frame analysis. In Chapter 11 we look at immigration as a social problem through an analysis of a case study of *The New York Times*. This chapter also introduces the concept of 'conditional hospitality' with its implications for race, ethnicity, sexual orientation, and gender. How does *The New York Times* frame social problems of immigration around the themes of justice, multiculturalism, governance, and social movements?

In all three chapters we consider the media's structuring of social problems as both a journalistic practice and a creative practice through the use of both various entertainment genres and news reporting as a means of highlighting social problems. Insofar as we attend to audiences, the emphasis is on implied audiences; that is, not only are issues framed by the media but they are also framed by audiences. News stories on poverty tend not to address the poor, stories on immigration tend not to address the immigrant, and stories on copyright tend not to address the creator.

9 Reporting on Social Problems

Learning Objectives

- To learn about the difference between personal problems and public issues
- To understand how social problems are constructed by the media
- To consider copyright, social networking, and gaming as media-constructed social problems
- To look at the role of gender in the definition and reporting of social problems
- To understand the mediation of crime and health as social problems
- To consider entertainment as mediator of social problems

Introduction

In this section we turn our interest to media reporting of **social problems**: how are they presented, are particular problems emphasized over others, and to whom are reports on social problems directed? You will recognize the source of these questions and the suggestion that the very concept of 'social problems' requires scrutiny. Sociology, and most especially critical sociology, demands that we consider accepted ways of looking at the world in relation to established institutions. The framing of certain behaviours as problematic and others as not is rooted in established interests, be they related to class, gender, ethnicity, or other social categories or to economic, political, and ideological concerns. True, interests do not remain fixed; in practice, their authority may decrease or increase, they may clash, they may overlap, or they may be redefined. Behaviours and relationships negatively framed by media and journalists as social problems are generally received by readers and viewers as innocent statements of fact. Facts are reported, but assembled in particular ways. In this and the next two chapters we deconstruct the framing around social problems. This chapter addresses social problems in general while giving particular attention to the way in which crime, health, gaming, social networking, and other common day-to-day events are presented as social problems and how gender factors into this presentation.

What Makes a Problem Social?

The question 'what makes a problem *social?*' suggests a distinction between social or collective problems and individual or private problems. Turning the sociological gaze toward social problems, C.W. Mills drew our attention to the question 50 years ago. He proposed a distinction between '*the personal troubles of milieu*' and '*the public issues of social structure*'. Consider poverty. If in a small town of 5,000 people one or two families and perhaps three or four children are living in poverty, more than likely their difficulties may be attributed to personal problems. If, on the other hand, 25 per cent of children in a city of three million are living in poverty, we are dealing with a major public issue. **Public issues** bring values, institutions, and social policies to mind and are the purview of sociology. For Mills 'this distinction is an essential tool of the sociological imagination and a feature of all classic work in sociology' (Mills, 1959: 8–11).

Public issues or social problems are reported on and discussed by sociologists through books, articles, and research reports and by the media in news, documentaries, drama, and comedy programming. Both sociology and media are expected to build knowledge about the world in which we find ourselves. Our knowledge of social problems and possible solutions is mediated through both sources. True enough, any of us may have found ourselves living through social problems, as the recipient of racist slurs or as one among many unemployed.

Before proceeding, it might be useful to examine in more detail the various ways in which the social sciences in general and sociology in particular address social problems. In his review and assessment of social problems Joel Best drew attention to three approaches current in the literature (Best, 2008). First are those who define social problems simply as harmful conditions. The difficulty with this approach is that what is considered harmful or controversial varies over time. Issues concerning gender equality provide a good example. In 1950 gender inequality was considered neither harmful nor controversial, nor did it appear as an issue in textbooks addressing social problems. The debates around gender issues did not become a noticeable part of discussions of social problems until the 1980s. The second definition, 'social problems as topics of concern', carries a similar difficulty. Today's concerns were not yesterday's concerns nor are the concerns of low-income people the same as those of high-income people. Best opted for a third position which he labelled 'social construction.' Designating a condition as a social problem

> involves a process of claims-making: that is, someone must bring the topic to the attention of others, by making a claim that there is a condition that should be recognized as troubling, that needs to be addressed. For constructionist sociologists, social problems are defined in terms of this claims-making process, because it is claims-making—and only claims-making—that all social problems have in common. (Best, 2008: 11–28)

The claims-making process, a process involving any number and variety of social actors and groups, is that which defines and mediates social problems. In accepting this definition we have included three crucial elements in our definition of a social problem: (1) we include a subjective element insofar as it is people and groups acting and making claims; (2) we have allowed for agency, that is, for the intervention of activists into structurally originating conditions; and (3) we have recognized the exercise of power in the process of defining social problems (Alvi, DeKeseredy, and Ellis, 2000: 5). Claims-making clearly occurs within a socio-cultural context. Various actors, groups, and institutions (the media, for example) come to imagine a social problem or multiple social problems. According to one prominent researcher in the field, 'the media provide access to and construct social problems for large numbers of audiences in many parts of the world and in turn themselves have become a social problem in view of their multiple and complex effects', both positive and negative (Kellner, 2004: 209).

To consider the process of mediation with respect to social problems is complex. It is complex in part because the role of both sociology and the

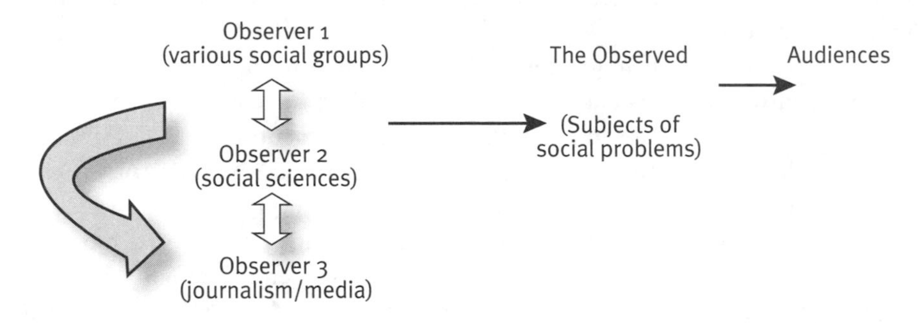

FIGURE 9.1 Mediation of Social Problems

media, including journalism, is to construct knowledge about their objects with reference to the real social world. Both come to conclusions and report on observations one step removed from everyday social life and both construct meaning about that life as a result of their observations of those who are actually acting out a lived reality, be that lived reality one of poverty, gender or sexual orientation victimization, or racism. But the similarity ends there inasmuch as sociology takes news and information as mediated forms of knowledge whereas traditional print journalism and media in general are enveloped by institutions that report, copy, and disseminate information and entertainment that engages, commercially for the most part, both narrow and mass publics depending on the medium. Whereas sociology looks to understand and explain the multiple voices that make up mediated society and sees that these voices are in a struggle to overcome constraints, mainstream journalism sees itself as a *neutral* reporter of news, and media have always treated news subjects as opportunities to create and re-create images of events. Together journalism and media argue that they present multiple points of view and tastes that help make up public opinion. Both sociology and journalism/media are contested in terms of their abilities to achieve their goals, but we propose that sociology has the added responsibility to ask the classic question regarding mediation: how do the observers observing the observed come between the subjects of social problems that are reported on and the audiences that are addressed?

Figure 9.1 characterizes the complex set of relations involved in the process of mediating social problems—a set of social relations or a subsystem which may be linked to the media system described in Chapter 3. In this case the link is between Observer 3 and the audience. Observer 3 captures the whole complex of the media system as discussed in Chapter 3. Journalists observe and report on, or frame, social problems with audiences in mind or imagined. In effect social problems are viewed 'as products of a process of collective definition . . . . A theory that views social problems as mere reflections of objective conditions' cannot explain why some conditions demand considerable attention and others do not (Hilgartner and Bosk, 1988: 53–4). Why, for example, does uranium drilling and mining, a process which exposes local populations to highly volatile toxins in northern Saskatchewan and eastern Ontario, receive little attention while tobacco use, which also exposes populations to dangerous toxins, receives considerable media and political attention? The answer lies in the power arrangements built into a complex set of actors and institutions involved in defining and communicating social problems, and thus, the link back to the media system.

Our interest is in the manner in which journalists and media in general frame social problems and assume particular readers or audiences. In this chapter we will consider the routes through which citizens as audiences acquire knowledge and make judgments regarding social problems as framed by journalism and media programming. We will look at the manner in which media defines and reports on social problems internal and external to itself and the use of drama to define and elaborate on social problems.

Reporting on Social Problems

All forms of media present stories on public issues and, in the process, define, review, evaluate, and rank social problems. Here we focus on social problems internal and external to media organizations. Problems internal to the media refer to public issues which are attributed to media itself. External problems refer to those social issues not attributed to media per se but brought to public attention by media reporting. Social problems directly associated with the media are legion. Most certainly the assumed negative effects of television and video games on children and young people are popularly defined as social problems. We might also include copyright legislation and music downloading, use of the Internet by sexual predators, pornography, and the assumed negative implications of social networking sites such as Facebook.

Social problems external to the media include urban decay and homelessness, crime, poverty, immigration, racism, and gender inequality, all of which are major occupiers of space and time in the news, in documentaries, and on the Internet. Internal or external, social problems have been the mainstay of news reporting. People who do not directly experience these issues receive their knowledge and understanding of social problems through the media. Those who do experience poverty or homelessness, racism, or gender bias often note the gap between their experience and the stories told and wonder who writes the stories for whom. This latter point is the subject of Chapters 10 and 11. Here we will look first at problems internal to the media, with an emphasis on copyright issues and problems associated with networking and violence.

Problems Internal to the Media

McKie and Singer have pointed out that, 'each time a new medium emerges, there is fear that it will have undue influence on society or will be inordinately influenced by powerful groups', as we saw in Chapter 4. They drew attention to US studies investigating the dangers of movies in the late 1920s and of comic books in the 1940s. There were investigations of TV in the United States during the 1960s and in Canada in the 1970s. Canadian studies carried out during the early 1990s were 'translated into new codes on TV violence announced by the Canadian Radio-television and Telecommunications Commission (CRTC) in 1993 to deal with the problem of gratuitous violence on Canadian TV screens' (McKie and Singer, 2001: 271). Throughout history technological changes, from steamships to railways and automobiles, from radio to television, and from television to the Internet, have been perceived as a threat to everyday life and, at times, as a threat to vested commercial interests. For example, a recent study suggested television addiction as a problem requiring attention, noting that scores of self-confessed TV addicts on a particular addiction scale 'were positively correlated with neuroticism' (McIlwraith, 1998: 381). As well, there is a fairly extensive literature on children's use of media and parental guidance (Van den Bulck and Van den Bergh, 2000), a witness to constant parental concern over the assumed negative effects of media use. We will direct our attention to copyright issues, social networking, and gaming as social problems internal to media organizations.

Copyright Issues

We begin with an examination of struggles over intellectual property as a social problem associated with media use.[1] This is especially appropriate because the presence of vested interests (creators versus users) is more apparent than in most social problems emanating from media itself. Referring back to the media system, copyright, insofar as it opposes creators and media corporations to users, reflects the structure of power within that system. Nevertheless, issues surrounding copyright—downloading music and movies and file sharing—are presented as a social problem. Judicial and law enforcement institutions become involved. Recent news stories suggest the scope of the problem:

- 'Canada a top copyright violator, U.S. group says', announced the CBC News on 12 February 2008. 'Canada has joined Russia and China as the biggest violators of U.S. copyright law, according to the U.S.-based International Intellectual Property Alliance . . . . The IIPA said Canada is the only country in the 30-member Organization for Economic Co-operation and Development that has yet to modernize its copyright law or meet the minimum global standards set out in the World Intellectual Property Organization treaty signed in 1996' (CBC, 2008a).

- 'Canada's iPod levy may yet face the music', wrote Michael Geist in the *Ottawa Citizen*. Referring to 'Canada's private copying levy, which adds 21 cents to the price of every blank CD to compensate the music industry for personal copying', he reported that Canada's Copyright Board had made a decision to 'reopen the door to placing a levy of up to $75 on iPods . . . [and further that this is] the second time that the Canadian Private Copying Collective, the collective that has pocketed more than $150 million from the levy since 2000, has sought to include iPods within the levy system' (Geist, 2007).
- Again from Michael Geist, a report that some governments, under pressure from "content lobby groups", [had] moved toward requiring Internet service providers to terminate subscribers if they engage in file sharing activities on three occasions. In recent weeks, however, it would appear that governments are beginning to have sober second thoughts. After a Swedish judge recommended adopting the three-strike policy, that country's ministers of justice and culture wrote a public opinion piece setting out their forthcoming policy that explicitly excluded the three strikes model' (Geist, 2008a).
- 'In April 2009 a Swedish court brought in a guilty verdict against the world's largest BitTorrent search website . . . four men behind the website were found guilty of breaking copyright laws in Sweden on Friday and were each sentenced to one year in prison. They must also pay $3.6 million U.S. in damages to entertainment companies, including Warner Bros., EMI and Columbia pictures' (Pilieci, 2009).

Copyright issues are a major news item in the daily press and on radio and television. *The Globe and Mail* averaged 46 articles on copyright issues during a three-month period from mid-January to mid-April 2009. *The New York Times* published 29 articles dealing with copyright between mid-March and mid-April 2009. Copyright issues involve millions, even billions, of dollars and the large media monopolies—Warner Brothers, EMI, and Columbia on one side and Google, BitTorrent, and other large search engines on the other. The actor omitted from most of the discussion on the issue is the user—the citizens using the search engines for information and entertainment. But just what is copyright?

According to the Government of Canada,

> The *Copyright Act* provides the legal framework within which creators and other rights holders are entitled to recognition and control of, and payment for, the use of their works. Examples of works protected by copyright are: films, novels, songs, information products and computer programs. Copyright establishes the

> economic and moral rights of creators and other rights holders to control the publication and commercial exploitation of their works, protect the integrity of their endeavours, and ensure that they are properly remunerated. (Canada, 2009: 1)

Canada's Copyright Act, a reasonable piece of legislation relative to US law, was passed in 1924 and was last amended in 1997. The federal government, under pressure to conform to the current US and world copyright laws, was reviewing the act in 2009; parliamentary debate on a new act is likely to begin during the late autumn of 2010. The Canadian copyright regimen recognizes users and sets out regulation for access to and use of copyrighted materials. For example:

> The Government is committed to ensuring that copyright law promotes both the creation and the dissemination of works. The objective of the *Copyright Act* is also to ensure appropriate access for all Canadians to works that enhance the cultural experience and enrich the Canadian social fabric. Access is assured through various means: by establishing simple rights clearance mechanisms; by devising alternate schemes that recognize copyright, e.g. the private copying regime; by allowing specific exemptions to aid users such as libraries, schools and archives to fulfill their vital institutional roles in Canadian society; and by other means that favour the circulation of information and cultural content for and by Canadians. Access is therefore an important public policy objective to consider when reviewing the copyright framework. (Canada, 2009: 2)

Thus, in a restricted fashion, access to and use of copyrighted materials are recognized as a necessary part of the system. Nevertheless, the tension between the rights of the creator and the rights of the user remains. James Boyle (http://james-boyle.com, 2008), in his discussion of intellectual property, drew attention to the proposition 'that *the line between* intellectual property and the public domain is important in every area of culture, science, and technology' (emphasis added). Note in the list of references at the end of this chapter that his book is available for reading or downloading online. It is also available for purchase on Amazon.com. It is this 'line between' that requires very careful thought on the part of lawmakers and media corporations. There is always the danger of falling too far on one side or the other, though falling on the side of the user would be a very rare occurrence.

It is the user who tends to get lost in reporting news items on copyright and intellectual property. With the exception of editorial commentaries, which often provide critical commentary combined with reporting, journalists frame stories on copyright according to their sources—courts, lawyers, and media corporations. Two articles in the *Ottawa Citizen* on a decision by Swedish courts well illustrate this point. Vincent Pilieci's article 'Fileshare four hit with jail sentence, 3.6M fine' (2009) referred to above and the article 'Guilty verdict sparks debate over website in Canada' (2009) report on the court decision, noting the effects of the decision on the accused, the benefits to the plaintiffs, and possible effects on other search engines such as Google, but ignore the user.

Social Network Issues

YouTube, MySpace, Facebook, Twitter, and other social network sites appear in various news headlines as social problems requiring public concern and action. This is another perceived problem area where media reports on media.

The tension between communication through Internet networking and privacy is frequently reported by media sources. Facebook appears to be a major offender, having recently moved to gain control over user data from user accounts. Indeed it is an issue which links back to copyright.

In addition to copyright/privacy and public/privacy issues, social networking is also portrayed as having detrimental effects on learning and the mental capabilities of users. Thus is another tension constructed—between the negative effects of misuse and overuse and the positive social effects of citizen communication.

Our Views: Exposing Ourselves (2008b)

A warning to those who upload every detail of their lives to the Internet: Those frat party pictures might amuse your buddies now, but digital indiscretions have a tendency to linger. The latest example of how difficult it can be to expunge our online alter egos comes courtesy of Facebook. The social networking website is drawing criticism for its reluctance to part with members' personal data. Other networking websites allow users to delete their profiles with one click. Facebook, however, requires parting members to erase data line by line. Even then, virtual crumbs remain.

Our Views: Privacy Dilemma (2009a)

Angry users say they, not Facebook, own everything they upload to the site—every photo, every comment, every status update—and if they delete their accounts (which they never do), everything should just disappear . . . . The Internet has complicated traditional notions of privacy. When people e-mail their friends, they expect those interactions will remain private. And they should. However, when people comment on Internet forums, they are declaring their opinions to the world. If they later regret it—too bad. They no longer own those words.

- **The Good:** 'A neuroscientist and gerontologist in California . . . found that older people who use Google create dynamic new brain circuitry that fights aging, just like doing crosswords or learning a second language. But that, he insisted, was just the beginning. [And] today's young people can do more things at once with their brains than their parents ever could, as a result of long training: TV, iPods, texting, homework all at once' (Spears, 2008).
- **The Bad:** But if we are more engrossed in things online, and spending less time face-to-face, then there's also the possibility of evolution down the wrong path. What follows, the neuroscientist says, is an actual weakening of some neural circuitry. The neurons are still there, but they aren't linking up into the sophisticated network that allows complex brain action in areas outside the computer world: 'Our social interactions may become awkward, and we tend to misinterpret, and even miss subtle, nonverbal messages' (Spears, 2008).
- **The Ugly:** A Facebook group launched to discuss a dispute between rival groups of students at a Summerside, PEI, high school has been shut down after threats were posted on it. 'It wasn't hurting anything but somebody hurt it [said the student affected by the decision]' (CBC, 2008b).

Media ambivalence about itself will, on occasion, condemn the technology as a source of social problems, especially in relation to youthful users. On other occasions it will condemn users for the misuse of the technology, especially the use of network sites for sexual material, vindictive behaviour, and simple overuse. In either situation, reports tend to overlook the socio-cultural context, in which overt sexuality or violence is common and parents of younger users tend to provide little advice and supervision.

Part of the problem and the context is well documented in Tamyra Pierce's study of the content of MySpace. She noted that before such sites as MySpace, 'few adolescents had the knowledge or capability to create their own homepages in which they could post [personal information and photos]' (2007: 4). With the advent of MySpace, teens, perhaps unaware that posted material is available to anyone who can log on to a site, posted sexually explicit material featuring themselves. In a survey of 700 randomly selected MySpace sites Pierce found that 59 per cent featured sexual poses (clothed but revealing) and 45 per cent featured partial frontal nudity (2007: 10). Sites link to more sophisticated pornographic sites and do indeed place users at considerable risk to themselves.

The media frames the social problems tied to social networking sites principally as a problem associated with adolescent behaviour—a problem to be solved by parental intervention or the intervention of educational institutions. That part of the problem firmly linked to the pornography industry on one hand and to large-scale commercial interests on the other is generally ignored. The same, more or less, holds with the way in which media frame violence as a problem.

Gaming and Violence

Violent and criminal behaviours as portrayed on television, in gaming, in film, and on the Internet are perhaps the most disapproved of events internal to media. Television, film, popular music lyrics, and comic books were among the first media outlets to receive considerable criticism for their portrayals of violence and crime. And, as might be expected, the principal concern was and continues to be over the influence on children and adolescents. Media programming is perceived as the source of violent behaviour. In 1998 in Arkansas a playground killing in which two boys, one 11 and one 13, killed four girls and wounded 11 other children and one teacher was explained away by the state governor as due to the role of television in creating 'a state of callousness and disregard'. Others blamed video games and Hollywood movies (Tate and McConnell, 2001: 273). A decade later it would appear that video gaming has become the main culprit—press headlines and documentaries addressing gaming are common news stories.

- 'It's Grand Theft Auto for girls: Players encouraged to skip class, spread rumours, try drugs in new video game, Coolest Girl in School': A controversial new video game for girls implies that stealing, sexual dalliances, drug use, and gossiping pave the path to teenage empowerment, with the express objective being to 'lie, bitch and flirt your way to the top of the high school ladder'. *Coolest Girl in School* is billed as the young woman's answer to *Grand Theft Auto*, the hugely popular series in which players steal cars, kill police officers, and indulge criminal impulses. The girl-centric role-playing game puts a magnifying glass to the darker side of school life, with participants encouraged to experiment with fashion, drugs, sexuality, cutting class, and spreading rumours in an effort to win. According to the game developer, 'teachers exist to he manipulated,' a looming parent signals potential 'social death', new clothes are procured by stealing from the mall, and bribery is an exit strategy for sticky situations (Harris, 2007).
- 'Gaming fixation could be linked to Ont. boy's disappearance: parents': 'The parents of an Ontario boy who has been missing for over a week said Tuesday they believe their son's obsession with a video game had something to do with his disappearance. Brandon Crisp, 15, had been spending virtually every waking hour playing the Xbox game *Call Of Duty 4: Modern Warfare*, his parents said. Steve and Angelika Crisp had, as a result, revoked his video game privileges on numerous occasions, they said. On Oct. 13, after an argument over the amount of time he spent playing the game, Crisp jumped on his bicycle and sped away from the family home in Barrie, Ont.' (CBC, 2008c).

Three weeks later Brandon Crisp's body was found. On 6 March 2009 a documentary, titled *Top Gun: When Video Gaming Obsession Turns to Addiction and Tragedy* (Findlay, 2009), was aired as a part of the CBC program *The Fifth Estate*. The program was described as revealing to parents 'a darker aspect to their children's gaming addiction'. Viewers were invited to 'go inside this virtual community—where gaming addiction can trump family and friends.' Note that gaming is being framed as an 'addiction'; this is supported with interviews of a family therapist and a psychologist. The framing is just a step short of classifying gaming as an illness requiring medical intervention.

Two years earlier CBC News (2007) was reporting on studies published in the *Journal of Adolescent Health* and the *Archives of Pediatrics & Adolescent Medicine*—an indication that gaming had been **medicalized** by professionals in the field. According to an abstract of the publication in the *Journal of Adolescent Health*,

> Of 1254 participants (53% female, 47% male), only 80 reported playing no electronic games in the previous 6 months. Of 1126 children who listed frequently played game titles, almost half (48.8%) played at least one violent (mature-rated) game regularly (67.9% of boys and 29.2% of girls). One third of boys and 10.7% of girls play games nearly every day; only 1 in 20 plays often or always with a parent. Playing M-rated games is positively correlated ($p < .001$) with being male, frequent game play, playing with strangers over the Internet, having a game system and computer in one's bedroom, and using games to manage anger. (Olson et al., 2007)

However, the story is not all that discouraging. During the same year the *Archives of Pediatrics & Adolescent Medicine* published a study designed to scrutinize video game playing among adolescents in the United States. They found that 'only 36% of adolescents played video games, and those who played did so for 1 to 1-1/2 hours on average.' The authors also noted that 'adolescents spend 3 times this amount of time watching TV [and that] gamers did not spend less time than nongamers interacting with parents and friends. These findings do not support the notion that adolescents who play video games are socially isolated' (Cummings and Vandewater, 2007: 684).

The framing of video gaming and its effects as a medical problem shifts a vaguely defined social problem from institutions related to media and entertainment to medical institutions, thereby increasing scrutiny and placing the activity on the same level as alcoholism and gambling. Addiction becomes the problem as the instituted gaze shifts from media to medicine.

The process of the medicalization of the Internet and video game playing draws attention to Figure 9.1 above. The principal social actors involved in the process—media organizations, medical research and related sources, and health care professionals—are Observers 1, 2, and 3. The observed are the *users*, adolescents and others using the technologies. The audience is composed of readers, listeners, and viewers. The system, as a complex of actors and institutions, locates a behavioural set and defines and mediates it as a social problem. Note, too, that media organizations stand to economically benefit. In February 2008 the following report appeared in the *Ottawa Citizen*:

> [W]hat happens to video games matters. According to the research firm NPD Group, sales of video games in the U.S. shattered records set in 2005, passing $12.5 billion U.S. last year. In Canada, sales of video games hit $1.5 billion, an increase of 56 per cent over 2006, or more than four times what Canadian movie theatres took in at the box office. While EA will be the first major game studio to eliminate the sticker price and offer its products for free, others are not far behind. Others are expected to follow Electronic Arts' lead with ad-supported games. (Pilieci, 2008a)

To 'solve' the problem, now mediated through news organizations and the medical establishment, requires attention to the users, who must be 'cured'. Media corporations stand on the outside in a neutral position.

Problems External to the Media

Now we shift our interest to social problems external to the media; that is, problems not usually attributed to media as the cause. Crime, poverty, immigration, racism, drug use, economic depression, epidemics, and many other issues are, if we base our conclusion on frequency of appearance in media outlets, the social problems of the day. The next two chapters will focus on poverty and immigration, examining newspapers in Montreal and New York City as a lens through which to consider the press and implied audiences. Here we will take a brief look at crime reporting. Stories about criminal activity, crimes committed, problems associated with the control of crime, and the activities of criminal courts occupy a good deal of space on radio and television and in newspapers (Voumvakis and Ericson, 1984).

The 'cop on the beat' is most certainly not going to be cited as a primary source, though he or she may actually act in that capacity. Police sources in crime reporting are thoroughly instructed as to how to act as a source. Ericson and others (1989: 98–9) provided the following example from the Metropolitan Toronto Police administrative procedures document's instructions regarding news communications to the duty officer:

> The Duty Officer
> Acts as co-ordinator for the dissemination of news releases.
> When dealing with members of the media [the Duty Officer must]
> - Acquaint himself [*sic*] with the individual member

- Attempts [*sic*] to create a credibility bond with them
- Show no favouritism between their members
- Promptly disseminate to members current information of all incidents
- Refer members to the appropriate officer when further information required
- When necessary, act as a liaison between members of the media and members of the Force
- Assembles essential information of major incidents as it becomes available

Ensures proper operation of the 'Media Broadcast System' by:

- Broadcasting 'bulletin type' information as soon as practical upon notification of:
  - a major incident (crime),
  - developments possibly leading to a major incident,
  - emergency or dangerous conditions for the public, and
  - developments possibly leading to emergency or dangerous conditions for the public.

Institutional sources used for the construction of news items are indeed well schooled and, where not specifically instructed as are the police, source organizations will have public relations staff to spin information or, as is the case with universities, will have designated faculty members for specified topics. Journalists build their stories around information from these sources; that is, for the most part they work within the media system. In their analysis of reports on attacks on women Voumvakis and Ericson (1984: 1) point out that

> on occasion news workers (including journalists and their sources) link together a series of crime incidents to create a wider framework and theme in the news. Either on their own or after talking with sources, journalists invoke lay theories about possible patterns which are indicated by several crime incidents. They initially 'test' these theories with their sources, and continue to do this until they themselves, as well as their editors and news competitors, decide that the 'newsworthiness' of doing so has been exhausted.

They continue, citing Cohen (1972) and observing that these practices on the part of journalists in interaction with their sources yield a sense of 'moral panic' within the public: 'Societies appear to be subject, every now and then, to periods of moral panic. A condition, episode, person or group of persons emerges to become defined as a threat to societal values [and] the moral barricades are manned by . . . socially accredited experts' (1984: 1–2). This kind of news-generated panic recently occurred around urban gangs and gangland slayings in Vancouver and Toronto and around terrorist activity in Toronto, London, UK, and New York.

The interaction of journalists and their sources, as each makes use of the other, may lead to panic over social problems other than crime. News media, in interaction with health professionals and laboratory scientists, constructed extensive and complicated scenarios around the emergence of the H1N1 flu virus in the spring of 2009. The content of any daily newspaper or any television newscast during the week of 26 April to 2 May 2009 will demonstrate panic in preparation. As an example, the following headlines appeared over several stories in the *Ottawa Citizen* on 28 April 2009:

- On page A1: 'Ottawa at the Ready'; '5 Ottawans being monitored as WHO signals "significant step toward pandemic"'; and 'Hospitals at edge of capacity'.
- On page A4: 'Canada braces for battle; expect some deaths, warn health officials' and 'Experts say flu may echo 1918 pandemic'.
- On page A5: 'The wages of fear: Pandemic threat rocks economy, but Canada well placed.'
- On page A6: 'Hospitals: Screening targets patients at risk' and 'Monitor: Clear plan lays out what to expect and what to do.'

Sources quoted included Ottawa's chief medical officer of health, the World Health Organization, a federal senator, the chair of the emergency health planning committee in the region, city officials, Public Health Canada officials, and many more. These experts and local journalists linked together to produce not simply a news story but a thematic treatment in which a particular social problem was framed and delivered, leaving their audiences in a near panic situation. Oddly enough, on the editorial page of the same issue of the *Ottawa Citizen* (2009) the editorial cartoon mocked the situation, and the lead editorial, titled 'Be afraid but not of the flu', warned against a miscalculation of the seriousness of the situation and noted that there were other health problems of far greater import. On 2 May 2009 CBC news announced: 'Potential pandemic or garden-variety flu? No agreement among experts'. Medical experts and world leaders seemed to be at odds as to the severity of the new H1N1 virus, with some experts saying it was no worse than your average seasonal flu. Similar press framing of events occurred again in the fall of 2009 in relation to the administration of vaccine. The 31 October *Globe and Mail* lead story drew attention to a shortage of the H1N1 vaccine while at the same time featuring celebrities discussing whether they would take advantage of the vaccine or not. Television news, blogs, and various Internet and social network sites tried to outdo each other in a cacophony of pro- and anti-vaccine information.

There are breaks in the system. Journalists will set up independent sources; in the case of crime and deviance reporting 'outside sources' will be located in the deviant community itself. In spite of this, the centre of power, and thus of authority, lies within the system. The commercial imperative is at the centre of the life of media corporations. Media elites intertwine with elites in government, finance, manufacturing, health care, and education. More likely than not, problems constructed and reported will be within the confines of the cultural outlook of major institutions. This observation does not mean that journalists do not report stories that will seriously disrupt linked institutions—law enforcement, government, education, and health care, for example. The attack, however, will remain within accepted norms of journalistic critique and overall societal norms. Historically, we can observe both press and public almost simultaneously moving from acceptance of capital punishment to calls for its elimination and, finally, legislation prohibiting capital punishment. In matters of crime and punishment, media is seldom ahead of the public.

Social Problems Imagined through Entertainment

'Is it just entertainment?' asks Joel Best (2008) in his analysis of social problems. Are news media the only vehicles through which social problems are located, defined, and framed? Entertainment programming, specifically comedy and drama on radio and television and in print, most certainly reflects social problems as seen by the public, but it also frames social problems. Problems perceived as public issues in the areas of health care, crime, racism, war and peace, nationalism and regionalism, and others are addressed via media entertainment.

Police procedural and detective novels and crime fiction in film and on television are prime sources for the exploration of criminal behaviour and crime as a public issue. Gwyn Symonds (2008: 113), citing Leitch's (2002: 300) work on crime movies, notes:

> In their quest to make entertainment out of taboo behaviour, they treat crime as both realistic and ritualistic, a shocking aberration and business as usual, a vehicle of social idealism and of social critique. But although the nature of the character who embodies the heroic role the genre prescribes can vary from one crime film to the next even in the same multiplex, the genre itself is best defined in terms of a single constitutive theme: the romance of criminal behaviour.

The fact that crime fiction is usually romantic in form does not preclude the social criticism it carries to its audiences. British crime fiction in print from Conan Doyle to P.D. James and Ian Rankin carries a fundamental critique of social class. Television crime fiction from *Dragnet* to *Law and Order* and *The Sopranos* romaticizes crime while simultaneously framing criminal activity as a social problem. Referring to Symonds' (2008: 120) analysis of *The Sopranos*, to date reviews of the show have pointed to 'the way the series develops its critique of American capitalism, psychiatry, and family suburban life in the context of the mob'. Media entertainment in the form of crime fiction not only frames crime itself as a social problem but creates a base for a critique of Western culture in general.

Entertainment programming other than crime fiction also frames social problems. Comedy, on both stage and television, is a genre well suited to social critique. Comedy, satire, and irony engage audiences in dialogue—whether the laughter is out of embarrassment, ridicule, recognition, or support it indicates deep cultural comprehension. A recent analysis of the CBC comedy show *This Hour Has 22 Minutes* (from its inception in 1993 to Season 6 in 1998) pointed to the show's elaboration of the economic, political, and social problems related to the dominant/subordinate relationship between rural and urban Canada and the tensions arising between eastern, western, and central Canada.[2]

> The predominant format of *This Hour* is a mock newscast that presents the four comedians—Cathy Jones, Rick Mercer, Greg Thomey, Mary Walsh—in the roles of newscasters and special correspondents. Each episode opens with an introductory news brief that over-extends the logic of some of the more ludicrous news items of the past week to demonstrate the inherent absurdities of social life or convey the ironical incongruities of free-market democracy. One such news brief is related by Greg Thomey in his character's usual deadpan manner: 'Molson brewery is closing a plant in Barrie, Ontario, putting 414 people out of work. The company is blaming the decline in Canada's beer drinking. Molson insiders are hoping, however, that with the massive lay-offs, beer drinking in the region will soon be on the rise!'
>
> Opinion pieces or critical commentary on social and political issues in the form of monologues abound in *This Hour*'s comedy. Certainly, Rick Mercer's 'Rant' is an impressive example of this comedic format. Others include Babe Bennett, Sexual Affairs Correspondent, whose 1940s get-up glibly frames her feminist stance on the sexes; Joe Crow, a Micmac native who regards his people's oppressed legacy with a wry sense of humour; the audacious Marg Delahunty, who, in one piece, jauntily states from the comfort of her bathtub: 'You know, the reason they say that there are not more women in politics in Ontario is because it's so hard to keep the make-up on two faces!'; Dakey Dunn, a Newfoundlander on welfare who waxes in the vernacular on subjects ranging from sex to literature; and Connie, the Prairie Correspondent, whose leftist critique of neo-liberalism is re-dressed as a right-wing conspiracy theory which has her wailing about such subjects as the evils of technology, 'Frankenfood and Farmageddon!', in a Tim Hortons coffee shop somewhere in Saskatchewan.

Regarding the centre/east/west tensions in Canadian social and political life, the players frequently drew attention to rural/urban and east/west tensions.

> A particularly explicit interpretation has Marge Delahunty dressed as a cowwoman, yipping it up and firing excitedly into the sky with toy guns in front of a

large oil rig: 'Well, my good times were all gone—it seemed to be time to be moving on. So I pulled up stakes, strapped on my side irons and hauled my sorry arse to ALBERTA!' Marge then visits the [provincial legislative] building to confront Premier Ralph Klein regarding the publicly disparaging remarks he made about federal transfer payments to the Maritimes. She good-naturedly launches an assault in her uniquely maritime brogue:

> Mr. Klein! I'm still cut to the quick about those remarks you made about us there, a little while ago, you know, when you called all us from the East Coast bums and thieves. I know, Ralph, you didn't mean it. And I know you're sorry about it now and so on behalf of the good people of the Atlantic Provinces, I accept your apology, and you know what? If you cut us one or two of those big Alberta heritage cheques, that could do an awful lot to assuage the guilt from the heart.

Marge's diatribe conveys a recurring theme in the comedy of *This Hour*, namely, Maritime alienation. In addition, the recurrent characterization of Jerry Boyle, a politician and sole member of the Newfoundland Separation Party, is both a wry and self-effacing nod to this long-standing alienation. His famous words, 'If you can mark an X, you're my kinda people!', attest to the prevalent cynicism among Newfoundlanders toward the democratic political process and, more darkly still, the sense of resignation to partisan politics in place of a shared political vision that encompasses all the regions of Canada.

Comedy is one of the most poignant ways of addressing social problems. The laughing audience slowly realizes it has been had—it is laughing at itself and real public issues which call for its intervention. Radio, too, through drama isolates and frames social problems. The CBC was broadcasting drama over radio at its inception in 1932 and continues to do so. *Afghanada* (2008–09) is moving into its third season. It features the adventures of Canadian soldiers posted in Kandahar province in Afghanistan and frames the issues of war and peace, the horror of war, and the ambiguity of Western military presence in Afghanistan. *Monsoon House* (2008) is a dramatic comedy presented as a family drama featuring second-generation Canadians whose parents migrated from India. Though focused on the family saga, it subtlety ironically raises issues of multiculturalism.

The tradition is a long one. Since its beginnings CBC radio drama has defined public issues. In addition to the contemporary works cited above, two examples from the past will serve to demonstrate the point. Following the conclusion of the Second World War in 1945, value orientations in Canada and the United States shifted from a collective orientation toward community and nation to an individual orientation to self and family. In addition, the experience with war had prompted changes in values such that a more open view of sexuality and the role of women slowly began to replace the hard-line Victorian/Edwardian value system in favour of a more open, transparent view. But the move from the old to the new was slow and the tensions between the two were great. Several CBC radio plays picked up on this, defining the movement in values as a major public issue.[3]

One of these plays, *Hilda Morgan* (written by Lister Sinclair, produced by Andrew Allan, and broadcast on 22 May 1949), was one of the most controversial of the plays aired during the first six years of the *CBC Stage* series. The issue addressed in the play—the choice among the abortion of a child conceived out of wedlock, the acceptance of the child, or its surrender for adoption—shocked many listeners. Angry letters followed to CBC officials, members of Parliament, and the prime minister. Individuals and organizations alike expressed their outrage. The rebroadcast a year later only served to increase the outrage. A reading of this correspondence suggests that those offended identified with the conservative position taken by Hilda's mother. The play framed a new role for women in the world depicted in the play—a world in which women have a choice, in which the double standard is seen for what it is, and in which love dominates over concern for reputation.

Another was the play *Mother Is Watching*, written by Patricia Joudry, produced by Andrew Allan, and aired on 23 November 1952. The play spoke with both bitterness and hope to the many young women trapped in the postwar suburbs which had sprung up on the outskirts of Canadian and American metropolitan centres. It was in these new middle-class communities that the struggle between consumerism and culture and between individualism and community expressed itself. The play was at once a commentary on the contradictory values of the new middle classes of the 1950s and on the profound effects of the new lifestyles on women, effects which, in retrospect, sowed the seeds for the feminist movement a decade later. Neither the theme of feminine emancipation nor the critique of suburban lifestyles was uncommon in the plays produced during the 1950s. *Mother Is Watching* was an especially penetrating example of the genre.

Television and radio entertainment have demonstrated considerable ambivalence in addressing issues related to gender equality. On the one hand, radio drama opened discussion on the inequality of women as early as the 1950s, and currently in dramas such as *Afghanada* and the new (April 2010) series *The Backbencher*, which features a female MP from Nova Scotia, and in television through comedy programming as exemplified in *This Hour Has 22 Minutes*. The trend in television drama has been toward portraying gender roles in a positive way, with more female characters cast as working outside of the home (Elasmar, Hasegawa, and Brian, 1999: 23). On the other hand, overall women continue to be presented in prime-time TV drama in roles featuring romance, family, and friends. This conclusion was reported in a fairly recent study of TV drama roles using a sample of 124 prime-time TV dramas broadcast during the 2005–06 season (Lauzen, Dozier, and Horan, 2008: 200).

Summary

This chapter opened by drawing our attention to a distinction made by C. Wright Mills (1959: 8) in his classic work, *The Sociological Imagination*. For Mills the difference between personal troubles and public issues highlighted the primary focal point of sociology as a discipline: the organization of the biographies of individuals 'into the institutions of an historical society as a whole'. Institutions define and direct human behaviour. Social problems—the principal fodder of news and entertainment media—are framed by media organizations. Copyright issues, gaming and violence, crime and health, and the role of women are public issues defined and redefined by news outlets and are up front one day and on the back page the next day.

The point of this chapter is that media have become the principal institutions now formulating and framing public issues. Public issues, as we perceive them, be they within the media itself or external to the media, are mediated through such outlets as the press, television, the Internet, and social networks. On the one hand, perhaps a certain feeling of malaise decreases as we become aware of the particular social problems bearing down upon us. On the other hand, the process through which the problems come to us, insofar as we are removed from such issues, involves a complex system of relations between corporations, journalists, and their sources, a process which may or may not enlighten us or may contribute to moral panic.

Accordingly, the media carries considerable responsibility in a democratic society to frame public issues for intelligent and rational discussion. It most certainly meets this responsibility, to a point. To go beyond that point requires an active and intelligent citizenry to call it to task when it fails to deconstruct the messages received. This places the citizenry in a very difficult position, a position in which the media frames social problems for the citizenry but the citizenry must be sufficiently alert to question and debate the process. Only then will citizen and media work hand in hand.

Enhanced Learning Activities

1. List the benefits and disadvantages of copyright rules for users and creators. Develop an argument favouring the benefits to creators and users respectively.
2. Select a metropolitan daily newspaper and, using any five-day period, count the number of crime stories appearing on the first three pages. Note the proportion of crime stories relative to the total number of stories. Discuss your findings in relation to the mediation of social problems by the media.

3. Select a television or radio drama or comedy program and discuss the manner in which it frames a social problem.

Annotated Further Reading

Joel Best, *Social Problems*. New York: W.W. Norton Company, 2008. This is a welcome new approach to textbooks on the subject. Rather than listing and discussing an array of social problems, this book focuses on process—the way in which issues become social problems.

James Boyle, *The Public Domain: Enclosing the Commons of the Mind*. http://jamesboyle.com, 2008. You do not have to buy this book, though you may if you wish. You can download it from the Internet free of charge and without worrying about copyright. It is a refreshing new look at intellectual property as a public issue by a lawyer working in the field.

Richard Ericson, Patricia M. Baranek, and Janet B.L. Chan. *Negotiating Control: A Study of News Sources*. Toronto: University of Toronto Press, 1989. Any publication from the Centre of Criminology at the University of Toronto is worth reading. This one is selected because it deals with the interaction between journalists and their sources in the process of framing social problems.

C. Wright Mills, *The Sociological Imagination*. New York: Oxford University Press, 1959. This work was referred to in earlier chapters. It is a classic in sociology. It is relevant here because of the attention given to private troubles and public issues. Chapter 1 is especially important in the context of a consideration of social problems.

Useful Media

National Film Board of Canada—*Roadsworth*
http://films.nfb.ca/roadsworth.ca

This website provides information on a documentary dealing with urban space and graffiti. The question behind the film, 'Who owns public spaces?', links with Chapter 2.

Cinema Politica
http://www.cinemapolitica.org/node/524

This is the website of Cinema Politica, a non-profit media arts network of community and campus screenings of independent political film and video. This site reviews the film *Rip: A Remix Manifesto*, a critique of copyright, with access to a 2.5-minute trailer.

National Film Board of Canada—*Of Hopscotch and Little Girls*
http://www.onf-nfb.gc.ca/eng/collection/film/index.php?id=33878

This site gives access to the National Film Board of Canada's award-winning film *Of Hopscotch and Little Girls*. Hopscotch is a universal game; girls around the world trace squares on the ground, and then hop through them, trying hard to reach the end. But all too often, through poverty, perversion, spite, ignorance, or superstition, adults shatter their dreams by denying girls the right to an education, entering them into forced labour, and subjecting them to mutilation, sexual abuse, and other injustices.

Real Injun
http://www.reelinjunthemovie.com/site/
As noted, media frame social problems. This website refers you to the film *Real Injun*, a documentary on how Hollywood movies have portrayed North American Aboriginal peoples over the past century.

Notes

1. Copyright is just one aspect of intellectual policy issues. Patents and trademarks are also considered as intellectual property. See James Boyle (2008).
2. The following material on *This Hour Has 22 Minutes* is an adaptation from Saxton, Rocher, and Jackson (2004).
3. The following material on CBC radio drama is adapted from Fink and Jackson (1987).

10

Journalism and Seriocomedy: Framing Poverty in Montreal Media[1]

Learning Objectives

- To provide a comparative case study to learn how journalism and television seriocomedy frame poverty as a social problem
- To assess sociological and media approaches to poverty
- To learn about frame analysis and the implied audience
- To learn how to deconstruct news and seriocomedy treatment of poverty as a social problem

Introduction

The quotes in the box are examples of how newspapers go about framing different forms of poverty to be understood as social problems and as public issues. Three contradictory claims are framed for the implied audience. The first quote is taken from a *La Presse* report on 20 or so homeless people who continue to sleep outdoors on the coldest day of the year, in –34 degree Celsius temperatures. We are called to witness the social problem of homelessness from the point of view of the homeless. Note that even though the homeless are directly quoted in the article, the article is not framed as an address to the homeless but to readers who likely have no experience of being without shelter under such conditions. The second quote is from *Le Devoir* two months earlier. It uses the voice of an executive of an association of developers lobbying

THE PRESS AND HOMELESSNESS

Alain, who is 50 and has AIDS, has lived on the street for 14 years. He lost his will to survive in the shelters and says, 'I am like a dog, and I always want to be outside.' Two young men, Simon and Donald, avoid shelters because their pet dogs are not allowed. As Simon says, 'I live in the street to keep my future open. In a house you only see your future through a window.' (Touzin, 2005: A8)

Jacques Primeau, the vice-president of the Partenariat du Quartier des spectacles (the economic association for the development of the new arts quarter in Montreal), states: 'the entrance to the sector is especially pitiful. Bleury Street is still scarred by vacant lots with dilapidated buildings housing homeless squatters . . . . Planning a city is a great cultural gesture, and vice versa. It is a fundamental choice to propose a negative or positive plan and when people came into the no-man's-land of vacant lots and abandoned buildings that were there before it presented the negative image of poverty.' (Baillargeon, 2005: B2)

But why the homeless? What have they done? Have they become a new danger to public security? To national security? No. The mortal sin of the homeless is that they exist and give the city and the neighborhood a bad image. Police tell us citizens no longer want to see them. So the police give themselves the noble mandate to clear the homeless out and provide a more agreeable urban aesthetics for the city. Should we applaud them . . . or vomit on them . . . . A society that encourages or tolerates the persecution of the homeless by the police is not civilized or guided by humanist values. No, it is a society of neglect, founded in egocentric values of the maximum accumulation of everyone for themselves. (Popovic, 2005: A11) to build downtown Montreal's new Arts Quarter and frames the homeless as a public issue in a city that fails to solve its social problems through planning. Although the article refers to the homeless, its implied audience would be one that shares little interest in the homeless except as a problem the City needs to get rid of. Finally, the third quote frames the homeless as victims of the City's repressive police apparatus that harasses them in attempts to control or liquidate their visibility. Even though the article makes a passionate plea in favour of justice for the homeless, it still does not address the homeless as an audience. Rather it speaks directly to those who would do them injustice in the name of justice.

A paradox of the mainstream media is that while the poor are represented regularly in supportive and often conditional tones of hospitality in newspaper reports, journalists rarely address the poor as their imagined or implied audiences (Nielsen, 2008). How citizens imagine poverty as a social problem in the city through mass media is thus an obvious yet also complex research object for critical sociology. To begin with, it is important to recall that sociology and media are both similar and different. Sociology and mass media represent their objects of study from second-level positions, that is, through constructing theories out of data analysis and observation for sociology, and information gathering, program development, and analysis for mass media (Luhmann, 2002). Both are second-level observation points in the sense that they represent real living actors or first-level observers. Given that the media can draw its inspiration for stories from almost any first-level observers, what Georg Simmel calls subjective culture (see Chapter 1), and sociology can take any institution or first-level social interaction as its object of study, then it stands to reason media and sociology enter into each other's research domains.

The sociology of media representations of social problems means examining norms about the common good in society. In reporting, representing, or explaining themes of poverty, sociology and media are both realist and constructivist insofar as the role of each is to construct knowledge about the object with reference to the real social world. For example, the sociological definition of extreme poverty is limited to the more than 20 per cent of the world's population that live with incomes of less than $1.00 a day, while moderate poverty includes another 20 per cent who live with less than $2.00 a day (Sachs, 2005; Davis, 2006). Neither group is easily reached by social assistance. In these definitions it may not be appropriate to calculate either extreme or moderate poverty for the poor who reportedly live in similar conditions in Montreal but may also have access to first-world social services, food, and shelter. Nonetheless, as we will see, images of 'the poorest of the poor' in the city are reported and framed in storytelling by journalists and in popular entertainment programs from various media.

The discussion that follows is about how poverty is variously represented as a social problem and social issue in a comparative study of print journalism and television seriocomedy in Montreal. The chapter illustrates the sociological relation between social problems, journalism, and entertainment media. To get a sense of how reports on poverty are framed, examples are drawn from daily online newspapers in 2005—*The Gazette*, *La Presse*, and *Le Devoir*—and from skits taken from the popular Radio-Canada television program about the underclass of poor 'have-nots' in east-end Montreal, *Les Bougons* (2003–05).

Keep in mind as the analysis proceeds that whereas **mainstream newspapers** engage the theme of poverty through conventional journalistic practices that include various levels of commitment to 'balance, accuracy, accountability, checks on profit motives, and editorial separation' (Entman, 2005: 54), seriocomedies like *Les Bougons* frame poverty through ironic and satirical treatments of current events that invert social status through a unique use of language and dialect (Bakhtin, 1984; see also Chapter 8). What is sociologically critical here is not the fact that these media each represent poverty but how they go about framing interpretations of what poverty is like *for those who are not poor*. Deconstructing examples of the journalist's and broadcaster's sense of the 'normal' and the 'not normal' dimension of poverty is needed in order to see how each communicates social problems to their implied readers or viewers.

Les Bougons: Seriocomedy and Poverty

As was discussed in Chapter 8, a culture of laughter has to do with how values and norms are implicated in shared emotions and a strong sense of belonging to a particular sense of 'we'. In Québec society the social problem of poverty has long been a central theme in the mass urban culture of laughter. A modern Québec culture of laughter can be traced as far back as private radio seriocomedies produced daily in Montreal beginning in the 1920s. Throughout the history of electronic media, seriocomedies have been known to play with the reversal of upper and lower social class accents and mannerisms and have frequently satirized the poverty and powerlessness of French Canadians. The implied audiences for these seriocomedies are clearly discernable in the response anticipated from playing on the deep tension between traditional and contemporary culture through the ironic use of sub-dialects, local oral traditions, and economically and socially stratified regional accents—all the while celebrating their ability to create and express themselves in vernacular language.

The *Les Bougons* television series from Radio-Canada (2003–05) needs to be understood as connected to this long history of social-problem-based seriocomedy produced in Montreal. At the same time the Bougon family is part of a more contemporary urban but not fictional underclass who endlessly scheme to make money illegally and to cheat the system in ways that could have never been imagined in previous forms of seriocomedy. It is a weekly half-hour program about a permanently unemployed poor family of six living in Montreal's traditional Francophone working-class east end. The implied audience gets a double message. On the one hand, the Bougons appear to be allies of the poor in a struggle against a corrupt system. On the other hand, they themselves are not poor, given the success of their illegal activities—although they are almost never seen spending money. For the Bougons, going to school, getting a job, going straight, and supporting political ideologies all represent debased values, whereas eliminating need and maximizing profit through elaborate bunco schemes and family teamwork constitute the highest values. They sometimes cheat each other and generally appear to be out for themselves as individuals whenever possible. But the **carnivalesque** spirit of their laughter lightens the moral message and also allows the series to empower the poor. They cheat the housing authority, the welfare office, the unemployment office, all social services and bureaucracies, and any municipal, provincial, or federal authority that might enter into the sphere of poverty. The characters buy as little as possible, steal almost everything they use, and never pay rent.

The following extract from first season illustrates a similar relativity in the concept of poverty as we saw above in the samples from the newspapers. The scene treats the question of the way the poor might imagine the poor as 'other' than themselves. The Bougons have won a contract to develop a pilot for a television series about a poor family. The pilot is at the stage where a focus group composed of imaginary poor people is invited to listen to the script. The pilot they have sold concerns the creation of a fake daycare for neighbourhood children for which the government pays five dollars a day. In the last phase of production before going on air, Rita Bougon, the mother of the Bougon family and the co-producer of the imaginary pilot, leads a discussion with a focus group to see if any last-minute changes are needed for the script. The focus group points out that the series is not funny or very realistic and is actually offensive toward the poor.

FOCUS GROUP: I felt they were laughing at the poor.

RITA: You thought they were laughing at you?

FOCUS GROUP: Not at us. At the poor.

PAUL BOUGON (head of the family, and co-producer) to Fred (his brother and script writer for the pilot): Looks like we are going to have to rewrite it a bit more positively.

FRED BOUGON: C'mon, Paul, these are just a couple of uneducated welfare bums, they don't know anything . . .

MARC LABRÈCHE (a famous Québec comedian who plays the Radio-Canada executive in the skit): But they are exactly the same people who watch our shows.

After the pilot airs Radio-Canada receives complaints that pick up on the same point raised in the focus group and cancels the series.

LABRÈCHE: Look, Paul, things have changed since yesterday. We were flooded with complaints about the show. The audience feels that the show is laughing at the poor. They don't think they speak that bad and that they don't dress that bad. The thing is they want a more positive image of the poor; the League for Anti-Poverty thinks it will make the real horror of poverty seem banal.

Unlike the newspapers cited above and others we discuss in more detail below, *Les Bougons* addresses its implied audience in two ways. In the first instance it empowers them through a more inclusive form of participation in that the laughter invites all of its audience into the fun. In this sense it is possible to imagine the poor themselves as part of the implied popular audience that the media provider (Radio-Canada) and the creators of the series are imagining. Here all social classes share inside jokes about the poor as if this were a distinguishing feature of what helps make up Québec society itself. The other way it addresses the implied audience is through shared knowledge that the system is no less corrupt than the characters scheming to set up the fake daycare centre. But this is no longer addressed toward everyone and becomes a very similar moral framework to the one cited in examples we will see from the newspapers below. That is, the poor do not recognize themselves as poor, but that the poor are seen as a social problem implies that the audience has to be other than poor. The implied audience is in agreement that television does not represent the 'real poor' and at the same time it participates in a destabilizing or 'undecidable' force as to whom and what poverty is about.

Studying Newspapers: Frame Analysis and Keyword Search

Frame analysis of content from each media provides a method for deconstructing the active relation to societal norms that authors and audiences negotiate inside and outside the content of the newspapers and seriocomedies. Frame analysis is traced back to Irving Goffman (1974), who examined the minute details involved in framing mundane everyday interactions. Over time frame analysis shifted from its ethnographic application to media studies in general (Tuchman, 1978; D'Angelo, 2002). According to one definition, frame analysis illustrates the participatory orientation of media by showing how news media involves actively 'selecting and highlighting some facets of events or issues, and making connections among them so as to promote a particular interpretation, evaluation, and solution' (Entman, 2004: 5). We adapt frame analysis to explain whether the journalist's or broadcaster's selection of moral terms and emotional tone supports the status quo, provides an alternative, or is critical of the event, issue, and agents that are the focus of the story. Deconstructing multiple relations of closeness or distance between the author, the subject of poverty as a social problem, and the implied audience means undoing their interconnections.

For example, a polemic in a newspaper or a seriocomedy may be directly addressed against a city official or government functionary named in the article or seriocomedy episode. This is a direct address to an **internal audience** or addressee inside the article or comedy episode. The serious or comic critique of the city official suggests distance from the author's sense of what the official should do for the poor. It is also a frame that draws the poor close to the opinion of the author. This proximity or sympathy with the poor frames the legitimacy of the story. At the same time the criticism or polemic in journalism, or the satirical irony in seriocomedy, addresses an externally implied audience about the city official and his or her responsibility to serve the poor. The implied audience has to do with how the author frames the address to an audience beyond the direct addressee inside the article or episode. Whereas the city official is distanced from both the author and the implied audience, the image of the poor is close to what the author sees as normal with the audience that is implied.

Unlike seriocomedies, newspapers negotiate the realm of public opinion more directly by anticipating an implied audience that is presupposed within their framing of reports on government policy, official statements, or claims from organizations or individuals who work for the poor or, far more rarely, the voices of the poor themselves. Although other media express identities that may be urban, they are not as rooted in the city as newspapers. Mainstream newspapers remain embedded in their cities even when they transform themselves into 'national', 'bi-national', or 'global' publications by going online. We are drawn far less to images or issues of our home city when we read newspapers from other cities or from abroad, and more to national or international issues we are mutually engaged in, even though these images are removed from the many nuanced opinions, tastes, and sensibilities expressed in our own local newspapers.

The selection of newspaper materials for analysis of poverty in the following sections was made by employing search engines using keyword selections from Biblio Branché, Factiva, and Proquest in 2005. The keywords included 'poverty' (pauvreté) and 'poor' (pauvre). Only articles from columns, editorials and op-eds, news reports, and feature articles were selected. The search was done in a way that ensured that results contained both 'Montreal' and one of the keywords in the same paragraph so as to focus the selection on the city. It was found that over a 10-year search the average flow of stories on the theme of poverty in Montreal in the three newspapers combined is 382 articles a year. A first reading of each of the 343 articles for 2005 was done for relevance and 112 articles were further selected as best suited to the more limited frame analysis with a focus on the Montreal context. From this group of articles, 20 are cited and grouped below as examples of the three strong themes that are submitted to further analysis.

Direct Talk in the Press: 'The Poorest of the Poor'

Our analysis of newspaper reports on poverty as a social problem begins by asking how the press named the poorest of the poor in Montreal in 2005. When journalists refer to macro aggregate data for authority to legitimate reports, the stories most often frame questions about policy and a politics of naming poverty through social facts. Who are the poor? How have they been counted and by whom? How many are homeless? Why is poverty persistent? How can poverty be eradicated? What are the global causes? How are the homeless mistreated? Emotional tones and moral terms of sympathy frame implied audiences in these articles through the surprise or shock effect of the data itself. Each type of article invites its implied audience to question just how prevalent poverty has become.

For example, one article in this 'face-centred' discourse claims that Montreal had 10 per cent unemployment, among the highest levels, in 2005. In the province of Québec, 40 per cent of salaries were less than $20,000, which hovers around the official definition of poverty levels for families of four in Canadian society. In the same year, it was reported that 340,000 people received social assistance (*La Presse*, 9 September 2005: A1). Estimates are reported of hundreds of thousands of meals served to the poor in the city over the year (Block, 2005: A8; Petits frères des pauvres, 2005) and of the relative size of the homeless population, which varies between the official count of 12,000 in 1998 (Sutherland, 2005a: A11) to upwards of possibly 60,000 in the summer of 2005. Between 1994 and 2004, the homeless accounted for more than 90 per cent of charges by police for public-nuisance misdemeanours. We are told that the data for 2004 represents a fourfold increase in infractions, with an average fine ranging from $102 to $371 if prison time is served (Cauchy, 2005: A1).

On the other hand, when newspapers frame their address toward the implied audiences through an ethnographic lens, attention is geared toward local voices and immediate contexts as well as to more individual cases and moral imperatives. Articles written in an ethnographic style include official and non-official voices that talk about the poor or homeless. Very few articles frame poverty as voiced by the poor themselves. At the same time, the majority of newspaper articles frame a hospitable or sympathetic orientation toward the poor and a negative image for relevant government agencies. Where, in the minority of cases, more intensely hostile assumptions about the poor and the homeless are addressed, they are expressed indirectly, as shown in the final section of the chapter.

Three highly compelling reports by Brian Myles for *Le Devoir* are about an estimated 350 homeless Aboriginals (Myles, 2005a: A1; Sansfaçon, 2005:

A6), who are presented to the anticipated reader as 'the poorest of the poor in Montréal' (Myles, 2005b: A1; Myles, 2005c: A4). Myles reports on the perspective of an amateur anthropologist, Emmanuel Morin, who first met Inuit street people while still a student and developed a lifelong compassionate relationship with them as an activist and social worker. We are told that First Nation males have no shelter or treatment centre of their own in Montreal, while there is one small shelter for females—even though more than 10,000 First Nation peoples live in the city. Aboriginals prefer not to use shelters run by whites because of their experience of racism, and even if they did want to use the shelters, they would generally not be eligible because the facilities require sobriety. In other words, they sleep outside and, as Morin says, 'the violence is there, the alcohol is there. And when it explodes it really explodes . . . .' It is so disappointing, he says, that whites have written off the Inuit, who are living in the harshest of third-world conditions. 'Sometimes it gives me the shivers', says Morin. 'These are the most messed-up people you can find. They are at the bottom of the bottom and live in the hour, not the everyday' (Myles, 2005c: A4).

Myles is among a minority of journalists (although he has had quite limited success) to attempt interviews with Aboriginal homeless people and to portray them in their own voice. He explains that there are multiple reasons why natives become homeless in the city. Causes are rooted in 'a corrosive cocktail of racism, bureaucracy and ignorance. For the poor it is difficult to find housing. For a poor Aboriginal it is almost impossible' (Myles, 2005: A1). While the Inuit make up 10 per cent of the native population in Montreal, 'they account for 43 per cent of the Aboriginal homeless in the city.' He situates the high rate of homelessness for Inuit in the context of their migration from Nunavut, where 'the suicide rate is six times higher than the Canadian average . . . and where 40% of Inuit children are victims of sexual assault. Inuit are drawn to the city because of phenomenal demographic growth while employment opportunities remain non-existent.' Violence, abuse, and exclusion increase as Inuit pour into the city: 'Through a cruel stroke of destiny the Inuit who live on the street live in the violence they thought they were free from . . . a violence that is especially brutal on women' (Myles, 2005: A1).

In the first article of the series, Myles tells the story of Hank, who is waiting for a band of natives from the West to come and 'take revenge' on the whites. It is Valentine's Day and a young Inuit woman is looking for Sebastian for a party while Hank eats sandwiches distributed by the Ka'wahse (Mohawk for 'where are you going?') patrol in Atwater Park next to the metro in downtown Montreal. Later they try to find a place for the night for Annie, who is always drunk, while all of them are nervous that Greg is going to come. Greg is a Métis 'who the Inuit instinctively mistrust', Myles tells us, and they are right! Greg has just 'served eight years in prison for having raped a seventeen-year-old girl in front of her mother, who was tied up . . . . This evening, fortunately, Greg is not there' (Myles, 2005a: A1).

It is important to recall that these articles are not engaged in a simple conversation between journalists and their actual readers but represent a more implicit exchange that takes place in the anticipation of an audience's imagined interest in their subject. Journalists frame their texts to meet that anticipation and in the process look to describe some element about the maximum level of poverty in the city. Framing the issue of poverty is done through emotional expressions arising from voices in the streets, which are situated against background facts on conditions in the North and racism in the South that lend legitimacy to the plea for much greater sympathy toward the poor, with fewer conditions. Having AIDS and living almost entirely outside in the dead of winter, or coming from Northern poverty and descending even further into its degradation in the Southern city, also supposes an understanding about the journalist's implied audience that it has no immediate experience of this kind of poverty.

These mainly secondary ethnographic reports shine a powerful light of hospitality and dignity on the poorest through contextual analyses. In some cases they establish a moving emotional tone through direct quotes from people in the street and especially from the best expert on the street (in the case of the ethnographer). The poorest of the poor in Montreal are presented as 'others' who also have basic rights to shelter, food, warmth, and medical care. Does this mean these reports offer a model for an unconditional journalistic hospitality toward the poor?

Framing is about highly selective choices made by journalists to highlight certain aspects of a story and to provide an interpretation or solution for the reader. For example, in Figure 10.1 we selected a sample of articles in 2007 that discuss poverty and Montreal, from the same three Montreal newspapers we studied in 2005, in order to determine whether or not journalists were generally positive in terms of the support they express for the poor. We asked coders to determine whether the interpretation or proposed solution for a given social problem related to poverty showed hospitality, conditional hospitality, or rejection of the poor: Was the judgment in favour of supporting the poor as long as some conditions were respected or imposed, even if the judgment agreed with some things but disagreed with others or imposed certain limits? A framed rejection meant that the subject of exclusion was rejected outright. Coders were also asked what considerations the judgment was based on. Were judgments named emotionally, that is, was the authority's judgment based on emotional considerations such as personal feelings and experiences? Was the judgment *moral*? Were the authority's judgments based on moral considerations, giving arguments such as 'because this is how things should be', or 'because this is the right thing to do'? Was the judgment *rational*: were the authority's judgments based on rational considerations: Was the authority maintaining a certain distance or neutrality when discussing the issue?

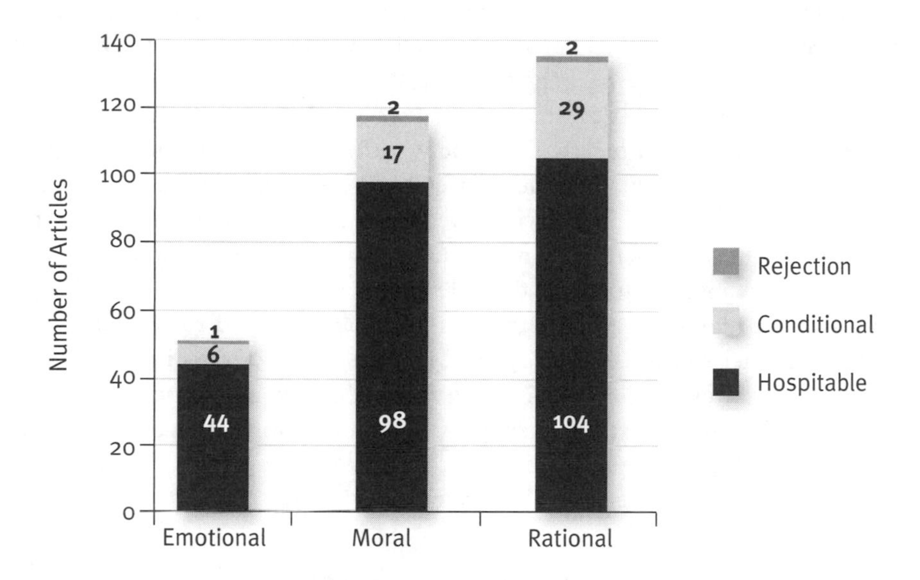

FIGURE 10.1 Number and Type of Judgments (n=221 articles)
Montreal Press, 2007: Poverty

'Our TV Poor' Are at Peace

There is no representation of extreme poverty in *Les Bougons*. Poverty is seen more like a party than a burden. The carnival or party ambiance can be seen in multiple parodies of the way in which Québec television imagines its audience would like to see poverty. In one such episode the Bougons are selected as the best example of a poor family in Montreal. The characters from *Les Bougons* live in a dilapidated second-storey apartment. Family members include Papa (Paul) and Mama (Rita); Mon Oncle Fred (Papa's brother); the invalid quasi-mute grandfather; Dolores, the eldest daughter, who practises prostitution out of her room in the family apartment; the son, Junior, who is an excellent thief; Mao, an illegal refugee, their androgynous eight-year-old Chinese daughter; and Ben Laden, the family dog. Prostitution, fraud, theft, and vice are noble endeavours directed against anyone who has money and especially against government agencies.

We are introduced to the characters through a television interview sketch episode in which the Bougons are informed that a mobile unit from a reality-style program, led by the popular host Monsieur Gagnon, will be visiting them. The sketch is both a parody of the reality show genre in that it demonstrates how scripted the format is, and a fantasy discussion on how the mainstream audience would like to see poverty represented. In preparation the 'Local Association for the Poor' has sent the Bougons an elaborate fruit basket to put in their refrigerator so as to give a 'good impression' to the television audience. The point, claims Papa Bougon, 'is not what you do in life but how you look on television, especially in politics!'

This sketch introduces the main characters of the program. Dolores, the sex-worker daughter, enters the apartment with two of her clients. They apologize for the interruption and in a series of double entendres excuse themselves to her bedroom. The television team thanks the family and leaves the apartment. On one level, the parody shows us the way television laughs at television. On another, it shows the sideways glance of the implied audience that is in the know along with *Les Bougons* about how bad reality television can be. In other words, the parody critiques the way poverty is imagined and the implied viewer is called to witness a form of everyday injustice within the media system itself. Like the newspaper articles on extreme images of poverty, *Les Bougons* calls on the implied viewer to witness the everyday injustice of media that transform the reality of poverty into fantasy.

Journalistic Polemics on Politicians, Developers, and the State

Exclusion of the poor as the audience of newspapers and seriocomedy has never been ethically or politically problematic for mainstream media. It has long been embedded in the understanding that news stories and entertainment programs should be addressed to the interest of the majority readership or viewer (Retief, 2002; Ward, 2006). Traditionally, the first responsibility of the journalist, and of television producers, is to examine and judge the newsworthiness or entertainment value of the story for this *marketable* audience, as was noted in Chapter 3. This postulate is so basic to the media industry that it raises the question of whether or not media itself is a monologic rather than dialogic form of address. Does the news industry systematically overlook how marginalized groups become subjects of news reports and yet remain strikingly distant from the audience that journalists and broadcasters imagine they are addressing?

Like *Les Bougons*, most of the newspaper articles are critical of local, provincial, and federal government agencies. Whereas newspapers and seriocomedies do appear monologic in the sense that their empirical audiences are not engaged in any direct question-and-answer exchange (except for highly selective letters to the editor or to the broadcaster, and more recently blogs), the fact that journalists and producers anticipate a response from an imaginary but not fictional sense of who they are addressing suggests a dialogic relationship. For example, newspapers also refer mostly to relative rather than extreme poverty in Montreal. Descriptions of poverty are most often framed in the voice of moral disappointment and backed by data or other third-person ethnography, expert testimony from workers in the field, or opinions from researchers. A completely opposite response to the 'expert' who speaks in the voice of the politician, police authority, or developer can also be framed in sarcasm and ridicule though the same form of indirect speech as seen in the TV sketch on poverty below. Along with the polemic on police actions against the homeless we saw at the beginning of the chapter, *Gazette* journalist Bill Brownstein provides another good example of the anti-institutional rant when he ridicules the downtown borough councillor from Ville-Marie who in 2005 proposed to increase a tax on street musicians by more than 800 per cent:

> Surely the councilors have more pressing matters to contend with in the downtown borough like littered sidewalks and busted recycling receptacles and the homeless . . . . Seems the borough mayor feels Place Jacques Cartier gets too jammed. Hello! Isn't it a good thing to have people pack the place in the summer? (Brownstein, 2005: D1)

Two other articles in *La Presse*, one by Marcel Sevigny, an activist and former municipal councillor, and another by Rima Elkouri, ridicule the coalition of developers promoting a version of commercial citizenship that would revitalize a rundown neighbourhood by moving the casino from its out-of-the-way location on Île Notre-Dame on the St Lawrence Seaway to the historically working-poor neighbourhood of Pointe-Saint-Charles, situated just south of the downtown area. Sevigny recalls that the Montreal Casino was put out of the way in the first place in order to protect communities from risks associated with gambling. Loto-Québec (the government lottery agency promoting the move) included the casino as one part of a plan for a massive shopping centre. Rima Elkouri is also very sarcastic about the plan to move the casino to the Point but is much more ironic in her utterance.

> **Sevigny:** What a great social project! Not only would the casino come and empty the pockets of the community's new gamblers from the Point and other Montrealers, but it also proposes a wasteful anti-ecological development organized around the use of automobiles . . . at the same time the City of Montreal has just announced its strategic plan for sustainable development. (2005: A23)
>
> **Elkouri:** Far be it from me to not celebrate or to turn my back on international development for Montreal, or to turn my nose up at the hordes of tourists who will descend on the futuristic entertainment complex costing 1.2 billion dollars. Far be it from me to spit on the 6450 jobs . . . . How could I possibly doubt the genius of Cirque du Soleil? Far be it from me to ever question its capacity to get Montreal to prosper like no other city. (2005: A5)

The sarcasm in these polemical rants lends the voices a doubled and contradictory quality through both an internal (a direct address to someone within the article) and externally implied audience. The external implied audience takes the same form in each example even though the journalists and commentators are talking about different issues. Each of the examples charges that the poor and homeless are victims of political and economic incompetence, greed, or plain stupidity. Charging buskers an outrageous tax, using the police to eliminate the homeless, moving the city's only casino into a poor neighbourhood are ultimate violations of the common good. Each of the rants claims superior reasoning through this ultimate argument about the common good in the name of the least well-off. Each directs the polemic against a single internal addressee and, at the same time, each pretends they are in some way inadequate judges of their adversaries. The internal sarcastic reversal of utterances distorts literal meanings for the external implied audience: when Sevigny says, 'What a great social project!' he means that moving the casino is the worst possible plan for the neighbourhood; when Elkouri exclaims, 'How could I possibly doubt the genius of Cirque de Soleil?' she means the Cirque is acting out of self-interest, which counters its legendary status as an international entertainment enterprise with strong community consciousness. When Popovic asks, as we saw earlier, why the police target the homeless, he is ironically reversing the question into a charge against the police.

Are these kinds of polemics a good example of advocacy for positive inclusion of the poor in society? In each of the above examples the rights of the poor are defended and yet in each case the references to the poor are of secondary importance compared to the agencies who claim to work for the common good and are the objects of attack. Although the direct address of moral, emotional outrage toward the interior audience in these examples appears to define a positive acceptance of the poor, note that the audience addressed inside the text, or the person or institution toward which the outrage is directed, is not the poor themselves. This seems banal and without consequence at first glance. After all, when we speak sarcastically and angrily to someone about our support for someone they are harming, we are not addressing that someone else but the someone to whom we are speaking.

Are the poor in fact used in each of these examples as a moral referent that frames their 'otherness', an 'otherness' that lies in an assumed moral condition of hospitality framed in the dialogue with the implied audience? In each case the rights of the poor are defended on a second level of observation and in each case the reference to the poor and the homeless is secondary to the agencies who claim to work for the common good.

Seriocomedy as Anarchy: Against the Common Good

For *Les Bourgons*, the most important point about the 'poorest of the poor' and these more relative images of poverty in anti-institutional rants is that their resolution is never in the system. They do not look to claim rights or impose obligations but to develop strategies to subvert gentrification, social assistance programs, the police, and all other institutions contributing to the common good. This is made clear in an episode entitled 'Citizen of the World', in which Papa Bougon gives an impassioned direct speech against his brother Fred (*mon oncle*) who announces a sense of pride on being called in for his first job interview. For the middle-aged Uncle Fred this is his first chance to finally become a 'real citizen' like everyone else. When asked by his brother, Papa Bougon, why he wants this, Fred's reply is simply: 'to contribute to my country.' This receives the following acerbic response: 'Your country? Have you ever asked what your country has done for you? Nothing but shit! Come on!!! A tiny elite of thugs that we never see runs your country!' The internal audience of the Bougon family listening to the rant provides relief to its serious tone for the external implied audience.

The internal audience engages a lighter comedy that clashes with a darker one and helps save the political speech from its serious gloominess and recover a joyous relativity. The audience listening inside the sketch already know the speech before the implied audience does. The speech is like a manifesto they have already internalized. They wait nervously and cynically for Papa to finish his fight with his brother so they can get back to having fun. On the other hand, the implied listener is piecing together a political argument against 'the system' that sees everyone but the rich as being exploited. The sideways glance between the implied audience and Papa works against Uncle Fred, who represents the logic of the system. The 'we' opposes any solution to end poverty that begins with the assumption that society has to create jobs. The poor as 'other' are constructs of the system. Getting a job is participating in the system that exploits everyone who does not subvert it.

Indirect Talk: Journalistic Accounts of Poor Reporting on Poor

Journalistic transgressions like bias, slander, plagiarism, and conflicts of interest are most often governed in-house but occasionally can erupt into public issues when posted as complaints to local **press councils**. More embedded constitutional rights legitimate everyday issues like the journalists' access to information, freedom of expression, and protection of sources (Russell, 2006). Neither press councils nor existing codes of conduct that govern journalistic ethics take into consideration the problem of the gap between the subject that is being reported on and the audiences to whom the reports are addressed. In this section we address examples of how this gap permits a type of indirect criticism of poverty without drawing attention to any 'ethical' violation or legal sanction.

No direct negative images or polemics against poverty and homelessness were found to unite journalists and implied audiences within the articles found in 2005. Two kinds of negative images of the poor are, however, derived indirectly by arguing either for the gentrification of neighbourhoods to eliminate poverty or a more common theme—comparing the 'authentic' homeless with 'inauthentic' homeless. In both cases journalists indirectly critique poverty and the poor as a negative value.

We saw a good example of the indirect negative image of poverty above that was reported on by *Le Devoir*'s Stéphane Baillargeon. The critique was aimed at government inertia regarding its plan to develop the Quartier du spectacles, or the Entertainment District, at the heart of the city's festival life. Another negative image that often appears in the news concerns the image the poor have of the poor, especially between cities, regions, and generations. Montreal is somewhat of a magnet for migrant homeless youth from across Québec, Canada, and the United States who drop into the city during summer festival season. Some estimates, according to Hugo Meunier, put the influx of people sleeping outdoors on any given night during this period at up to 40,000, whereas the local homeless population fluctuates between 20,000 and 30,000. Some leave jobs and home to party in the city for a while and live in the streets before returning to their lives. According to Meunier,

> The locals call them 'shrimps'. They are temporary homeless who come in and make good money off the street, then leave. André, a local for the last eight years, is quoted as saying, 'It really pisses me off when I see those imbeciles from Ontario, Manitoba, and Vancouver do their squeegee number.' André, another local, claims, 'The visitors are mainly junkies and see us locals as bums so we have to be aggressive sometimes just to protect our space. The streets have really changed since the squeegees invaded us.' (Meunier, 2005: A2)

The sense of authentic street credibility has its own version in the straight world, as can be seen in stories from the *Gazette*. Ann Sutherland writes on the front page about an out-of-town visitor who had his possessions stolen from his car, including his much-valued in-line skates. He noticed a homeless shelter nearby and went in to ask the nun at the desk for help and posted a reward. Apparently the skates and most of his possessions appeared at the front desk anonymously a little while later, demonstrating an unexpected moral code between the shelter and the street (Sutherland, 2005b: A1).

Another front-page cover story on the theme of codes of honour is about a 'wealthy' Toronto panhandler selling happy faces on the Montreal streets. According to journalist Catherine Solyom, the woman was reported as being seen in front of the Eaton Centre in Toronto selling stickers; she commuted there from Hamilton in a Volkswagen Jetta. The story illustrates the moral question of 'real street people' versus ordinary thieves masquerading in poverty in order to profit: '"I don't make much money, and I'm just one person trying to live." Hebert says she budgets to make about $75 a day—which fluctuates according to the weather. She paid $300 in taxes last year, she says proudly. And she insists she is always honest with potential benefactors about what the money is for: to feed and clothe her two children. Never mind [that] one of her two children is 25 years old and apparently living on her own in Toronto' (Solyom, 2005: A1).

Distinguishing real poor from pretend poor frames a conditional acceptance of the poor in two ways. First it confirms a shared value judgment that a fraud carried out in the name of the poor is among the lowest transgressions. The fake panhandler and squeegee punks are the most fraudulent and the least valued respectively. The poor in the shelter are authentic and deserve a measure of forgiveness for sharing a moral reference, as seen in the return of the stolen goods through the medium of the nun. The seemingly wealthy panhandler from Toronto has no credibility and is universally condemned. The seasoned regulars on the street are given a significant edge in value over the ephemeral suburban or out-of-town street youth, who are seen as less credible.

The **doubling of discourse** carries a scale of values that creates a conditional hospitality toward the poor and homeless. In the case of the regular 'down and out', the otherness of the poor is secured in the internal understanding offered them through the press, while their implied audience is encouraged to reject the second group of 'others' as inauthentic and as having violated conditions these values set for hospitality. Unlike the authentic poor and homeless, the second group of outsiders does not take responsibility for their disregard of the territory of the city's 'authentic poor'. Through their actions, the outsiders degrade the common good and transgress its existing condition of hospitality.

Summary

When presenting poverty as a social problem, journalism moves between a social realism and moral allegory and seriocomedy travels through an imaginary realism and a local living culture of urban laughter in consummating its relationship with its mainly urban audiences. Journalists and television producers anticipate their audience's intrinsic interests and frame their texts accordingly but they tend not to imply that the poor themselves are the audience. For journalists, voices of the poor or, more often, of the agencies, groups, or individuals who speak for the poor, are most often framed in tones of moral disappointment and argued through independent macro data, micro ethnography, expert testimony, or opinion from scholarly sources. Broadcasts of seriocomedy have historically framed its implied audiences with knowing conditional understandings about poverty and the common good and use a variety of poetic devices that converge or bring into collision the serious and the comic, ironically reversing social hierarchies. While seriocomedy can imply a more inclusive audience than journalism, this is not always the case. The juxtaposition of the seriocomedy and stories that treat poverty seriously in newspapers in Montreal reveals a more important point about the way in which comic and serious discourse can be seen as extensions of each other. Comparing the implied audiences for the two media indicates complementary but different public discourses of sympathy toward the poor and to a lesser extent about how the poor see the public. At the same time both the newspapers and seriocomedy and their implied audiences demonstrate important reservations and conditional sensibilities about Montreal's urban citizenship in showing the limits of authentic rights claims.

The comparative analysis shows that the journalist or entertainment broadcaster, whether consciously or not, does not innocently report on or portray an event. On one level, as seen especially in the final section, the assumption between both media and their implied audience is hospitable but it is also conditional in the sense that the poor are never seen as meeting their obligation to be self-determining. They are framed as dependent 'others' who by implication risk living in various states of inauthenticity, as was seen in the way the implied audience is addressed when the poor speak of the poor. Unlike the newspaper reporting, though, *Les Bougons* can empower the poor by showing the corruption of the entire system. The assumption with its audience is that the 'we' in the welfare culture of laughter (or the underclass black market of social assistance) can reverse hierarchy, subvert conventional norms, and do things you can't do in 'straight' life. If 'we' can do it, anyone can do it. On the other hand, we also saw a conditional comic sense of how the institution of television imagines television imagining how its audience would like to see the poor in the city. Images of the implied audience for the newspapers is also seen in a variety of anti-institutional and pro-poverty rants that correspond neatly with the same implied audience in the anti-nationalist speech from *Les Bougons*. Unlike the editorial pieces, though, *Les Bougons* argues against both the system of social benefits and development or nationally improved employment prospects as solutions to the problem of poverty.

What can be concluded from the deconstruction of the gap between the subjects of poverty and the audiences that creators and media providers appear to address? For critical sociology, the answer is not about a common class or category of tastes shared between the actual audiences but rather about how each implied audience can be seen as an extension of the media discourse. How the address toward the implied audiences structures the reception for the actual audiences remains a separate research question, but it can at least be concluded that the framing of a discourse on public hospitality by the two media toward urban have-nots in Montreal needs to be understood as overwhelmingly addressed toward the haves of the same city. The address is almost unique given that seriocomedy can address a more universal audience but only in a carnivalesque mode. Our analysis shows that presentation of the poor in their own voice measures one pole of positive sympathetic communicative power that exists in mediated society while at the other pole, stories that frame the poor talking about the poor in both media warn of the limits of authenticity and thus infer definite conditions and obligations on their citizenship practices. We conclude that examining this kind of difference and commonality between each media and their implied audiences indicates the way mediated society both pleads for the right of the poor to have right and at the same time excludes their voices from the realm of public discourse.

Enhanced Learning Activities

1. Compare the description in the chapter on *Les Bougons* with the CTV series *Trailer Park Boys*. What are the seriocomedy features they share and how are their sociological portraits of poverty the same or different?
2. Do a keyword search with Factiva or ProQuest that will draw on the word 'poverty' and the name of a city in your region in the same paragraph. Compare the results over a period of two or three years. Read all the articles and count which ones would be relevant for the kind of sociological analysis we see in this chapter.
3. Take five newspaper articles that address poverty and give a brief description of how they frame their implied audience. Do they support or contradict the argument in this chapter that the press rarely frames its direct address to the poor themselves?

Annotated Further Reading

Mike Davis, *Planet of Slums*. London, UK: Verso, 2006. This source provides an overview of the problem of extreme and relative urban and rural poverty in global terms as reported by the United Nations Human Settlement Programme in *The Challenge of Slums*. Davies argues that if things remain the same over the next 50 years more than 70 per cent of the world population will be forced to live in mega urban slums.

Herbert Gans, *The War Against the Poor: The Underclass and Antipoverty Policy*. New York, NY: Basic Books, 1995. This is a classic study that provides an example of how labelling theory is used by the press. It examines how the underclass are named and stigmatized in mediated society through an examination of both the press and public policy.

Erving Goffman, *Frame Analysis: An Essay on the Organization of Experience*. Cambridge, MA: Harvard University Press, 1974. This is a modern sociological classic that introduces and defines frame analysis in greater detail for the study of social interaction.

Gaye Tuchman, *Making the News*. New York, NY: Free Press, 1978. This is an early study that applies Goffman's frame analysis to news content and provides an ethnography of the complex division of labour in the newsroom.

Useful Media

Online databases, such as Factiva for international printed media (http://factiva.com), ProQuest for English-Canadian printed media (http://www.proquest.com), and Eureka for French-Canadian printed media (http://www.eureka.cc), offer easy access to entire collections of newspapers and journals. They include powerful search engines which facilitate browsing the media for specific themes or keywords. Instead of having to browse through each publication's own archive (if available), one can use a single database to search multiple items. By using standardized search engines, these sites facilitate comparative research on printed media (though one has to be aware of the differences in their search engines when using different databases).

Canadian Journalism Project
http://www.j-source.ca/english_new/page.php?p=7

The Canadian Journalism Project (CJP) and its websites, J-Source.ca (English) and ProjetJ.ca (French), are projects of the Canadian Journalism Foundation in collaboration with leading journalism schools and organizations across Canada. Students are invited to join in an ongoing dialogue 'about the achievement of, and challenges to, excellence in Canadian journalism and provide a convenient and trustworthy source of information and commentary'. Launched in the spring of 2007, the site provides a source for news, research, commentary, advice, discussion, and resources. It also includes links to other organizations that recognize and support excellence in journalism.

Note

1. This chapter is in part based on a revision of material that first appeared in an article by Greg Nielsen (2008).

11 Framing Immigration as a Social Problem in *The New York Times*[1]

Learning Objectives

- To critically assess how journalism frames immigration as a social problem in the US context
- To define illegal, non-documented, and non-status immigrants
- To review the background to US immigration and the case of New York City
- To consider the origins of conditional hospitality and how ancient laws apply to contemporary immigrants
- To learn how *The New York Times* frames social problems of immigration around the themes of justice, multiculturalism, governance, and social movements
- To consider how public journalism helps reduce the gap between the audiences that journalists write for and those who are the subjects of social problems they write about

Introduction

> There is the father from Panama, a cleaning contractor in his 50s, who had lived and worked in the United States for more than 19 years. One morning, he woke to the sound of loud banging on his door. He went to answer it and was greeted by armed immigration agents. (Danticat, 2007: A12)
>
> She is a made-in-Queens mix of devotion and defiance, this slim, dark-eyed adolescent who arrived in Astoria with her family at age 5. In her round schoolgirl handwriting, she has compiled lists of favorite prayers and pious resolutions . . . . But when she recalls how FBI agents questioned her religious lifestyle, her voice drips typical teenage scorn: 'Like, I'm supposed to live for you guys?' (Bernstein, 2005a: B5)
>
> Facing the prospect of major layoffs of farm workers during harvest season, growers and lawmakers from agricultural states spoke in dire terms yesterday about new measures by the Bush administration to crack down on employers of illegal immigrants. (Preston, 2007: A10)
>
> American critics of open borders speak in terms of national sovereignty and cultural cohesion. If the United States is to retain its cultural identity, the argument goes, it cannot accept everyone who wants to come here. (Rieff, 2005: 15)

These recent quotes from *The New York Times* construct a series of contemporary social problems for their implied audience by opposing citizens and non-citizens in the US context. What would happen if illegal fathers were deported? What would happen to their children? What happens when children, like the teenager from Queens, are expelled and not their parents? What would happen with the workers doing jobs no one else will do? Should non-citizens get state benefits like health care and other social services when they are in need? These are not stories about a few cheaters jumping to the front of the line or over a fence. Rather these are stories about personal troubles that include millions of people and so need to be understood as public issues with significant policy implications. Behind the undecidable opposition between the 'legal' and 'illegal' citizen is an everyday father or worker, a child, a neighbour, a member of a community. In the US context millions of non-status residents like these are intimidated with rumours about crackdowns, imprisonment, and deportations without appeal and are often exempted from many social services, including welfare, health care, and education.

This chapter examines how journalism frames undocumented immigration as a social problem in the US with a special focus on New York City. The social problem is narrated through four public issues: *justice*, *multiculturalism*, *governance*, and *social movements*. We prepare for this discussion in the first section below by describing the generally inhospitable or conditional contexts that have intensified against undocumented immigration in the US and go on to contrast it with the more hospitable context of the New York City region. We then present the theoretical approaches that inform the concept of conditional hospitality in the following section before developing sections on each of the four areas of social problems mentioned above.

In mediated societies around the world it is more and more apparent that the term 'illegal', when applied to citizen status, designates a series of social problems that are said to threaten the economic, cultural, and political centre of society. For critical sociology the unity of a given society is paradoxical. Unity normalizes differences but differences are always pushing back against territorializing forces. More neutral terms like 'undocumented' or 'non-status' emerge to deterritorialize the sense of a unified culture of citizenship. To be without documents suggests one is there and might eventually gain status, as in waiting to qualify, or preparing for an application, or paying some kind of fine so as to become eligible. The terms 'illegal', 'undocumented', and 'non-status' depend on each other to establish different levels in the definition of the social problem. Each term engages various levels of emotional intensity and moral rectitude. On the one hand, the term 'illegal' attacks the formal status of citizenship by opposing obligations like paying taxes against rights to benefits, like health care. If followed all the way through, the designation 'illegal' would supersede even basic human rights. 'Pro-immigration' activists argue for comprehensive immigration reform for the 'undocumented' and for a compromise process that would allow many to be gradually integrated into legal citizenship status. Opponents argue vigorously against 'illegality' as well as 'amnesty', and pleas are repeated almost daily for more checkpoints, border patrols, security agents, fences, deportations, fines, arrests, and prison terms for 'illegal aliens' and their accomplices.

The terms 'illegal' and 'undocumented' or 'non-status' oppose each other at both the substantive and formal levels of citizenship. Formal citizenship status is directly linked to a closed-off cultural unity that reduces the 'illegal alien's' capacity to respond politically. Reform would allow the 'undocumented' or non-status person to be included and eventually heard in a future cultural diversity that might define the nation another way. A third term comes out of the opposition between 'illegal' and 'undocumented' and transforms both terms into undecidables.

Our critical sociology seeks to illustrate not only the levels of judgment that journalists employ in reporting on these subjects but also to pinpoint the gap between the imaginary but not fictional audience and the non-status citizens who are the subjects of the controversies but not the implied readers of the stories. To critical sociologists looking to deconstruct the journalists' sense of social problems and of the sense of 'normal' in the city, this gap poses a striking contradiction. Think about it this way: if the mainstream media regularly discuss the social problems of poverty or undocumented immigrants in positive but conditionally hospitable terms and their reportage rarely addresses them directly as their readers, does it not follow that public understanding of the experience of immigration is diminished, even when the media passionately pleads in the name of democracy for greater hospitality and refuge? We address this latter question in the final section of the chapter, where suggestions are revived from the reform movement in public journalism that could improve journalism's capacity to address the position of marginal groups in the context of the malaise over the meaning of citizenship that defines the present context.

On US Immigration and New York City

It is important to situate the personal problems of non-citizens in the historical context of immigration understood as a public issue. The current inhospitable attitude toward the undocumented in the US began in the policy shift away from European ethnic quotas that allowed only those ethnic groups to immigrate who already had established communities. This policy was enforced until 1965, when it changed in order to allow migrants with much needed skills who came from other areas of the world not commonly established in the US (Chavez, 2001). A large influx of migrant workers, mainly from Latin America and Asia, led to the 1996 reform to allow members of extended families to migrate and to increase economic-based programs. The reform also provided amnesty for three million mostly non-European migrant workers who had entered the country after the 1965 reform but without documentation. The 1996 reform also put in place severe new restrictions on the civil rights of the undocumented. In the US, an anti-immigration climate took hold more aggressively following three referenda in California on the status of the Latino population in the state: Proposition 187 (which denied public benefits to the undocumented, adding teeth to the federal reform of immigration law in 1996); Proposition 209 (ending affirmative action); and Proposition 227 (against bilingual education).

By 2005 the estimated population of non-status immigrants had risen to more than 11 million. By the spring of 2006, protests and mass mobilization of millions of undocumented migrants and their supporters erupted against the background of a decade of anti-immigration legislation and public political discourse. Articles in *The New York Times* on immigration between June and December 2005, and the spike that occurred between March and May 2006, need to be understood in this historical context. While a relative decline in coverage on immigration followed the May 2006 boycott against anti-immigration legislation, the issue re-emerged several times in the US House of Representatives with tentative bipartisan proposals that were aggressively debated on both sides for brief periods and then set aside again for more pressing issues. The issue, along with the debate, returns aggressively under the Obama administration.

Our analysis below will focus on stories from New York City and will illustrate the paradox by which journalists frame a mainly positive and supportive but also conditional hospitality for undocumented immigrants in the US, notably in the context of New York City. That New York would differ from the rest of the US is not surprising. Although New York is a cultural centre of the United States, it is widely considered to be unlike the rest of the US. As seen in Figure 11.1, articles about the undocumented in New York express a mainly welcoming hospitality while a minority demand conditions or reject them outright. Coders were asked to indicate levels of rejection, conditions placed on hospitality, and a general sense of hospitable welcome toward non-citizens as reported in rational, moral, or emotional tones.

At first glance, the framing of poverty in the Montreal press we saw in Chapter 10 and the framing of immigration in the New York press seem unconnected. After all, these are different cities, different cultures, different nations, and different social problems. And yet it helps to understand the New York case if we consider some of the social facts about both cities and especially if we keep in mind the way stories are constructed for implied readers who are not the subjects of the reports. Both New York and Montreal are well-known around the world for their openness to immigration and cultural diversity, and both serve as unique metropolitan centres that struggle with poverty despite their pockets of extraordinary affluence (Bratt et al., 2006; Arnold, 2004; Simon, 2006). Both cities have about the same proportion of

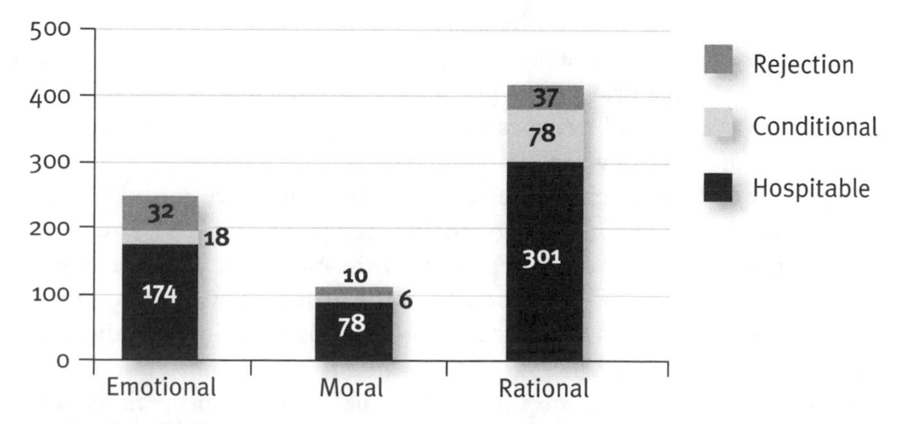

FIGURE 11.1 Immigration Judgments, New York, 2007 (n=237 articles)

foreign-born citizens (29 per cent and 35 per cent respectively), which is significantly less than Miami (59.5 per cent) or Toronto (51 per cent) (Legros, 2008); both have approximately the same portion of their population living under the poverty line; both have similar proportions of English and non-English speakers (US Bureau of Statistics, 2006; Statistics Canada, 2006); and in both cities divisions over language, race, gender, class, and ethnicity distinguish neighbourhoods and quality-of-life options as well as access to schools, work, and status (Germaine and Rose, 2000; Simon, 2006).

Unlike Montreal, New York is a global centre for English-language media, a financial hub, a service centre for world commerce, and a cultural centre of the United States. Like New York, Montreal is a centre of Canadian culture and politics, but it is widely regarded as different from the rest of Canada. While Montreal remains a second-tier city, or a city that is not a global financial centre, it is the metropole for a Francophone national minority and a global centre for French-language media that is fully engaged in national and international debates over immigration (Abrahamson, 2004). Finally, for both cities, despite over a decade of economic growth leading up to the 2008 recession, median family incomes have decreased and public funding for homelessness lags significantly behind each city's national average (Foundation of Greater Montreal, 2006; NYPIRG Homeless Project, 2007).

What Is Conditional Hospitality?

History is full of shocking examples where powerful groups and sometimes whole societies have defined other humans or societies as non-humans on the basis of their skin colour, class or ethnic origins, sexual orientation, religion, or even gender. In a similar way, societies on the scale of nation-states are built from social divisions linked to historical forms of discrimination generally inhospitable toward those who do not hold the legal status of citizenship. To repeat the point, inhospitable acts of discrimination or prejudice occur against citizens and non-citizens alike when any number of informal conditions that reproduce social division emerge: being identified with the wrong racialized class, ethnic or gender orientation; not having a fixed address, a telephone, or identification papers; and not speaking a language or speaking it poorly are only a few of the most obvious.

Media also help keep citizens and non-citizens in place through conditions that are embedded in ways journalists report or write to an audience. Journalists write about non-status citizens to audiences who are citizens and generally not the other way around. Critical sociology seeks to unravel how conditions for hospitality toward non-citizens work in journalism and to point to where we can begin to think about how a more public form of journalism could overcome this basic social division in mediated society. Public journalism, defined further in the final section of the chapter, examines how we might propose ways to include the voices of non-citizens and also address those voices as audiences in ways that encourage wider civic participation.

The concept of hospitality is classically used to explain an ethical approach toward solving the social problem of the 'foreigner', the 'stranger', or simply 'the other' who doesn't share the same customs, laws, food, or religion as the host society. Hermann Cohen, founder of the Marburg school of philosophy in Germany at the beginning of the nineteenth century, argues that the Western origin of the question concerning the hospitality a society offers toward the 'other' is seen in the origins of monotheist religion. The idea of creating a city of refuge to help solve the social problem of violence against 'others' who do not belong is recorded in Deuteronomy, where Moses proclaims it as a law so that the person 'fleeing unto one of these cities . . . might live' (Levinas, 1994: 34). From the beginning, monotheism struggled to solve the problem of how to deal with the stranger who did not share the belief in one deity: 'The stranger is not thought of as a slave, but as a guest-friend, who requires the piety of guest-friendship' (Cohen, 1972: 120). The guest-friend can be excused from strict observance of the customs. Eventually the guest-friend evolves into a more legal status. Here, a foreigner-stranger, much like the contemporary landed immigrant, may enter into another's territory and be recognized as having the same legal rights without necessarily sharing full citizenship.

Social theory has long been divided over whether or not 'hospitality' or the offer of refuge to the foreigner, the stranger, or the outsider is a universal right or a relative moral principle. Immanuel Kant, for example, provides a modern twist to the ancient right to asylum in a 1784 text where he states that hospitality toward the foreigner is never unconditional but is rather an obligation of universal justice dependent on domestic law (Kant, 1983). In other words, hospitality should be offered to all those who need refuge, but those who accept hospitality are also bound by the condition that they respect the 'right' local custom or conduct. Kwame Anthony Appiah extends a similar distinction for the contemporary post-9/11 context, arguing that hospitality cannot be offered by just any 'us' to just any 'them'; instead it is limited to those who would enter dialogue between 'different ways of life' (Appiah, 2006).

The genealogy of values that inform conditions placed on the immigrant by the 'host' society in exchange for hospitality is most provocatively challenged by Jacques Derrida. While he recognizes the practical and legal difficulties of accepting the 'other' without conditions, he argues that a society which abandons the principle of unconditional hospitality toward the refugee, the homeless, or the outcast loses its relation to justice. Thus, for Derrida the term 'hospitality' also entails a contradictory sense of hostility toward the 'other' given the possibility of the 'others'' failure or refusal to meet the expectation of the condition (Derrida, 2001, 2002).

The deconstruction of the strongest themes from *The New York Times* articles on immigration discussed in the following sections reveals a series of different levels of hospitality that journalists express toward immigrant-others. It also depicts conditions journalists propose or direct toward their implied audiences in order to avoid social problems caused by immigration. The first section below considers articles published in 2005 that present a series of just and unjust cases related mainly to crime and immigration. The articles address 'worst-case' scenarios for undocumented immigrants and report on the most extreme cases of injustice against immigrants or committed by immigrants. The next section shifts to discussions of multiculturalism and the changing face of the city that immigration has generated, and then reviews the implied audiences for official political debates that both support the cause of immigration and add conditions to its future governance. Finally, we examine the heated March to May 2006 period and how implied audiences are addressed in tones of astonishment regarding the new social movement for undocumented immigrants and activist demands for unconditional hospitality that developed along with, and to provide counterpoint to, the official political debate.

Just, Unjust, and Extreme

One of the oldest conditions for hospitality toward strangers is that they be law-abiding. Yet, being law-abiding can also be distinguished from being treated justly. Immigrants are variously portrayed as illegal and committing crimes as well as being legal and suffering from injustice. Articles on crime most often involve either a penal or a civil violation alleged against an undocumented immigrant or an official such as a New York City police officer or government employee. A straightforward example of the latter type of story is the report of a rookie police officer put on probation for killing an unarmed African immigrant during a botched raid in Chelsea on a CD/DVD counterfeit ring. According to the judge, 'Mr. Conroy, who was relatively inexperienced, was insufficiently trained, insufficiently supervised, insufficiently led on the day in question, by people who had the responsibility to make sure he did nothing but protect and serve rather than end up taking a life' (Hartocollis, 2005: 1). Reports like these derive their authority by quoting the external authority of the judge's decision. They establish balance by quoting the official police spokesman's response in contrast to the judge's decision and then add emotional and moral intensity through a quote from the victim's family. This tripartite reference to authority (the judge, the police spokesman, and the family representative) addresses the audience in terms of an emotional sympathy and moral plea for justice tempered by legal realism. That the rookie police officer killed an unarmed immigrant 'other' is still evidence of the city's unjust shootings and massive arrest incidents of people of colour in New York. The implied audience is not the undocumented or African-American minority, but a more general audience of citizens who are assumed to share a horizon of understanding and expectation about violence in the city whenever a questionable shooting involving a police officer occurs. In other words, New York City itself, along with its crime problems, racial tensions, and widely publicized incidents of police misconduct, is an unsaid mediating element shaping the meaning of conditional hospitality toward undocumented immigrants.

Sometimes civil and penal components of a crime and their relation to immigration in New York City are mixed together. The story of an undocumented immigrant who commits a heinous crime is found in a report about the arrest of a police sergeant for shooting his wife. It is not immediately clear from the headline, 'Officer arrested in killing of his children's mother', that this is a story that links crime with immigration in New York City. Initially, the story is framed in a moral tone set against an estranged, violent husband who brutally kills his wife to escape spousal support payments and regain custody of his children. The tripartite authority that frames the address toward the audience in this case does not become clear until much further along in the story. The first part of the article mentions that the wife had just got a job as an Immigration and Customs agent. Three-quarters of the way into the article we learn that the sergeant himself was an 'illegal immigrant' who 'fraudulently obtained United States citizenship through a sham marriage'. The framing technique that links the crime to illegal immigration uses emotional quotes from the wife's family, who are celebrating the justice of the sergeant's arrest, and then regains balance by referring to expert testimony from the New York cold case squad and a Department of Immigration official (Rashbaum, 2005: B4).

An example of a civil case involving criminal elements, in which officials are charged with violating immigrants' rights, is seen in the report on a lawsuit brought against the then attorney general and the head of the FBI for violating the rights of two Muslim immigrants. Here the plea for hospitality is not couched in condition. The two plaintiffs were held in a federal detention centre in Brooklyn for eight months, where they claim to have been seriously abused. On the issue of journalistic balance, the article provides an interesting illustration of how references to an external context, along with a mixture of varied emotional and moral tones from the subjects of the story, frame the article for the implied reader. The journalist constructs the event within a critique of the state's post-9/11 moral authority as a rationale for abuse. He quotes expert testimony from the judge's decision to deny the accused motions for dismissal as well as the plaintiffs' emotional and graphic descriptions of the abuse: 'They said they were kicked and punched until they bled, cursed as "terrorists" and "Muslim bastards", and subjected to multiple unnecessary body-cavity searches, including one in which correction officers inserted a flashlight into Mr. Elmaghraby's rectum, making him bleed.' After getting a statement from the detention centre to establish journalistic balance, the framing is completed with a quote from an expert constitutional lawyer, who braces the implied audience for the political struggle needed to combat extreme measures and attitudes of repressive state institutions against innocent victims: 'The judge understood that this isn't just a case about individuals being abused in detention. These are people who were singled out according to a policy created on the highest levels of government' (Bernstein, 2005c: B4).

A similar case maintains a conditional hospitality in its reporting. It also crosses from themes of injustice committed by the legal system toward the most extreme forms of injustice committed against immigrants in the post-9/11 moral-authority context of New York City. Two teenaged Muslim girls from Queens were reported in *The New York Times* as suspects in planning suicide bombings. One of the girls grew up in Queens but was not born in the US and was not a citizen. Following a request to the police from her despondent father, who discovered she had run away with a young man, the girl was arrested and held on evidence from Internet chat sites, school diaries, and questionable FBI interrogation tactics. This led to information regarding her alleged consumption of Islamic clerical broadcasts from London. After her unexpected arrest her father went into hiding while the mother left the country. The second girl was released much earlier, while the undocumented teenager was detained for seven weeks before being released on the condition that she leave the country.

The framing of this story provides a good example of how *The New York Times* opposes anti-immigration acts by the legal system but at the same time, in the interest of balance, also establishes the 'understandable' condition of necessary security in the post-9/11 context, used by the FBI in defence of its tactics. At the same time, the first sentence frames the story in ironic tones by describing the utter bewilderment of this young girl. The context is framed in the contrasting figure of an encultured but undocumented New York teenager who is suddenly displaced from her life in New York City to a third-world city where she has been exiled. The opening paragraph reads: 'Dhaka, Bangladesh—Slumped at the edge of the bed she would have to share with four relatives that night, the 16-year-old girl from Queens looked stunned.' This is quickly juxtaposed with a description of the pastoral but urban setting the teen was forced to leave in Queens—'a neighborhood of tidy lawns and American flags'. The second ironic layer is the framing of an emotional tone of sympathy toward the protagonist that is set by the article's clash over the implication linking teenage angst with radical Islamic suicide bombers. 'She is a made-in-Queens mix of devotion and defiance, this slim, dark-eyed adolescent who arrived in Astoria with her family at age 5. In her round schoolgirl handwriting, she has compiled lists of favorite prayers and pious resolutions . . . . But when she recalls how FBI agents questioned her religious lifestyle, her voice drips typical teenage scorn: "Like, I'm supposed to live for you guys?"' (Bernstein, 2005a: B5).

Stories about the extreme abuse of basic civil rights in the post-9/11 context of moral authority include the arrest of other Muslims under similar conditions as the teenagers from Queens (Bernstein, 2005a: B5), polemics against random searches in New York City subways after the London bombings (*NY Times*, 26 July 2005), and the plight of 60,000 undocumented high school students in the New York area (*NY Times*, 19 June 2005). Two other stories, both from the same issue, are about extreme abuse; they include a man who had his green card revoked because he could not read English and a family of homeless immigrants who ride the shuttle bus back and forth all night between JFK Airport and Manhattan to stay warm in the winter (*NY Times*, 14 November 2005).

Two shocking extremes on the theme of severe immigrant abuse involve cases of Chinese immigrants, who constitute the highest number of undocumented people in the New York region. One case is the abuse of undocumented citizens by another immigrant. In 1993, Sister Ping was charged as a ringleader in a human smuggling operation that led to the death of 10 immigrants from drowning as they attempted to swim ashore to the United States. Human trafficking in the Chinese community often involves a 'snakehead, or immigrant smuggler [who] charges as much as $40,000 per passenger for a trip to New York from Asia' (Feuer, 2005: B3). Once landed, the immigrant is then often indentured to the handler for many years until the fee is paid off, with interest.

One of the worst cases of abuse of an undocumented immigrant was the tragic fate of a Chinese-food deliveryman stranded in a jammed Manhattan elevator for 81 hours. He was afraid to call out for fear he would then be exposed as an undocumented worker. Once rescued, he received psychiatric care to help him cope with his fear of immigration officials, of the dark, and of closed spaces: 'Psychiatrists call such symptoms classic hallmarks of post-traumatic stress disorder, and spoke of barriers to treatment like language, culture and money. But for Mr. Chen, who is deeply indebted for his passage to the United States . . . , his illness mainly represents a disastrous obstacle to delivery work in the nationwide network of Chinese restaurants where illegal immigrants like him are dispatched from New York to toil night and day, six days a week' (Bernstein, 2005b: B1).

Each of the above stories is framed in similar procedural and substantive processes that cascade from external referents of authority and balance both hospitable and conditional tones. As described above, each framing in turn addresses implied readers in sympathetic emotional tones of hospitality toward the immigrant while at the same time underlining the exceptional conditions that have led to the event. In this way, a context of public suspicion is maintained and the suspension of civil liberties becomes a partially normalized condition placed on hospitality toward immigration.

Multicultural Practices and Changing Faces

Articles on multicultural practices and the changing face of New York include stories on the various waves of legal and illegal immigration to the city (*NY Times*, 20 July 2005; 29 July 2005, 6 August 2005); the changing ethnic and racial makeup of neighbourhoods (30 June 2005; 9 October 2005); evolving economic and demographic variables in housing, labour, and business (31 July 2005; 4 August 2005; 13 December 2005; 25 December 2005; 18 December 2005); and densities of cultural diversity (30 December 2005). Several of these articles reporting on the theme of new immigrants changing the face of New York City offer a particular focus on the relation between race and immigration.

The first article in the heightened period of immigrant protest from April to May 2006 is a pro-immigration piece that makes a counter-intuitive argument about the likelihood of crime increasing as the number of immigrants coming into New York City declines. Citing a Pew Hispanic Center study, the reporter points out that immigrant flows to New York City have receded since 2001, 'while the homicide rate has leveled off and seems now to be creeping up' (Sampson, 2006: A15). The argument announces the complexity of the issue of race and ethnicity in New York and at the same time the special status New York holds in the history of world immigration. 'It is no longer tenable to assume that immigration automatically leads to chaos and crime. New York is a magnet for immigration, yet it has for a decade ranked as one of America's safest cities' (Sampson, 2006: A15).

A second, longer essay also refers to a similar conflux of the theme of changing faces and crime. This article challenges the implied audience's allegiance to political correctness by evoking an emotionally volatile tone against cultural explanations of young African-American males that might explain how they lost out on jobs to ambitious immigrants during the 1990s boom. The byline tells readers that the author is a Harvard sociologist, which leads the implied audience into the familiar terrain of the expert social scientist who often frames narratives with expressions like 'several recent studies say'. The article states that African Americans need to re-examine their rates of exclusion in the city and begin to take responsibility for their own self-determination. It first demonstrates the correlation between low education and poverty, and poverty and the disproportionally high rates of homicide, incarceration, and absent fathers among African-American males. Missing out on 'the economic boom years of the 90s makes it impossible to ignore the effects of culture'. But what does this mean? Is the failure to compete with immigrants for low-paying jobs caused by a misguided African-American hip-hop culture, as he would seem to suggest? The author counters that he is not 'blaming the victims' but rather pleading for an understanding of historical conditions in the African-American community in order to expose the abusive behaviour that victims themselves exert in order to change them: 'The tragedy unfolding in our inner cities is a time-slice of a deep historical process that runs back through the cataracts and deluge of our racist past. In academia, we need a new, multidisciplinary approach toward understanding what makes young black men behave so self destructively' (Patterson, 2006: D13).

The long essay is a form that can address an issue more directly to the excluded group, especially if the author focuses on the perspective of the group's ethos. Framing an article in the complex language and citations of the expert lends legitimacy to the story, while the direct address of the author to an excluded group lends an intense emotional and moral tone. The example is unique in the sense that the implied audience is the insider African American, but also the non-insider who looks on from an outside lifeworld. Although the article is focused on the African-American minority and not on immigration, it references immigration as a measure of how well the community is doing, suggesting that the thorny hierarchy of race and ethnicity is never far from the surface in discussions about immigration in New York City.

In addition to the two examples of extremely degrading conditions experienced by 'illegals' described above, there are only two other articles about the Chinese immigrant community in 2006 (*NY Times*, 13 March 2006, 17 March 2006). At first glance, the small number of articles on Chinese immigration is a bit surprising given that they are the largest undocumented immigrant group in the New York region. In reporting on immigration, the point that returns most often is that no single group dominates statistically in New York City and that there is a finely balanced sense of equitable pluralism. This is a condition that in part defines New York's special historical hospitality toward immigration. Several articles describe the strength of cultural pluralism among immigrants in New York City that serves to make the city unlike any other metropolitan centre of similar stature.

One example stands out: the influential march by illegal Irish immigrants in Yonkers in April 2006. The illegal Irish constitute only a tiny minority of the more than 700,000 estimated illegal immigrants in New York State, but their presence in the city generates major interest. 'Some in the immigrant coalitions resent being passed over', says the *New York Times* journalist, 'and worry the Irish are angling for a separate deal . . . . Others welcome the clout and razzmatazz and extraordinary track record they bring, like the creation of thousands of special visas in the 1990s that one historian calls "affirmative action for white Europeans"' (Bernstein, 2006a: A1). The fascination also seems disproportionate because the overall number of illegals in the US is usually pegged at 11 million, of which 78 per cent are Hispanic.

Articles on the changing face of the city do not address immigrants directly, nor do they record their voices in any significant way. They are, however, mainly hospitable toward the undocumented. The first article, which linked crime and declining rather than ascending immigration levels, addresses its implied audience by challenging the conditional assumption of ideal immigration limits for New York City. The argument neatly removes the stigma applied to the 'foreigner', which gives immigrants a negative image upon arrival in the community but at the same time re-stigmatizes the indigenous African-American minority and poor whites. Now these groups are the 'new' rising and most criminal 'others,' not the immigrants. The articles on African Americans, the situation with Chinese illegals, and the special clout of the Irish all link class and race as conditions that need to be considered when weighing the benefits of immigration. When thinking about the implied audiences these articles address, it is important to recall the heated context in which they were written. The unexpected rise of a massive social movement supporting immigration that was sparked by intense political reactions reverberated throughout the US and in New York City in particular, as described in the next two sets of examples.

Governance: Official Discourse and Political Shocks

Here the framing of immigration concerns the sense of shock that government policy and debate among politicians evoke in the way they formulate the problem of illegal immigration and in the solutions they propose. Each side is framed as if overwhelmed by the scope of the illegal-immigration debate, and each side is presented as astonished by its opponents' proposed solutions. Debates in the government and among politicians over the definition of the problem of undocumented immigrants, and the possible solutions that might bring about a consensus for resolving it, are mirrored almost step by step in events unfolding daily in the streets. In the tripartite framing of these articles, one official side is constructed in a way that cannot help but define itself in relation to the other. These two official discourses are balanced against one another while they also cross over and/or draw from the emotional-volitional currents of popular demonstrators.

From the beginning of this current debate, most Republicans as well as some Democrats were officially divided over the criminalization of undocumented immigrants, a division that would eventually give way to a crackdown against illegal immigrants (*NY Times*, 29 March 2006). They were also divided over exactly how to go about integrating illegals into programs that would eventually lead to citizenship. The minority of hard-core anti-illegalists (*NY Times*, 11 March 2006) continue to argue for deportation and even imprisonment of illegals, and would prefer to make it a crime for any organization or individual to assist them. These anti-illegalists also argue for massively increased customs patrols, a complete barrier fence on the Mexican border, and no amnesty or possibility of applying for citizenship for illegals already residing in the United States. The sense of shock in their statements at the numbers of illegal passages across the border is especially acute and the provocative language of fencing is often framed as a proportionate, if not responsible, response.

The Catholic Church in 2006 was one of the first mainstream forces in civil society reported to oppose the anti-illegal immigrationists. Cardinal McCarrick of Washington 'said he and other leaders decided they could not stay silent after witnessing the hardships endured by illegal immigrants . . . . This is a justice issue.' In response, Republican Tom Tancredo takes issue with Catholic leaders for 'evoking God when arguing for a blanket amnesty' while others 'question whether the church should maintain its tax exempt status' (Swarns, 2006a: D4). Pro–immigrant rights figures like New York City Mayor Michael Bloomberg and then New York Senator Hillary Clinton are against the proposed immigration law on criminalization and look to return the legal status of those who are undocumented to a civil violation (Bernstein, 2006b: B5). They both oppose increased border controls and promote amnesty or some similar approach to provide a path to citizenship for undocumented individuals residing in the United States. One article satirized the two extremes this way: 'self described patriots call them "terrorists"; on combative talk shows the term is "illegal aliens"; and advocates for immigrants prefer . . . "economic refugees"' (Vitello, 2006: A5).

In April 2006 *The New York Times* reported on how the logjam of offering a solution to illegal immigration in the Republican and Democrat dispute broke in Congress, and that a compromise was on the verge of acceptance that favoured the Bush administration plan (Swarns, 2006d: A21). It included two main categories for immigration: the immediate deportation of any illegal immigrant who had lived in the US for less than two years, and an increase in border security, including the construction of a partial fence. The compromise soon evaporated, but a year later the debate returned in a framing similar to the one in which it had first been conceived (*NY Times*, 7 April 2006).

The framing of the official government voices of pro- and anti-immigration sentiment address the implied national and urban audience as if they should expect a clear-cut debate between the right and the left over the status of the undocumented, with varying shades of compromise in between. Each side is presented as if it symbolically embodies the emotional and factual orientations of its constituencies. Each side stands for justice, the law, and the national good. Each side assumes it is acting as responsibly as possible toward reinforcing the regime of citizenship. In the dispute, the implied audience is caught up in the need for solutions and the variety of proposals: no fence, complete amnesty, and porous borders, or conversely, more fence, arrests, and closed borders with military and paramilitary controls. To summarize, stories are mainly framed through a bifurcated official sense of political shock concerning the dimensions of the problem and the proposed solutions from each side.

Social Movements: The Astonishment of Social Solidarity

Our final example concerns the sense of astonishment addressed toward the implied audiences regarding the show of solidarity in civil society that opposes the government. This is the second most common theme during the period that led to the national one-day strike on 1 May 2006 by the undocumented and their supporters. The event serves as an emotional and volitional rejoinder to themes that are on opposing sides in the official debate. Popular rejoinders appear mainly in the form of reports on the scope of the demonstrations during or leading up to the strike that are framed using quotes or reports from their organizations and from the variations between cities in terms of their meaning. Reports address implied audiences with a sense of astonishment at the new popular awareness of diversity in the American polis on the one hand, and fear of the hostile backlash and crackdown that rejects claims to citizenship and threatens the undocumented with imprisonment or deportation on the other hand. Reports on massive demonstrations (*NY Times*, 12 April 2006) not seen since the days of the civil-rights movement and the anti–Vietnam War protests give another sense of justice than the one debated in Congress and among politicians through the media. 'No human being is illegal', they argue, and all favour complete amnesty, political recognition, and full citizenship: '"We are inseparable, indivisible, and impossible to take out of America," Chung-Wha Hong, Director of the New York Immigration Coalition, told the crowd, which she greeted in English, Spanish, Chinese, French and Korean' (Swarns, 2006c: A1).

Numerous sub-genres of tragic life histories mainly of individual undocumented Latino immigrants either accompany or appear alongside articles on the mass demonstrations leading up to the May boycott. Undocumented workers tell their compelling stories in the form of moral counterpoints to the crackdowns against them. One commentator noted: 'Imagine turning more than 11 million people into criminals and then add five-year sentences to anyone that helped them' (Swarns, 2006b: A1). Leading up to the 1 May strike, about 2,000 undocumented people were detained, 175 mostly violent criminals were imprisoned, and another small number were deported (Lipton, 2006: A1). A disproportionate panic and fear spread quickly among the undocumented, who were in turn depicted as driven by opposition to rhetoric from the official discourse discussed above, but also from the reactions of the immigrant organizations themselves. The internal dialogue between the journalist and the implied audiences thus follows a series of tightly wound rejoinders between the voices of the popular coalition and official announcements and official debates.

The implied audience is captivated by the excitement of people rising up against conventions of justice that have become unjust. But another side of the journalist's implied audience is explicitly hostile toward the idea 'no one is illegal'. The political subject in the phrase 'no human is illegal' sees the conditional barrier of citizenship as based in the nation-state and the rule of law. Mass demonstrations in favour of the peoples caught in the interstices of various symbolic and physical boundaries mark the US and global contexts and yet, as these stories suggest, it is not the rule of law or status that draws our attention to injustices. It is, rather, 'acts that enact us/them as citizens, strangers, outsiders or aliens' (Isin and Nielsen, 2008: 3). Can it be concluded that the press is covering this kind of political subject? Or the acts themselves that are claiming, questioning, resisting, or demanding these mass demonstrations and the resulting debates? Does the mainstream press have any of the right concepts to begin to explain how experiences are transformed into these kinds of acts?

How Can Public Journalism Reduce the Gap?

To this point our analysis asks what happens when newspapers seek to be authoritative in their reports on immigration as a social problem in the US, with a special focus on New York. What emotional and moral tones frame the implied audience? What response is anticipated in these reports? What is the gap between the implied audiences and the subjects being reported on? The purpose of presenting the examples above is to get at the image of otherness which journalists frame in their dialogue with implied audiences about the subject of non-status immigrants. It is important to recall that this dialogue on otherness is not a simple conversation but a broader exchange that takes place in anticipation of an implied audience's imaginary response to the subject matter. Journalists actively frame their texts to meet that anticipation, and framing builds an understanding through the relation among the journalist, the implied audience, and the subject of the report. The unsaid acknowledgement here is that the implied audience has no immediate experience of immigration. The question remains to be asked: How might what has been called public journalism reduce the gap between the implied audiences and the subjects they report on?

The public journalism movement has sought to address audience members as citizens who can engage in public life in order to respond to these questions. In other words, public journalism recognizes the gap between the subjects being reported on and the imaginary-but-not-fictional audience that journalists address. Reducing the gap means reporting on acts the subjects of the reports are engaged in and drawing them into the dialogue with the implied audience. The discussion on public journalism began in a symposium on a question posed by the Ethics and Excellence in Journalism Foundation in Oklahoma City in 1994. Journalists and researchers were asked to explore answers to 'what extent the ethical journalist is an isolated "individualist", and to what extent he or she is a member of the wider community' (Black,

1997: v). Is the journalist an individual who reports on the personal troubles of non-citizens to a community of citizens, and what responsibility, if any, does the journalist have toward the community being reported on?

A series of debates and innovations with focus groups representing communities which had not been previously addressed were carried out with some urban newspapers in various US cities. The debates drew hard-line polemics around the professional principles of objectivity, fairness, and balance in ways that sought to draw mainstream journalism more directly into cultures it reported on (Lambeth et al., 1998; Esterowicz et al., 2000). As the movement declined, prominent corporate media editors claimed victory, arguing that public journalism was redundant given that the mandate of the urban newspaper already included extensive reporting on communities and that the issue was about the majority empirical audience and not a minority (Rosen, 1999). Other critics argued that the news industry is motivated by profit and loss and that stories emerge primarily because they sell, so the majority empirical audience is actually a commodity (Compton, 2000). Those most invested in expanding the role of the journalistic address toward more inclusive forums, while maintaining professional standards, argue that the movement simply shifted online to citizen journalism, blogging, crowd-sourcing, and other new media platforms. Others argue that the ethical concern about the role of journalists in 'public discourse' 'is not about the wondrous addition of citizen media, but the decline of the full time, professional monitoring of powerful institutions' (Kovach and Rosentiel, 2007: 185).

Framing analyses in Chapters 10 and 11 have shown that journalists do not innocently report or comment on an ongoing social problem without being selective and actively orientating the story toward an implied audience. Would journalism necessarily be less rigorously veridical, accurate, and balanced if the craft were turned into a commitment to social justice and addressing subjects of social exclusion as audiences in a broader social issue rather than to abstract principles of objectivity, balance, and fairness? According to advocates of public journalism, shifting to a commitment to the story and expanding the address can still be consistent with traditional benchmarks of good journalism.

Following critical sociology, we argue further that in order to reduce or re-address the gap between groups being reported on and the journalist's implied audience, the journalist would need to derive reporting from where acts of citizens or non-citizens are enacted. This does not mean abandoning accuracy, balance, or fairness in reporting, but rather making assumptions about bias and framing more explicitly. Balance and accuracy in journalism provide ethical guidelines to prevent the 'serious' press from falling into a 'pack mentality' or from becoming an instrument of 'mass mystification', as classical critiques have accused. If balance, however, means simply not 'taking a side', it may not be enough of a guideline, as it would simply mean another innovation in the principle of neutrality that reinforces the false assumption of passive transmission of a message toward an equally passive receiver.

This does not mean sources do not have to be verified or that rigour of procedure and accuracy should be loosened. On the one hand, the principle of reporting from where the subjects are is partially seen in *The New York Times*' articles on social problems, in the section on the changing face of New York City and conflicts over immigration and work. On the other hand, there is less of a sense in these articles of provoking more conversation directly with the subjects and therefore less of a sense of gaining ideas about further rejoinders or solutions. If the journalist could reduce the gap between the implied audience and the subjects being reported on, it follows that public culture could be understood as an ongoing conversation between speakers. But conversation means adding not only authenticated but also performative propositions to keep the conversation alive. In other words, journalists would need to accept more responsibility to intervene in order to increase the quality of dialogue and the scope of inclusion. This is partially seen in reports that express shock about official policies proposed by governments or their oppositional counter-proposals. Yet these reports frame the same distance between the implied reader and the immigrants who are being discussed. The same is also the case in those articles that express hospitality toward the most excluded but are also committed to demonstrating the conditions of authenticity placed on them. Using strongly slanted emotional-volitional tones derived from where the subjects themselves are situated in their lifeworlds provides an uncanny hook effect, but it is usually not enough to provoke a civic dialogue. What is needed is to bring the interlocutors together into a deeper exchange in order to expand the criteria of inclusivity that haunt the present malaise around citizenship in order to begin to express a greater diversity of voices in the public conversation. To accomplish this, journalists would need to be more adversarial. This should not mean more one-sided, ideological, or monologic writing. Their responsibility would rather be to openly and directly contribute to the deliberative, multi-voiced democratic process through exercising their skills of research and communicative action to provide balance and fairness in dialogue rather than neutral and passive detachment.

Summary

Reading the American debate about 'illegal' or 'undocumented' immigration through *The New York Times* leaves a sense of informed familiarity with a specific set of social problems but without the depth of having entered more directly into conversation with the immigrants being discussed. We get a New York sense of urban citizenship and the extraordinary tensions around extreme forms of injustice, the changing face of the city brought about by immigration, the New York bias in the two-sided national debate over governance, and the astonishment of a new solidarity among non-status people in the heart of the American polis. Portraying shock on both sides of the argument over the 'illegal' or 'undocumented' frames a set form of conditions for hospitality on one side, and pleas for limiting conditions and expanding hospitality on the other. We learn about the extremes between law and justice, racial hierarchy, multiculturalism in the city, and popular forces from New York, but we never get all the way through to the experiences of the subjects being discussed in the reports.

Journalists perform acts of citizenship by claiming the right of immigrants to have rights through direct and indirect discussions about non-status citizens with their implied, have-status audiences. Mainly, however, journalists do not address the subjects produced by these acts as their audience and in so doing also reinforce social division by constructing their subjects' voices as 'other'. We learn about this otherness through balanced framing and emotional reminders to implied audiences about the just or unjust conditions attached to immigrants themselves. In addition, most of the articles present positive emotions in their framing to support agencies or actors that lobby agencies to display a greater hospitality toward immigrants. The assumption between the journalists and their audience is hospitable, but it is also conditional and even hostile toward immigrants under certain circumstances. We are reminded of the extraordinary circumstances of 9/11 that need to be considered and of the criteria of authenticity as strict conditions measured against hospitality toward immigrants.

A final question can be posed. Given that stories often quote undocumented immigrants while rarely addressing them directly, how might they shift their framing to include a broader diversity of cultural expression of the subjects they report on? In other words, can it be enough to provide accurate and balanced reports about just or unjust crimes committed by immigrants or against them; about the shifting cultural practices and hierarchy of race in the city; about official debates over the rights and wrongs of immigration or mass refusals of the rule of law? Or should the mainstream press engage itself more directly with the acts it reports on, but also with the acts of citizenship or ruptures from *habitus* when non-citizens rise up to claim rights to have rights? If journalism could begin from there, would it not engage more diverse claims for justice and cultural expression within these formations that would not only increase the audibility of have-not citizens in public culture but also participate in their demands for recognition? And if so, then what would this mean for the subjects that the acts create?

Enhanced Learning Activities

1. Do a keyword search with Factiva on *The New York Times* that will draw on the word 'immigration' and the name of a city you are interested in within the same paragraph. Compare the results over a period of two or three years. Read all the articles and count which ones would be relevant for the

kind of analysis we see in this chapter.

2. Take five newspaper articles that address immigration and give a brief description of how they frame their implied audience. Code them as hospitable, conditional, or rejections and whether or not they are expressed in emotional, rational, or moral tones. Do the articles support or contradict the argument in this chapter that the press rarely frames its direct address to immigrants themselves?

Annotated Further Reading

Leo Chavez, *Covering Immigration: Popular Images and the Politics of the Nation*. Berkeley: University of California Press, 2001. This volume is a study of the historical context of immigration in the US and analyses of how immigration is represented in mediated society.

Engin Isin and Greg Nielsen, *Acts of Citizenship*. New York: Zed Publications, 2008. This collection of essays provides a sociological and interdisciplinary critique of the traditional concept of citizenship. Acts of citizenship are investigated as events or ruptures that create new subjects who claim rights in emotionally charged tones and challenge the established order of justice and law through enduring arguments.

Jay Rosen, *What Are Journalists For?* New Haven: Yale University Press, 1999. This is a good summary of the history, theory, and practice of public journalism in the US context. It has clear presentations of various theories of public space and multiple examples of American newspapers that attempted experiments in public journalism.

Bill Kovach and Tom Rosenstiel, *The Elements of Journalism: What Newspeople Should Know and the Public Should Expect*. New York: Random House, 2007. This book provides an overview of the craft, politics, economics, ethics, and sociology of contemporary journalism.

Useful Media

Online databases, such as Factiva (for international printed media), ProQuest (for English-Canadian printed media) and Eureka (for French-Canadian printed media), offer easy access to entire collections of newspapers and journals. They include powerful search engines which facilitate browsing the media for specific themes or keywords. Instead of having to browse through each publication's own archive (if available), one can use a single database to search multiple items. By using standardized search engines, the sites facilitate comparative research on printed media (though one has to be aware of the differences in their search engines when using different databases).

Note

1. This chapter is in part based on material from Nielsen (2009).

Glossary

Absent nation This describes the fictional nature of the *one Canada* and the lack of a strong, primordial idea of a particular ethno-national culture about what English Canada is.

Aestheticizing of political life Observing the Nazi regime, Benjamin cautioned against seizing political power and winning people's support by beautifying, glorifying, and thus mystifying the intent and agenda of political violence.

Agency On some occasions you may feel that you are acting of your own volition, free of the social and cultural constraints of established values and norms. This is agency in contrast with structure; agency is the power of self-determination.

Alienation In Marx's view, alienation is an action through which people are estranged from (1) the results or products of their own activities, (2) the social surrounding in which they live, (3) all other human beings, and (4) themselves. Alienation therefore is also self-alienation.

Bourgeoisie In the Marxist tradition, the bourgeoisie are the economically dominant class who also control cultural production and government. This social class is in opposition to and in conflict with the working class. In today's terms the bourgeoisie are sometimes referred to as the 'dominant economic class' and sometimes simply as the 'upper middle class'.

Bureaucracy Bureaucracy is a key term in the sociology of organization. Weber gives shape to this term by denoting a type of government and a system of administration continuously carried out by trained professionals according to prescribed rules.

Carnivalesque Refers to the transposition of carnival laughter into media content. In the Middle Ages popular carnivals had a special sense of time and place that allowed people to dress and laugh in ways they would not do normally, somewhat similar to today's Mardi Gras celebrations. Features of the carnival spirit that can be observed in contemporary media content include a call to participate in the fun, the comic reversal of the body and of social hierarchies, and a turning of social divisions from absolute to relative differences through imaginative usage of forbidden words (Bakhtin, 1984).

Civil society All institutions in society related to voluntary associations that are not part of the state or government apparatus.

CNN effect This term refers to the intensive Cyclops or monocular gaze providing information directly and shaping the directions of public discourse and opinion indirectly.

Commodification The action of turning something into or treating something as a commodity. The real audience watching a TV program is composed of real persons. Commercial and, to some extent, public broadcasters (especially Canada's CBC) treat you as a saleable commodity, selling the number of viewers of a certain type watching at a certain time to commercial advertisers.

Commodities Usually refers to any products that can be bought or sold, but may also refer to services which can be bought and sold in a commercial marketplace.

Commodity fetishism When consumers project a value onto a commodity as if the value came from the commodity itself rather than the labour that produced it (Marx, 1970).

Communicative actions Rationally motivated attempts to move toward shared understanding between people (Habermas, 1990).

Conspicuous consumption This broadly refers to consumption patterns prompted by symbolic significance more than material utility.

Corporate media Large-scale monopoly-style, profit-orientated media, non-publicly funded (Goodman and Goodman, 2006).

Creative formations This refers to groupings of various social roles (artists, musicians, writers, directors, etc.) involved in the making of advertising, drama, newscasts, etc.

Critical sociology Sociology that puts into question dominant social practices and that serves the principle that a better world is possible. Both a science and an art, it applies explanation and understanding to events in developing knowledge that provokes theories of the possible rather than testing hypotheses that end in technical knowledge about structures or practical descriptions of social interaction (Habermas, 1970).

Crown corporation Corporations owned by Canadian federal and provincial governments; the Canadian Broadcasting Corporation (CBC) and Television Ontario (TVO) are examples.

Cultural intermediaries This is a key concept in Pierre Bourdieu's work. Experts give consultation to the middle classes about correct styles, appropriate images, and standard ways of living. This not only defines the middle classes' social role through habitual practices of consumption but also maintains their status and position by cultivating specific knowledge, expertise, contacts, and networks.

Deconstruction A school of philosophy that originated in France during the 1960s, principally influenced by Jacques Derrida. Deconstruction is an analytical process which questions all central concepts and propositions in a discourse with the objective being to expose the problematic nature of current and accepted ways of thinking. This is the making undecidable of any norm or explanation of purity, or any naming of something as truth (Powell, 1970).

Demos This refers to a political community; citizenship is usually defined in relation to a demos.

Deterritorialize To uproot and displace from any given territory; re-territorialize means to spread out over a new territory or plateau (Deleuze and Guattari, 1986).

Dialogical An adjective of or relating to dialogue and referring to a conversation or discourse in which different positions or participants are recognized and in which each recognizes the competing position of the other.

Discourse This includes the spoken and the written word, formal and informal speech. Sociologists refer to communities of discourse. Communities in the broadest sense share ways of thinking, speaking, and writing. For example, in the health sector patients are increasingly referred to as 'consumers' rather than patients, indicating a shift in the community of discourse from person-centred to commodity-centred, from a medical to a commercial community.

Disenchantment One of Max Weber's key concepts describing modernity, in which myth and religion no longer govern society; this is also the process in which science and reason are considered to have the capacity to reveal truth, state and bureaucracy replace religious institutions in organizing social relations, and industrial production and capitalism dominate economic life.

Docudrama This term generally refers to a dramatized TV film or radio play based on real events. Here we are referring to a combination of documentary and feature film techniques to mediatize historical events. As the replacement for the classical historical TV documentary, it entails ritualistic, event-specific, and entertaining modes of narrative construction.

Dystopia A terrifying and outlandish vision of society; the opposite to utopia.

Effacement This refers to a framing technique that makes the victims faceless, non-auditable, and closed to grief. It denies the victims' sufferings, demands, and even existence.

Emancipation In the Marxist tradition, freedom is not the absence of interference but the removal of obstacles to the development of human capacities and powers. This process is emancipation because it aims at a social life worthy of living. Obstacles include the conditions of wage labour and capitalist exploitation.

Encoding and decoding Encoding refers to the placing of meaning in a message. Decoding is the extracting of meaning by the receiver. The receiver may well change or distort the encoded message in the process.

Established and establishing Both carry their everyday meaning but, as used here, 'established' refers specifically to accepted norms, values, and institutions. 'Establishing' refers to a process of reforming established norms and values or creating new ones, implying a critical stance.

Ethos This refers to the world view or 'spirit' of a people or community.

False consciousness In the Marxist tradition, false consciousness is about misrecognizing the nature of commodities. It is also about misidentifying property ownership and consumption as the means of individual empowerment.

First and second levels of observation Sociology and mass media represent their environments from second-level positions, that is, through theory construction for sociology, and information gathering, program development, and analysis for mass media. Both are second-level observation points that mediate acts carried out by first-level observers (Luhmann, 2002).

Framing Framing in a communication text is to accentuate some aspects of a perceived social phenomenon in order to insert particular interpretations, evaluation, and treatment for a specific problem.

Global south and global north The division between the global south and global north refers to the one between the poorer (south) and wealthier (north) countries with regard to urban-industrial development. The division is not strictly geographical, although most of the northern countries are located in the Northern Hemisphere (except countries like Singapore, Australia, and New Zealand). In addition, the division is loosely used in social, political, and economic contrasts and conflicts between dominant/exploitive and dominated/resistant forces in the processes wherein global capitalism operates.

Globalization Facilitated by media and communication technologies, globalization is characterized by intensified connections and accelerated networks in both physical and virtual senses. Far from being a homogenous system or complete entity, globalization is an uneven process of movement of economic, political, informational, and human resources across national boundaries. While nation-states and nationalism continue, challenges from globalization generate contrasting or paradoxical social phenomena such as domination and resistance, integration and disconnection, and heterogeneity and homogeneity.

Glocalization This term refers to the interconnected and intermingled processes of global and local initiatives, flows, and transformations. It challenges the misconception that the global, the national, and the local are fixed structures in which one fits into the other like Russian dolls.

Grand narrative A narrative is a spoken or written story or, more technically, the telling of an event or connected sequence of events by a narrator. A grand narrative, sometimes referred to as a master narrative, is an all-inclusive, overriding story absorbing 'little', or local, stories as a way of capturing and securing adherence to a particular world view.

Have-nots This term refers to those who have no ownership of the means of production or who have little or no capital (Gans, 1996).

Hyperreal Simulated images that seem more real than the real (Baudrillard, 1983).

Imagined political community This refers to Benedict Anderson's (2006) influential notion about the creation of the nation as an imagined political community. It is imagined because most of the members only have the image of their communion in mind. This requires mass-mediated communication as a source of imagination and the thread linking political members together.

Implied audience Similar to 'imaginary audience, this refers to the audience that the creator(s) of the text or program imagine and imply they are addressing (Nielsen, 2008, 2009).

Instituted and instituting 'Institute' is used here as a verb. Instituted interaction patterns and ways of doing and seeing things are those already established. Instituting is the process of establishing ways of doing and seeing things. (See also *Established and establishing*)

Institution A pattern of linked actions supported by administrative and instituted ways of doing and experiencing things as well as creative formations and possibilities of instituting new ways of doing and experiencing things (Castoriadis, 1987).

Interlocutor This refers to a performer onstage who calls for and engages others in conversation. Here we refer to radio or any other communications medium as engaging others in conversation.

Internal audience The agency that is addressed inside the story as opposed to the external implied audience.

Leisure class A key concept in Thorstein Veblen's work on consumption. It denotes a social class of non-industrial people from diversified occupations. The common traits of the leisure class include ownership in the broader processes of industrialization and commodification, and the ability to enjoy luxury and comforts in life.

Lifeworlds The everyday culture of feelings, background convictions, and subjective beliefs of a group, class, or society (Habermas, 1984).

Mainstream newspapers This refers to large, mass-circulated corporate-owned newspapers.

Mediated citizenship Citizenship is a multi-faceted concept referring to a complex of social roles. Media tend to place the emphasis on the legal and individualized citizen, thereby ignoring the collective and public facet of citizenship. (See also *Mediated society*)

Mediated society A concept we invented to help capture the paradox in which contemporary media seem more and more capable of representing all and any aspects of society and lifeworld experiences, and yet our own voices and private thoughts remain separate from media. Or do they?

Medicalization A process of recasting a non-medical problem into a medical discourse. For example, an obsession with gaming becomes an 'addiction' and is so treated.

'The medium is the message' Central to McLuhan's technological determinism, this phrase denotes the significance of the form of a medium because the characteristics of the medium influence the reception and perception of the message. (See also *Encoding and decoding*)

Mennipean satire The original literary genre of the seriocomedy, named after the Greek philosopher Mennipus of Gadara, who lived in the third century BCE (Bakhtin, 1984).

Monological discourse Mikhail Bakhtin's concept about the manner in which one does not recognize the other's thoughts and ideas. At the same time, everything ideological is divided into affirmation or reputation.

Multicultural As an adjective 'multicultura' refers to an observed state of affairs, as in 'this country contains several cultural traditions.' It is also used to refer to the content of laws, public policies, rules, and regulations overseeing the relations between cultures within a given jurisdiction.

New media In our era, new media in the global north refer to computation and digitalization of media technologies which allow greater convergence and interconnectedness. New media includes Web 2.0 or social networking technologies. In the global south, cellular phone technologies overcoming the barriers of landline infrastructures are considered to be new media. From a historical perspective, new media give rise to hopes and fears in social imaginaries because their transformation of and challenges to existing social institutions, practices, and individual subjectivity remain unknown.

Norms The implicit standards that help guide or discipline acts.

Objective and subjective culture The products of culture and the internal thoughts, emotions, and will of cultural agents (Simmel, 1998).

Phantasmagoria For Marx, this concept is about the depreciation of the value of productive labour by the exchange value of commodities. For Benjamin, the dazzling effects of technological advancement is phantasmagoria, as if they perform a magic lantern show and create optical illusions.

Powerful banality This concept denotes profound social transformation due to the popularity and omnipresence of media technologies in mundane, everyday life.

Press councils These are provincial organizations in Canada composed of volunteer members from a wide spectrum of society who evaluate complaints against newspapers.

Public issues C. Wright Mills referred to public issues as issues relating to social structure; that is, issues having to do with matters that are over and above personal concerns (Mills, 1959: 8).

Public spaces and public sphere The public sphere (see *Publics and public opinion* below), a concept put forward by Jürgen Habermas (1991), has come to mean a place where discussion is carried out about what goods and services should be transformed or kept, regulated or deregulated, about what laws should be changed or reinforced, about what languages should be encouraged, what religious practices should be accommodated, and where schools should be built, among any other number of subjects concerning the common good. The concept of public spaces was advanced by Charles Taylor (1995) in referring to the common space in which people meet, through a variety of media (print, radio, TV, the Internet) and also face-to-face, to discuss matters of common interest and are thus able to form a common position.

Publics and public opinion 'Publics' refers to domains or gatherings of private individuals considering a variety of issues. 'Public opinion' refers to positions taken which have been elaborated through discussion and so recognized and were elaborated outside of official, hierarchical, and established structures (Taylor, 1995: 216–17). In this sense public opinion is not the result of polling, a marketing and political device presented as public opinion by the press and electronic media.

Re-enchantment For Benjamin, modern people are re-enchanted by the euphoric spell of consumers' desire and excitement while being pushed deeper into an individual isolated state of alienation.

Rhetoric Specifically, this refers to persuasive public speaking or writing where the objective is to win over or guide an audience.

Ritual media events This may be understood as mediatized rituals carried out through staging and mediating the 'sacred' centre in order to facilitate social integration or national cohesion.

Simulation The act of copying copies that imitate reality (Baudrillard, 1983).

Social problems If a designated issue perceived as a problem brings values, institutions, and social policies into play it is correctly called a social problem. (See also *Public issues*)

Sociological imagination Derived from sociologist C. Wright Mills, the sociological imagination is the intellectual process and capacity of making sense of individual experiences in larger social and historical contexts. Social theorists exercise sociological imagination in order to develop conceptual tools and analytical frameworks for a better understanding of individuals and society beyond common senses and underneath social imaginaries of collective understandings.

State or governing violence This refers to Jacques Derrida's notion concerning the violence that establishes law in the service and interests of state authority.

Structure Social structure refers to given social arrangements, interaction patterns, norms, values, and institutions. (See also *Agency*)

System or social system This refers to a set of interacting elements (roles, statuses, groups, institutions) moving in some discernable direction or exhibiting some function. Social systems are always open, linking in one way or another with other subsystems and systems in their environs. Various institutions are coordinated or linked together to form a society.

Technological determinism This is a simplified conviction that technology is a powerful independent variable which can change other social factors in a cause–effect relation.

Two-sided answerability Refers to communication, speech, or gestures that have a general or universal meaning for which the sender assumes responsibility and that invite a specific subjective response from the receiver.

Undecidables Created whenever we put into question the naming or defining of something and defer any final decision about its meaning (Powel, 2007).

Utopia A vision of a perfect society where all social and economic relations are in perfect harmony; the opposite to dystopia.

Values The shared feelings about what is desirable in a culture.

References

Abercrombie, Nicholas, Stephen Hill, and Bryan Turner. 1980. *The Dominant Ideology Thesis*. London: George Allen & Unwin.

Abrahamson, Mark. 2004. *Global Cities*. New York: Oxford University Press.

Achter, Paul. 2008. 'Comedy in Unfunny Times: News Parody and Carnival After 9/11', *Critical Studies in Media Communication* 25 (3): 274–303.

Adorno, Theodor W. 1991. *The Culture Industry*, J.M. Bernstein, ed. London: Routledge.

———. 2007. 'Letters to Walter Benjamin', in *Aesthetics and Politics*. London: Verso.

Alasuutari, Pertti, ed. 1999. *Rethinking the Media Audience*. London: Sage Publications.

Alexander, Jeffrey. 2006. *The Civil Sphere*. New York: Oxford.

Allor, Martin. 1988. 'Relocating the Site of the Audience', *Critical Studies in Mass Communications* 5 (3): 217–33.

Alvi, Shahid, Walter DeKeseredy, and Desmond Ellis. 2000. *Contemporary Social Problems in North America*. Don Mills, ON: Addison-Wesley.

Angus, Ian. 1996. *A Border Within: National Identity, Cultural Plurality, and Wilderness*. Montreal and Kingston: McGill-Queen's University Press.

Appadurai, Arjun. 2006. *Fear of Small Numbers: An Essay on the Geography of Anger*. Durham: Duke University Press.

Appiah, Kwame Anthony. 2006. *Cosmopolitanism: Ethics in a World of Strangers*. New York, NY: Norton.

Archer, Margaret. 1988. *Culture and Agency: The Place of Culture in Social Theory*. Cambridge, UK: Cambridge University Press.

Arnold, Kathleen. 2004. *Homelessness, Citizenship and Identity: The Uncanniness of Late Modernity*. Albany: SUNY.

Baillargeon, Stéphane. 2005. 'Le Quartier des spectacles critique l'inaction des gouvernements'. *Le Devoir*, 21 October: B2.

Bakhtin, Mikhail. 1968. *Rabelais and His World*, H. Iswolsky, trans. Bloomington: Indiana University Press.

———. 1981. *The Dialogic Imagination*, Michael Holquist and Caryl Emerson, ed. and trans. Austin: University of Texas Press.

———. 1984a [1929/1963]. *Dostoevsky's Poetics*. Minneapolis: University of Minnesota Press.

———. 1984b. *Problems of Dostoevsky's Poetics*, Caryl Emerson and Wayne Booth, ed. and trans. Minneapolis: University of Minnesota Press.

———. 1993. *Toward a Philosophy of the Act*, Vadim Liapunow, trans., Michael Holquist, ed. Austin: University of Texas Press.

———. 1996. *Speech Genres and Other Late Essays*. Austin: Texas University Press.

Barry, Dan. 2006. 'Wriggling through the cracks in the urban façade', *New York Times*, 29 March: B1.

Baudrillard, Jean. 1970. *La Société de consummation*. Paris: Gallimard.

———. 1983. *Simulations*, P. Foss et al., trans. New York: Semiotext

———. 2005. *The System of Objects*. London: Verso.

Becker, Lee B. 1998. 'Conflicting Goals, Confused Elites, Active Audiences: Some Thoughts on Canadian Media Policy', in Joel Smith, ed., *Media Policy, National Identity and Citizenry in Changing Democratic Societies: The Case of Canada*. Durham, NC: Canadian Studies Centre, Duke University.

Benjamin, Walter. 1969. *Illuminations: Essays and Reflection*, Hannah Arendt, ed. New York: Shoken.

Bernstein, Alina, and Neil Blain. 2003. *Sport, Media, Culture: Global and Local Dimensions*. London: F. Cass.

Bernstein, Nina. 2005a. 'Questions, bitterness and exile for Queens girl in terror case', *The New York Times*, 17 June: B5.

———. 2005b. 'Deliveryman relives the fear of 81 hour ordeal in elevator', *The New York Times*, 17 August: B1.

———. 2005c. 'Top officials told to testify in Muslims' suit', *The New York Times*, 29 September: B4.

———. 2005d. 'Immigrant victims of abuse are illegally denied benefts, suit says', *New York Times*, 13 December: B1.

———. 2006a. 'An Irish face on the cause of citizenship', *The New York Times*, 16 March: A1.

———. 2006b. 'Mrs. Clinton says G.O.P.'s immigration plan is at odds with the Bible', *New York Times*, 23 March: B5

Best, Joel. 2008. *Social Problems*. New York: W.W. Norton.

Bird, Roger. 1997. *The End of News*. Toronto: Irwin Publishing.

Black, Jay. 1997. *Mixed News: The Public/Civic/Communitarian Journalism Debate*.

New Jersey: Lawrence Erlbaum Associates.

Block, Irwin. 2005. 'Quebec food bank use second-highest in Canada: Province has anti-poverty law; 50% increase in number of working people needing help, Harvest Montreal says', *The Gazette*, 24 November: A8.

Borradori, Giovanna. 2003. *Philosophy in a Time of Terror: Dialogues with Jürgen Habermas and Jacques Derrida*. Chicago: University of Chicago Press.

Boudreau, Julie-Anne. 2000. *The Mega City Saga: Democracy and Citizenship in This Global Age*. Montreal: Blackrose Books.

Bourdieu, Pierre. 1984. *Distinction: A Social Critique of the Judgment of Taste*. London: Routledge.

Boyd-Barrett, Olivier. 1977. 'Media Imperialism: Towards an International Framework for the Analysis of Media System', in J. Curran, M. Gurevitch, and J. Woollacott, eds, *Mass Communication and Society*. London: Open University Press.

Boyle, James. 2008. *The Public Domain: Enclosing the Commons of the Mind*. Available online at http://james-boyle.com.

Bratt, Rachel, Michael E. Stone, and Chester Hartman, eds. 2006. *A Right to Social Housing: Foundation for a New Social Agenda*. Philadelphia, PA: Temple University Press.

Brown, Wendy. 2006. *Regulating Aversion: Tolerance in the Age of Identity and Empire*. Princeton, NJ: Princeton University Press.

Brownstein, Bill. 2005. 'Philistines would dim music in the streets', *The Gazette*, 11 May: D1.

Buck-Morris, Susan. 1991. *The Dialectics of Seeing. Walter Benjamin and the Arcades Project*. Cambridge, MA: MIT.

———. 2002. *Dreamworld and Catastrophe*. Cambridge, MA: MIT.

Bureau of Broadcast Measurement. 2000. *Bureau of Broadcast Management, Electronic Book, Fall 2000 Radio* (including Fall '99, Spring '00, Summer '00), 12 November.

Butler, Judith. 2004. *Undoing Gender*. New York: Routledge.

———. 2005. *Giving an Account of Oneself*. New York: Fordham University.

———. 2006. *Precarious Life*. London: Verso.

———. 2008. *The Work of Art in the Age of Its Technological Reproducibility and Other Writings on Media*. Cambridge, MA: Belknap/Harvard Press.

Canada. 1986. Report of the Task Force on Broadcasting Policy. Ottawa: Minister of Supply & Services.

———. 1991. *Broadcasting Act* 1991, C.11. Available online at http://lois.justice.gc.ca/en/B-9.01/6760.html#rid-6767.

———. 2009. *A Framework for Copyright Reform*. Copyright Reform Process, Archives. Available online at http://www.ic.gc.ca/eic/site/crp-prda.nsf/eng/rp01101.html.

Carey, James W. 1989. *Communication as Culture: Essays on Media and Society*. Boston: Unwin Hyman.

Castells, Manuel, ed. 2004. *The Network Society: A Cross-Cultural Perspective*. Cheltenham, UK: Edward Elgar Publishing.

Castoriadis, Cornelius. 1978. *The Imaginary Institution of Society*. London: Polity.

Cauchy, Clairandrée. 2005. 'Contraventions et prison pour les itinérants', *Le Devoir*, 4 May: A1.

Cavanagh, Allison. 2007. *Sociology in the Age of the Internet*. Berkshire, UK: Open University Press.

CBC News. 2008. 'Union urges CRTC to curb internet interference by Bell, Rogers', *CBC News Online*, 28 March. Available online at http://www.cbc.ca/technology/story/2008/03/28.

CBC News. 2007. 'Video gamers virtually violent but socially active, studies say: High numbers of teens playing M-rated games', 3 July.

CBC News. 2008a. 'Canada a top copyright violator, U.S. group says', 12 February.

CBC News. 2008b. 'Facebook group in school dispute shut down', 26 February.

CBC News. 2008c. 'Gaming fixation could be linked to Ont. boy's disappearance: Parents', 22 October.

CBC News. 2009. 'Potential pandemic or garden-variety flu?', 2 May.

CBC *Times. Eastern Region*. 1948–53. Available in the Concordia University Centre for Broadcasting Studies CBC Archives.

Chambers, Gretta. 2000. 'A government addicted to reform', *The Gazette*, 15 December: B3.

Chan, Sewell. 2006. 'Mayor calls main idea on immigration unrealistic', *New York Times*, 31 March: B6.

Chavez, Leo. 2001. *Covering Immigration: Popular Images and the Politics of the Nation*. Berkeley: University of California Press.

Cheslow, Jerry. 2005. 'Blending two cities into one', *New York* Times, 9 October: B7.

Chun, Wendy Hui Kyong. 2005. 'Introduction', in Wendy Hui Kyong Chun and Thomas Keenan, eds, *New Media, Old Media: A History and Theory Reader*. New York: Routledge.

Classen, Christoph. 2007. 'Thoughts on the

Significance of Mass Media Communications in the Third Reich and the GDR', *Totalitarian Movements and Political Religions* 8 (3/4): 547–62.

Clement, Wallace. 1975. *Canadian Corporate Elite: An Analysis of Economic Power*. Toronto: McClelland and Stewart.

Cohen, S. 1972. *Folk Devils and Moral Panics*. London: MacGibbon and Kee.

Compton, James. 2000. 'Communicative Politics and Public Journalism', *Journalism Studies*, 1 (3): 449–67.

comScore. 2009. Available online at http://www.comscore.com/Press_Events/Press_Releases.

Cottle, Simon. 2006. 'Mediatized Rituals: Beyond Manufacturing Consent', *Media, Society & Culture* 28 (3): 411–32.

Couldry, Nick. 2006. *Listening Beyond the Echoes: Media, Ethics, and Agency in an Uncertain World*. Boulder: Paradigm Publishers.

Cummings, Hope M., and Elizabeth A. Vandewater. 2007. 'Relation of Adolescent Video Game Play to Time Spent in Other Activities', *Archives of Pediatrics & Adolescent Medicine*. Available online at http://archpedi.ama-assn.org/contents-by-date.2007.dtl.

Curran, James. 2005. 'Media and Cultural Theory in the Age of Market Liberalism', in James Curran and David Morley, eds, *Media and Cultural Theory*. London: Routledge, 129–48.

Cusson, Marie. 2004. 'Du Soldat au Danse à Dix: Représentation des rapports sociaux de pouvoir et du pluralisme urbain dans *les Bye-Bye*', *Frequency: Journal for the Study of Canadian Radio and Television* 11–12: 227–51.

———. 2004b. 'Canadian Radio Satire', in Christopher H. Sterling and Michael C. Keith, eds, *The Museum of Broadcast Communications Encyclopedia of Radio*, Vol. 1. New York: Fitzroy Dearborn, 285–9.

Cusson, Marie, and Greg Nielsen. 2001. 'La satire à la radio publique et à la radio privée au Québec', *Canadart II: Revista do nucleo de estudos canadenses* 8: 83–105.

D'Angelo, Paul. 2002. 'News Framing as a Multiparadigmatic Research Program: A Response to Entman', *Journal of Communication* 52 (4): 870–88.

Danticat, Edwidge. 2007. 'Impounded fathers', *The New York Times*, 17 June: A12.

Davis, Mike. 2006. *Planet of Slums*. London: Verso.

Dayan, Daniel, and Elihu Katz. 1992. *Media Events: The Live Broadcasting of History*. Cambridge, MA: Harvard University Press.

Debord, Guy. 1995. *The Society of the Spectacle*. New York: Zone Books.

de Certeau, Michel. 1984/1988. *The Practice of Everyday Life*, Steven Rendall, trans. Berkley: University of California Press.

Deleuze, Gilles, and Felix Guattari. 1987. *Thousand Plateau: Capitalism and Schizophrenia*. Minneapolis: University of Minnesota Press.

Derrida, Jacques. 1992. 'Force of Law: The Mystical Foundation of Authority', in *Deconstruction and the Possibility of Justice*, Drucilla Cornell et al., trans. London: Routledge, 1–67.

———. 1997. *Politics of Friendship*. London: Verso.

———. 2001. *On Cosmopolitanism and Forgiveness*. London, UK: Routledge.

———. 2002. *Without Alibi*. Stanford: Stanford University Press.

———. 2005. *Rogues*. Stanford: Stanford University Press.

Dowd, Maureen. 2006. 'W's mixed messages', *New York Times*, 11 March: A15.

Durkheim, Émile. 1966. *The Rules of Sociological Method*. New York: Free Press.

Ebbrecht, Tobias. 2007. 'History, Public Memory and Media Event: Codes and Conventions of Historical Event-Television in Germany', *Media History* 13(2/3): 221–34.

Edelman, Murray. 1988. *Constructing the Political Spectacle*. Chicago: Chicago University Press.

Edwards, Tim. 2000. *Contradictions of Consumption: Concepts, Practices and Politics of Consumption*. London: Open University.

Elasmer, Michael G., K. Hasegawa, and M. Brian. 1999. 'The Portrayal of Women in U.S. Prime Time Television' *Journal of Broadcasting & Electronic Media* 43 (1): 20–34.

Elkouri, Rima. 2005. 'Le cadeau de Grec', *La Presse*, 23 June: A5.

Entman, Robert M. 1993. 'Framing: Toward Clarification of a Fractured Paradigm', *Journal of Communication* 7 (1): 69–93.

———. 2004. *Projections of Power: Framing News, Public Opinion, and U.S. Foreign Policy*. Chicago: University of Chicago Press.

———. 2005. 'The Nature and Sources of News', in *The Press*, Geneva Overholser and Kathleen H. Jamieson, eds. New York: Oxford University Press, 48–65.

Ericson, Richard, Patricia M. Baranek, and Janet B.L. Chan. 1987. *Visualizing Deviance: A Study of News Organization*. Toronto: University of Toronto Press.

———. 1989. *Negotiating Control: A Study of News Sources*. Toronto: University of Toronto Press.

Esterowicz, Anthony, and Robert N. Roberts. 2000. *Public Journalism and Political Knowledge*. New York: Rowman and Littlefield.

Evans, Fred. 2008. *The Multivoiced Body: Society and Communication in the Age of Diversity*. New York: Columbia University Press.

Fanon, Frantz. 1995. *A Dying Colonialism*. New York: Grove Press.

Farzad, Roben. 2005. 'Housing boom brings jobs and, sometimes, abuse', *New York Times*, 20 July: A1.

Featherstone, Mike. 1995. *Global Modernities*, M. Featherstone, S. Lash, and R. Robertson, eds. London: Thousand Oaks.

Feuer, Alan. 2005. 'Businesswoman known as Sister Ping is found guilty on federal conspiracy charges', *The New York Times*, 23 June: B3.

Findlay, Gillian. 2009. 'Top gun: When video gaming obsession turns to addiction and tragedy', *The Fifth Estate*, CBC News, 6 March.

Fine, Janet. 2007. 'Alternative Viewpoints: The Indian Media Perspective on the 9/11 Attacks', in *How the World's News Media Reacted to 9/11: Essays from Around the Globe*, T. Pludowski, ed. Spokane, WA: Marquette.

Fink, Howard, and John Jackson, eds. 1987. *All the Bright Company: Radio Drama Produced by Andrew Allan*. Kingston and Toronto: Quarry Press and CBC Enterprises, 67–101, 170–202.

Fiske, John. 1989. *Understanding Popular Culture*. New York: Routledge.

———. 1994. 'Audiencing: Cultural Practice and Cultural Studies', in Norman K. Denzin and Yvonne S. Lincoln, eds, *Handbook of Qualitative Research*. London: Sage Publications.

Florida, Richard, and Elizabeth Currid. 2005. 'Bohemian Rhapsody', *New York Times*, 31 July: A4.

Fossum, John Eric, and Philip Schlesinger. 2007. *The European Union and the Public Sphere*. New York: Routledge

Foucault, Michel. 2003. *Society Must Be Defended: Lectures at the Collège de France, 1975–76*, David Macey, trans. New York: Picador.

Foundation of Greater Montreal. 2006. *Greater Montreal's Vital Signs*. Montreal, QC.

Fraser, Nancy. 1992. 'Rethinking the Public Sphere: A Contribution to the Critique of Actual Existing Democracy', in *Habermas and the Public Sphere*, C. Calhoun, ed. Cambridge, MA: MIT Press, 109–42.

Fried, Joseph P. 2005. 'Keeping son in mind in quest for second job', *New York Times*, 14 November: B6.

Frye, Northrop. 1962. 'The Nature of Satire', in *Satire Theory and Practice*, Charles A. Allen and George D. Stephens, eds. Belmont, CA: Wadsworth.

Gagné, Gilles, and Simon Langlois. 2002. *Les raisons fortes: Nature et signification de l'appui à la souveraineté*. Montreal: Les Presses de l'Université de Montréal.

Gagnon, Alain, ed. 2009. *Contemporary Canadian Federalism*. Toronto: University of Toronto Press.

Gallagher, Margaret. 2003. 'Feminist Media Perspectives', in *A Companion to Media Studies*, A.N. Valdivia, ed. Malden, MA: Blackwell, p.19–39.

Gans, Herbert. 1995. *The War Against the Poor: The Underclass and Antipoverty Policy*. New York, NY: Basic Books.

Gardiner, Sue. 2008. 'Web 2.0 and Beyond'. Unpublished paper presented at the RIPE Conference, Mainz, Germany, 9 October 2008. Available online at http://www.uta.fi/jour/ripe/index.html.

Geist, Michael. 2007. *Ottawa Citizen*, 7 August: D1, D8.

———. 2008a. *Ottawa Citizen*, 22 April: F1, F6.

———. 2008b. *Ottawa Citizen*, 21 October: B1, B6.

Gazette. 2000. 'Mayors fume as Bill 170 becomes law', 21 December: A6.

Germaine, Annick, and Damaris, Rose. 2000. *Montréal: The Quest for Metropolis*. New York: John Wiley and Sons.

Gillwald A., ed. 2005. *Towards an African e-Index; Household and Individual ICT Access and Usage across 10 countries in Africa*. Johannesburg: The Link Centre, Witwatersrand University.

Goffman, Erving. 1974. *Frame Analysis: An Essay on the Organization of Experience*. London: Harper and Row.

Goode, Luke. 2005. *Jürgen Habermas: Democracy Beyond the Public Sphere*. Ann Arbor: Pluto Press.

Goodleaf, Donna. 1995. *Entering the War Zone: A Mohawk Perspective on Resisting Invasions*. Penticton, BC: Theytus Books.

Goodman, Amy, and David Goodman. 2006. *Static: Government Liars, Media Cheerleaders, and the People Who Fight*

Back. New York: Hyperion Books.

Gray, Ann. 1999. 'Audience Reception Research in Retrospect: The Trouble with Audiences' in *Rethinking the Media Audience*, Pertti Alasuutari, ed. London: Sage Publications.

Grossberg, L. 1988. 'Wandering Audiences, Nomadic Critics', *Cultural Studies* 2 (3): 377–91.

Haberman, Clyde. 2005. 'In melting pot, it takes time to buddy up', *New York Times*, 30 December: B1.

Habermas, Jürgen. 1987. *The Theory of Communicative Action,* Volume 2, *Lifeworld and System: A Critique of Functionalist Reasoning*. Boston: Beacon Press.

———. 1990. *Moral Consciousness and Communicative Action*. Boston: MIT Press.

———. 1991. *The Structural Transformation of the Public Sphere*. Cambridge, MA: MIT Press.

Hall, Stuart. 1974. 'Encoding and Decoding in the Television Discourse'. Centre for Contemporary Cultural Studies, Occasional Papers No. 7. Birmingham, UK: University of Birmingham.

Hannes, Allison. 2000. 'Future a mystery for libraries: Megacity bound to tap into well-stocked suburban networks under municipal merger', *The Gazette*, 8 December: A3.

Hansen, Miriam. 1993. 'Of Mice and Ducks: Benjamin and Adorno on Disney', *South Atlantic Quarterly* 92 (January): 27–61.

Harding, Robert. 2006. 'Historical Representations of Aboriginal People in the Canadian News Media', *Discourse & Society* 17 (2): 205–35.

Harris, Misty. 2007. 'It's Grand Theft Auto for girls *Ottawa Citizen*, 22 November: A3.

Hart, William, and Fran Hassencahl. 2002. 'Dehumanizing the Enemy in Editorial Cartoons', in *Communication and Terrorism: Public and Media Responses to 9/11*, B. Greenberg, ed. Cresskill, NJ: Hampton Press, 137–55.

Hartley, M. 2009. 'Reality check for social networks', *Globe and Mail*, 3 January: A10.

Hartocollis, Anemona. 2005. 'Former officer gets probation in homicide', *The New York Times*, 10 December: 1.

Hassan, Robert, and Thomas, Julian, eds. 2006. *The New Media Theory Reader*. New York: Open University Press.

Hilgartner, Stephen, and Charles L. Bosk. 1988. 'The Rise and fall of Social Problems: A Public Arenas Model', *American Journal of Sociology* 1: 53–8.

Hobsbawm, E.J. 1990. *Nations and Nationalism Since 1780*. New York: Cambridge University Press.

Horkheimer, Max, and Theodor Adorno. 2002. *The Dialectic of Enlightenment: Philosophical Fragments*. Stanford, CA: University of Stanford Press.

Housefeather, Anthony. 2000. 'The cause isn't lost: It's up to citizens to fight the PQ government's municipal-merger plan', *The Gazette*, 18 November: B5.

Innis, Harold A. 1956. *Essays in Canadian Economic History*. Toronto: University of Toronto Press.

———. 1972. *Empire and Communications*. Toronto: University of Toronto Press.

Isin, Engin. 2000. 'Governing Cities Without Government', in *Democracy, Citizenship and the Global City*, Engin Isin, ed. London: Routledge, 148–68.

Isin, Engin, and Greg Nielsen, eds. 2008. *Acts of Citizenship*. London: Zed Books.

ITU. 2007. Available online at http://www.itu.int/osg/spu/newslog/ct.

Jackson, John. 2002. 'From Cultural Relativity to Multiculturalism: The CBC's "The Ways of Mankind" Series, 1953', *Fréquence/Frequency* 9–10: 95–107.

Jackson, John, and Michael Rosenberg. 2004. *Recognition and Mis-recognition: Radio as Interlocutor*. Montreal: Concordia University, Centre for Broadcasting Studies.

Jackson, John, and Mary Vipond. 2003. 'The Public./Private Tension in Broadcasting: The Canadian Experience with Convergence', in *Broadcasting and Convergence: New Articulations of the Public Service Remit*, Gregory Ferrel Lowe and Taisto Hujanen, eds. Göteborg, Norway: Nordicom, 69–82.

James, Susan Donaldson. 2005. 'For illegal immigrants, a harsh lesson', *New York Times*, 19 June: A1.

Jensen, Klaus B. 1990. 'The Politics of Polysemy: Television News, Everyday Consciousness and Political Action', *Media, Culture and Society. 12 (1): 57–77.*

Johnston, David, Deborah Johnston, and Sunny Handa. 1995. *Getting Canada on Line: Understanding the Information Highway*. Toronto: Stoddart.

Kamhawi, Rasha, and M.E. Grabe. 2008. 'Engaging the Female Audience: An Evolutionary Psychology Perspective on Gendered Responses to News Valence Frames', *Journal of Broadcasting and Electronic Media* 52 (1): 33–49.

Karim, Karim H. 2000. *Islamic Peril: Media and Global Violence*. Montreal: Black Rose.

Katz, Elihu, and Paul Lazarsfeld. 1955. *Personal Influence*. Glencoe, IL: Free Press.

Keane, John. 2005. *Global Civil Society*. Cambridge: Cambridge University Press.

Kellner, Douglas. 2004. 'Spectacle and Media Propaganda in the War on Iraq: A Critique of U.S. Broadcasting Network', in *War, Media, and Propaganda: A Global Perspective*, Y.R. Kamalipur and N. Snow, eds. Boulder: Rowman & Littlefield.

Kent, Raymond, ed. 1994. *Measuring Media Audiences*. London: Routledge.

Kovach, Bill, and Tom Rosenstiel. 2007. *The Elements of Journalism: What Newspeople Should Know and the Public Should Expect*. New York: Random House.

Kymlicka, Will. 1998. *Finding Our Way: Rethinking Ethnocultural Relations in Canada*. Toronto: Oxford University Press Canada.

Lambeth, Edmund, Philip E. Meyer, and Esther Thorson, eds. 1998. *Assessing Public Journalism*. Columbia: University of Missouri Press.

La Presse. 2005. 'Petits frères des pauvres', *La Presse*, 29 March: 6.

Lauzen, Martha M., David Dozier, and Nora Horan. 2008. 'Constructing Gender Stereotypes Through Social Roles In Prime-Time Television', *Journal of Broadcasting and Electronic Media* 52 (2): 200–14.

Lee, Chin-Chuan, Joseph Man Chan, Zhongdang Pan, and Clement Y.K So. 2002. *Global Media Spectacle*. Albany: State University of New York.

Legros, Domminique. 2008. '0.45% Cosmopolitan', *St. Thomas Law Review* 20: 490–512.

Leitch, Thomas. 2002. 'Crime Films', in *Genres in American Cinema*, Barry Keith Grant, ed. Cambridge: Cambridge University Press.

Levinas, Emmanuel. 1994. *Beyond the Verse*, G.D. Mole, trans. London: Continuum.

Leys, Colin. 2001. *Market-Driven Politics: Neoliberal Democracy and the Public Interest*. London: Verso.

Lipton, Eric. 2006. 'U.S. crackdown set over hiring of immigrants', *New York Times*, 7 April: A1.

Lucy, Niall. 2004. *A Derrida Dictionary*. London: Blackwell.

Lueck, Thomas J. 2005. 'Enclave is called more tolerant than in '86', *New York Times*, 30 June: B8.

Luhmann, Niklas. 1995. *Social Systems*. Stanford, CA: Stanford University Press.

———. 2000. *The Reality of the Mass Media*, K. Cross, trans. Stanford, CA: University of Stanford Press.

Lukacs, Georg. 1971. *Theory of the Novel: A Historico-Philosophical Essay on the Forms of Great Epic Literature*. London: Polity.

Maguire, Joseph, Sarah Barnard, Katie Butler, and Peter Golding. 2008. '"Celebrate Humanity" or "Consumers?": A Critical Evaluation of a Brand in Motion', *Social Identities* 14 (1): 63–76.

Marchessault, Janine. 2001. 'Film Scenes: Paris, New York, Toronto', *Public* 22–23: 59–82.

Marvin, Carolyn. 1990. *When Old Technologies Were New: Thinking about Electric Communication in the Late Nineteenth Century*. New York: Oxford University Press.

———. 1987. 'Dazzling the Multitude: Imagining the Electric Light as a Communications Medium', in *Mass Communication Review Yearbook*, Vol. 6. Beverly Hills, CA: Sage.

Marx, Karl. 1978. *The Marx-Engels Reader*, Robert C. Tucker, ed. New York: Norton.

———. 1990. *Capital*, Volume 1. London: Penguin.

McChesney, Robert. 1999. *Rich Media, Poor Democracy: Communication Politics in Dubious Times*. Urbana: University of Illinois Press.

McCluhan, Marshall. 1967. *Quentin Fiore: The Medium Is the Message: An Inventory of Effects*. Toronto: Bantam.

———. 1994. *Understanding Media: The Extension of Men*. Cambridge, MA: MIT.

McIlwraith, Robert D. 1998. '"I'm Addicted to Television": The Personality, Imagination, and TV Watching Patterns of Self-Identified TV Addicts', *Journal of Broadcasting & Electronic Media* 42 (3): 371–86.

McKie, Craig, and Benjamin D. Singer, eds. 2001. *Communications in Canadian Society*, 5th ed. Toronto: Thompson Educational Publishing.

McQuail, Denis. 2006. 'On the Mediatization of War: A Review Article', *International Communication Gazette* 68 (2): 107–18.

Mead, G.H. 1934. *Mind, Self and Society from the Point of View of a Social Behaviorist*. Charles Morris, ed. Chicago: University of Chicago Press.

Medina, Jennifer. 2005. 'Shoppers in a parallel paradise', *New York Times*, 30 December: B1.

Meehan, Eileen R. 1984. 'Ratings and the Institutional Approach: A Third Answer to the Commodity Question', *Critical Studies in Mass Communication* 1 (2): 216–25.

Merton, Robert. 1946. *Mass Persuasion*. New York: Free Press.

Meunier, Hugo. 2005. 'Le festival de la "crevette"', *La Presse*, 18 July: A2.

Mills, C. Wright. 1959. *The Sociological*

Imagination. New York: Oxford University Press

Monsoon House. 2008. Radio play produced by Thomas Anniko. Available online at http://www.cbc.ca/monsoonhouse/index.html.

Mosco, Vincent 1996. *The Political Economy of Communication*. London: Sage Publications.

———. 2004. *The Digital Sublime: Myth, Power, and Cyberspace*. Cambridge, MA: MIT Press.

Mosco, Vincent, and L. Kaye. 2000. 'Questioning the Concept of the Audience', in *Consuming Audiences? Production and Reception in Media Research*, I. Hagen and J. Wasko, eds. Cresskill, NJ: Hampton Press.

Murdock, Graham. 1990. 'Television and Citizenship: In Defence Of Public Broadcasting', in *Consumption, Identity, and Style: Marketing, Meanings, And The Package Of Pleasure*, Alan Tomlinson, ed. London: Routledge.

Museum of Broadcast Communications. Available online at http:www.museum.tv/archives/etv/A/htm/A.

Myles, Brian. 2005a. 'Le Tiers-Monde au bout de la rue', *Le Devoir*, 26 February: A1.

———. 2005b. 'Les autochtones laissés à eux-mêmes', *Le Devoir*, 28 February: A1.

———. 2005c. 'Un Blanc parmi les Inuits', *Le Devoir*, 28 February: A4.

Napoli, Philip M. 2003. *Audience Economics: Media Institutions and the Audience Marketplace*. New York: Columbia University Press.

Nathan, Debbie. 2005. 'Long-distance love', *New York Times*, 18 December: B14.

New York Times. 2005a. 'Terrorism and the random search', *New York Times*, 26 July: A16.

———. 2005b. 'The poor endure with the city', *New York Times*, 14 November: A14.

———. 2006. 'People power', *New York Times*, 12 April: A20.

Nielsen, Greg M. 1994. *Le Canada de Radio-Canada: Sociologie critique et dialogisme culturel*. Toronto: Éditions du GREF.

———. 1995. 'L'impasse Canada-Québec et le sort de Radio-Canada: L'autonomie culturelle ou la mort!', *Cahiers de recherches sociologiques* 25: 181–212.

———. 1999. 'Two Countries, One State, Two Social Imaginations: A Comparison of CBC and Radio-Canada Seriocomedy', *Journal of Radio Studies* 6 (1): 150–58.

———. 2002. *The Norms of Answerability: Social Theory Between Bakhtin and Habermas*. Albany: State University of New York Press.

———. 2004. 'The Third Phase in the Seriocomedy Project', *Frequency: Journal for the Study of Canadian Radio and Television* 11–12: 174–81.

———. 2008. 'Conditional Hospitality: Framing Dialogue on Poverty in Montréal Newspapers', *Canadian Journal of Communication* 33 (4): 605–19.

———. 2009. 'Framing Immigration in the New York Times', *Aether: The Journal of Media Geography* 4: 37–57.

Nielsen, Greg M. 2007. 'Imagine-Nation in the City: Seriocomedy and Local Democracy', in *Urban Enigmas: Toronto-Montreal Comparisons*, J. Sloan, ed. McGill-Queen's University Press, 144–77.

Nielsen, Greg M., and John D. Jackson. 1991. 'Cultural Studies, a Sociological Poetics: Institutions of the Canadian Imaginary', *Canadian Review of Sociology and Anthropology* 28 (2): 280–2.

Nielsen, Greg M., Yon Hsu, and Louis Jacob. 2002. 'Public Culture and the Dialogics of Democracy: Reading the Montréal and Toronto Amalgamation Debates', *Canadian Journal of Urban Research* 2 (1): 111–40.

NYPIRG Homeless Project. 2007. *Facts and Statistics*. Available online at http://www.nypirg.org/homeless/facts.html.

Olson, Cheryl K., Lawrence A. Kutner, Dorothy E. Warner, et al. 2007. 'Factors Correlated with Violent Video Game Use by Adolescent Boys and Girls', *Journal of Adolescent Health* 41 (1). Available online at http://www.johonline.org/issues#2007.

Ottawa Citizen. 2008a. Advertisement for a conference titled, 'What happens online pays offline'. 6 September: H3.

———. 2008b. 'Our Views: Exposing ourselves', *Ottawa Citizen*, 16 February: B6.

———. 2009. 'Our Views: Privacy dilemma', *Ottawa Citizen*, 21 February: B6.

———. 2009. Various headlines quoted. 28 April: A1, 4, 5, 6, 12.

Pagé, Pierre, with Renée Legris. 1979. *Le comique et l'humour à la radio québécoise: Aperçu historique et textes choisi, 1930–1970*, Vol. 1–2. Montreal: Fides.

Palmer, Jerry. 2000. *Spinning into Control: News Values and Source Strategies*. London: Leicester University Press.

Parsons, Talcott. 1951. *The Social System*. Glencoe, IL: Free Press.

Patterson, Orlando. 2006. 'A poverty of the mind', *The New York Times*, 26 March: D13.

Perez-Pena, Richard. 2009. 'US newspaper circulation falls 10%', *New York Times*, 27

October: B3.

Perigoe, Ross. 2007. 'September 11 in Canada: Representation of Muslims in the Gazette', in *How the World's News Media Reacted to 9/11: Essays from Around the Globe*, T. Pludowski, ed. Spokane, WA: Marquette.

Pierce, Tamyra. 2007. 'X-Posed on MySpace: A Content Analysis of "MySpace" Social Networking Sites', *Journal of Media Psychology* 12 (1). Available online at http://www.calstatela.edu/faculty/sfischo/x-posed_on_MySoace.htm.

Pilieci, Vito. 2008a. 'How Battlefield is leading the charge to free gaming', *Ottawa Citizen*, 18 February: A1, A2.

———. 2008b. 'Recording industry speaks out against Internet levy proposal', *Ottawa Citizen*, 23 February: D2.

———. 2009. 'Guilty verdict sparks debate over website in Canada', *Ottawa Citizen*, 18 April: D3.

Popovic, Alexandre. 2005. 'Pourquoi les sans-abri?', *La Presse*, 5 June: A11.

Porter, Eduardo. 2006. 'Immigrants wanted: legal would be nice, but illegal will suffice', *New York Times*, 23 March: C1.

Porter, John. 1966. *The Vertical Mosaic: An Analysis of Social Class and Power in Canada*. Toronto: University of Toronto Press.

Postman, Neil. 1986. *Amusing Ourselves to Death: Public Discourse in the Age of Show Business*. New York: Penguin.

Powell, Jim. 2007. *Deconstruction for Beginners*. Documentary Comic Book.

Powers, Shawn, and Eytan Gilboa. 2007. 'The Public Diplomacy of Al Jazeera', in *New Media and the New Middle East*, Philip Seib, ed. New York: Palgrave.

Preston, Julia. 2006. 'Ringleader gets 35-year term in smuggling of immigrants', *New York Times*, 17 March: B2.

———. 2007. 'Farmers call crackdown on illegal workers unfair', *The New York Times*, 11 August: A10.

Purnick, Joyce. 2006. 'Two killings that didn't make news', *New York Times*, 13 March: B1.

Raboy, Marc. 1990. *Missed Opportunities: The Story of Canada's Broadcasting Policy*. Montreal: McGill-Queen's University Press.

Radway, Janice. 1984. *Reading the Romance*. Chapel Hill: University of North Carolina Press.

———. 1988. 'Reception Study: Ethnography and the Problems of Dispersed Audiences and Nomadic Subjects', *Cultural Studies* 2 (3): 359–76.

Rao, Shakuntala, and Seow Ting Lee. 2005. 'Global Media Ethics? An Assessment of Universal Ethics among International Political Journalists, *Journal of Mass Media Ethics* 20 (2&3): 99–120.

Rashbaum, William K. 2005. 'Officer Arrested in Killing of his children's mother', *The New York Times*, 15 June: B4.

Retief, Johan. 2002. *Media Ethics: An Introduction to Responsible Journalism*. New York, NY: Oxford University Press.

Rieff, David. 2005. 'The Way We Live Now: Migrant Worry', *New York Times*, 6 November: S6, 16.

Roberts, Sam. 2005. 'Castle garden set stage for Ellis Island'. *New York Times*, 29 July: A1

Robinson, Gertrude. 1998. *Constructing the Quebec Referendum: French and English Media Voices*. Toronto: University of Toronto Press.

Rosen, Jay. 1999. *What Are Journalists For?* New Haven: Yale University Press.

Roski, Edgar. 2007. 'A Genocide Without Images: White Film Noirs', *The Media and the Rwanda Genocide*, A. Thompson, ed. London: Pluto.

Ross, Andrew. 2004. *Low Pay, High Profile: The Global Push for Fair Labor*. New York: New Press.

Ross, K., and V. Nightingale. 2003. *Media and Audiences: New Perspectives*. Maidenhead, UK: Open University Press.

Roy, James, and Beverly Cooper, producers. 2008–09. *Afghanada*. Available online at http://www.cbc.ca/afghanada/index.htm.

Royal Commission on Aboriginal Peoples. 1996. *Final Report*. Vol. 4, *Public Education: Building Awareness and Understanding*. Ottawa: Canada Communications Group.

Russell, Nick. 2006. *Morals and the Media: Ethics in Canadian Journalism*. Vancouver: UBC Press.

Sachs, Jeffrey D. 2005. *The End of Poverty: Economic Possibilities for Our Time*. New York: Penguin Books.

Sampson, Robert J. 2006. 'Open doors don't invite criminals', *New York Times*, 11 March: A15.

Sancton, Andrew. 2000. *Merger Mania: The Assault on Local Government*. Montreal and Kingston: McGill-Queen's University Press.

Sansfaçon, Jean-Robert. 2005. 'Une grande détresse', *Le Devoir*, 1 March: A6.

Saxton, Tammy, Donavan Rocher, and John Jackson. 2004. 'This Hour Has 22 Minutes: The Centre-Periphery Problematic and Gender Performance', *Fréquence/Frequency* 11–12: 182–98.

Sebusang, S., S. Masupe, and J. Chumai. 2005. 'Botswana', in *Towards an African e-Index; Household and Individual ICT Access and Usage across 10 Countries in Africa*, A. Gillwald, ed. Johannesburg: The Link Centre, Witwatersrand University.

Seib, Philip. 2004. 'The New Media and "the Clash of Civilizations"', *Parameters* (Winter): 71–85.

———. 2007. *New Media and the New Middle East*. New York: Palgrave.

———. 2008. *The Al Jazeera Effect: How the New Global Media Are Reshaping World Politics*. Washington, DC: Potomac Books.

Sevigny, Marcel. 2005. 'NON: Ce serait une "aubaine" pour le crime organisé', *La Presse*, 16 June: A23.

Shattuck, Jennifer. 2005. 'Housing boom echoes in all corners of the city', *New York Times*, 6 August: A1.

Silverstone, Roger. 1999. 'What's New about New Media?', *New Media and Society*, 1 (1): 10–82.

———. 2004. 'Editorial: 9/11 and New Media', *New Media & Society* 6 (5): 587–90.

———. 2007. *Media and Morality: On the Rise of the Mediapolis*. London: Polity.

Simmel, Georg. 1971. *On Individuality and Social Forms*. Chicago: Chicago University Press.

———. 1998. *Georg Simmel on Culture*, D. Frisby and M. Featherstone, eds. London: Sage.

Simon, Sherry. 2006. *Translating Montreal: Episodes in the Life of a Divided City*. Montreal: McGill-Queen's University Press.

Slevin, James. 2000. *The Internet and Society*. Cambridge, UK: Polity Press.

Smythe, Dallas W. 1977. 'Communications: Blindspot of Western Marxism', *Canadian Journal of Political and Social Theory* 1 (3): 1–28.

Solyom, Catherine. 2005. 'Sticker lady hits streets of Montreal: Ontario panhandler has nice home, car', *The Gazette*, 22 January: A1.

Spears, Tom. 2008. 'Book Reviews', *Ottawa Citizen*, 21 December: B1, B2.

Statistics Canada. 2006. 2001 Community Profiles. Available online at http://www12.statcan.ca/english/Profil01/CP01/Details/Page.cfm?Lang=E&Geo1=CSD&Code1=2466025&Geo2=PR&Code2=24&Data=Count&SearchText=montreal&SearchType=Begins&SearchPR=01&B1=All&Custom=.

Stein, David Lewis. 1996. *Toronto Star*, A8.

Sutherland, Anne. 2005a. 'First Stop targets vulnerable runaways: Booth at bus station offers advice, contacts', *The Gazette*, 20 October: A11.

———. 2005b. 'Stolen skates returned—too late', *The Gazette*, 12 September: A1.

Swarns, Rachel L. 2006a. 'The nation: rift on immigration widens for conservatives and cardinals', *The New York Times*, 19 March: D4.

———. 2006b. 'A G.O.P. split on immigration vexes a senator', *New York Times*, 26 March: A1.

———. 2006c. 'Split over immigration reflects nation's struggle', *New York Times*, 29 March: A17.

———. 2006d. 'Senate republicans strike immigration deal', *New York Times*, 6 April: A21.

———. 2006e. 'Senate deal set for immigration, but then falters', *New York Times*, 7 April: A1.

Symonds, Gwyn. 2008. *The Aesthetics of Violence in Contemporary Media*. London: Continuum International Publishing Group.

Talaga, Tanya. 1996. '3 mayors dig in for vote on megacity', *Toronto Star*, December 31: A3.

Tate, Eugene D., and Kathleen McConnell. 2001. 'The Mass Media and Violence', in *Communications in Canadian Society*, 5th ed, C. McKie and B.D. Singer, eds. Toronto: Thompson Educational Publishing, 273–94.

Taylor, Charles. 1995. *Philosophical Arguments*. Cambridge, MA: Harvard University Press.

Thompson, Allan. 2007. 'The Responsibility to Report: A New Journalistic Paradigm', in *The Media and the Rwanda Genocide*, A. Thompson, ed. London: Pluto, 436–9.

Thompson, John B. 1990. *Ideology and Modern Culture*. Stanford, CA: Stanford University Press.

———. 1995. *The Media and Modernity: A Social Theory of the Media*. Cambridge: Polity Press.

Thomson, Andrew. 2007. 'Somali debates return to war-torn land', *Ottawa Citizen*, 14 August: C1.

Thussu, Daya. 2005. 'Selling Neo-Imperial Conflicts: Television and US Public Diplomacy', in *Mass Media and Society*, J. Curran and M. Gurevitch, eds. London: Hodder Arnold.

Tompkins, Jane P., ed. 1980. *Reader Response Criticism*. Baltimore: John Hopkins University Press.

Toronto Star. 1996a. 'Annoying extras and mayors, councilors denied what they now tout', *Toronto Star*, 21 December: E3.

———. 1996b. 'Supercity savings', *Toronto Star*, 26 December: A46.

———. 1996c. 'Cheerleading the demise of democracy', *Toronto Star*, 30 December: A20.

Toronto Sun. 1997. Unsigned editorial, 5 November: 12.

Touzin, Caroline. 2005. 'Sans abri, la journée la plus froide depuis le début de l'année', *La Presse*, 19 January: A8.

Tuchman, Gaye. 1978. *Making the News*. New York, NY: Free Press.

US Census Bureau. 2006. Available online at http://quickfacts.census.gov/qfd/states/36/3651000.html.

Van den Bulck, Jan, and Bea Van den Bergh. 2000. 'The Influence of Perceived Parental Guidance Patterns on Children's Media Use: Gender Differences and Media Displacement', *Journal of Broadcasting & Electronic Media* 44 (3): 329–48.

van Ginneken, Japp. 1998. *Understanding Global News*. London: Sage.

Veblen, Thorstein. 1994. *The Theory of the Leisure Class*. New York: Dover.

Vitello, Paul. 2006. 'Kiss me, I'm illegal', *New York Times*, 26 March: A5.

Voumvakis, Sophia E., and Richard Ericson. 1984. 'News Accounts of Attacks on Women: A Comparison of Three Toronto Newspapers', *Research Report of the Centre of Criminology*. Toronto: University of Toronto.

WAN (World Association of Newspapers). 2008. *World Press Trends: Newspapers Are a Growth Business*. Available online at http://www.wan-press.org.

Ward, Stephan. 2006. *The Invention of Journalism Ethics: The Path to Objectivity and Beyond*. Montréal: McGill-Queen's University Press.

Weber, Max. 1978. *Economy and Society: An Outline of Interpretive Sociology*, Günter Roth and Claus Wittich, eds. Berkeley: University of California Press.

West, Emily. 2002. 'Selling Canada to Canadians: Collective Memory, National Identity, and Popular Culture', *Critical Studies in Media Communication* 19 (2): 212–29.

Wilk, Richard. 2006. 'The Pure Commodity in the Age of Branding', *Journal of Consumer Culture* 6: 303–25.

Winship, Janice. 1987. *Inside Women's Magazines*. London: Pandora.

Young, David. 2001. 'Celine Dion, National Unity and the English-Language Press in Canada', *Media, Culture and Society* 23 (5): 647–63.

Young, Iris M. 2005. *On Female Body Experience: 'Throwing Like a Girl' and Other Essays*. New York: Oxford University Press.

———. 2007. *Global Challenges: War, Self Determination and Responsibility for Justice*. London: Polity.

Zipes, Jack. 1999. *When Dreams Came True: Classical Fairy Tales and Their Tradition*. New York: Routledge.

Zylinska, Joanna. 2004. 'Mediating Murder: Ethics, Trauma and the Price of Death', *Journal for Cultural Research* 8 (3): 227–46.

Index